Spanish for Human Resources Managers

William C. Harvey, M.S.

D1606197

BARRON'S

All inquiries should be addressed to:
Barron's Educational Series, Inc.
250 Wireless Boulevard
Hauppauge, NY 11788

International Standard Book No. 0-8120-9887-0

Library of Congress Catalog Card No. 97-73107

PRINTED IN THE UNITED STATES OF AMERICA

9 8 7 6 5 4 3 2 1

Contents

Introduction

A Note from the Author

Having taught Spanish for almost 20 years, I've discovered that one of the most prominent fields of employment in need of Spanish language skills is the management of human resources.

In essence, the job of a Human Resources Manager is to communicate effectively. From hiring and training to evaluating and advising, these busy professionals must know which Spanish words to use for each unique situation. More importantly, they need to understand what the Spanish-speaking employee is saying in order to meet his or her particular needs.

This guidebook is designed for managers who must meet the needs of the growing number of Spanish speakers in today's workforce.

Once the language and cultural barriers are removed, many problems disappear and business improves. From what I have observed, learning Spanish is definitely the right career move!

How to Use this Guidebook

Spanish for Human Resources Managers teaches how to understand and speak to Spanish-speaking employees. This book provides Spanish vocabulary and phrases needed to recruit, interview, train, counsel, and discharge employees, as well as to converse socially about everyday activities. All Spanish language skills are taught gradually, and then are reinforced systematically through practice and review.

To get the most out of this book, either use the convenient specialized dictionary in the back, or try focusing on the icons provided on the next page. They can be helpful when you are working on a specific skill or topic of interest. Simply scan the pages for the corresponding icon, and locate whatever you need.

¡Información! (*Information*—tips and suggestions)

 Temas culturales (*Cultural subjects*—insights on Hispanic cultural characteristics)

 ¡Ordenes! (*Orders!*—Spanish command words)

 Palabras activas (*Action words*—basic Spanish verb tenses)

 Más fácil (*Simplify*—key phrases that combine with verb forms)

 Listos para practicar (*Exercises*)

Great News!

If you're a little fearful about learning Spanish, here's good news:

• Grammar and pronunciation don't have to be "perfect" in order to be understood.

• Thousands of words are similar in both English and Spanish, which makes it easier for you to remember vocabulary.

• Messages in Spanish can be communicated with only a few simple expressions.

Believe me. By following the proven suggestions mentioned in this guidebook, you can pick up lots of **español** *(eh-spah-'nyohl)* in no time at all!

Chapter One

Capítulo Uno

(kah-'pee-too-loh 'oo-noh)

Let's Get Started

Vamos a empezar

('vah-mohs ah ehm-peh-'sahr)

The sounds of Spanish
Los sonidos del español
(lohs soh-'nee-dohs dehl eh-spah-'nyohl)

As a beginner, your first step is to learn what Spanish sounds like. Fortunately, you don't have to pronounce everything correctly in order to be understood. Not only are people generally forgiving, but in reality there aren't that many differences between the two sound systems. In fact, you need to remember only *five* sounds in order to speak well enough to be understood. These are the vowels, which, unlike their English equivalents, are pronounced the way they are written. Go ahead—read each letter aloud, and follow the corresponding pronunciation guide.

> **a** *(ah)* as in *yacht*
> **e** *(eh)* as in *met*
> **i** *(ee)* as in *keep*
> **o** *(oh)* as in *open*
> **u** *(oo)* as in *tool*

Now, let's learn how to pronounce all the other letters.

Spanish letter	*English sound*
c (after an **e** or **i**)	*s* as in *sit* (**cigarro**) *(see-'gah-rroh)*
g (after an **e** or **i**)	*h* as in *hop* (**general**) *(heh-neh-'rahl)*
h	silent, like *k* in *knife* (**hombre**) *('ohm-breh)*
j	*h* as in *hat* (**Julio**) *('hoo-lee-oh)*
ll	*y* as in *yes* (**pollo**) *('poh-yoh)*
ñ	*ny* as in *canyon* (**señor**) *(seh-'nyohr)*
q	*k* as in *kit* (**tequila**) *(teh-'kee-lah)*
rr	the "rolled" *r* sound (**burro**) *('boo-rroh)*
z	*s* as in *son* (**zapato**) *(sah-'pah-toh)*

Although some dialects may vary slightly, the rest of the letters in Spanish are similar to their equivalents in English:

b	**bueno** *('bweh-noh)*	**l**	**leña** *('lehn-yah)*
d	**dinero** *(dee-'neh-roh)*	**m**	**mucho** *('moo-choh)*
f	**flan** *(flahn)*	**n**	**nada** *('nah-dah)*

p	**pronto** *('prohn-toh)*	**v**	**vaca** *('vah-kah)*
r	**tres** *(trehs)*	**x**	**mixto** *('meeks-toh)*
s	**sí** *(see)*	**y**	**yo** *(yoh)*
t	**taco** *('tah-koh)*		

Now, read the following words aloud, and then guess at their meanings. Don't forget that each letter needs to be pronounced the way it was introduced earlier:

amigo *(ah-'mee-goh)*
burrito *(boo-'rree-toh)*
Cinco de Mayo *('seen-koh deh 'mah-yoh)*
español *(eh-spah-'nyohl)*
excelente *(ehk-seh-'lehn-teh)*
Feliz Navidad *(feh-'lees nah-vee-'dahd)*

fiesta *(fee-'eh-stah)*
problema *(proh-'bleh-mah)*
televisión *(teh-leh-vee-see-'ohn)*
tortilla *(tohr-'tee-yah)*
vino *('vee-noh)*

 ¡Información! *(een-fohr-mah-see-'ohn)*
Information

• Any part of a word with an accent mark (´) needs to be pronounced LOUDER and with more emphasis (i.e., María) *(mah-'ree-ah)*. If there's no accent mark, say the last part of the word louder and with more emphasis (i.e., Beatriz) *(beh-ah-'trees)*. For words ending in a vowel, or in **n** or **s**, the next to the last part of the word is stressed (i.e., Fernando) *(fehr-'nahn-doh)*.

• In some cases, the letter **u** *(oo)* doesn't make the **oo** sound (i.e., guitarra *(gee-'tah-rrah)* or **guerra** *('geh-rrah)*).

 Listos para practicar
('lee-stohs 'pah-rah prahk-tee-'kahr)
Exercises

If you're having problems with the sounds of Spanish, try listening to the language for a few minutes each day. Spanish radio and TV stations or audio- and videocassettes are fun yet effective ways to become familiar with your new pronunciation patterns.

Key expressions

Expresiones claves *(ehk-spreh-see-'oh-nehs 'klah-vehs)*

The best way to get started in Spanish is to try out your new sounds in everyday conversations. Regardless of your situation, these basic expressions are a must for every Spanish student.

And you?	**¿Y usted?** *(ee oo-'stehd)*
Bless you!	**¡Salud!** *(sah-'lood)*
Excuse me!	**¡Con permiso!** *('kohn pehr-'mee-soh)*
Fine, thanks!	**¡Bien, gracias!** *(bee-'ehn, 'grah-see-ahs)*
Go ahead!	**¡Pase!** *('pah-seh)*
Good afternoon!	**¡Buenas tardes!** *('bweh-nahs 'tahr-dehs)*
Goodbye!	**¡Adiós!** *(ah-dee-'ohs)*
Good evening!/ Good night!	**¡Buenas noches!** *('bweh-nahs 'noh-chehs)*
Good morning!	**¡Buenos días!** *('bweh-nohs 'dee-ahs)*
Hi!	**¡Hola!** *('oh-lah)*
How are you?	**¿Cómo está?** *('koh-moh eh-'stah)*
How's it going?	**¿Qué tal?** *(keh tahl)*
I'm sorry!	**¡Lo siento!** *(loh see-'ehn-toh)*
Nice to meet you!	**¡Mucho gusto!** *('moo-choh 'goo-stoh)*
Please!	**¡Por favor!** *(pohr fah-'vohr)*
See you later!	**¡Hasta luego!** *('ah-stah 'lweh-goh)*
Thanks a lot!	**¡Muchas gracias!** *('moo-chahs 'grah-see-ahs)*
Very good!	**¡Muy bien!** *('moo-ee bee-'ehn)*
What's happening?	**¿Qué pasa?** *(keh 'pah-sah)*
Yes!	**¡Sí!** *(see)*
You're welcome!	**¡De nada!** *(deh 'nah-dah)*

¡Información!

- Several words in English are spelled the same in Spanish, and they usually have the same meaning. But, watch out! They are NOT pronounced the same!

chocolate *(choh-koh-'lah-teh)*   **idea** *(ee-'deh-ah)*
color *(koh-'lohr)*   **natural** *(nah-too-'rahl)*
final *(fee-'nahl)*   **terror** *(teh-'rrohr)*

- The upside-down exclamation point (¡) and question mark (¿) are found at the beginning of sentences, and must be used when you write in Spanish.

- Scan these other "excuse me" phrases:
Excuse me (if you cough or sneeze)
¡Perdón! *(pehr-'dohn)*
Excuse me (if you need someone's attention)
¡Disculpe! *(dee-'skool-peh)*

- Look! Some words change meanings if you drop the accent mark:

yes	**sí** *(see)*	if	**si** *(see)*
how	**cómo** *('koh-moh)*	I eat	**como** *('koh-moh)*
give	**dé** *(deh)*	from	**de** *(deh)*

Temas culturales

('teh-mahs kool-too-'rah-lehs)
Cultural subjects

Friendly greetings in Spanish are used all day long. Being courteous is the key to establishing trust with your employee. Throughout the Spanish-speaking world, a smile and a pleasant word can lead to respect and complete cooperation.

Do you speak Spanish?

¿Habla español? *('ah-blah eh-spah-'nyohl)*

Once you finish with the greetings and common courtesies, you will face the inevitable problem of not being able to understand one another. To make things easier, learn a few of these one-liners. They send the message that you are doing the best you can!

Again.	**Otra vez** *('oh-trah vehs)*
Do you understand?	**¿Entiende?** *(ehn-tee-'ehn-deh)*
How do you say it?	**¿Cómo se dice?** *('koh-moh seh 'dee-seh)*
How do you spell it?	**¿Cómo se deletrea?** *('koh-moh seh deh-leh-'treh-ah)*
I don't understand!	**¡No entiendo!** *(noh ehn-tee-'ehn-doh)*
I'm learning Spanish.	**Estoy aprendiendo el español** *(eh-'stoh-ee ah-prehn-dee-'ehn-doh ehl eh-spah-'nyohl)*
I speak little Spanish.	**Hablo poquito español.** *('ah-bloh poh-'kee-toh eh-spah-'nyohl)*
More slowly!	**¡Más despacio!** *(mahs deh'-spah-see·oh)*
Thanks for your patience.	**Gracias por su paciencia.** *('grah-see-ahs pohr soo pah-see-'ehn-see-ah)*
What does it mean?	**¿Qué significa?** *(keh seeg-nee-'fee-kah)*
Word by word!	**¡Palabra por palabra!** *(pah-'lah-brah pohr pah-'lah-brah)*

More essential phrases
Más frases esenciales
(mahs 'frah-sehs eh-sehn-see-'ah-lehs)

Spanish is full of common expressions. A lot can be communicated simply by saying a few simple phrases. Interject one of these whenever it is appropriate:

Don't worry.	**No se preocupe.** *(noh seh preh-oh-'koo-peh)*
Good idea.	**Buena idea.** *(bweh-nah ee-'deh-ah)*
I see.	**Ya veo.** *(yah 'veh-oh)*
I think so.	**Creo que sí.** *('kreh-oh keh see)*
Maybe.	**Quizás.** *(kee-'sahs)*
More or less.	**Más o menos.** *(mahs oh 'meh-nohs)*
Not yet.	**Todavía no.** *(toh-dah-'vee-ah noh)*
Ready?	**¿Listo?** *('lee-stoh)*

| Sure. | **Claro.** *('klah-roh)* |
| That depends. | **Depende.** *(deh-'pehn-deh)* |

Put a little more emotion into these!

Congratulations!	**¡Felicitaciones!** *(feh-lee-see-tah-see-'oh-nehs)*
Good luck!	**¡Buena suerte!** *('bweh-nah 'swehr-teh)*
Go with God!	**¡Vaya con Dios!** *('vah-yah kohn 'dee-ohs)*
Happy Birthday!	**¡Feliz cumpleaños!** *(feh-'lees koom-pleh-'ah-nyohs)*
Have a nice day!	**¡Qué le vaya bien!** *(keh-leh-'vah-yah bee-'ehn)*
Right away!	**¡En seguida!** *(ehn seh-'gee-dah)*
That's great!	**¡Qué bueno!** *(keh 'bweh-noh)*
Welcome!	**¡Bienvenidos!** *(bee-ehn veh-'nee-dohs)*
What a shame!	**¡Qué lástima!** *(keh 'lah-stee-mah)*
Wow!	**¡Caramba!** *(kah-'rahm-bah)*

Bear in mind that most idiomatic expressions cannot be translated word for word. Therefore, try to memorize each phrase as one long string of individual sounds.

¡Información!

Read over this next set of one-liners. You never know when you'll need them:

Above all...	**Sobre todo...** *('soh-breh 'toh-doh)*
At first...	**Al principio...** *(ahl preen-'see-pee-oh)*
At last...	**Por fin...** *(pohr feen)*
At least...	**Por lo menos...** *(pohr loh 'meh-nohs)*
By the way...	**A propósito...** *(ah proh-'poh-see-toh)*
For example...	**Por ejemplo...** *(pohr eh-'hehm-ploh)*
In general...	**En general...** *(ehn heh-neh-'rahl)*
That is...	**Es decir...** *(ehs deh-'seer)*
On the other hand...	**En cambio...** *(ehn 'kahm-bee-oh)*

Try some:

En general, estoy bien.
(ehn heh-neh-'rahl eh-'stoh-ee bee-'ehn)
A propósito, _____ (fill blank)
(ah proh-'poh-see-toh)
Al principio, venga al trabajo.
(ahl preen-'see-pee-oh 'vehn-gah ahl trah-'bah-hoh)
En cambio, _____ (fill blank)
(ehn 'kahm-bee-oh)

Listos para practicar

Connect each phrase with its appropriate response:

¿Cómo está? *('koh-moh eh-'stah)*
¿Entiende? *(ehn-tee-'ehn-deh)*
Gracias. *('grah-see-ahs)*
Hasta luego.
('ah-stah 'lweh-goh)
¿Listo? *('lee-stoh)*

Adiós. *(ah-dee-'ohs)*
No, hablo poquito español.
(noh, 'ah-bloh poh-'kee-toh eh-spah-'nyohl)
De nada. *(deh 'nah-dah)*
Bien. ¿Y usted?
('bee-ehn ee oo-'stehd)
Sí, en seguida.
(see, ehn seh-'gee-dah)

¡Información!

• Notice that the names for people, places, and things are either masculine or feminine, and so have either **el** *(ehl)* or **la** *(lah)* in front. **El** and **la** mean *the*. Generally, if the word ends in the letter **o** there's an **el** in front (i.e., **el cuarto** *(ehl 'kwahr-toh)*, **el niño** *(ehl 'nee-nyoh)*. Conversely, if the word ends in an **a** there's a **la** in front (i.e., **la mesa** *[lah 'meh-sah]*, **la persona** *[lah pehr-'soh-nah]*). Some Spanish words are exceptions: **el agua** *(ehl 'ah-gwah)*, **la mano** *(lah 'mah-noh)*, **el sofá** *(ehl soh-'fah)*.

• Words not ending in either an **o** or **a** need to be memorized (i.e., **el amor** *(ehl ah-'mohr)*, **la paz** *(lah pahs)*. In the case of single objects, use **el** and **la** much like the word *the* in English: The house is big (**La casa es grande**) *(lah 'kah-sah ehs 'grahn-deh)*.

• Remember too, that **el** and **la** are used in Spanish to indicate a person's sex. **El doctor** *(ehl dohk-'tohr)* is a male doctor, while **la doctora** *(lah dohk-'toh-rah)* is a female doctor. Here's how we change words to refer to the female gender: **la muchacha** *(lah moo-'chah-chah)*, **la niña** *(lah 'nee-nyah)*, **la bebé** *(lah beh-'beh)*.

Necessary vocabulary
El vocabulario necesario
(ehl voh-kah-boo-'lah-ree·oh neh-seh-'sah-ree·oh)

It's impossible to carry on intelligent conversation in Spanish without the basic vocabulary words. To learn them quickly, let's list the terms under specific categories. As you read each series, try to pronounce everything correctly.

Everyday things
Las cosas diarias *(lahs 'koh-sahs dee-'ah-ree·ahs)*

bathroom	**el baño** *(ehl 'bah-nyoh)*
bed	**la cama** *(lah 'kah-mah)*
book	**el libro** *(ehl 'lee-broh)*
car	**el carro** *(ehl 'kah-rroh)*
chair	**la silla** *(lah 'see-yah)*
door	**la puerta** *(lah 'pwehr-tah)*
floor	**el piso** *(ehl 'pee-soh)*
food	**la comida** *(lah koh-'mee-dah)*
house	**la casa** *(lah 'kah-sah)*
key	**la llave** *(lah 'yah-veh)*
light	**la luz** *(lah loos)*
paper	**el papel** *(ehl pah-'pehl)*
pen	**el lapicero** *(ehl lah-pee-'seh-roh)*
pencil	**el lápiz** *(ehl 'lah-pees)*
room	**el cuarto** *(ehl 'kwahr-toh)*

table	**la mesa** *(lah 'meh-sah)*
trash	**la basura** *(lah bah-'soo-rah)*
water	**el agua** *(ehl 'ah-gwah)*
window	**la ventana** *(lah vehn-'tah-nah)*
work	**el trabajo** *(ehl trah-'bah-hoh)*

People
La gente *(lah 'hehn-teh)*

baby	**el bebé** *(ehl beh-'beh)*
boy	**el niño** *(ehl 'nee-nyoh)*
girl	**la niña** *(lah 'nee-nyah)*
man	**el hombre** *(ehl 'ohm-breh)*
person	**la persona** *(lah pehr-'soh-nah)*
teenager (female)	**la muchacha** *(lah moo-'chah-chah)*
teenager (male)	**el muchacho** *(ehl moo-'chah-choh)*
woman	**la mujer** *(lah moo-'hehr)*

Colors
Los colores *(lohs koh-'loh-rehs)*

black	**negro** *('neh-groh)*
blue	**azul** *(ah-'sool)*
brown	**café** *(kah-'feh)*
green	**verde** *('vehr-deh)*
orange	**anaranjado** *(ah-nah-rahn-'hah-doh)*
purple	**morado** *(moh-'rah-doh)*
red	**rojo** *('roh-hoh)*
white	**blanco** *('blahn-koh)*
yellow	**amarillo** *(ah-mah-'ree-yoh)*

More important words
Más palabras importantes
(mahs pah-'lah-brahs eem-pohr-'tahn-tehs)

big	**grande** *('grahn-deh)*
small	**pequeño** *(peh-'keh-nyoh)*
good	**bueno** *('bweh-noh)*
bad	**malo** *('mah-loh)*

many	**muchos** *('moo-chohs)*
all	**todo** *('toh-doh)*
a few	**pocos** *('poh-kohs)*
more	**más** *(mahs)*
less	**menos** *('meh-nohs)*
much	**mucho** *('moo-choh)*
a little	**poco** *('poh-koh)*

Be aware that there are other names in Spanish for the items listed here. Most languages have more than one dialect. Here are a few "synonyms" you should know:

bathroom	**el servicio** *(ehl sehr-'vee-see-oh)*
car	**el coche** *(ehl 'koh-cheh)*
man (respectful address)	**el señor** *(ehl seh-'nyohr)*
pen	**la pluma** *(lah 'ploo-mah)*
woman (respectful address)	**la señora** *(lah seh-'nyoh-rah)*

Listos para practicar

Fill in the blank with an English translation:

el libro *(ehl 'lee-broh)* _____

la mesa *(lah 'meh-sah)* _____

el trabajo *(ehl trah-'bah-hoh)* _____

Now match the opposites:

pequeño *(peh-'keh-nyoh)*	**mujer** *(moo-'hehr)*
hombre *('ohm-breh)*	**negro** *('neh-groh)*
blanco *('blahn-koh)*	**grande** *('grahn-deh)*

Numbers

Los números *(lohs 'noo-meh-rohs)*

0	**cero** *('seh-roh)*	14	**catorce** *(kah-'tohr-seh)*
1	**uno** *('oo-noh)*	15	**quince** *('keen-seh)*
2	**dos** *(dohs)*	16	**dieciséis** *(dee-ehs-ee-'seh-ees)*
3	**tres** *(trehs)*	17	**diecisiete** *(dee-ehs-ee-see-'eh-teh)*
4	**cuatro** *('kwah-troh)*	18	**dieciocho** *(dee-ehs-ee-'oh-choh)*
5	**cinco** *('seen-koh)*	19	**diecinueve** *(dee-ehs-ee-noo-'eh-veh)*
6	**seis** *('seh·ees)*	20	**veinte** *('veh·een-teh)*
7	**siete** *(see-'eh-teh)*	30	**treinta** *('treh-een-tah)*
8	**ocho** *('oh-choh)*	40	**cuarenta** *(kwah-'rehn-tah)*
9	**nueve** *(noo-'eh-veh)*	50	**cincuenta** *(seen-'kwehn-tah)*
10	**diez** *(dee·'ehs)*	60	**sesenta** *(seh-'sehn-tah)*
11	**once** *('ohn-seh)*	70	**setenta** *(seh-'tehn-tah)*
12	**doce** *('doh-seh)*	80	**ochenta** *(oh-'chehn-tah)*
13	**trece** *('treh-seh)*	90	**noventa** *(noh-'vehn-tah)*

For all the numbers in-between, just add **y** *(ee)*, which means *and:*

21 **veinte y uno** *('veh·een-teh ee 'oo-noh)*
22 **veinte y dos** *('veh·een-teh ee 'dohs)*
23 **veinte y tres** *('veh·een-teh ee 'trehs)*

Sooner or later, you'll also need to know how to say the larger numbers in Spanish. They aren't that difficult, so practice aloud:

100	**cien** *(see·'ehn)*
200	**doscientos** *(dohs-see-'ehn-tohs)*
300	**trescientos** *(trehs-see-'ehn-tohs)*
400	**cuatrocientos** *(kwah-troh-see-'ehn-tohs)*
500	**quinientos** *(keen-ee-'ehn-tohs)*
600	**seiscientos** *(sehs-see-'ehn-tohs)*
700	**setecientos** *(seh-teh-see-'ehn-tohs)*
800	**ochocientos** *(oh-choh-see-'ehn-tohs)*
900	**novecientos** *(noh-veh-see-'ehn-tohs)*
1000	**mil** *(meel)*

¡Información!

- The cardinal numbers are valuable too! Practice:

first	**primero** *(pree-'meh-roh)*
I'm first.	**Soy el primero.** *('soh-ee ehl pree-'meh-roh)*
second	**segundo** *(seh-'goon-doh)*
I'm second.	_____
third	**tercero** *(tehr-'seh-roh)*
I'm third.	_____
fourth	**cuarto** *('kwahr-toh)*
I'm fourth	_____
fifth	**quinto** *('keen-toh)*
I'm fifth	_____
sixth	**sexto** *('sehks-toh)*
I'm sixth	_____
seventh	**séptimo** *('sehp-tee-moh)*
I'm seventh	_____
eighth	**octavo** *(ohk-'tah-voh)*
I'm eighth	_____
ninth	**noveno** *(noh-'veh-noh)*
I'm ninth	_____
tenth	**décimo** *('deh-see-moh)*
I'm tenth	_____

- A basic set of job-related vocabulary may also help get you started, so work on these for a while:

business	**los negocios** *(lohs neh-'goh-see-ohs)*
company	**la compañía** *(lah kohm-pah-'nyee-ah)*
department	**el departamento** *(ehl deh-pahr-tah-'mehn-toh)*
employee	**el empleado/la empleada**
	(ehl ehm-pleh-'ah-doh, lah ehm-pleh-'ah-dah)
Human Resources	**Los Recursos Humanos**
	(lohs reh-'koor-sohs oo-'mah-nohs)
manager	**el gerente/la gerente**
	(ehl heh-'rehn-teh, lah heh-'rehn-teh)
office	**la oficina** *(lah oh-fee-'see-nah)*
personnel	**el personal** *(ehl pehr-soh-'nahl)*

All together
¡Todos juntos! *('toh-dohs 'hoon-tohs)*
• Are you ready to form a few phrases? You'll need the following:

for	**para**	**para el trabajo**
	('pah-rah)	*('pah-rah ehl trah-'bah-hoh)*
in, on, at	**en** *(ehn)*	**en el cuarto** *(ehn ehl 'kwahr-toh)*
of, from	**de** *(deh)*	**de la persona** *(deh lah pehr-'soh-nah)*
to	**a** *(ah)*	**a la oficina** *(ah lah oh-fee-'see-nah)*
with	**con** *(kohn)*	**con el agua** *(kohn ehl 'ah-gwah)*
without	**sin** *(seen)*	**sin el carro** *(seen ehl 'kah-rroh)*

• There are only two contractions in Spanish:

| to the | **al** *(ahl)* | **al hombre** *(ahl 'ohm-breh)* |
| of the, from the | **del** *(dehl)* | **del libro** *(dehl 'lee-broh)* |

• Use these words to link everything together:

and = **y** *(ee)*   or = **o** *(oh)*   but = **pero** *('peh-roh)*

Thank you and goodbye!

¡Gracias y adiós! *('grah-see-ahs ee ah-dee-'ohs)*

 Temas culturales

If you have problems in the middle of a phrase or sentence, don't be afraid to send messages using hand gestures or facial expressions. Body signals are used frequently in conversations throughout the Spanish-speaking world. And remember, there's nothing wrong with repeating your message several times until you're understood!

Follow the rules!
¡Siga las reglas! *('see-gah lahs 'reh-glahs)*
No matter what the language, certain grammatical rules must be followed in order for you to be clearly understood.

1. The Reverse Order Rule:
As you begin to link your Spanish words together, you will find that often words are positioned in reverse order. This reverse rule is applied

when you give a description: *The descriptive word goes after the word being described.* Study these examples.

The big house	**La casa grande** *(lah 'kah-sah 'grahn-deh)*
The green chair	**La silla verde** *('lah 'see-yah 'vehr-deh)*
The important man	**El hombre importante**
	(ehl 'ohm-breh eem-pohr-'tahn-teh)

2. The Agreement Rule:

First, when you are referring to more than one item in Spanish, the words **el** and **la** (see page 9), become **los** *(lohs)* and **las** *(lahs)*, respectively.

el baño *(ehl 'bah-nyoh)*	**los baños** *(lohs 'bah-nyohs)*
el muchacho	**los muchachos**
(ehl moo-'chah-choh)	*(lohs moo-'chah-chohs)*
la mesa *(lah 'meh-sah)*	**las mesas** *(lahs 'meh-sahs)*
la silla *(lah 'see-yah)*	**las sillas** *(lahs 'see-yahs)*

Second, not only do all the nouns and adjectives need to end in s or **es** to make the sentence plural, but, when they are used together, the genders must match as well.

Two white doors	**Dos puertas blancas** *(dohs 'pwehr-tahs 'blahn-kahs)*
Many red cars	**Muchos carros rojos** *('moo-chohs 'kah-rrohs 'roh-hohs)*
Six little children	**Seis niños pequeños**
	('seh-ees 'nee-nyohs peh-'keh-nyohs)

By the way, to say *a* or *an* in Spanish, use **un** *(oon)* or **una** *('oo-nah)*:

A floor	**Un piso** *(oon 'pee-soh)*
	Un piso azul *(oon 'pee-soh ah-'sool)*
A window	**Una ventana** *('oo-nah vehn-'tah-nah)*
	Una ventana grande *('oo-nah vehn-'tah-nah 'grahn-deh)*

And to say *some* or *a few,* use **unos** *('oo-nohs)* or **unas** *('oo-nahs)*:

Some floors	**Unos pisos** *('oo-nohs 'pee-sohs)*
	Unos pisos azules *('oo-nohs 'pee-sohs ah-'soo-lehs)*
A few windows	**Unas ventanas** *('oo-nahs vehn-'tah-nahs)*
	Unas ventanas grandes
	('oo-nahs vehn-'tah-nahs 'grahn-dehs)

Listos para practicar

Fill in the missing number in each series:

treinta *('treh-eehn-tah)*, **cuarenta** *(kwah-'rehn-tah)*,
_____, **sesenta** *(seh-'sehn-tah)*
primero *(pree-'meh-roh)*, **segundo** *(seh-'goon-doh)*, **tercero**
(tehr-'seh-roh), _____
_____, **cinco** *('seen-koh)*, **seis** *('seh-ees)*, **siete** *(see-'eh-teh)*

Write the Spanish translation for these words:

with _____
on _____
to the _____

Follow the example. Change these from the singular to the plural:

El carro grande *(ehl 'kah-rroh 'grahn-deh)*
Los carros grandes *(lohs 'kah-rrohs 'grahn-dehs)*
La silla amarilla *(lah 'see-yah ah-mah-'ree-yah)*

_____

Un hombre importante *(oon 'ohm-breh eem-pohr-'tahn-teh)*

_____

La oficina blanca *(lah oh-fee-'see-nah 'blahn-kah)*

_____

The question words
Las preguntas *(lahs preh-'goon-tahs)*

The following set of Spanish questions should be memorized right away.
See if you can recognize any of these from the expressions we learned
earlier:

How many?	**¿Cuántos?** *('kwahn-tohs)*
How much?	**¿Cuánto?** *('kwahn-toh)*
How?	**¿Cómo?** *('koh-moh)*
What?	**¿Qué?** *(keh)*
When?	**¿Cuándo?** *('kwahn-doh)*
Where?	**¿Dónde?** *('dohn-deh)*

Which?	¿Cuál? *(kwahl)*
Who?	¿Quién? *(kee-'ehn)*
Whose?	¿De quién? *(deh kee-'ehn)*
Why?	¿Por qué? *(pohr keh)*

¡Información!

A few questions are actually common one-liners used regularly in simple conversations. Notice how they are not literal translations.

How's it going?	¡Qué tal! *(keh tahl)*
What's your name?	¿Cómo se llama? *('koh-moh seh 'yah-mah)*
How old are you?	¿Cuántos años tiene?
	('kwahn-tohs 'ah-nyohs tee-'eh-neh)

Powerful pronouns
Pronombres poderosos
(proh-'nohm-brehs poh-deh-'roh-sohs)

To effectively answer questions about *who* or *whose,* pronouns will be required. These are the basic words you'll need:

I	Yo *(yoh)*
We	Nosotros *(noh-'soh-trohs)*
You	Usted *(oo-'stehd)*
You (plural)	Ustedes *(oo-'steh-dehs)*
She	Ella *('eh-yah)*
He	Él *(ehl)*
They (feminine)	Ellas *('eh-yahs)*
They (masculine)	Ellos *('eh-yohs)*

Practice:

How are you?	¿Cómo está usted? *('koh-moh eh-'stah oo-'stehd)*
I am fine.	Yo estoy bien. *(yoh eh-'stoh-ee 'bee-ehn)*
How are you guys?	¿Cómo están ustedes?
	('koh-moh eh-'stahn oo-'steh-dehs)

We are fine.   **Nosotros estamos bien.**
(noh-'soh-trohs eh-'stah-mohs 'bee·ehn)

¡Información!

Nosotras *(noh-'soh-trahs)* is *we* feminine:
We are (female) supervisors.
Nosotras somos supervisoras
(noh-'soh-trahs 'soh-mohs soo-pehr-vee-'soh-rahs).

Whose is it?

¿De quién es? *(deh kee-'ehn ehs)*

A similar group of Spanish words is used to indicate possession. They
tell us *whose* it is:

It's *my* house.   **Es *mi* casa.** *(ehs mee 'kah-sah)*
It's *your, his, her*
  or *their* house.   **Es *su* casa.** *(ehs soo 'kah-sah)*
It's *our* house.   **Es *nuestra* casa.** *(ehs 'nweh-strah 'kah sah)*

Notice what happens to pronouns when you talk about more than one:

mi casa *(mee 'kah-sah)*   **mis casas** *(mees 'kah-sahs)*
su casa *(soo 'kah-sah)*   **sus casas** *(soos 'kah-sahs)*
nuestra casa *('nweh-strah 'kah-sah)* **nuestras casas** *('nweh-strahs 'kah-sahs)*

Now try these other possessive words. Are you able to translate?

mine   **mío** or **mía** *('mee-oh, 'mee-ah)*
                        Es mío. *(ehs 'mee-oh)*
yours, his, hers, theirs **suyo** or **suya** *('soo-yoh, 'soo-yah)*
                        Es suya. *(ehs 'soo-yah)*

If something *belongs to* someone else, use *de* to indicate possession:

It's Mary's.   **Es de María.** *(ehs deh mah-'ree-ah)*
It's the company's.   **Es de la compañía.**
                          (ehs deh lah kohm-pah-'nyee-ah)
It's his.   **Es de él.** *(ehs deh ehl)*

Is
Está *(eh-'stah)* and Es *(ehs)*

Now that you can form short phrases on your own, it's time to join all of your words together. To accomplish this, you'll need to understand the difference between **está** *(eh-'stah)* and **es** *(ehs)*. Both words mean *is*, but they're used differently.

The word **está** *(eh-'stah)* expresses a temporary state, condition, or location:

The girl is fine.	**La niña está bien.**
	(lah 'nee-nyah ehs-'tah 'bee-ehn)
The girl is in the room.	**La niña está en el cuarto.**
	(lah 'nee-nyah ehs-'tah ehn ehl 'kwahr-toh)

The word **es** *(ehs)* expresses an inherent characteristic or quality, including origin and ownership.

The girl is small.	**La niña es pequeña.**
	(lah 'nee-nyah ehs peh-'keh-nyah)
The girl is Maria	**La niña es María.** *(lah 'nee-nyah ehs mah-'ree-ah)*
The girl is American.	**La niña es americana.**
	(lah 'nee-nyah ehs ah-meh-ree-'kah-nah)
The girl is my friend.	**La niña es mi amiga.**
	(lah 'nee-nyah ehs mee ah-'mee-gah)

Are
Están *(eh-'stahn)* and Son *(sohn)*

You just saw how helpful **está** and **es** were. Countless sentences can be made with them. However, you'll also need to talk about more than one person, place, or thing. To do so, replace **está** with **están** *(eh-'stahn)*, and **es** with **son** *(sohn)*. And don't forget that words must agree when you change to plurals.

The book is on the table.	**El libro está en la mesa.**
	(ehl 'lee-broh eh-'stah ehn lah 'meh-sah)
The books are on the table.	**Los libros están en la mesa.**
	(lohs 'lee-brohs eh-'stahn ehn lah 'meh-sah)

The book is important.	**El libro es importante.** *(ehl 'lee-broh ehs eem-pohr-'tahn-teh)*
The books are important.	**Los libros son importantes.** *(lohs 'lee-brohs sohn eem-pohr-'tahn-tehs)*

Check out these other examples. Read them aloud as you focus on their structure and meaning.

The chairs are black.	**Las sillas son negras.** *(lahs 'see-yahs sohn 'neh-grahs)*
The papers are in the house.	**Los papeles están en la casa.** *(lohs pah-'peh-lehs eh-'stahn ehn lah 'kah-sah)*
They are not friends.	**No son amigos.** *(noh sohn ah-'mee-gohs)*
Are they good?	**¿Están buenos?** *(eh-'stahn 'bweh-nohs)*

The best way to learn how to use these words correctly is to listen to Spanish-speakers in real-life conversations. They constantly use **es, está, son,** and **están** to communicate simple messages.

This house, that house
Esta casa, esa casa
('eh-stah 'kah-sah, 'eh-sah 'kah-sah)

A lot more can be said when you learn these vocabulary terms. Remember they change according to gender:

that	**ese** *('eh-seh)* or **esa** *('eh-sah)* **Ese muchacho está aquí.** *('eh-seh moo-'chah-choh ehs-'tah ah-'kee)*
these	**estos** *('eh-stohs)* or **estas** *('eh-stahs)* **Estos tacos están malos.** *('eh-stohs 'tah-kohs ehs-'tahn 'mah-lohs)*
this	**este** *('eh-steh)* or **esta** *('eh-stah)* **Este es mi papel amarillo.** *('eh-steh ehs mee pah-'pehl ah-mah-'ree-yoh)*
those	**esos** *('eh-sohs)* or **esas** *('eh-sahs)* **Esos son hombres buenos.** *('eh-sohs sohn 'ohm-brehs 'bweh-nohs)*

I am and we are
Estoy *(eh-'stoh·ee)*/Soy *('soh·ee)* y
Estamos *(eh-'stah-mohs)*/Somos *('soh-mohs)*

To say *I am* and *We are* in Spanish, you must also acquire their different forms. As with **está** *(eh-'stah)* and **están** *(eh-'stahn)*, the words **estoy** *(eh-'stoh·ee)* and **estamos** *(eh-'stah-mohs)* refer to the location or condition of a person, place, or thing. And just like **es** *(ehs)* and **son** *(sohn)*, the words **soy** *('soh·ee)* and **somos** *('soh-mohs)* are used with everything else.

I am fine.	**Estoy bien.** *(eh-'stoh·ee 'bee·ehn)*
We are in the room.	**Estamos en el cuarto.**
	(eh-'stah-mohs ehn ehl 'kwahr-toh)
I am Lupe.	**Soy Lupe.** *('soh·ee 'loo-peh)*
We are Cuban.	**Somos cubanos.** *('soh-mohs koo-'bah-nohs)*

Now let's group all of these forms together. Look over the present tense forms of the verbs **ESTAR** *(eh-'stahr)* and **SER** *(sehr)*.

TO BE	*ESTAR (eh-'stahr)*	*SER (sehr)*
I'm	**estoy** *(eh-'stoh·ee)*	**soy** *('soh-ee)*
You're, He's, She's	**está** *(eh-'stah)*	**es** *(ehs)*
You're (pl.), They're	**están** *(eh-'stahn)*	**son** *(sohn)*
We're	**estamos** *(eh-'stah-mohs)*	**somos** *('soh-mohs)*

¡Información!

• You don't have to use the subject pronouns in every sentence. It's usually understood who's involved:

> **Nosotros somos** *(noh-'soh-trohs 'soh-mohs)* and **somos** *('soh-mohs)* both mean *we are.*

• Two other words, **estás** *(eh-'stahs)* and **eres** *('eh-rehs)*, may also be used to mean *you are* among family, friends, and small children. However, since most of your begining conversations will be between yourself and an employee, try focusing primarily on the eight words mentioned above.

• *There is* and *there are* are very simple. In both cases you use the little word, **hay** *('ah·ee):*

There's one bathroom.	**Hay un baño.**
	('ah·ee oon 'bah-nyoh)
There are two bathrooms.	**Hay dos baños.**
	('ah·ee dohs 'bah-nyohs)

Listos para practicar

Join the subject pronouns with their possessive forms:

Ella *('eh-yah)*	**mi** *(mee)*
Yo *(yoh)*	**nuestro** *('nweh-stroh)*
Nosotros *(noh-'soh-trohs)*	**su** *(soo)*

Translate into English:

¿Quién? *(kee-'ehn)* _____

¿Cuántos? *('kwahn-tohs)* _____

¿Dónde? *('dohn-deh)* _____

Fill in each blank with the appropriate verb form:

está *(eh-'stah),* **son** *(sohn),* **hay** *('ah·ee),* **estoy** *(eh-'stoh·ee),* **somos** *('soh-mohs)*

Estos _____ **muy buenos.**
('eh-stohs____ 'moo·ee 'bwehn-nohs)

Pedro _____ **en la oficina.**
('peh-droh ____ ehn lah oh-fee-'see-nah)

Ella y yo _____ **amigas.** *('eh-yah ee yoh ___ ah-'mee-gahs)*

No _____ **trabajo.** *(noh ___ trah-'bah-hoh)*

Yo _____ **bien.** *(yoh___ 'bee-ehn)*

To have
Tener *(teh-'nehr)*

Tener *(teh-'nehr)* (to have) is another common linking word in Spanish, and its forms will become more necessary as you begin to create Spanish sentences on your own. Although these words will be discussed in more detail later, here are the basics to get you started:

I have	**tengo** *('tehn-goh)*
You have, He has, She has	**tiene** *(tee-'eh-neh)*
You have (pl.), They have	**tienen** *(tee-'eh-nehn)*
We have	**tenemos** *(teh-'neh-mohs)*

Study these examples:

I have a problem. **Tengo un problema.**
('tehn-go oon proh-'bleh-mah)

She has a white car. **Tiene un carro blanco.**
(tee-'eh-neh oon 'kah-rroh 'blahn-koh)

They have four children. **Tienen cuatro niños.**
(tee-'eh-nehn 'kwah-troh 'nee-nyohs)

We have the office. **Tenemos la oficina.**
(teh-'neh-mohs lah oh-fee-'see-nah)

¡Información!

- Even though **tener** literally means *to have*, sometimes it is used instead of the verb **estar** to express a temporary condition:

(I am) afraid	**(tengo) miedo** *('tehn-goh mee-'eh-doh)*
(we are) at fault	**(tenemos) la culpa** *(teh-'neh-mohs lah 'kool-pah)*
(they are) cold	**(tienen) frío** *(tee-'eh-nehn 'free-oh)*
(she is) 15 years old	**(tiene) quince años** *('tee-'eh-neh keen-seh 'ah-nyohs)*
(I am) hot	**(tengo) calor** *('tehn-goh kah-'lohr)*
(they are) hungry	**(tienen) hambre** *(tee-'eh-nehn 'ahm-breh)*
(he is) sleepy	**(tiene) sueño** *(tee-'eh-neh 'sweh-nyoh)*
(we are) thirsty	**(tenemos) sed** *(teh-'neh-mohs sehd)*

- To say *not* in Spanish, interject the word **no** in front of the verb:

José is not my friend.	**José no es mi amigo.**
	('hoh-seh noh ehs mee ah-'mee-goh)
I do not have the job.	**No tengo el trabajo.**
	(noh 'tehn-goh ehl trah-'bah-hoh)
There are no more.	**No hay más.** *(noh 'ah·ee mahs)*

- **Tienes** is the informal way to say *you have.*

My friend, do you have the key?	**¿Amigo, tienes la llave?**
	(ah-'mee-goh, tee-'eh-nehs lah 'yah-veh)

More Spanish verbs
Más verbos en español
(mahs 'vehr-bohs ehn eh-spah-'nyohl)

Putting a few words together in a new language is a thrilling experience, but real communication begins once you start using verbs, or "action words." Although **estar, ser,** and **tener** are extremely useful, they do not express action. Learning how to use Spanish verbs will allow us to talk about what's going on in the world around us.

Spend a few moments memorizing this brief list of helpful beginning verbs. Notice that Spanish action words end in the letters **ar, er,** or **ir:**

to come	**venir** *(veh-'neer)*
to drive	**manejar** *(mah-neh-'hahr)*
to eat	**comer** *(koh-'mehr)*
to drink	**beber** *(beh-'behr)*
to follow	**seguir** *(seh-'geer)*
to go	**ir** *(eer)*
to listen	**escuchar** *(eh-skoo-'chahr)*
to look	**mirar** *(mee-'rahr)*
to read	**leer** *(leh-'ehr)*
to repeat	**repetir** *(reh-peh-'teer)*
to run	**correr** *(koh-'rrehr)*
to sleep	**dormir** *(dohr-'meer)*
to speak	**hablar** *(ah-'blahr)*
to walk	**caminar** *(kah-mee-'nahr)*

to wait	**esperar** *(eh-speh-'rahr)*
to work	**trabajar** *(trah-bah-'hahr)*
to write	**escribir** *(eh-skree-'beer)*

¡Información!

• You can never learn enough action words in Spanish. Over one hundred verbs are listed in the specialized dictionary at the end of this book, so use it as a reference tool. When you come across a verb as you study and practice, look it up in Spanish or English to learn its base form and meaning.

• Many Spanish verb infinitives that relate to human resources are similar to English. Look at these examples:

to investigate	**investigar** *(een-veh-stee-'gahr)*
to observe	**observar** *(ohb-sehr-'vahr)*
to consult	**consultar** *(kohn-sool-'tahr)*
to repair	**reparar** *(reh-pah-'rahr)*
to move	**mover** *(moh-'vehr)*

Más fácil *(mahs 'fah-seel)*
Simplify

One of the most effective ways to put your verbs into action is to combine them with simple phrases that create complete commands. For example, look what happens when you add these verb infinitives to **Favor de...** *(fah-'vohr deh)*, which implies, *Would you please...*:

Please...	**Favor de...** *(fah-'vohr deh)*
write everything	**escribir todo** *(eh-skree-'beer 'toh-doh)*
read the paper	**leer el papel** *(leh-'ehr ehl pah-'pehl)*
speak in English	**hablar en inglés** *(ah-'blahr ehn een-'glehs)*

Here's another shortcut. By adding the word **no** in front of the verb, you communicate the command *don't.*

Please don't read the paper.
Favor de no leer el papel.
(fah-'vohr deh noh leh-'ehr ehl pah-'pehl)

Favor de is one of several key expressions that can be found in chapter segments entitled **Más fácil.** These phrases are combined with basic verb forms in order to improve your language skills at a faster pace!

Listos para practicar

Use forms of **tener** *(teh-'nehr)* to translate the following:

They are cold. _____
I don't have the job. _____
We are hungry. _____

Insert the verb infinitive that *best* fits each sentence:

comer, hablar, manejar, leer, escuchar
(koh-'mehr, ah-'blahr, mah-neh-'hahr, leh-'ehr, eh-skoo-'chahr)

Favor de _____ **el carro.** *(fah-'vohr deh ___ ehl 'kah-rroh)*
No _____ **el libro.** *(noh ___ ehl 'lee-broh)*
Favor de _____ **español.** *(fah-'vohr deh ___ eh-spah-'nyohl)*
No _____ **en el restaurante.**
(noh ___ ehn ehl reh-stow-'rahn-teh)
Favor de _____ **la radio.** *(fah-'vohr deh ___ lah 'rah-dee-oh)*

Palabras activas
(pah-'lah-brahs ahk-'tee-vahs)
Action words

To express your thoughts clearly in Spanish, you'll need to learn as many verb tenses as possible. Throughout this book, in sections entitled, **Palabras activas,** you will be introduced to a variety of conjugated verb forms. By practicing the patterns, you'll soon be able to discuss past, present, and future events.

Let's begin with one of the easiest verb forms to use. It's the Present Progressive tense, and it refers to actions that are taking place at this moment. It is similar to our *-ing* form in English. Simply change the base verb ending slightly, and then combine the new form with the four forms of the verb **estar** *(eh-'stahr)*. The **ar** verbs become **-ando** *('ahn-doh)*, while the **er** and **ir** verbs become **-iendo** *('yehn-doh)*. Study these examples closely:

work	**trabajar** *(trah-bah-'hahr)*
working	**trabajando** *(trah-bah-'hahn-doh)*
We're working.	***Estamos*** **trabajando.**
	(eh-'stah-mohs trah-bah-'hahn-doh)
eat	**comer** *(koh-'mehr)*
eating	**comiendo** *(koh-mee-'ehn-doh)*
The man *is* eating.	**El hombre *está* comiendo.**
	(ehl 'ohm-breh eh-'stah koh-mee-'ehn-doh)
write	**escribir** *(eh-skree-'beer)*
writing	**escribiendo** *(eh-skree-bee-'ehn-doh)*
I'm writing on the paper.	***Estoy*** **escribiendo en el papel.**
	(eh-'stoh-ee eh-skree-bee-'ehn-doh ehn ehl pah-'pehl)

☞ **¡Información!**

Some verbs change in spelling and pronunciation when you add the **-ndo** ending. Look at these examples:

follow	**seguir** *(seh-'geer)*
following	**siguiendo** *(see-gee-'ehn-doh)*
sleep	**dormir** *(dohr-'meer)*
sleeping	**durmiendo** *(duhr-mee-'ehn-doh)*
read	**leer** *(leh-'ehr)*
reading	**leyendo** *(leh-'yehn-doh)*

¡Ordenes! *('ohr-deh-nehs)*
Orders!

As long as we're talking about working with Spanish-speaking employees, review the following important command or request words. They are unique forms of verbs that can be used all by themselves. Try using them in work-related situations—and always say **por favor** *(pohr fah-'vohr)*:

Please...	**Por favor...** *(pohr fah-vohr)*
come	**venga** *('vehn-gah)*
listen	**escuche** *(eh-'skoo-cheh)*
go	**vaya** *('vah-yah)*
hurry up	**apúrese** *(ah-'poo-reh-seh)*
run	**corra** *('koh-rrah)*
sit down	**siéntese** *(see-'ehn-teh-seh)*
stand up	**levántese** *(leh-'vahn-teh-seh)*
stop	**párese** *('pah-reh-seh)*
wait	**espere** *(eh-'speh-reh)*
walk	**camine** *(kah-'mee-neh)*
watch	**mire** *('mee-reh)*

There's no better way to learn than by doing. That's why each chapter in *Spanish for Human Resources Managers* includes a section entitled **¡Ordenes!** where learners receive new lists of command words, followed by tips on how to practice them with Spanish speakers. Watch out for the icon depicted above to learn more command expressions.

¡Información!

• Do not try to translate the **se** ending on some commands. It is found throughout Spanish, and has a number of unique meanings. It's probably best if you attempt to say these words now, and ask questions about grammar later!

• Any vocabulary item can be learned quickly if it's practiced in conjunction with a command word. For example, to pick up the names for furniture, have a native Spanish speaker command you to touch, look at, or point to things throughout the office. This exercise really works, and more importantly, it can be lots of fun:

Touch...	**Toque...** (*'toh-keh*)	
Look at...	**Mire...** (*'mee-reh*)	...the desk
Point to...	**Señale...** (*seh-'nyah-leh*)	**(el escritorio)**
		(*ehl ehs-kree-'toh-ree-oh*)

Listos para practicar

Follow the pattern as you practice:

manejar	**manejando**	**Estoy manejando**
trabajar	_____	_____
hablar	_____	_____
consultar	_____	_____

Connect the opposites:

Siéntese (*see-'ehn-teh-seh*)	**Vaya** (*'vah-yah*)
Venga (*'vehn-gah*)	**Camine** (*kah-'mee-neh*)
Corra (*'koh-rrah*)	**Levántese** (*leh-'vahn-teh-seh*)

Chapter Two

Capítulo Dos
(kah-'pee-too-loh dohs)

The Employee
El empleado
(ehl ehm-pleh-'ah-doh)

To call, interview, and hire
Llamar, entrevistar y contratar
(yah-'mahr, ehn-treh-vee-'stahr ee kohn-trah-'tahr)

Before you take on any more Spanish, read over and practice the basic language material found in Chapter One because this next series of skills builds upon the fundamentals. You are now going to develop sentences that meet your specific needs.

Let's start with your initial contact with someone. Greet, and then ask how he or she is doing:

Hi. How are you?	**Hola. ¿Cómo está?** *('oh-lah 'koh-moh eh-'stah)*
I am...	**Estoy...** *(eh-'stoh·ee)*
bored	**aburrido (a)** *(ah-boo-'rree-doh)*
fine	**bien** *('bee·ehn)*
happy	**contento (a)** *(kohn-'tehn-toh)*
nervous	**nervioso (a)** *(nehr-vee-'oh-soh)*
sad	**triste** *('tree-steh)*
sick	**enfermo (a)** *(ehn-'fehr-moh)*
surprised	**sorprendido (a)** *(sohr-prehn-'dee-doh)*
tired	**cansado (a)** *(kahn-'sah-doh)*
upset	**enojado (a)** *(eh-noh-'hah-doh)*
worried	**preocupado (a)** *(preh-oh-koo-'pah-doh)*
Are you...?	**¿Está...** *(eh-'stah)*
available	**disponible** *(dee-spoh-'nee-bleh)*
interested	**interesado(a)** *(een-teh-reh-'sah-doh)*
busy	**ocupado(a)** *(oh-koo-'pah-doh)*

> All of the above adjectives are masculine and most end in **o**. When the adjective is feminine, in most cases you delete the **o** and add an **a** (**aburrido-aburrida, contento-contenta**). Some, such as **triste** and **disponible** remain unchanged.

After you greet, use this sample sentence to introduce yourself:

My name is _____.
Me llamo _____. *(meh 'yah-moh ____)*

I'm from the _____ company.

Soy de la compañía de _____.

('soh·ee deh lah kohm-pah-'nyee-ah deh ____)

I'm _____, from the Human Resources Department.

Soy _____, del Departamento de Recursos Humanos.

('soh·ee ____ dehl deh-pahr-tah-'mehn-toh deh reh-'koor-sohs oo-'mah-nohs)

Now, let the person know the nature of your business. There are several new action words here, so pay attention. For review, all of these base forms will be introduced again at the end of the chapter:

I would like...	**Quisiera...** *(kee-see-'eh-rah)*
to hire you	**contratarle** *(kohn-trah-'tahr-leh)*
to explain the test	**explicar la prueba**
	(ehks-plee-'kahr lah proo-'eh-bah)
to read your resume	**leer su curriculum**
	(leh-'ehr soo koo-ree-koo-'loom)
to send you something	**mandarle algo** *(mahn-'dahr-leh 'ahl-goh)*
to describe the position	**describir el puesto**
	(deh-skree-'beer ehl 'pweh-stoh)
to offer you a job	**ofrecerle un trabajo**
	(oh-freh-'sehr-leh oon trah-'bah-hoh)
to know if you're interested	**saber si está interesado (a)**
	(sah-'behr see ehs-'tah een-teh-reh-'sah-doh)
to see if you're available	**ver si está disponible**
	(vehr see eh-'stah dee-spoh-'nee-bleh)
to have some information	**tener alguna información**
	(teh-'nehr ahl-'goo-nah een-fohr-mah-see-'ohn)
to interview you	**darle una entrevista**
	('dahr-leh 'oo-nah ehn-treh-'vee-stah)
to talk to your boss	**hablar con su jefe**
	(ah-'blahr kohn soo 'heh-feh)
to call you later	**llamarle más tarde**
	(yah-'mahr-leh mahs 'tahr-deh)
to give you the opportunity	**darle la oportunidad**
	('dahr-leh lah oh-pohr-too-nee-'dahd)

to discuss the details	**discutir los detalles**
	(dee-skoo-'teer lohs deh-'tah-yehs)
to recommend a place	**recomendar un sitio**
	(reh-koh-mehn-'dahr oon 'see-tee·oh)
to check these references	**verificar estas referencias**
	(veh-ree-fee-'kahr 'eh-stahs reh-feh-'rehn-see·ahs)
to have a second interview	**tener una segunda entrevista**
	(teh-'nehr 'oo-nah seh-'goon-dah ehn-treh-'vee-stah)

 ## ¡Información!

One effective method to remember the names for things is to write their names on removable stickers and then place them on the objects you are trying to remember.

Please fill out this form
Favor de llenar este formulario
(fah-'vohr deh yeh-'nahr 'eh-steh fohr-moo-'lah-ree·oh)

Once your prospective employee understands your intentions, hand him or her the proper application forms. To gather all the information you can, start off with a standard questionnaire. In Spanish, the structure is a breeze. Simply continue with the basic pattern:

What is your...?	**¿Cuál es su...?** *(kwahl ehs soo)*
address	**dirección** *(dee-rehk-see-'ohn)*
date of birth	**fecha de nacimiento**
	('feh-chah deh nah see-mee-'ehn-toh)
first language	**lengua materna**
	('lehn-gwah mah-'tehr-nah)
full name	**nombre y apellido**
	('nohm-breh ee ah-peh-'yee-doh)
insurance company	**compañía de seguros**
	(kohm-pah-'nyee-ah deh seh-'goo-rohs)
last name	**apellido** *(ah-peh-'yee-doh)*

last place of employment	**último lugar de empleo**
	('ool-tee-moh loo-'gahr deh ehm-'pleh-oh)
license number	**número de licencia**
	('noo-meh-roh deh lee-'sehn-see·ah)
maiden name	**nombre de soltera**
	('nohm-breh deh sohl-'teh-rah)
marital status	**estado civil** *(eh-'stah-doh see-'veel)*
middle initial	**segunda inicial**
	(seh-'goon-dah ee-nee-see-'ahl)
name	**nombre** *('nohm-breh)*
nationality	**nacionalidad** *(nah-see·oh-nah-lee-'dahd)*
place of birth	**lugar de nacimiento**
	(loo-'gahr deh nah-see-mee-'ehn-toh)
relationship	**relación** *(reh-lah-see-'ohn)*
religion	**religión** *(reh-lee-hee-'ohn)*
social security number	**número de seguro social**
	('noo-meh-roh deh seh-'goo-roh soh-see-'ahl)
telephone number	**número de teléfono**
	('noo-meh-roh deh teh-'leh-foh-noh)
zip code	**zona postal** *('soh-nah poh-'stahl)*

Keep going—pronounce each word as you practice:

What's your...?	**¿Cuál es su...?** *(kwahl ehs soo)*
height	**altura** *(ahl-'too-rah)*
weight	**peso** *('peh-soh)*
blood type	**tipo de sangre** *('tee-poh deh 'sahn-greh)*
signature	**firma** *('feer-mah)*

 ## Temas culturales

When referring to others by name, it really helps if you are able to pronounce people's names correctly, as it makes them feel much more at ease. Always remember that Spanish is pronounced the way it is written. Also, it is not uncommon for someone in Spain or Latin America to have two last names. Don't get confused. Here's the order:

First name	Father's last name	Mother's last name
primer nombre	**apellido paterno**	**apellido materno**
(pree-'mehr	*(ah-peh-'yee-doh*	*(ah-peh-'yee-doh*
'nohm-breh)	*pah-'tehr-noh)*	*mah-'tehr-noh)*
Juan Carlos	**Espinoza**	**García**
(wahn 'kahr-lohs)	*(eh-spee-'noh-sah)*	*(gahr-'see-ah)*

¡Información!

- The popular phrase **¿Cómo se llama?** *('koh-moh seh 'yah-mah)* is usually translated to mean *What's your name?* However, you may also hear **¿Cuál es su nombre?** *(kwahl ehs soo 'nohm-breh)*, which means *Which is your name?*

- Not all Hispanic people have two first names, and there is no "middle name" as we know it.

- Often, when a woman marries, she keeps her father's last name, followed by her husband's.

- Learn these abbreviations:

Mr.	**Sr.** *(seh-'nyohr)*
Mrs.	**Sra.** *(seh-'nyoh-rah)*
Miss	**Srta.** *(seh-nyoh-'ree-tah)*

Listos para practicar

Complete this form with answers about yourself. Can you do it without checking for translations?

nombre completo *('nohm-breh kohm-'pleh-toh)*

_____

fecha de nacimiento *('feh-chah deh nah-see-mee-'ehn-toh)*

_____

número de teléfono *('noo-meh-roh deh teh-'leh-foh-noh)*

_____

dirección *(dee-rehk-see-'ohn)* _____
firma *('feer-mah)* _____

Match these opposites:

contento (kohn-'tehn-toh)   **aburrido** (ah-boo-'rree-doh)
interesado (een-teh-reh-'sah-doh) **triste** ('tree-steh)
enfermo (ehn-'fehr-moh)   **bien** (bee-'ehn)

Finish this pattern using one of the phrases you learned:

I would like...   **Quisiera...** (kee-see-'eh-rah)
to interview you   _____
to call you later   _____
to offer you a job   _____

A few more questions

Unas preguntas más ('oo-nahs preh-'goon-tahs mahs)

Continue collecting information with more "question words." You should know many of these words already. Again, pronounce each sentence correctly and try to memorize any unfamiliar vocabulary:

What's your...?	**¿Cuál es su...?** (kwahl ehs soo)
business	**negocio** (neh-góh-see·oh)
field	**campo de trabajo** ('kahm-poh deh trah-'bah-hoh)
level	**nivel** (nee-'vehl)
preference	**preferencia** (preh-feh-'rehn-see·ah)
skill	**habilidad** (ah-bee-lee-'dahd)
specialty	**especialidad** (eh-speh-see-ah-lee-'dahd)
talent	**talento** (tah-'lehn-toh)
title	**título** ('tee-too-loh)
Who's your...?	**¿Quién es su...?** (kee-'ehn ehs soo)
boss	**jefe** ('heh-feh)
closest relative	**pariente más cercano** (pah-ree-'ehn-teh mahs sehr-'kah-noh)
family physician	**médico familiar** ('meh-dee-koh fah-mee-lee-'ahr)
friend	**amigo** (ah-'mee-goh)
manager	**gerente** (heh-'rehn-teh)
neighbor	**vecino** (veh-'see-noh)

previous employer	**empleador previo** *(ehm-pleh-ah-'dohr 'preh-vee·oh)*
reference	**referencia** *(reh-feh-'rehn-see·ah)*
spouse	**esposo(a)** *(eh-'spoh-soh/ah)*
supervisor	**supervisor** *(soo-pehr-vee-'sohr)*
How much...?	**¿Cuánto/a...?** *('kwahn-toh/ah)*
can you tell me	**¿Cuánto puede decirme?** *('kwahn-toh 'pweh-deh deh-'seer-meh)*
does it cost	**¿Cuánto cuesta?** *('kwahn-toh 'kweh-stah)*
do you earn	**¿Cuánto gana usted?** *('kwahn-tah 'gah-nah oo-'stehd)*
education	**¿Cuánta educación?** *('kwahn-tah eh-doo-kah-see-'ohn)*
experience	**¿Cuánta experiencia?** *('kwahn-tah ehk-speh-ree-'ehn-see·ah)*
time	**¿Cuánto tiempo?** *('kwahn-toh tee-'ehm-poh)*
training	**¿Cuánto entrenamiento?** *('kwahn-toh ehn-treh-nah-mee-'ehn-toh)*
work	**¿Cuánto trabajo?** *('kwahn-toh trah-'bah-hoh)*
When...?	**¿Cuándo...?** *('kwahn-doh)*
can you meet	**puede reunirse** *('pweh-deh reh-oo-'neer-seh)*
can you start	**puede empezar** *('pweh-deh ehm-peh-'sahr)*
can you work	**puede trabajar** *('pweh-deh trah-bah-'hahr)*
did you finish	**terminó** *(tehr-mee-'noh)*
did you leave	**salió** *(sah-lee-'oh)*
did you quit	**renunció** *(reh-noon-see-'oh)*
did you retire	**jubiló** *(hoo-bee-'loh)*
did you start	**empezó** *(ehm-peh-'soh)*
did you work there	**trabajó ahí** *(trah-bah-'hoh ah-'ee)*
Where...?	**¿Dónde...?** *('dohn-deh)*
did you study	**estudió** *(eh-stoo-dee-'oh)*
did you work before	**trabajó antes** *(trah-bah-'hoh 'ahn-tehs)*
do you live	**vive** *('vee-veh)*
do you work now	**trabaja ahora** *(trah-'bah-hah ah-'oh-rah)*
were you born	**nació** *(nah-see-'oh)*

Why...?	¿Por qué...? *(pohr keh)*
aren't you working	**no está trabajando**
	(noh eh-'stah trah-bah-'hahn-doh)
are you applying	**está solicitando trabajo**
	(eh-'stah soh-lee-see-'tahn-doh trah-'bah-hoh)
are you quitting	**está renunciando**
	(eh-'stah reh-noon-see-'ahn-doh)
should I hire you	**debo contratarle**
	('deh-boh kohn-trah-'tahr-leh)
were you fired	**le (la) despidieron**
	(leh/lah deh-spee-dee-'eh-rohn)

¡Información!

• Do not get frustrated by all the different verb forms. They'll be discussed in the pages ahead!

• *Time* in general is **el tiempo** *(ehl tee-'ehm-poh)*. The *specific time* is **la hora** *(lah 'oh-rah)*. *Time* in reference to an occurrence is **la vez** *(lah vehs)*.

• Check out these popular variations of the word, **dónde** *('dohn-deh)*:

Where are you from?	**¿De dónde es?** *(deh 'dohn-deh ehs)*
Where did you go?	**¿Adónde fue?** *(ah-'dohn-deh fweh)*

• Don't be afraid to ask about citizenship:

Are you a U.S. citizen?

¿Es usted un (una) ciudadano(a) de los Estados Unidos?
(ehs oo-'stehd oon/oonah see-oo-dah-'dah-noh/nah deh lohs eh-'stah-dohs oo-'nee-dohs)

What's your resident number?

¿Cuál es su número de residente?
(kwahl ehs soo 'noo-meh-roh deh reh-see-'dehn-teh)

Do you have a green card?

¿Tiene usted una tarjeta de residente permanente?
(tee-'eh-neh 'oo-nah tahr-'heh-tah deh reh-see-'dehn-teh pehr-mah-'nehn-teh)

Are you a naturalized citizen?
¿Es usted ciudadano(a) naturalizado(a)?
(ehs oo-'stehd see-oo-dah-'dah-noh/nah nah-too-rah-lee-'sah-doh/dah)

Do you have a work permit?
¿Tiene usted un permiso de trabajo?
(tee-'eh-neh oo-'stehd oon pehr-'mee-soh deh trah-'bah-hoh)

Listos para practicar

Write the word that best fits each sentence, and then read everything aloud:

entrenamiento, gerente, vive, está renunciando *(ehn-treh-nah-mee-'ehn-toh, heh-'rehn-teh, 'vee-veh, eh-'stah reh-noon-see-'ahn-doh)*

¿Por qué _____? *(pohr keh)*
¿Quién es su _____? *(kee-'ehn ehs soo)*
¿Cuánto _____? *('kwahn-toh)*
¿Dónde _____? *('dohn-deh)*

Now try it with these verb forms:

Estudió, Trabajó, Salió *(eh-stoo-dee-'oh, trah-bah-'hoh, sah-lee-'oh)*

You, he, she studied _____
You, he, she worked _____
You, he, she left _____

Translate:

negocio *(neh-'goh-see·oh)* _____
tiempo *(tee-'ehm-poh)* _____
habilidad *(ah-bee-lee-'dahd)* _____

Do you have it?
¿Lo tiene? *(loh tee-'eh-neh)*

As we learned in Chapter One, the word **¿Tiene...?** *(tee-'eh-neh)* is often used to mean *Do you have...?* Look at how valuable this word can be during the hiring process. As you speak, listen for the answers, **sí** or **no:**

Do you have (the)...?	**¿Tiene...?** *(tee-'eh-neh)*
appointment	**la cita** *(lah 'see-tah)*
approval	**la aprobación** *(lah ah-proh-bah-see-'ohn)*
date	**la fecha** *(lah 'feh-chah)*
education	**la educación** *(lah eh-doo-kah-see-'ohn)*
employment	**el empleo** *(ehl ehm-'pleh-oh)*
experience	**la experiencia** *(lah ehk-speh-ree-'ehn-see·ah)*
interview	**la entrevista** *(lah ehn-treh-'vee-stah)*
location	**el lugar** *(ehl loo-'gahr)*
meeting	**la reunión** *(lah reh-oo-nee-'ohn)*
name	**el nombre** *(ehl 'nohm-breh)*
number	**el número** *(ehl 'noo-meh-roh)*
time	**la hora** *(lah 'oh-rah)*
training	**el entrenamiento** *(ehl ehn-treh-nah-mee-'ehn-toh)*
transportation	**el transporte** *(ehl trahn-'spohr-teh)*
I have (the)...	**Tengo...** *('tehn-goh)*
application	**la solicitud** *(lah soh-lee-see-'tood)*
card	**la tarjeta** *(lah tahr-'heh-tah)*
certificate	**el certificado** *(ehl sehr-tee-fee-'kah-doh)*
contract	**el contrato** *(ehl kohn-'trah-toh)*
diploma	**el diploma** *(ehl dee-'ploh-mah)*
driver's license	**la licencia de manejar** *(lah lee-'sehn-see·ah deh mah-neh-'hahr)*
equipment	**el equipo** *(ehl eh-'kee-poh)*
form	**el formulario** *(ehl fohr-moo-'lah-ree·oh)*
identification	**la identificación** *(lah ee-dehn-tee-fee-kah-see-'ohn)*
insurance	**el seguro** *(ehl seh-'goo-roh)*
record	**el registro** *(ehl 'reh-'gee-stroh)*
references	**las referencias** *(lahs reh-feh-'rehn-see·ahs)*
requirements	**los requisitos** *(lohs reh-kee-'see-tohs)*
results	**los resultados** *(lohs reh-sool-'tah-dohs)*
resume	**el currículum, el resumé** *(ehl koo-ree-koo-'loom, ehl reh-soo-'meh)*
schedule	**el horario** *(ehl oh-'rah-ree·oh)*

tools	**las herramientas** *(lahs eh-rrah-mee-'ehn-tahs)*
transcripts	**las transcripciones**
	(lahs trahn-skreep-see-'oh-nehs)
uniform	**el uniforme** *(ehl oo-nee-'fohr-meh)*

¡Información!

• Try out a few of the more delicate questions:

Do you drink?	**¿Toma licor?** *('toh-mah lee-'kohr)*
Do you smoke?	**¿Fuma?** *('foo-mah)*
Do you take drugs?	**¿Toma drogas?** *('toh-mah 'droh-gahs)*
Let's talk about (the)...	**Vamos a hablar de...** *('vah-mohs ah-'blahr deh)*
appearance	**el aspecto** *(ehl ah-'spehk-toh)*
credit problems	**los problemas con el crédito** *(lohs proh-'bleh-mahs kohn ehl 'kreh-dee-toh)*
grades in school	**las notas en la escuela** *(lahs 'noh-tahs ehn lah eh-'skweh-lah)*
language proficiency	**la competencia en el lenguaje** *(lah kohm-peh-'tehn-see-ah ehn ehl lehn-'gwah-heh)*
medical problems	**los problemas médicos** *(lohs proh-'bleh-mahs 'meh-dee-kohs)*
military service	**el servicio militar** *(ehl sehr-'vee-see-oh mee-lee-'tahr)*
physical requirements	**los requisitos físicos** *(lohs reh-kee-'see-tohs 'fee-see-kohs)*

• One unique form of the verb **haber** allows you to ask what the applicant has or has not done in the past. Be careful with your pronunciation as you try out the pattern below:

Have you...?	**¿Ha...?** *(ah)*
been arrested	**sido arrestado** *('see-doh ah-'rreh-stah-doh)*

been looking for a job	**estado buscando un trabajo**
	(eh-'stah-doh boo-'skahn-doh oon trah-'bah-hoh)
completed high school	**terminado la escuela secundaria**
	(tehr-mee-'nah-doh lah eh-'skweh-lah seh-koon-'dah-ree-ah)
had experience	**tenido experiencia**
	(teh-'nee-doh ehk-speh-ree-'ehn-see-ah)
had training	**tenido entrenamiento**
	(teh-'nee-doh ehn-treh-nah-mee-'ehn-toh)
seen the classified ad	**visto el anuncio clasificado**
	('vee-stoh ehl ah-'noon-see-oh klah-see-fee-'kah-doh)
taken courses in college	**tomado cursos en la universidad**
	(toh-'mah-doh 'koor-sohs ehn lah oo-nee-vehr-see-'dahd)
used that machine	**usado esa máquina**
	(oo-'sah-doh 'eh-sah 'mah-kee-nah)
worked here before	**trabajado aquí antes**
	(trah-bah-'hah-doh ah-'kee 'ahn-tehs)

How did you hear about the job?

¿Cómo aprendió del trabajo?

('koh-moh ah-prehn-dee-'oh dehl trah-'bah-hoh)

employment office	**la agencia de trabajo**
	(lah ah-'hehn-see-ah deh trah-'bah-hoh)
friends, family	**los amigos, la familia**
	(lohs ah-'mee-gohs, lah fah-'mee-lee-ah)
newspaper, magazine	**el periódico, la revista**
	(ehl peh-ree-'oh-dee-koh, lah reh-'vee-stah)
television, radio	**la televisión, la radio**
	(lah teh-leh-vee-see-'ohn, lah 'rah-dee-oh)
want ads	**los anuncios de trabajos**
	(lohs ah-'noon-see-ohs deh trah-'bah-hohs)

Do you know?
¿Sabe? *('sah-beh)*

In Spanish, there are two primary ways to say *to know. To know something* requires the verb **saber,** *(sah-'behr)* while *to know someone* requires the verb **conocer.** Instead of working on all the conjugated forms of these new verbs, why not put them to practical use. Next time you need *to know,* pull a line from the sentences below:

I don't know.	**No sé.** *(noh seh)*
I don't know him.	**No le conozco.** *(noh leh koh-'noh-skoh)*
Do you know English?	**¿Sabe usted inglés?** *('sah-beh oo-'stehd een-'glehs)*
Do you know her?	**¿La conoce a ella?** *(lah koh-'noh-seh ah 'eh-yah)*
I didn't know it.	**No lo sabía.** *(noh loh sah-'bee-ah)*
I didn't know him.	**No le conocía a él.** *(noh leh koh-noh-'see-ah ah ehl)*

Obviously, **saber** *(sah-'behr)* works wonders at an interview. Ask your candidates about their professional skills:

Do you know how to speak English?	**¿Sabe hablar inglés?** *('sah-beh ah-'blahr een-'glehs)*
Do you know how to read and write?	**¿Sabe leer y escribir?** *('sah-beh leh-'ehr ee eh-skree-'beer)*
Do you know how to do it?	**¿Sabe hacerlo?** *('sah-beh ah-'sehr-loh)*

 ## ¡Información!

You've probably noticed that some Spanish words are listed again in a different group of vocabulary items. That's because they are used frequently in more than one topic of conversation. Just think of it as a chance to get more practice with the same terminology!

appointment date	**la fecha de la cita** *(lah 'feh-chah deh lah 'see-tah)*

business card	**la tarjeta de negocios**
	(lah tahr-'heh-tah deh neh-'goh-see·ohs)
contact person	**la persona de contacto**
	(lah pehr-'soh-nah deh kohn-'tahk-toh)
cover letter	**la carta de presentación**
	(lah 'kahr-tah deh preh-sehn-tah-see-'ohn)
education background	**la historia educacional**
	(lah ee-'stoh-ree·ah eh-doo-kah-see-oh-'nahl)
entry-level	**de nivel básico** *(deh nee-'vehl 'bah-see-koh)*
equal opportunities	**la igualdad de oportunidades**
	(lah ee-gwahl-'dahd deh oh-pohr-too-nee-'dah-dehs)
hiring procedure	**el procedimiento para contratar**
	(ehl proh-seh-dee-mee-'ehn-toh 'pah-rah kohn-trah-'tahr)
hours of work	**las horas de trabajo**
	(lahs 'oh-rahs de trah-'bah-hoh)
job description	**la descripción del trabajo**
	(lah deh-skreep-see-'ohn dehl trah-'bah-hoh)
job placement	**la contratación de personal**
	(lah kohn-trah-tah-see-'ohn deh pehr-soh-'nahl)
job-related	**relacionada con el trabajo**
	(reh-lah-see·oh-'nah-dah kohn ehl trah-'bah-hoh)
office location	**la localidad de la oficina**
	(lah loh-kah-lee-'dahd deh lah oh-fee-'see-nah)
pre-employment	**antes de tener empleo**
	('ahn-tehs deh teh-'nehr ehm-'pleh-oh)
room number	**el número del cuarto**
	(ehl 'noo-meh-roh dehl 'kwahr-toh)
work experience	**la experiencia con el trabajo**
	(lah ehk-speh-ree-'ehn-see·ah kohn ehl trah-'bah-hoh)
work schedule	**el horario de trabajo**
	(ehl oh-'rah-ree·oh dehl trah-'bah-hoh)

Listos para practicar

Join each English word with its correct Spanish translation:

appointment	**la entrevista** *(lah ehn-treh-'vee-stah)*
interview	**la tarjeta** *(lah tahr-'heh-tah)*
date	**la fecha** *(lah 'feh-chah)*
card	**el seguro** *(ehl seh-'goo-roh)*
insurance	**la cita** *(lah 'see-tah)*

Write in the translation as quickly as you can. These are very easy:

la referencia *(lah reh-feh-'rehn-see-ah)* _____

la identificación _____
   (lah ee-dehn-tee-fee-kah-see-'ohn)

el problema *(ehl proh-'bleh-mah)* _____

el uniforme *(ehl oo-nee-'fohr-meh)* _____

la experiencia *(lah ehk-speh-ree-'ehn-see-ah)* _____

Dozens of verbs have been introduced in this chapter so far. How many of these opposites can you recognize? Go ahead and connect!

contratar *(kohn-trah-'tahr)*   **mandar** *(mahn-'dahr)*

empezar *(ehm-peh-'sahr)*   **tomar** *(toh-'mahr)*

dar *(dahr)*   **terminar** *(tehr-mee-'nahr)*

recibir *(reh-see-'beer)*   **despedirse** *(deh-speh-'deer-seh)*

Can you explain the main difference between these two verbs?

SABER *(sah-'behr)* _____

CONOCER *(koh-noh-'sehr)* _____

The top ten questions
Las diez preguntas más importantes
(lahs dee-'ehs preh-'goon-tahs mahs eem-pohr-'tahn-tehs)

Now that you've got a list of questions to use when hiring Spanish-speaking employees, why not prepare for these key questions that they might ask you. Here are ten **preguntas** that are asked all the time.

How much do you pay?	**¿Cuánto pagan?** *('kwahn-toh 'pah-gahn)*
When can I start?	**¿Cuándo puedo empezar?**
	('kwahn-doh 'pweh-doh ehm-peh-'sahr)

Is it part-time or full-time?	**¿Es tiempo completo o tiempo parcial?** *(ehs tee-'ehm-poh kohm-'pleh-toh oh tee-'ehm-poh pahr-see-'ahl)*
What kinds of benefits?	**¿Cuáles son los beneficios?** *('kwah-lehs sohn lohs beh-neh-'fee-see·ohs)*
What's my shift?	**¿Cuál es mi turno de trabajo?** *(kwahl ehs mee 'toor-noh deh trah-'bah-hoh)*
What are my days off?	**¿Cuáles son mis días de descanso?** *('kwah-lehs sohn mees 'dee-ahs deh deh-'skahn-soh)*
How many hours a week?	**¿Cuántas horas por semana?** *('kwahn-tahs 'oh-rahs pohr seh-'mah-nah)*
When will you be hiring?	**¿Cuándo estarán contratando?** *('kwahn-doh eh-stah-'rahn kohn-trah-'tahn-doh)*
What skills do I need?	**¿Qué habilidades necesito?** *(keh ah-bee-lee-'dah-dehs neh-seh-'see-toh)*
When can I get a raise?	**¿Cuándo recibiré un aumento de sueldo?** *('kwahn-doh reh-see-bee-'reh oon ow-'mehn-toh deh 'swehl-doh)*

• Break down the job into pieces:

It's (the)...	**Es...** *(ehs)*
chore	**la faena** *(lah fah-'eh-nah)*
duty	**la obligación** *(lah ohb-lee-gah-see-'ohn)*
errand	**el encargo** *(ehl ehn-'kahr-goh)*
job	**el trabajo** *(ehl trah-'bah-hoh)*
service	**el servicio** *(ehl sehr-'vee-see·oh)*
task	**la tarea** *(lah tah-'reh-ah)*

Bad news!

¡Malas noticias! *('mah-lahs noh-'tee-see·ahs)*

Not everyone gets the job, so be sure you learn how to give the bad news:

I'm sorry,	**Lo siento,**
we hired someone else	**contratamos a otra persona**
	(kohn-trah-'tah-mohs ah 'oh-trah pehr-'soh-nah)
we're not hiring	**no estamos contratando**
	(noh eh-'stah-mohs kohn-trah-'tahn-doh)
try back next month	**regrese el próximo mes**
	(reh-'greh-seh ehl 'prohk-see-moh mehs)
you need more experience	**necesita más experiencia**
	(neh-seh-'see-tah mahs ehk-speh-ree-'ehn-see·ah)
we're looking for a ____	**estamos buscando un/una ____**
	(eh-'stah-mohs boo-'skahn-doh oon/'oo-nah)
the position has been filled	**ya no hay vacante**
	(yah noh 'ah·ee vah-'kahn-teh)
you should try with another company	**debería tratar con otra compañía**
	(deh-beh-'ree-ah trah-'tahr kohn 'oh-trah kohm-pah-'nyee-ah)
maybe later	**quizás más tarde**
	(kee-'sahs mahs 'tahr-deh)

Learn all the one-liners you can!

Think about it.	**Piense en eso.**
	(pee-'ehn-seh ehn 'eh-soh)
Call me at this number.	**Llámeme a este número.**
	('yah-meh-meh ah 'eh-steh 'noo-meh-roh)
Talk to your family.	**Hable con su familia.**
	('ah-bleh kohn soo fah-'mee-lee·ah)
It's a great job offer.	**Es una oferta de trabajo muy buena.**
	(ehs 'oo-nah oh-'fehr-tah deh trah-'bah-hoh 'moo·ee 'bweh-nah)
You're a good candidate.	**Usted es un buen candidato.**
	(oo-'stehd ehs oon bwehn kahn-dee-'dah-toh)
Sign this agreement.	**Firme este contrato.**
	('feer-meh 'eh-steh kohn-'trah-toh)

Temas culturales

Did your employee just move to this country? Is he or she a bit confused about our language and culture? When you find the time, share a few insights on U.S. customs toward tipping, dress, dating, holidays, and social skills. Make them feel welcome by respecting their perspective, and watch your relationship grow!

Words that tell *where*
Palabras que expresan *dónde*
(pah-'lah-brahs keh ehk-'spreh-sahn 'dohn-deh)
All the job applicants are bound to ask where things are located.

Where's the office?	**¿Dónde está la oficina?**
	('dohn-deh eh-'stah lah oh-fee-'see-nah)
Where are the tools?	**¿Donde están las herramientas?**
	('dohn-deh eh-'stahn lahs en-rah-mee-'ehn-tahs)
Where is the lavatory?	**¿Donde está el baño?**
	('dohn-deh eh-'stah ehl 'bahn-yoh)

Use the words and phrases below to direct everyone in the right direction. These work great as quick responses:

It's...	**Está...** *(eh-'stah)*
above	**encima** *(ehn-'see-mah)*
at the bottom	**en el fondo** *(ehn ehl 'fohn-doh)*
behind	**detrás** *(deh-'trahs)*
down	**abajo** *(ah-'bah-hoh)*
far	**lejos** *('leh-hohs)*
here	**aquí** *(ah-'kee)*
in front of	**en frente de** *(ehn 'frehn-teh deh)*
inside	**adentro** *(ah-'dehn-troh)*
next to	**al lado de** *(ahl 'lah-doh deh)*
outside	**afuera** *(ah-'fweh-rah)*
over there	**allá** *(ah-'yah)*
straight ahead	**adelante** *(ah-deh-'lahn-teh)*
there	**allí** *(ah-'yee)*

to the left	**a la izquierda** *(ah lah ee-skee-'ehr-dah)*
near	**cerca** *('sehr-kah)*
to the right	**a la derecha** *(ah lah deh-'reh-chah)*
up	**arriba** *(ah-'rree-bah)*

If a map is required, send everybody this way:

east	**este** *('eh-steh)*
north	**norte** *('nohr-teh)*
south	**sur** *(soor)*
west	**oeste** *(oh-'eh-steh)*

¡Información!

• You'll need this pattern for larger facilities:

first floor	**primer piso** *(pree-'mehr 'pee-soh)*
second floor	**segundo piso** *(seh-'goon-doh 'pee-soh)*
third floor	**tercer piso** *(tehr-'sehr 'pee-soh)*

• By the way, **en** *(ehn) (in, on, at)* is one of the most commonly used words in Spanish. Watch:

She's in her office, on the second floor, at her desk.
Está en su oficina *(eh-'stah ehn soo oh-fee-'see-nah),*
en el segundo piso *(ehn ehl seh-'goon-doh 'pee-soh),*
en su escritorio *(ehn soo eh-skree-'toh-ree-oh).*

• And always use **estar** *(eh-'stahr)* instead of **ser** *(sehr)* to tell where someone is located.

The man is here.	**El hombre está aquí.**
	(ehl 'ohm-breh eh-'stah ah-'kee)

• Be familiar with as many location words as you can:

face down	**boca abajo** *('boh-kah ah-'bah-hoh)*
face up	**boca arriba** *('boh-kah ah-'rree-bah)*
on its way	**en camino** *(ehn kah-'mee-noh)*
toward the back	**hacia atrás** *('ah-see-ah ah-'trahs)*
backwards, inside out, or upside down	**al revés** *(ahl reh-'vehs)*

Listos para practicar

Let's review some of the top phrases used by HR staff members. Look the words up as you fill in these translations:

We're not hiring. _____

Call me at this number. _____

Full-time or part-time? _____

This group of opposites should be simple. Just draw a line to connect each pair:

adentro *(ah-'dehn-troh)*	**derecha** *(deh-'reh-chah)*
abajo *(ah-'bah-hoh)*	**arriba** *(ah-'rree-bah)*
izquierda *(ee-skee-'ehr-dah)*	**norte** *('nohr-teh)*
sur *(soor)*	**cerca** *('sehr-kah)*
lejos *('leh-hohs)*	**afuera** *(ah-'fweh-rah)*

Words that tell *when*
Palabras que expresan *cuándo*
(pah-'lah-brahs keh ehk-'spreh-sahn 'kwahn-doh)

One of the most frequently asked questions in Spanish is *When?* (**¿Cuándo?**) *(kwahn-doh)*, so you'll need to be prepared when it comes time to answer. Begin by learning a few of the most popular responses:

A.M.	**de la mañana** *(deh lah mah-'nyah-nah)*
P.M.	**de la tarde** *(deh lah 'tahr-deh)*
afterward	**después** *(deh-'spwehs)*
already	**ya** *(yah)*
always	**siempre** *(see-'ehm-preh)*
at dawn	**a la madrugada** *(ah lah mah-droo-'gah-dah)*
at dusk	**al anochecer** *(ahl ah-noh-cheh-'sehr)*
at sunset	**a la puesta del sol** *(ah lah 'pweh-stah dehl sohl)*
before	**antes** *('ahn-tehs)*
daily	**a diario** *(ah dee-'ah-ree-oh)*
each day	**cada día** *('kah-dah 'dee-ah)*
early	**temprano** *(tehm-'prah-noh)*

every day	**todos los días** *('toh-dohs lohs 'dee-ahs)*
in a moment	**en un momento** *(ehn oon moh-'mehn-toh)*
in a while	**en un rato** *(ehn oon 'rah-toh)*
just	**apenas** *(ah-'peh-nahs)*
last month	**el mes pasado** *(ehl mehs pah-'sah-doh)*
last night	**anoche** *(ah-'noh-cheh)*
last week	**la semana pasada**
	(lah seh-'mah-nah pah-'sah-dah)
late	**tarde** *('tahr-deh)*
later	**más tarde** *(mahs 'tahr-deh)*
lots of times	**muchas veces** *('moo-chahs 'veh-sehs)*
never	**nunca** *('noon-kah)*
next month	**el próximo mes** *(ehl 'prohk-see-moh mehs)*
next week	**la próxima semana**
	(lah 'prohk-see-mah seh-'mah-nah)
now	**ahora** *(ah-'oh-rah)*
once	**una vez** *('oo-nah vehs)*
on time	**a tiempo** *(ah tee-'ehm-poh)*
right now	**ahorita** *(ah-oh-'ree-tah)*
sometimes	**a veces** *(ah 'veh-sehs)*
soon	**pronto** *('prohn-toh)*
the day after tomorrow	**pasado mañana**
	(pah-'sah-doh mah-'nyah-nah)
the day before yesterday	**anteayer** *(ahn-teh-ah-'yehr)*
then	**entonces** *(ehn-'tohn-sehs)*
today	**hoy** *('oh-ee)*
tomorrow	**mañana** *(mah-'nyah-nah)*
tomorrow morning	**mañana por la mañana**
	(mah-'nyah-nah pohr lah mah-'nyah-nah)
tonight	**esta noche** *('eh-stah 'noh-cheh)*
yesterday	**ayer** *(ah-'yehr)*
yet	**todavía** *(toh-dah-'vee-ah)*

This is how these special words can be used:

Are you working today?
¿Está trabajando hoy? *(eh-'stah trah-bah-'hahn-doh 'oh-ee)*

Come right now!

¡Venga ahorita! *('vehn-gah ah-oh-'ree-tah)*

Sometimes I have problems with my car.

A veces tengo problemas con mi carro.

  (ah 'veh-sehs 'tehn-goh proh-'bleh-mahs kohn mee 'kah-rroh)

¡Información!

Understanding and using words like *where* and *when* in Spanish is crucial in gathering information. The best way to learn how to use question words in a foreign language is to focus on the first word of each sentence and then try to get a general feel for what the person might be asking. Attempting to translate every word will only lead to frustration.

Time telling!

¡Decir la hora! *(deh-'seer lah 'oh-rah)*

You can't discuss employment without mentioning the clock. Everyone has to check in or out sometime. To read the clock in Spanish, simply give the hour, followed by the word **y** *(ee)* (and), and the minutes. For example, 8:15 is **ocho y quince** *('oh-choh ee 'keen-seh)*.

What time is it?	**¿Qué hora es?** *(keh 'oh-rah ehs)*
At what time?	**¿A qué hora?** *(ah keh 'oh-rah)*
It's...	**Son las...** *(sohn lahs)*
At...	**A las...** *(ah lahs)*
10:40	**diez y cuarenta** *(dee-'ehs ee kwah-'rehn-tah)*
3:25	**tres y veinte y cinco**
	(trehs ee 'veh·een-teh ee 'seen-koh)
12:05 A.M.	**doce y cinco de la mañana**
	('doh-seh ee 'seen-koh deh lah mah-'nyah-nah)
4:00 P.M.	**cuatro de la tarde** *('kwah-troh deh lah 'tahr-deh)*
9:30 P.M.	**nueve y treinta de la noche**
	(noo-'eh-veh ee 'treh·een-tah deh lah 'noh-cheh)

¡Información!

For 1:00–1:59, use **Es la...** *(ehs lah)* instead of **Son las...** *(sohn lahs)*. For example:

It's one o'clock.	**Es la una.** *(ehs lah 'oo-nah)*
It's one-thirty.	**Es la una y treinta.**
	(ehs lah 'oo-nah ee 'treh·een-tah)

What day?
¿Qué día? *(keh 'dee-ah)*

Spend a few minutes looking over the following Spanish words. They'll allow you to say things about the calendar and work schedules. Then stress each sound as you pronounce them aloud:

The days of the week	**Los días de la semana**
	(lohs 'dee-ahs deh lah seh-'mah-nah)
Monday	**lunes** *('loo-nehs)*
Tuesday	**martes** *('mahr-tehs)*
Wednesday	**miércoles** *(mee-'ehr-koh-lehs)*
Thursday	**jueves** *(hoo-'eh-vehs)*
Friday	**viernes** *(vee-'ehr-nehs)*
Saturday	**sábado** *('sah-bah-doh)*
Sunday	**domingo** *(doh-'meen-goh)*

Now, read these questions and answers. See how **los días** *(lohs 'dee-ahs)* function as one-word responses to *when* questions:

When do I get paid?
¿Cuándo me pagan? *('kwahn-doh meh 'pah-gahn)*
Viernes. *(vee-'ehr-nehs)*
When do I start?
¿Cuándo empiezo? *('kwahn-doh ehm-pee-'eh-soh)*
Sábado. *('sah-bah-doh)*
When do I work?
¿Cuándo trabajo? *('kwahn-doh trah-'bah-hoh)*
Martes y jueves. *('mahr-tehs ee hoo-'eh-vehs)*

¡Información!

• Most students of Spanish get confused when using the words **por** *(pohr)* and **para** *('pah-rah)* because they are similar in meaning. The differences between the two are not easy to explain, so it may be best to listen to Spanish speakers as they use them, and then try them out in short, practical phrases.

by Friday	**para el viernes** *('pah-rah ehl vee-'ehr-nehs)*
for two days	**por dos días** *(pohr dohs 'dee-ahs)*
in order to apply	**para solicitar** *('pah-rah soh-lee-see-'tahr)*
throughout the afternoon	**por la tarde** *(pohr lah 'tahr-deh)*

• *On Friday* is **el viernes** *(ehl vee-'ehr-nehs)* but *on Fridays* is **los viernes** *(lohs vee-'ehr-nehs)*.

• If you want, you can interject the following expressions:

the next one	**el próximo** *(ehl 'prohk-see-moh)*
the past one	**el pasado** *(ehl pah-'sah-doh)*
the weekend	**el fin de semana** *(ehl feen deh seh-'mah-nah)*

• Use **¿Hace cuánto?** *('ah-seh 'kwahn-toh)* for *How long ago?*

How long ago?	**¿Hace cuánto?** *('ah-seh 'kwahn-toh)*
Two weeks ago.	**Hace dos semanas.** *('ah-seh dohs seh-'mah-nahs)*

What month?
¿Qué mes? *(keh mehs)*

As far as the months are concerned, just remember that most words are similar in both Spanish and English.

The months of the year
Los meses del año *(lohs 'meh-sehs dehl 'ah-nyoh)*

January	**enero** *(eh-'neh-roh)*
February	**febrero** *(feh-'breh-roh)*
March	**marzo** *('mahr-soh)*
April	**abril** *(ah-'breel)*
May	**mayo** *('mah-yoh)*
June	**junio** *('hoo-nee·oh)*
July	**julio** *('hoo-lee·oh)*
August	**agosto** *(ah-'goh-stoh)*
September	**septiembre** *(sehp-tee-'ehm-breh)*
October	**octubre** *(ohk-'too-breh)*
November	**noviembre** *(noh-vee-'ehm-breh)*
December	**diciembre** *(dee-see-'ehm-breh)*

What's the date?
¿Cuál es la fecha? *(kwahl ehs lah 'feh-chah)*

To give the date, reverse the order of your words. For example, February 2nd is **el dos de febrero** *(ehl dohs deh feh-'breh-roh)*.

• And this is how you say *the first* in Spanish:

el primero *(ehl pree-'meh-roh)*
January 1st
el primero de enero *(ehl pree-'meh-roh deh eh-'neh-roh)*

• The year is often read as one large number:

1999
mil novecientos noventa y nueve
(meel noh-veh-see-'ehn-tohs noh-'vehn-tah ee noo-'eh-veh)

• Can you give today's date in Spanish? Use a calendar to practice all of your new vocabulary!

Listos para practicar

Choose the best word to complete each series:

mes, ayer, a veces *(mehs, ah-'yehr, ah 'veh-sehs)*

   siempre, nunca, *(see-'ehm-preh, 'noon-kah)* _____

   hoy, mañana, *('oh-ee, mah-'nyah-nah)* _____

   día, semana, *('dee-ah, seh-'mah-nah)* _____

Try to complete these lists, but without any help:

   lunes, martes, miércoles *('loo-nehs, 'mahr-tehs, mee-'ehr-koh-lehs)*

   _____

   enero, febrero, marzo, *(eh-'neh-roh, feh-'breh-roh, 'mahr-soh)*

   _____

Say these dates and times in Spanish:

   At 6:00 A.M.   _____

   June 6, 1999   _____

   It's 9:30 P.M.   _____

 ## Temas culturales

Not all folks panic when it comes to tardiness—some cultures put less emphasis on beating the clock than others. Be direct and explain the importance of punctuality in certain areas of employment.

You have to arrive early.

Tiene que llegar temprano. *(tee-'eh-neh keh yeh-'gahr tehm-'prah-noh)*

Don't be late!

¡No llegue tarde! *(noh 'yeh-geh 'tahr-deh)*

If you're late again, I'll have to let you go.

Si llega tarde otra vez, tendré que despedirle.

  (see 'yeh-gah 'tahr-deh 'oh-trah vehs, tehn-'dreh keh deh-speh-'deer-leh)

If missing work is a problem, or if there's a request for a day off, the best way to handle things is to ask about the problem, and then focus only on the words as you both work out a solution.

What's the problem?
¿Cuál es el problema? *('kwahl ehs ehl proh-'bleh-mah)*

Tell me about yourself!
¡Dígame de usted mismo!
('dee-gah-meh deh oo-'stehd 'mees-moh)

As a beginner in Spanish, perhaps the toughest group of interview questions will be the personal ones. Although we've covered a few already, this next selection will really open things up during a conversation:

Are you...?	**¿Es usted...?** *(ehs oo-'stehd)*
divorced	**divorciado(a)** *(dee-vohr-see-'ah-doh/dah)*
married	**casado(a)** *(kah-'sah-doh/dah)*
separated	**separado(a)** *(seh-pah-'rah-doh/dah)*
single	**soltero(a)** *(sohl-'teh-roh/rah)*
widowed	**viudo(a)** *(vee-'oo-doh/dah)*
Canadian	**canadiense** *(kah-nah-dee-'ehn-seh)*
Cuban	**cubano(a)** *(koo-'bah-noh/nah)*
Mexican	**mexicano(a)** *(meh-hee-'kah-noh/nah)*
Puerto Rican	**puertorriqueño(a)** *(pwehr-toh-rree-'keh-nyoh/nyah)*
Spanish	**español(a)** *(eh-spah-'nyohl/nah)*

Again, all of the above words ending in **o** are meant for males. Change the ending to **a** to address females.

I am...	**Soy...** *('soh-ee)*
Catholic	**católico(a)** *(kah-'toh-lee-koh/kah)*
Christian	**cristiano(a)** *(kree-stee-'ah-noh/nah)*
Jewish	**judío(a)** *(hoo-'dee-oh/ah)*
Moslem	**musulmán(a)** *(moo-sool-'mahn/nah)*

¡Información!

• Get to know the person you're looking to hire. Take an interest in their responses, and work hard to control your tone and non-verbal actions. The more comfortable they feel, the more information they will share. Here are some great things to say:

You are very...	Usted es muy... *(oo-'stehd ehs 'moo-ee)*
skillful	**hábil** *(ah-beel)*
capable	**capaz** *(kah-'pahs)*
qualified	**calificado** *('kah-lee-fee-'kah-doh)*

• Learn these two important expressions right away. You will need them soon enough!

You are...	Usted está... *(oo-'stehd eh-'stah)*
hired	**contratado** *(kohn-trah-'tah-doh)*
fired	**despedido** *(deh-speh-'dee-doh)*

What kind of person?
¿Qué tipo de persona?
(keh 'tee-poh deh pehr-'soh-nah)

Care to know more about the person you're hiring? Utilize the words below, and remember that descriptive word endings change from an **o** to an **a** when they refer to females:

Is he...?	¿Es...? *(ehs)*
ambitious	**ambicioso** *(ahm-bee-see-'oh-soh)*
brave	**valiente** *(vah-lee-'ehn-teh)*
bright	**despierto** *(dehs-pee-'ehr-toh)*
cruel	**cruel** *(kroo-'ehl)*
famous	**famoso** *(fah-'moh-soh)*
fast	**rápido** *('rah-pee-doh)*
fat	**gordo** *('gohr-doh)*
funny	**chistoso** *(chee-'stoh-soh)*
good-looking	**guapo** *('gwah-poh)*
healthy	**saludable** *(sah-loo-'dah-bleh)*
industrious	**trabajador** *(trah-bah-hah-'dohr)*

intelligent	**inteligente** *(een-teh-lee-'hehn-teh)*
lazy	**perezoso** *(peh-reh-'soh-soh)*
mature	**maduro** *(mah-'doo-roh)*
new	**nuevo** *('nweh-voh)*
nice	**simpático** *(seem-'pah-tee-koh)*
old	**viejo** *(vee-'eh-hoh)*
older	**mayor** *(mah-'yohr)*
patient	**paciente** *(pah-see-'ehn-teh)*
polite	**cortés** *(kohr-'tehs)*
poor	**pobre** *('poh-breh)*
quiet	**quieto** *(kee-'eh-toh)*
rich	**rico** *('ree-koh)*
short (in height)	**bajo** *('bah-hoh)*
slow	**lento** *('lehn-toh)*
strange	**raro** *('rah-roh)*
strong	**fuerte** *('fwehr-teh)*
sure	**seguro** *(seh-'goo-roh)*
tall	**alto** *('ahl-toh)*
thin	**delgado** *(dehl-'gah-doh)*
valuable	**valioso** *(vah-lee-'oh-soh)*

Describe things

Describa las cosas *(deh-skree-bah lahs 'koh-sahs)*

Work on expanding your descriptive vocabulary by reading the list of opposites below.

It's...	**Es...** *(ehs)*
	Está... *(eh-'stah)*
cheap	**barato** *(bah-'rah-toh)*
expensive	**caro** *('kah-roh)*
clean	**limpio** *('leem-pee·oh)*
dirty	**sucio** *('soo-see·oh)*
deep	**profundo** *(proh-'foon-doh)*
shallow	**bajo** *('bah-hoh)*

difficult	**difícil** *(dee-'fee-seel)*
easy	**fácil** *('fah-seel)*
hard	**duro** *('doo-roh)*
soft	**blando** *('blahn-doh)*
long	**largo** *('lahr-goh)*
short (in length)	**corto** *('kohr-toh)*
narrow	**estrecho** *(eh-'streh-choh)*
wide	**ancho** *('ahn-choh)*
pretty	**bonito** *(boh-'nee-toh)*
ugly	**feo** *('feh-oh)*
rough	**áspero** *('ah-speh-roh)*
smooth	**liso** *('lee-soh)*
dry	**seco** *('seh-koh)*
wet	**mojado** *(moh-'hah-doh)*
thin	**delgado** *(dehl-'gah-doh)*
thick	**grueso** *(groo-'eh-soh)*

Keep in mind that in Spanish, the adjective (the word used to describe anything) usually goes after the noun. Here are some more vocabulary words:

It's an _____ job.   **Es un trabajo _____.**
                        (ehs oon trah-'bah-hoh)

excellent   **excelente** *(ehk-seh-'lehn-teh)*
important   **importante** *(eem-pohr-'tahn-teh)*
interesting   **interesante** *(een-teh-reh-'sahn-teh)*

He's a _____ man.   **Es un hombre _____.**
                       (ehs oon 'ohm-breh)

bald   **calvo** *('kahl-voh)*
blond   **rubio** *('roo-bee-oh)*
dark-haired   **moreno** *(moh-'reh-noh)*

She is a _____ woman. **Es una mujer _____.**
(ehs 'oo-nah moo-'hehr)

bad   **mala** *('mah-lah)*
good   **buena** *(boo-'eh-nah)*
prepared   **preparada** *(preh-pah-'rah-dah)*

• Description words that begin with "no," "in," or "des" oftentimes refer to an opposite:

qualified **(calificado)** *(kah-lee-fee-'kah-doh)*
unqualified **(no calificado)** *(noh kah-lee-fee-'kah-doh)*
correct **(correcto)** *(koh-'rrehk-toh)*
incorrect **(incorrecto)** *(een-koh-'rrehk-toh)*
employed **(empleado)** *(ehm-pleh-'ah-doh)*
unemployed **(desempleado)** *(dehs-ehm-pleh-'ah-doh)*

• Use these little words to compare things:

a little big   **un poco grande** *(oon 'poh-koh 'grahn-deh)*
as big as   **tan grande como** *(tahn 'grahn-deh 'koh-moh)*
bigger than   **más grande que** *(mahs 'grahn-deh keh)*
biggest   **el (or la) más grande** *(ehl (or lah) mahs 'grahn-deh)*
so big   **tan grande** *(tahn 'grahn-deh)*
too big   **demasiado grande** *(deh-mah-see-'ah-doh 'grahn-deh)*
very big   **muy grande** *('moo-ee 'grahn-deh)*

Carlos es más grande que Samuel.
('kahr-lohs ehs mahs 'grahn-deh keh sah-moo-'ehl)
Samuel es tan grande como una casa.
(sah-moo-'ehl ehs tahn 'grahn-deh 'koh-moh 'oo-nah 'kah-sah)
Felipe es el más grande.
(feh-'lee-peh ehs ehl mahs 'grahn-deh)

Listos para practicar

Name three nationalities in Spanish:

_____

_____

_____

Here are some more opposites to practice. You know what to do:

gordo *('gohr-doh)*   **seco** *('seh-koh)*
nuevo *('nweh-voh)*   **viejo** *(vee-'eh-hoh)*
rápido *('rah-pee-doh)*   **fácil** *('fah-seel)*
limpio *('leem-pee·oh)*   **bonito** *(boh-'nee-toh)*
difícil *(dee-'fee-seel)*   **bajo** *('bah-hoh)*
feo *('feh-oh)*   **corto** *('kohr-toh)*
pobre *('poh-breh)*   **lento** *('lehn-toh)*
largo *('lahr-goh)*   **delgado** *(dehl-'gah-doh)*
alto *('ahl-toh)*   **sucio** *('soo-see·oh)*
mojado *(moh-'hah-doh)*   **rico** *('ree-koh)*

Can you create sentences using the descriptions you have learned?

Es un trabajo *(ehs oon trah-'bah-hoh)* _____.
Es un hombre *(ehs oon 'ohm-breh)* _____.
Es una oficina *(ehs 'oo-nah oh-fee-'see-nah)* _____.

What's your occupation?
¿Cuál es su ocupación?
(kwahl ehs soo oh-koo-pah-see-'ohn)

Besides giving description, the word *es (ehs)* is also used to identify a person's occupation. Continue interviewing folks about their areas of expertise. Are you making the switch when it's a female?

We need (the)...   **Necesitamos...** *(neh-seh-see-'tah-mohs)*
We're hiring (the)...   **Estamos contratando...**
                          (eh-'stah-mohs kohn-trah-'tahn-doh)
artist   **el artista** *(ehl ahr-'tee-stah)*

bartender	**el cantinero** *(ehl kahn-tee-'neh-roh)*
bellhop	**el botones** *(ehl boh-'toh-nehs)*
busboy	**el ayudante de camarero** *(ehl ah-yoo-'dahn-teh deh kah-mah-'reh-roh)*
carpenter	**el carpintero** *(ehl kahr-peen-'teh-roh)*
cashier	**el cajero** *(ehl kah-'heh-roh)*
clerk	**el dependiente** *(ehl deh-pehn-dee-'ehn teh)*
cook	**el cocinero** *(ehl koh-see-'neh-roh)*
dishwasher	**el lavaplatos** *(ehl lah-vah 'plah-tohs)*
driver	**el chofer** *(ehl choh-'fehr)*
gardener	**el jardinero** *(ehl hahr-dee-'neh-roh)*
guide	**el guía** *(ehl 'gee-ah)*
helper	**el ayudante** *(ehl ah-yoo-'dahn-teh)*
janitor	**el conserje** *(ehl kohn-'sehr-heh)*
laborer	**el obrero** *(ehl oh-'breh-roh)*
mechanic	**el mecánico** *(ehl meh-'kah-nee-koh)*
painter	**el pintor** *(ehl peen-'tohr)*
plumber	**el plomero** *(ehl ploh-'meh-roh)*
receptionist	**el recepcionista** *(ehl reh-sehp-see-oh-'nee-stah)*
salesman	**el vendedor** *(ehl vehn-deh-'dohr)*
secretary	**el secretario** *(ehl seh-kreh-'tah-ree-oh)*
servant	**el criado** *(ehl kree-'ah-doh)*
operator	**el telefonista** *(ehl teh-leh-foh-'nee-stah)*
truck driver	**el camionero** *(ehl kah-mee-oh-'neh-roh)*
typist	**el mecanógrafo** *(ehl meh-kah-'noh-grah-foh)*
waiter	**el mesero** *(ehl meh-'seh-roh)*
worker	**el trabajador** *(ehl trah-bah-hah-'dohr)*

Here are some more standard professions. Try them with **soy** *('soh-ee)*:

I'm the...	**Soy...** *('soh·ee)*
architect	**el arquitecto** *(ehl ahr-kee-'tehk-toh)*
dentist	**el dentista** *(ehl dehn-'tee-stah)*
doctor	**el doctor** *(ehl dohk-'tohr)*
engineer	**el ingeniero** *(ehl een-heh-nee-'eh-roh)*
farmer	**el campesino** *(ehl kahm-peh-'see-noh)*
firefighter	**el bombero** *(ehl bohm-'beh-roh)*

lawyer	**el abogado** *(ehl ah-boh-'gah-doh)*
librarian	**el bibliotecario**
	(ehl bee-blee·oh-teh-'kah-ree·oh)
mail carrier	**el cartero** *(ehl kahr-'teh-roh)*
musician	**el músico** *(ehl 'moo-see-koh)*
nurse	**el enfermero** *(ehl ehn-fehr-'meh-roh)*
pilot	**el piloto** *(ehl pee-'loh-toh)*
police officer	**el policía** *(ehl poh-lee-'see-ah)*
priest	**el sacerdote** *(ehl sah-sehr-'doh-teh)*
soldier	**el soldado** *(ehl sohl-'dah-doh)*
student	**el estudiante** *(ehl eh-'stoo-dee-'ahn-teh)*
surgeon	**el cirujano** *(ehl see-roo-'hah-noh)*
tailor	**el sastre** *(ehl 'sah-streh)*
teacher	**el maestro** *(ehl mah-'eh-stroh)*

¡Información!

• You might have to do a little research to find the names for everyone:

mechanical engineer	**el ingeniero mecánico**
	(ehl een-heh-nee-'eh-roh meh-'kah-nee-koh)
subcontractor	**el subcontratista**
	(ehl soob-kohn-trah-'tee-stah)
auto worker	**el obrero automotriz**
	(ehl oh-'breh-roh ow-tow-moh-'trees)

• Practice these new words in sentences.

| chief | **el jefe** *(ehl 'heh-feh)* |
| | **la jefa** *(lah 'heh-fah)* |

Carlos es un jefe importante.
('kahr-lohs ehs uhn 'heh-feh eem-pohr-'tahn-teh)
María es la jefa aquí.
(Mah-'ree-ah ehs lah 'heh-fah ah-'kee)

| employer | **el empresario** *(ehl ehm-preh-'sah-ree-oh)* |
| | **la empresaria** *(lah ehm-preh-'sah-ree-ah)* |

¿Quién es el empresario?
(kee-'ehn ehs ehl ehm-preh-'sah-ree-oh)
La empresaria es Sandra.
(lah ehm-preh-'sah-ree-ah ehs 'sahn-drah)

owner	**el dueño** *(ehl 'dweh-nyoh)*
	la dueña *(lah 'dweh-nyah)*

Soy el dueño de la compañía.
('soh-ee ehl 'dweh-nyoh deh lah kom-pah-'nyee-ah)
Ana es la dueña de la silla.
('ah-nah ehs lah 'dweh-nyah deh lah 'see-yah)

• Check out these other useful terms for Human Resources personnel:

Talk to (the)...	**Hable con...** *('ah-bleh kohn)*
apprentice	**el aprendiz** *(ehl ah-prehn-'dees)*
boss	**el patrón** *(ehl pah-'trohn)*
client	**el cliente** *(ehl klee-'ehn-teh)*
employee	**el empleado** *(ehl ehm-pleh-'ah-doh)*
foreman	**el capataz** *(ehl kah-pah-'tahs)*
graduate	**el graduado** *(ehl grah-doo-'ah-doh)*
interpreter	**el intérprete** *(ehl een-'tehr-preh-teh)*
journeyman	**el artesano** *(ehl ahr-teh-'sah-noh)*
leader	**el líder** *(ehl 'lee-dehr)*
manager	**el gerente** *(ehl heh-'rehn-teh)*
supervisor	**el supervisor** *(ehl soo-pehr-vee-'sohr)*
translator	**el traductor** *(ehl trah-dook-'tohr)*

• Now learn the titles of each superior:

administrator	**el administrador**
	(ehl ahd-mee-nee-strah-'dohr)
executive	**el ejecutivo** *(ehl eh-heh-koo-'tee-voh)*
president	**el presidente** *(ehl preh-see-'dehn-teh)*
top	**la alta gerencia**
management	*(lah 'ahl-tah heh-'rehn-see-ah)*
vice-president	**el vicepresidente**
	(ehl vee-seh-preh-see-'dehn-teh)

Listos para practicar

This exercise should only take a few minutes. Translate these titles just as fast as you can, and then change them to females!

el vendedor *(ehl vehn-deh-'dohr)*   salesman   **la vendedora**
                                           (lah vehn-deh-'doh-rah)

el secretario *(ehl seh-kreh-'tah-ree·oh)* _____ _____

el piloto *(ehl pee-'loh-toh)* _____ _____

el carpintero *(ehl kahr-peen-'teh-roh)* _____ _____

el estudiante *(ehl eh-stoo-dee-'ahn-teh)* _____ _____

el supervisor *(ehl soo-pehr-vee-'sohr)* _____ _____

el doctor *(ehl dohk-'tohr)* _____ _____

el artista *(ehl ahr-'tee-stah)* _____ _____

el dentista *(ehl dehn-'tee-stah)* _____ _____

Más fácil

To handle any interview situation, make sure you've set aside all the appropriate Spanish verbs that relate to the hiring process. Remember how these are used:

Please...	**Favor de...** *(fah-'vohr deh)*
Don't...	**No...** *(noh)*
answer	**contestar** *(kohn-teh-'stahr)*
arrive	**llegar** *('yeh-gahr)*
ask	**preguntar** *(preh-goon-'tahr)*
begin	**empezar** *(ehm-peh-'sahr)*
call	**llamar** *(yah-'mahr)*
explain	**explicar** *(ehk-splee-'kahr)*
finish	**terminar** *(tehr-mee-'nahr)*
help	**ayudar** *(ah-yoo-'dahr)*
look for	**buscar** *(boo-'skahr)*
return	**regresar** *(reh-greh-'sahr)*
send	**mandar** *(mahn-'dahr)*
sign	**firmar** *(feer-'mahr)*
take	**tomar** *(toh-'mahr)*

Please write your name. **Favor de escribir su nombre.**
(fah-'vohr deh eh-skree-'beer soo 'nohm-breh)

Consider this next set of expressions. By adding the word **que** *(keh)*, to the verb, **tener** *(teh-'nehr)*, you create a new action phrase, **tener que** *(teh-'nehr keh), to have to.* Watch:

I have to	**Tengo que** *('tehn-goh keh)*
You have to; He or She has to	**Tiene que** *(tee-'eh-neh keh)*
They have to, You (pl.) have to	**Tienen que** *(tee-'eh-nehn keh)*
We have to	**Tenemos que** *(teh-'neh-mohs keh)*

Now bring in a few verbs from the list above, and look what you can say:

I have to explain the interview.
Tengo que explicar la entrevista.
('tehn-goh keh ehk-splee-'kahr lah ehn-treh-'vee-stah)
You have to work on Saturday.
Tiene que trabajar el sábado.
(tee-'eh-neh keh trah-bah-'hahr ehl 'sah-bah-doh)
They have to call.
Tienen que llamar.
(tee-'eh-nehn keh yah-'mahr)
We have to look for the paper.
Tenemos que buscar el papel.
(teh-'neh-mohs keh boo-'skahr ehl pah-'pehl)

 ¡Información!

• These other verbs popped up earlier in this chapter and should be set aside for practice as soon as possible:

to accept	**aceptar** *(ah-sehp-'tahr)*
to apply	**solicitar** *(soh-lee-see-'tahr)*
to check	**averiguar** *(ah-veh-ree-'gwahr)*
to describe	**describir** *(deh-skree-'beer)*
to discuss	**conversar** *(kohn-vehr-'sahr)*
to give	**dar** *(dahr)*
to help	**ayudar** *(ah-yoo-'dahr)*

to hire	**contratar** *(kohn-trah-'tahr)*
to live	**vivir** *(vee-'veer)*
to quit	**renunciar** *(reh-noon-see-'ahr)*
to receive	**recibir** *(reh-see-'beer)*
to recommend	**recomendar** *(reh-koh-mehn-'dahr)*
to recruit	**reclutar** *(reh-kloo-'tahr)*
to select	**seleccionar** *(seh-lehk-see-oh-'nahr)*
to smoke	**fumar** *(foo-'mahr)*
to study	**estudiar** *(ehe-stoo-dee-'ahr)*

• Always be on the lookout for verbs with **se**:

| to retire | **retirarse** *(reh-tee-'rahr-seh)* |
| to meet | **reunirse** *(reh-oo-'neer-seh)* |

• This shortcut technique of putting one-liners in front of base verbs will be repeated throughout this guidebook. Here are a few more examples that are very helpful for HR staff:

I want to...	**Quiero...** *(kee-'eh-roh)*
I'd like to...	**Quisiera...** *(kee-see-'eh-rah)*
I'm going to...	**Voy a...** *('voh-ee ah)*
I could...	**Podría...** *(poh-'dree-ah)*
I need to...	**Necesito...** *(neh-seh-'see-toh)*
...ask.	**...preguntar.** *(preh-goon-'tahr)*

• These next three phrases may also be used in place of **tiene que** *(tee-'eh-neh keh)*:

One must...	**Hay que...** *('ah-ee keh)*
One must work.	**Hay que trabajar.**
	('ah-ee keh trah-bah-'hahr)
You should...	**Debe...** *('deh-beh)*
You should read.	**Debe leer.** *('deh-beh lee-'ehr)*
You need to...	**Necesita** *(neh-seh-'see-tah)*
You need to write.	**Necesita escribir.**
	(neh-seh-'see-tah eh-skree-'beer)

Palabras activas

We have learned that our Spanish verbs change when we talk about current action. Just like English, we alter our endings slightly:

To speak	**hablar** *(ah-'blahr)*
I'm speaking.	**Estoy hablando.** *(eh-'stoh·ee ah-'blahn-doh)*
To eat	**comer** *(koh-'mehr)*
We're eating.	**Estamos comiendo.**
	(eh-'stah-mohs koh-mee-'ehn-doh)
To write	**escribir** *(eh-skree-'beer)*
He's writing.	**Está escribiendo.** *(eh-'stah eh-skree-bee-'ehn-doh)*

The same thing happens consistently when we refer to everyday activities. However, this time the verbs shift according to who completes the action. This next pattern is the same for most action words:

TO SPEAK	**HABLAR** *(ah-'blahr)*
I speak	**hablo** *('ah-bloh)*
you speak; he, she speaks	**habla** *('ah-blah)*
you (plural), they speak	**hablan** *('ah-blahn)*
we speak	**hablamos** *(ah-'blah-mohs)*
TO EAT	**COMER** *(koh-'mehr)*
I eat	**como** *('koh-moh)*
you eat; he, she eats	**come** *('koh-meh)*
you (plural), they eat	**comen** *('koh-mehn)*
we eat	**comemos** *(koh-'meh-mohs)*
TO WRITE	**ESCRIBIR** *(eh-skree-'beer)*
I write	**escribo** *(eh-'skree-boh)*
you write; he, she writes	**escribe** *(eh-'skree-beh)*
you (plural), they write	**escriben** *(eh-'skree-behn)*
we write	**escribimos** *(eh-skree-'bee-mohs)*

Notice how the **ar** verb, **hablar** *(ah-'blahr),* doesn't change the same as the **er** and **ir** verbs! This tip will be helpful as you pick up more action forms later on.

¡Información!

• Many verbs are considered irregular because they don't follow the pattern above. We'll discuss many of their changes in the pages ahead.

to begin	**empezar** *(ehm-peh-'sahr)*
I begin	**Empiezo** *(ehm-pee-'eh-soh)*
to think	**pensar** *(pehn-'sahr)*
I think	**Pienso** *(pee-'ehn-soh)*
to leave	**salir** *(sah-'leer)*
I leave	**Salgo** *('sahl-goh)*
to tell	**decir** *(deh-'seer)*
I tell	**Digo** *('dee-goh)*
to see	**ver** *(vehr)*
I see	**Veo** *('veh-oh)*
to give	**dar** *(dahr)*
I give	**Doy** *('doh-ee)*
to find	**encontrar** *(ehk-kohn-'trahr)*
I find	**Encuentro** *(ehn-'kwehn-troh)*
to fire	**despedir** *(deh-speh-'deer)*
I fire	**Despido** *(deh-'spee-doh)*
to offer	**ofrecer** *(oh-freh-'sehr)*
I offer	**Ofrezco** *(oh-'freh-skoh)*
to do	**hacer** *(ah-'sehr)*
I do	**Hago** *('ah-goh)*
to bring	**traer** *(trah-'ehr)*
I bring	**Traigo** *('trah-ee-goh)*
to understand	**entender** *(ehn-tehn-'dehr)*
I understand	**Entiendo** *(ehn-tee-'ehn-doh)*

• To describe an action word in Spanish, try one of these. Do you note any pattern?

completely	**completamente** *(kohm-pleh-tah-'mehn-teh)*
quickly	**rápidamente** *(rah-pee-dah-'mehn-teh)*
slowly	**lentamente** *(lehn-tah-'mehn-teh)*
partially	**parcialmente** *(pahr-see-'ahl-mehn-teh)*

- This is how you ask a question in the PRESENT TENSE:

Are they working?	**¿Están trabajando?**
	(eh-'stahn trah-bah-'hahn-doh)
Do they work?	**¿Trabajan?** *(trah-'bah-hahn)*

¡Ordenes!

Nothing will get done without those command words and phrases. Read through these first few examples and then create some expressions of your own:

Answer	**Conteste** *(kohn-'teh-steh)*
Answer in English.	**Conteste en inglés.**
	(kohn-'teh-steh ehn een-'glehs)
Bring	**Traiga** *('trah-ee-gah)*
Bring the form.	**Traiga el formulario.**
	('trah-ee-gah ehl fohr-moo-'lah-ree-oh)
Call	**Llame** *('yah-meh)*
Call your supervisor.	**Llame a su supervisor.**
	('yah-meh ah soo soo-pehr-vee-'sohr)
Listen	**Escuche** *(eh-'skoo-cheh)*
Listen to the question.	**Escuche la pregunta.**
	(eh-'skoo-cheh lah preh-'goon-tah)
Read	**Lea** *('leh-ah)*
Read the application.	**Lea la solicitud.** *('leh-ah lah soh-lee-see-'tood)*
Return	**Regrese** *(reh-'greh-seh)*
Return tomorrow.	**Regrese mañana.**
	(reh-'greh-seh mah-'nyah-nah)
Sign	**Firme** *('feer-meh)*
Sign here.	**Firme aquí.** *('feer-meh ah-'kee)*
Speak	**Hable** *('ah-bleh)*
Speak more slowly.	**Hable más despacio.**
	('ah-bleh mahs deh-'spah-see-oh)
Take	**Tome** *('toh-meh)*
Take a seat.	**Tome un asiento.**
	('toh-meh oon ah-see-'ehn-toh)

And now, write the information yourself.	**Y ahora, escriba usted la información.** *(ee ah-'oh-vah eh-'skree-bah oos-'tehd lah een-fohr-mah-see-'ohn)*
Describe	**Describa** *(deh-'skree-bah)*
Explain	**Explique** *(ehk-'splee-keh)*
Do	**Haga** *('ah-gah)*
Help	**Ayude** *(ah-'yoo-deh)*
Give	**Dé** *(deh)*
Send	**Mande** *('mahn-deh)*
Follow	**Siga** *('see-gah)*
Look for	**Busque** *('boo-skeh)*
Leave	**Salga** *('sahl-gah)*
Tell	**Diga** *('dee-gah)*

☞ ¡Información!

Commands can be strings of words, also. Say these out loud!

Listen to me	**Escúcheme** *(eh-'skoo-cheh-meh)*
Explain to me	**Explíqueme** *(ehk-'splee-keh-meh)*
Tell me	**Dígame** *('dee-gah-meh)*
Call me	**Llámeme** *('yah-meh-meh)*
Give me	**Déme** *('deh-meh)*
Send me	**Mándeme** *('mahn-deh-meh)*
Answer me	**Contésteme** *(kohn-'teh-steh-meh)*
Bring me	**Tráigame** *('trah-ee-gah-meh)*

Listos para practicar

Select the correct verb infinitive from the list provided:

ayudar, salir, llamar, estudiar, solicitar, buscar *(ah-yoo-'dahr, sah-'leer, yah-'mahr, eh-stoo-dee-'ahr, soh-lee-see-'tahr, boo-'skahr)*

¿Dónde está el papel? *('dohn-deh eh-'stah ehl pah-'pehl)*

Tengo que *('tehn-goh keh)* _____.

¡Ya son las ocho! *('yah sohn lahs 'oh-choh)*

Tengo que _____. *('tehn-goh keh___)*

Mi familia no tiene dinero.

(mee fah-'mee-lee-ah noh tee-'eh-neh dee-'neh-roh)

Tengo que _____. *('tehn-goh keh___)*

Soy estudiante. *('soh·ee eh-stoo-dee-'ahn-teh)*

Tengo que _____. *('tehn-goh keh___)*

El trabajo es muy bueno. *(ehl trah-'bah-hoh ehs 'bweh-noh)*

Tengo que _____. *('tehn-goh keh___)*

Aquí está el teléfono. *(ah-'kee eh-'stah ehl teh-'leh-foh-noh)*

Tengo que _____. *('tehn-goh keh___)*

Using what you learned about the new Present Tense forms in Spanish, make changes to these verbs and then translate to English.

Here's an example:

TERMINAR *(tehr-mee-'nahr)* (to finish)

Yo termino temprano.

(yoh tehr-'mee-noh tehm-'prah-noh) (I finish early.)

FUMAR *(foo-'mahr)* (to smoke)

Ella _____ mucho. *('eh-yah _____ 'moo-choh)* (_____)

MANDAR *(mahn-'dahr)* (to send)

Nosotros _____ el dinero. *(noh-'soh-trohs _____ ehl dee-'neh-roh)* (_____)

REGRESAR *(reh-greh-'sahr)* (to return)

Ellos _____ tarde. *('eh-yohs _____ 'tahr-deh)* (_____)

RECIBIR *(reh-see-'beer)* (to receive)

Yo _____ la información. *(yoh _____ lah een-fohr-mah-see-'ohn)* (_____)

Now choose the best command word!

Lea, Llame, Conteste, Firme, Traiga

('leh-ah, 'yah-meh, kohn-'teh-steh, 'feer-meh, 'trah-ee-gah)

_____ **la pregunta.** *(lah preh-'goon-tah)*

_____ **el libro.** *(ehl 'lee-broh)*

_____ **su nombre.** *(soo 'nohm-breh)*

_____ **a su casa.** *(ah soo 'kah-sah)*

_____ **la silla.** *(lah 'see-yah)*

Chapter Three

Capítulo Tres
(kah-'pee-too-loh trehs)

The Benefits
Los beneficios
(lohs beh-neh-'fee-see·ohs)

The package

El paquete *(ehl pah-'keh-teh)*

Now that you've hired the new employee, we'll look at the HR Department's responsibility of sharing the benefit and insurance information with Spanish-speaking employees. As we learned earlier, the fastest way to take on new words and phrases is to acquire them as parts of complete phrases, sentences, or expressions. Here's a start-up series that covers the topic in detail:

On this date, you receive (the)...	**En esta fecha, recibe usted...** *(ehn 'eh-stah 'feh-chah, reh-'see-beh oo-'stehd)*
check	**el cheque** *(ehl 'cheh-keh)*
commission	**la comisión** *(lah koh-mee-see-'ohn)*
earnings	**las ganancias** *(lahs gah-'nahn-see·ahs)*
paycheck	**la paga** *('lah 'pah-gah)*
payment	**el pago** *(ehl 'pah-goh)*
raise	**el aumento de sueldo** *(ehl ow-'mehn-toh deh 'swehl-doh)*
salary	**el salario** *(ehl sah-'lah-ree·oh)*
tips	**las propinas** *(lahs proh-'pee-nahs)*
wages	**el sueldo** *(ehl 'swehl-doh)*
Benefits include (the)...	**Los beneficios incluyen...** *(lohs beh-neh-'fee-see·ohs een-'kloo-yehn)*
back pay	**los pagos atrasados** *(lohs 'pah-gohs ah-trah-'sah-dohs)*
bonuses	**las pagas primas** *(lahs 'pah-gahs 'pree-mahs)*
breaks	**las pausas para descansar** *(lahs 'pow-sahs 'pah-rah deh-skahn-sahr)*
child care	**la guardería infantil** *(lah gwahr-deh-'ree-ah een-fahn-'teel)*
days off	**los días de descanso** *(lohs 'dee-ahs deh deh-'skahn-soh)*
incentive scheme	**el plan de incentivos** *(ehl plahn deh een-sehn-'tee-vohs)*

maternity pay	**el subsidio de maternidad**
	(ehl soob-'see-dee-oh deh mah-tehr-nee-'dahd)
medical insurance	**el seguro médico**
	(ehl seh-'goo-roh 'meh-dee-koh)
memberships	**las afiliaciones**
	(lahs ah-fee-lee-ah-see-'oh-nehs)
parking space	**el aparcamiento**
	(ehl ah-pahr-kah-mee-'ehn-toh)
pension funds	**los fondos de jubilación**
	(lohs 'fohn-dohs deh hoo-bee-lah-see-'ohn)
perks	**los beneficios adicionales**
	(lohs beh-neh-'fee-see·ohs ah-dee-see·oh-'nah-lehs)
profit sharing	**la participación en los beneficios**
	(lah pahr-tee-see-pah-see-'ohn ehn lohs beh-neh-'fee-see·ohs)
promotions	**los ascensos** *(lohs ah-'sehn-sohs)*
retirement package	**el paquete de jubilación**
	(ehl pah-'keh-teh deh hoo-bee-lah-see-'ohn)
severance pay	**la indemnización por despedida**
	(lah een-dehm-nee-sah-see-'ohn pohr deh-speh-'dee-dah)
sick leave	**los días pagados por enfermedad**
	(lohs 'dee-ahs pah-'gah-dohs pohr ehn-fehr-meh-'dahd)
time off for bereavement	**los días libres por luto**
	(lohs 'dee-ahs 'lee-brehs pohr 'loo-toh)
Worker's Compensation	**la compensación de obrero**
	(lah kohm-pehn-sah-see-'ohn deh oh-'breh-roh)
Social Security Insurance	**el seguro de seguridad social**
	(ehl seh-'goo-roh deh seh-goo-ree-'dahd soh-see-'ahl)

Now read through this next list of fringe benefits. Start with the ones you need right away:

You can...	**Usted puede...** *(oo-'stehd 'pweh-deh)*
attend special events	**asistir a eventos especiales** *(ah-see-'steer ah eh-'vehn-tohs eh-speh-see-'ah-lehs)*
get an allowance	**conseguir una asignación** *(kohn-seh-'geer 'oo-nah ah-seeg-nah-see-'ohn)*
have the keys	**tener las llaves** *(teh-'nehr lahs 'yah-vehs)*
join the union	**inscribirse con el sindicato** *(een-skree-'beer-seh kohn ehl seen-dee-'kah-toh)*
open an expense account	**abrir una cuenta de gastos** *(ah-'breer 'oo-nah 'kwehn-tah deh 'gah-stohs)*
park for free	**estacionar sin pagar** *(eh-stah-see·oh-'nahr seen pah-'gahr)*
receive a discount	**recibir un descuento** *(reh-see-'beer oon deh-'skwehn-toh)*
take a year's sabbatical	**tomar un año de sabático** *(toh-'mahr oon 'ah-nyoh deh sah-'bah-tee-koh)*
travel by carpool	**viajar en grupo** *(vee-ah-'hahr ehn 'groo-poh)*
use the gym	**usar el gimnasio** *(oo-'sahr ehl heem-'nah-see·oh)*
There is/are...	**Hay...** *('ah·ee)*
compressed work weeks	**semanas de trabajo condensadas** *(seh-'mah-nahs deh trah-'bah-hoh kohn-dehn-'sah-dahs)*
excellent security	**excelente protección** *(ehk-seh-'lehn-teh proh-tehk-see-'ohn)*
flexible schedules	**horarios flexibles** *(oh-'rah-ree·ohs flehk-'see-blehs)*
four-day work weeks	**cuatro días de trabajo por semana** *('kwah-troh 'dee-ahs deh trah-'bah-hoh pohr seh-'mah-nah)*

job rotation	**rotación de tareas**
	(roh-ta-see-'ohn deh tah-'reh-ahs)
job sharing	**trabajos compartidos**
	(trah-'bah-hohs kohm-pahr-'tee-dohs)
overtime pay	**pago por sobretiempo**
	('pah-goh pohr soh-bre-tee-'ehm-poh)
paid holidays	**días de fiesta pagados**
	('dee-ahs deh fee-'eh-stah pah-'gah-dohs)
paid leaves of absence	**períodos de licencia pagados**
	(peh-'ree-oh-dohs deh lee-'sehn-see-ah pah-'gah-dohs)
paid vacations	**vacaciones pagadas**
	(vah-kah-see-'oh-nehs pah-'gah-dahs)
tax deductions	**deducciones de impuestos**
	(deh-dook-see-'oh-nehs deh eem-'pweh-stohs)

¡Información!

We'll tackle the world of health insurance just ahead. Here's a set of other insurance concerns:

The job doesn't include...	**El trabajo no incluye...**
	(ehl trah-'bah-hoh noh een-'kloo-yeh)
auto insurance	**el seguro de carro**
	(ehl seh-'goo-roh deh 'kah-rroh)
dental insurance	**el seguro dental**
	(ehl seh-'goo-roh dehn-'tahl)
disability insurance	**el seguro de incapacidad**
	(ehl seh-'goo-roh deh een-kah-pah-see-'dahd)
home insurance	**el seguro de casa**
	(ehl seh-'goo-roh deh 'kah-sah)
life insurance	**el seguro de vida**
	(ehl seh-'goo-roh deh 'vee-dah)
unemployment insurance	**el seguro de desempleo**
	(ehl seh-'goo-roh deh dehs-ehm-'pleh-oh)

Temas culturales

One of the most difficult things to discuss in a foreign language concerns social ethics and values. Your personal feelings, attitudes, and beliefs cannot be communicated in a few short sentences. Therefore, the best way to express any serious matter such as spending or financial need is either through an interpreter or by preparing a written note. Be sure that your employee knows exactly what you consider a "right" or "wrong."

Accounting
Contabilidad *(kohn-tah-bee-lee-'dahd)*

Payday's the big topic, so sit down with your Spanish-speaking staff and brief them on financial matters. This list of terms will allow you to elaborate:

Talk to (the)...	**Hable con...** *('ah-bleh kohn)*
accounting department	**el departamento de contabilidad** *(ehl deh-pahr-tah-'mehn-toh deh kohn-tah-bee-lee-'dahd)*
billing department	**el departamento de facturación** *(ehl deh-pahr-tah-'mehn-toh deh fahk-'too-rah-see-'ohn)*
payroll department	**el departamento de pagos** *(ehl deh-pahr-tah-'mehn-toh deh 'pah-gohs)*
Ask about (the)...	**Pregunte acerca de (the)...** *(preh-'goon-teh ah-'sehr-kah deh)*
advance	**el anticipo** *(ehl ahn-tee-'see-poh)*
amount	**la suma** *(lah 'soo-mah)*
balance	**el saldo** *(ehl 'sahl-doh)*
charges	**los cargos** *(lohs 'kahr-gohs)*
cost	**el costo** *(ehl 'koh-stoh)*
expenditures	**los gastos** *(lohs 'gah-stohs)*
fee	**el honorario** *(ehl oh-noh-'rah-ree·oh)*
funds	**los fondos** *(lohs 'fohn-dohs)*

refund	**el reembolso** *(ehl reh-ehm-'bohl-soh)*
taxes	**los impuestos** *(lohs eem-'pweh-stohs)*

Continue practicing with this new phrase:

Look at (the)...	**Mire...** *('mee-reh)*
bill	**la cuenta** *(lah 'kwehn-tah)*
invoice	**la factura** *(lah fahk-'too-rah)*
purchase order	**la orden de compra** *(lah 'ohr-dehn deh kohm-'prah)*
receipt	**el recibo** *(ehl reh-'see-boh)*
stub	**el talón del cheque** *(ehl tah-'lohn deh 'cheh-keh)*

One effective way to learn the words you need is to break them into related vocabulary groups. Here are some examples:

It's (the)...	**Es...** *(ehs)*
hourly pay	**el pago por hora** *(ehl 'pah-goh pohr 'oh-rah)*
monthly salary	**el salario por mes** *(ehl sah-'lah-ree-oh pohr mehs)*
weekly wage	**el sueldo por semana** *(ehl 'swehl-doh pohr seh-'mah-nah)*
base pay	**el sueldo inicial** *(ehl 'swehl-doh ee-nee-see-'ahl)*
pay day	**el día de paga** *(ehl 'dee-ah deh 'pah-gah)*
pay period	**el período de paga** *(ehl peh-'ree-oh-doh deh 'pah-gah)*
minimum wage	**el salario mínimo** *(ehl sah-'lah-ree-oh 'mee-nee-moh)*
overtime rate	**el salario por sobretiempo** *(ehl sah-'lah-ree-oh 'pohr soh-breh-tee-'ehm-poh)*
time and a half	**el salario por tiempo y medio** *(ehl sah-'lah-ree-oh pohr tee-'ehm-poh ee 'meh-dee-oh)*
cost of living increase	**el aumento por el costo de vida** *(ehl ow-'mehn-toh pohr ehl 'koh-stoh deh 'vee-dah)*

pay cut	**la reducción de sueldo** *(lah reh-dook-see-'ohn deh 'swehl-doh)*
pay hike	**el aumento de sueldo** *(ehl ow-'mehn-toh deh 'swehl-doh)*
gross income	**los ingresos brutos** *(lohs een-'greh-sohs 'broo-tohs)*
net income	**los ingresos netos** *(lohs een-'greh-sohs 'neh-tohs)*
revenue	**los ingresos** *(lohs een-'greh-sohs)*

¡Información!

• Did you mention every detail concerning payments? Try these.

You need (the)...	**Necesita...** *(neh-seh-'see-tah)*
copy	**la copia** *(lah 'koh-pee·ah)*
endorsement	**el endoso** *(ehl ehn-'doh-soh)*
ID	**la identificación** *(lah ee-dehn-tee-fee-kah-see-'ohn)*
pay envelope	**el sobre de paga** *(ehl 'soh-breh deh 'pah-gah)*
request	**la petición** *(lah peh-tee-see-'ohn)*
signature	**la firma** *(lah 'feer-mah)*
transfer	**la transferencia** *(lah trahns-feh-'rehn-see·ah)*

• Some of the workers' earnings may be directed elsewhere. Ask or explain the following:

We need money for (the)...	**Necesitamos el dinero para...** *(neh-seh-see-'tah-mohs ehl dee-'neh-roh 'pah-rah)*
charity	**la caridad** *(lah kah-ree-'dahd)*
contributions	**las contribuciones** *(lahs kohn-tree-boo-see-'oh-nehs)*
donation	**la donación** *(lah doh-nah-see-'ohn)*
fundraising	**la colección de fondos** *(lah koh-lehk-see-'ohn deh 'fohn-dohs)*

gifts	**los regalos** *(lohs reh-'gah-lohs)*
prizes	**los premios** *(lohs 'preh-mee·ohs)*
rewards	**las recompensas**
	(lahs reh-kohm-'pehn-sahs)

• Some questions are a little awkward, so be courteous:

Do you receive (the)...?	**¿Recibe usted...?** *(reh-'see-bee oo-'stehd)*
child support	**el mantenimiento de los hijos**
	(ehl mahn-teh-nee-mee-'ehn-toh deh lohs 'ee-hohs)
food stamps	**los cupones para alimentos**
	(lohs koo-'poh-nehs 'pah-rah ah-lee-'mehn-tohs)
welfare	**la asistencia social**
	(lah ah-sees-'tehn-see-ah soh-see-'ahl)

• And how's your math?

add	**sumar** *(soo-'mahr)*
average	**promedio** *(proh-'meh-dee-oh)*
divide	**dividir** *(dee-vee-'deer)*
fraction	**fracción** *(frahk-see-'ohn)*
multiply	**multiplicar** *(mool-tee-plee-'kahr)*
percent	**por ciento** *(pohr see-'ehn-toh)*
subtract	**restar** *(reh-'stahr)*

Listos para practicar

Join each word with its translation:

payment	**la suma** *(lah 'soo-mah)*
revenue	**los ingresos** *(lohs een-'greh-sohs)*
accounting	**el saldo** *(ehl 'sahl-doh)*
wage	**las cuentas** *(lahs 'kwehn-tahs)*
balance	**el promedio** *(ehl proh-'meh-dee·oh)*
amount	**el pago** *(ehl 'pah-goh)*
average	**el sueldo** *(ehl 'swehl-doh)*

The credit union
El banco cooperativo
(ehl 'bahn-koh koh-oh-peh-rah-'tee-voh)

Human Resources managers are sometimes requested to help employees who struggle with personal finances. This may involve guiding personnel through bank or credit union procedures. The following words and phrases are important openers:

Do you know something about (the)...?	**¿Sabe usted algo de...?** *('sah-bee oo-'stehd 'ahl-goh deh)*
annuities	**las anualidades** *(lahs ah-noo-ah-lee-'dah-dehs)*
assets	**los bienes** *(lohs bee-'eh-nehs)*
bonds	**los bonos** *(lohs 'boh-nohs)*
budgets	**los presupuestos** *(lohs preh-soo-'pweh-stohs)*
certificates	**los certificados** *(lohs sehr-tee-fee-'kah-dohs)*
checking accounts	**las cuentas de cheques** *(lahs 'kwehn-tahs deh 'cheh-kehs)*
commodities	**las mercancías** *(lahs mehr-kahn-'see-ahs)*
credit ratings	**las clasificaciones de crédito** *(lahs klah-see-fee-kah-see-'oh-nehs deh 'kreh-dee-toh)*
dividends	**los dividendos** *(lohs dee-vee-'dehn-dohs)*
down payment	**el pago inicial** *(ehl 'pah-goh ee-nee-see-'ahl)*
interest rates	**las tasas de interés** *(lahs 'tah-sahs deh een-teh-'rehs)*
investments	**las inversiones** *(lahs een-vehr-see-'oh-nehs)*
leases	**los alquileres** *(lohs ahl-kee-'leh-rehs)*
liabilities	**las deudas** *(lahs 'deh-oo-dahs)*
loans	**los préstamos** *(lohs 'preh-stah-mohs)*
money markets	**los mercados de valores** *(lohs mehr-'kah-dohs deh vah-'loh-rehs)*
mortgages	**las hipotecas** *(lahs ee-poh-'teh-kahs)*
mutual funds	**los fondos mutualistas** *(lohs 'fohn-dohs moo-twah-'lees-tahs)*
real estate	**las propiedades** *(lahs proh-pee-eh-'dah-dehs)*
rollovers	**las renovaciones** *(lahs reh-noh-'vah-see-'oh-nehs)*

savings accounts	**las cuentas de ahorros**
	(lahs 'kwehn-tahs deh ah-'oh-rrohs)
stocks	**las acciones** *(lahs ahk-see-'oh-nehs)*
trust funds	**los fondos fiduciarios**
	(lohs 'fohn-dohs fee-duh-see-'ah-ree-ohs)
You need...	**Necesita usted...** *(neh-seh-'see-tah oo-'stehd)*
financial planning	**la planificación financiera**
	(lah plah-nee-fee-kah-see-'ohn fee-nahn-see-'eh-rah)
money	**la administración de sus fondos** *(lahs ahd-*
management	*mee-nees-trah-see-'ohn deh soos 'fohn-dohs)*
financial services	**los servicios financieros**
	(lohs sehr-'vee-see-ohs fee-nahn-see-'eh-rohs)

Money matters
Asuntos monetarios
(ah-'soon-tohs moh-neh-'tah-ree-ohs)

Focus on each of the following sets of question phrases:

Do you have (the)...?	**¿Tiene...?** *(tee-'eh-neh)*
bills	**los billetes** *(lohs bee-'yeh-tehs)*
cash	**el efectivo** *(ehl eh-fehk-'tee-voh)*
cents	**los centavos** *(lohs sehn-'tah-vohs)*
change	**el cambio** *(ehl 'kahm-bee-oh)*
check	**el cheque** *(ehl 'cheh-keh)*
coins	**las monedas** *(lahs moh-'neh-dahs)*
credit card	**la tarjeta de crédito**
	(lah tahr-'heh-tah deh 'kreh-dee-toh)
dollars	**los dólares** *(lohs 'doh-lah-rehs)*
Do you know (the)...?	**¿Le conoce a...?** *(leh koh-'noh-seh ah)*
analyst	**el analista** *(ehl ah-nah-'lee-stah)*
attorney	**el abogado** *(ehl ah-boh-'gah-doh)*
auditor	**el auditor** *(ehl ow-dee-'tohr)*
beneficiary	**el beneficiario** *(ehl beh-neh-fee-see-'ah-ree-oh)*
bookkeeper	**el contable** *(ehl kohn-'tah-bleh)*
broker	**el corredor** *(ehl koh-rreh-'dohr)*
cashier	**el cajero** *(ehl kah-'heh-roh)*

clerk	**el dependiente** *(ehl deh-pehn-dee-'ehn-teh)*
CPA	**el contador público** *(ehl kohn-tah-'dohr 'poo-blee-koh)*
member	**el miembro** *(ehl mee-'ehm-broh)*
notary public	**el notario público** *(ehl noh-'tah-ree-oh 'poo-blee-koh)*
partner	**el socio** *(ehl 'soh-see·oh)*
trustee	**el fideicomisario** *(ehl fee-deh-ee-koh-mee-'sah-ree·oh)*
Is it...?	**¿Es...?** *(ehs)*
a fiscal year	**un año financiero** *(oon 'ah-nyoh fee-nahn-see-'eh-roh)*
bi-monthly	**cada dos meses** *('kah-dah dohs 'meh-sehs)*
long-term	**a largo plazo** *(ah 'lahr-goh 'plah-soh)*
quarterly	**cuatro veces al año** *('kwah-troh 'meh-sehs ahl 'ah-nyoh)*
semi-annual	**semianual** *(seh-mee-ah-noo-'ahl)*
short-term	**a corto plazo** *(ah 'kohr-toh 'plah-soh)*
Is it...?	**¿Está...?** *(eh-'stah)*
accrued	**acumulado** *(ah-koo-moo-'lah-doh)*
active	**activo** *(ahk-'tee-voh)*
eligible	**elegible** *(eh-lee-'hee-bleh)*
fixed	**fijo** *('fee-hoh)*
variable	**variable** *(vah-ree-'ah-bleh)*
What's the...?	**¿Cuál es...?** *(kwahl ehs)*
adjustment	**el ajuste** *(ehl ah-'hoo-steh)*
appreciation	**la revalorización** *(lah reh-vah-loh-ree-sah-see-'ohn)*
cycle	**el ciclo** *(ehl 'see-kloh)*
estimate	**el estimado** *(ehl eh-stee-'mah-doh)*
expiration date	**la fecha de vencimiento** *(lah 'feh-chah deh vehn-see-mee-'ehn-toh)*
growth	**el crecimiento** *(ehl kreh-see-mee-'ehn-toh)*
index	**el índice** *(ehl 'een-dee-seh)*
limit	**el límite** *(ehl 'lee-mee-teh)*

penalty	**la sanción** *(lah sah-see-'ohn)*
regulation	**el reglamento** *(ehl reh-glah-'mehn-toh)*
requirement	**el requisito** *(ehl reh-kee-'see-toh)*
term	**el término** *(ehl 'tehr-mee-noh)*
value	**el valor** *(ehl vah-'lohr)*
yield	**el rendimiento** *(ehl rehn-dee-mee-'ehn-toh)*

☞ # ¡Información!

• Spend a few minutes reviewing this group of terms. The topic of taxes is unavoidable when it comes to payroll:

tax return	**el rembolso impositivo** *(ehl rehm-'bohl-soh eem-poh-see-'tee-voh)*
withholding tax	**el impuesto retenido** *(ehl eem-'pweh-stoh reh-teh-'nee-doh)*
federal income tax	**el impuesto federal sobre la renta** *(ehl eem-'pweh-stoh feh-deh-'rahl 'soh-breh lah 'rehn-tah)*
state income tax	**el impuesto estatal sobre la renta** *(ehl eem-'pweh-stoh eh-stah-'tahl 'soh-breh lah 'rehn-tah)*
tax shelter	**la protección contra los impuestos** *(lah proh-tehk-see-'ohn 'kohn-trah lohs eem-'pweh-stohs)*
deferred taxes	**los impuestos diferidos** *(lohs eem-'pweh-stohs dee-feh-'ree-dohs)*

• Keep collecting words that are similar in both languages:

restriction	**la restricción** *(lah reh-streek-see-'ohn)*
inflation	**la inflación** *(lah een-flah-see-'ohn)*
transaction	**la transacción** *(lah trahns-ahk-see-'ohn)*

• You may need to send some financial information by mail, so refer to these items in Spanish every day:

post office	**la oficina de correos** *(lah oh-fee-'see-nah deh koh-'rreh-ohs)*

air mail	**el correo aéreo**
	(ehl koh-'rreh-oh ah-'eh-reh-oh)
letter	**la carta** *(lah 'kahr-tah)*
stamps	**las estampillas** *(lahs eh-stahm-'pee-yahs)*
mailbox	**el buzón** *(ehl boo-'sohn)*
envelope	**el sobre** *(ehl 'soh-breh)*
delivery	**la entrega** *(lah ehn-'treh-gah)*
package	**el paquete** *(ehl pah-'keh-teh)*

• Some terms are so specialized or typical of this country that Spanish speakers will understand you better if you leave them untranslated

el T-Bill
el IRA
el 401K
el CD
el FDIC
el IRS

• Notice all the action words you'll need to discuss **dinero** matters.

How many can you remember?

accrue	**acumular** *(ah-koo-moo-'lahr)*
adjust	**ajustar** *(ah-hoo-'stahr)*
approve	**aprobar** *(ah-proh-'bahr)*
authorize	**autorizar** *(ow-toh-ree-'sahr)*
borrow	**pedir prestado** *(peh-'deer preh-'stah-doh)*
buy	**comprar** *(kohm-'prahr)*
calculate	**calcular** *(kahl-koo-'lahr)*
cancel	**cancelar** *(kahn-seh-'lahr)*
collect	**recolectar** *(reh-koh-lehk-'tahr)*
confirm	**confirmar** *(kohn-feer-'mahr)*
contribute	**contribuir** *(kohn-tree-boo-'eer)*
deliver	**repartir** *(reh-pahr-'teer)*
deposit	**depositar** *(deh-poh-see-'tahr)*
distribute	**distribuir** *(dee-stree-boo-'eer)*
diversify	**diversificar** *(dee-vehr-see-fee-'kahr)*

exchange	**cambiar** *(kahm-bee-'ahr)*
expire	**vencer** *(vehn-'sehr)*
get	**conseguir** *(kohn-seh-'geer)*
grow	**crecer** *(kreh-'sehr)*
invest	**invertir** *(een-vehr-'teer)*
join	**unir** *(oo-'neer)*
lose	**perder** *(pehr-'dehr)*
notify	**notificar** *(noh-tee-fee-'kahr)*
pay	**pagar** *(pah-'gahr)*
rent	**alquilar** *(ahl-kee-'lahr)*
save	**ahorrar** *(ah-oh-'rrahr)*
sell	**vender** *(vehn-'dehr)*
share	**compartir** *(kohm-pahr-'teer)*
transfer	**transferir** *(trahns-feh-'reer)*
withdraw	**sacar** *(sah-'kahr)*

Temas culturales

Personal expenses often include spending money on major family events. At times, much of the paycheck is spent on the following:

anniversary	**el aniversario** *(ehl ah-nee-vehr-'sah-ree-oh)*
birth	**el nacimiento** *(ehl nah-see-mee-'ehn-toh)*
birthday	**el cumpleaños** *(ehl koom-pleh-'ah-nyohs)*
engagement	**el compromiso** *(ehl kohm-proh-'mee-soh)*
funeral	**el funeral** *(ehl foo-neh-'rahl)*
shower	**el shower** *(ehl 'shah-wehr)*
15-year-old-daughter's "coming out" party	**la quinceañera** *(lah keen-seh-ah-'nyeh-rah)*
wedding	**el casamiento** *(ehl kah-sah-mee-'ehn-toh)*

Financial troubles
Problemas financieros
(proh-'bleh-mahs fee-nahn-see-'eh-rohs)

When things go wrong, listen for these terms:

It's (the)...	**Es...** *(ehs)*
audit	**la verificación contable** *(lah veh-ree-fee-kah-see-'ohn kohn-'tah-bleh)*
bankruptcy	**la bancarrota** *(lah bahn-kah-'rroh-tah)*
collection	**la cobranza** *(lah koh-'brahn-sah)*
debt	**la deuda** *(lah deh-'oo-dah)*
delay	**la demora** *(lah deh-'moh-rah)*
error	**el error** *(ehl eh-'rrohr)*
expense	**el gasto** *(ehl 'gah-stoh)*
extortion	**la extorsión** *(lah ehks-tohr-see-'ohn)*
forgery	**la falsificación** *(lah fahl-see-fee-kah-see-'ohn)*
fraud	**el fraude** *(ehl 'frah-oo-deh)*
insufficient funds	**los fondos insuficientes** *(lohs 'fohn-dohs een-soo-fee-see-'ehn-tehs)*
liability	**la obligación** *(lah ohb-lee-gah-see-'ohn)*
loss	**la pérdida** *(lah 'pehr-dee-dah)*
penalty	**la multa** *(lah mool-tah)*
reduction	**la reducción** *(lah reh-dook-see-'ohn)*
robbery	**el robo** *(ehl 'roh-boh)*

Listos para practicar

Fill in the blanks with the word that best fits the series:

fondo mutualista, dependiente, billete, estampilla, valor, extorsión *('fohn-doh moo-twah-'lees-tah, deh-pehn-dee-'ehn-teh, bee-'yeh-teh, eh-stahm-'pee-yah, vah-'lohr, ehks-tohr-see-'ohn)*

    fraude, robo, falsificación, _____
    ('frah-oo-deh, 'roh-boh, fahl-see-fee-kah-see-'ohn)

centavo, moneda, dólar, _____
(sehn-'tah-voh, moh-'neh-dah, 'doh-lahr)
carta, sobre, buzón, _____
('kahr-tah, 'soh-breh, boo-'sohn)
contador, corredor, cajero, _____
(kohn-tah-'dohr, koh-rreh-'dohr, kah-'heh-roh)
ciclo, índice, término, _____
('see-kloh, 'een-dee-seh, 'tehr-mee-noh)
bono, acción, certificado, _____
('boh-noh, ahk-see-'ohn, sehr-tee-fee-'kah-doh)

List three Spanish verbs that relate to financial affairs:

_____

_____

_____

Medical insurance
El seguro médico
(ehl seh-'goo-roh 'meh-dee-koh)

As your new employees finish up with their financial forms, set aside a selection of Spanish phrases that relate to health care insurance. If possible, get all legal documents translated. It'll make your job a whole lot easier. Now, simply brief everyone using the patterns below:

Here is (the)...	**Aquí tiene...** (ah-'kee-tee-'eh-neh)
claim form	**el formulario del reclamante** (ehl fohr-moo-'lah-ree-oh dehl reh-klah-'mahn-teh)
co-pay amount	**el monto del pago compartido** (ehl 'mohn-toh dehl 'pah-goh kohm-pahr-'tee-doh)
date of service	**la fecha de servicio** (lah 'feh-chah deh sehr-'vee-see-oh)
deductible	**el deducible** (ehl deh-doo-'see-bleh)
family policy	**la póliza para la familia** (lah 'poh-lee-sah 'pah-rah lah fah-'mee-lee-ah)

group number	**el número del grupo** *(ehl 'noo-meh-roh dehl 'groo-poh)*
health plan	**el plan de salud** *(ehl plahn deh sah-'lood)*
insurance card	**la tarjeta de seguro** *(lah tahr-'heh-tah deh seh-'goo-roh)*
insurance company	**la compañía de seguros** *(lah kohm-pah-'nyee-ah deh seh-'goo-rohs)*
list of doctors	**la lista de médicos** *(lah 'lee-stah deh 'meh-dee-kohs)*
premium	**la prima** *(lah 'pree-mah)*
procedure code	**el código de procedimiento** *(ehl 'koh-dee-goh deh proh-seh-dee-mee-'ehn-toh)*
Are you (the)...?	**¿Es usted...?** *(ehs oo-'stehd)*
claimant	**el reclamante** *(ehl reh-klah-'mahn-teh)*
dependent	**el dependiente** *(ehl deh-pehn-dee-'ehn-teh)*
nurse	**el enfermero** *(ehl ehn-fehr-'meh-roh)*
patient	**el paciente** *(ehl pah-see-'ehn-teh)*
physician	**el médico** *(ehl 'meh-dee-koh)*
representative	**el representante** *(ehl reh-preh-sehn-'tahn-teh)*
specialist	**el especialista** *(ehl eh-speh-see-ah-'lee-stah)*
The hospital needs the...	**El hospital necesita...** *(ehl oh-spee-'tahl neh-seh-'see-tah)*
dental insurance	**el seguro dental** *(ehl seh-'goo-roh dehn-'tahl)*
disability insurance	**el seguro de incapacidad** *(ehl seh-goo-roh deh een-kah-pah-see-'dahd)*
eye care insurance	**el seguro para la vista** *(ehl seh-'goo-roh 'pah-rah lah 'vee-stah)*
mental health insurance	**el seguro de salud mental** *(ehl seh-'goo-roh deh sah-'lood mehn-'tahl)*
personal insurance	**el seguro personal** *(ehl seh-'goo-roh pehr-soh-'nahl)*

Now make sure that all questions are answered:

Do you understand (the)...?	**¿Entiende...?** *(ehn-tee-'ehn-deh)*
coverage	**la cobertura** *(lah koh-behr-'too-rah)*

monthly payments	**los pagos mensuales**
	(lohs 'pah-gohs mehn-soo-'ah-lehs)
restrictions	**las restricciones**
	(lahs reh-streek-see-'oh-nehs)
terms	**los términos** *(lohs 'tehr-mee-nohs)*
waiver	**la exención** *(lah ehks-ehn-see-'ohn)*
Do you want...?	**¿Quiere...?** *(kee-'eh-reh)*
to cancel	**cancelar** *(kahn-seh-'lahr)*
to change	**cambiar** *(kahm-bee-'ahr)*
to check	**averiguar** *(ah-veh-ree-'gwahr)*
to enroll	**matricularse** *(mah-tree-koo-'lahr-seh)*
to file	**reportar** *(reh-pohr-'tahr)*
to verify	**verificar** *(veh-ree-fee-'kahr)*

¡Información!

• And what about life insurance? Add these words to your vocabulary list:

It's (the)...	**Es...** *(ehs)*
beneficiary	**el beneficiario** *(ehl beh-neh-fee-see-'ah-ree-oh)*
certificate	**el certificado** *(ehl sehr-tee-fee-'kah-doh)*
death benefit	**la indemnización por muerte**
	(lah een-dehm-nee-sah-see-'ohn pohr 'mwehr-teh)

• Be prepared to answer a few questions. Start with these:

What kind of coverage?
¿Qué tipo de cobertura? *(keh 'tee-poh deh koh-behr-'too-rah)*
What are my options?
¿Cuáles son mis opciones? *('kwah-lehs sohn mees ohp-see-'oh-nehs)*
What does it include?
¿Qué incluye? *(keh een-'kloo-yeh)*

• And remember to use your English:

el Blue Shield	el Medicaid
el Blue Cross	el HMO
el Medicare	el PPO

The policy
La póliza *(lah 'poh-lee-sah)*

The Human Resources Department is responsible for explaining all insurance policies and procedures, so save these terms and expressions for your next employee briefing:

We have...	**Tenemos...** *(teh-'neh-mohs)*
affordable payments	**pagos a su alcance** *('pah-gohs ah soo ahl-'kahn-seh)*
comprehensive coverage	**cobertura completa** *(koh-behr-'too-rah kohm-'pleh-tah)*
easy access	**una localidad conveniente** *('oo-nah loh-kah-lee-'dahd kohn-veh-nee-'ehn-teh)*
individual health plans	**planes de salud individuales** *('plah-nehs deh sah-'lood een-dee-vee-'dwah-lehs)*
special rates	**tarifas especiales** *(tah-'ree-fahs eh-speh-see-'ah-lehs)*
statewide network	**una red interestatal** *(oo-nah rehd een-tehr-ehs-tah-'tahl)*
24-hour service	**servicio de 24 horas** *(sehr-'vee-see-oh deh 'veh·een-teh ee 'kwah-troh 'oh-rahs)*
wide selection	**una amplia selección** *('oo-nah 'ahm-plee-ah seh-lehk-see-'ohn)*
It also includes...	**También incluye...** *(tahm-bee-'ehn een-'kloo-yeh)*
ambulance service	**el servicio de ambulancia** *(ehl sehr-'vee-see-oh deh ahm-boo-'lahn-see-ah)*
convalescent clinics	**las clínicas para convalecientes** *(lahs 'klee-nee-kahs 'pah-rah kohn-vah-leh-see-'ehn-tehs)*
examinations	**los exámenes** *(lohs ehk-'sah-meh-nehs)*
home health care	**el cuidado médico en el hogar** *(ehl kwee-'dah-doh 'meh-dee-koh ehn ehl oh-'gahr)*
immunizations	**las vacunas** *(lahs vah-'koo-nahs)*
major surgery	**la cirugía hospitalaria** *(lah see-roo-'hee-ah ohs-pee-tah-'lah-ree-ah)*

office visits	**las citas al médico**
	(lahs 'see-tahs ahl 'meh-dee-koh)
physical checkups	**exámenes médicos generales** *(ehk-'sah-*
	meh-nehs 'meh-dee-kohs heh-neh-'rah-lehs)
prescriptions	**las recetas médicas**
	(lahs reh-'seh-tahs 'meh-dee-kahs)
treatments	**los tratamientos**
	(lohs trah-tah-mee-'ehn-tohs)

Listos para practicar

Translate the following key questions without looking for help:

¿Tiene usted el formulario del reclamante?
(tee-'eh-neh oo-'stehd ehl fohr-moo-'lah-ree-oh dehl reh-klah-'mahn-teh)

¿Qué tipo de cobertura? *(keh 'tee-poh deh koh-behr-'too-rah)*

¿Es usted el médico? *(ehs oo-'stehd ehl 'meh-dee-koh)*

¿Entiende las restricciones?
(ehn-tee-'ehn-deh lahs reh-'streek-see-'oh-nehs)

¿Quiere matricularse? *(kee-'eh-reh mah-tree-koo-'lahr-seh)*

¿Incluye las recetas médicas?
(een-'kloo-yeh lahs reh-'seh-tahs 'meh-dee-kahs)

Temas culturales

Many cultures are somewhat suspicious about insurance coverage. If you have new immigrants on staff, they may request cash instead of a payroll deduction when they have a health care need. Be prepared to face employee fears and lack of trust.

The physical examination
El examen físico
(ehl ehk-'sah-mehn 'fee-see-koh)

No one's getting anything until they pass the physical exam! Use this series of questions as a checklist with Spanish-speaking employees. (However, for some of the more serious questions, it's always best to use a fluent interpreter.) These questions only require a **sí** or a **no** for an answer:

Do you have...?	¿Tiene...? *(tee-'eh-neh)*
a contagious disease	**una enfermedad contagiosa** *('oo-nah ehn-fehr-meh-'dahd kohn-tah-hee-'oh-sah)*
allergies	**alergias** *(ah-'lehr-hee-ahs)*
backaches	**dolores de espalda** *(doh-'loh-rehs deh eh-'spahl-dah)*
diabetes	**diabetes** *(dee-ah-'beh-tehs)*
dizziness	**mareos** *(mah-'reh-ohs)*
headaches	**dolores de cabeza** *(doh-'loh-rehs deh kah-'beh-sah)*
heart trouble	**problemas cardíacos** *(proh-'bleh-mahs kahr-'dee-ah-kohs)*
high blood pressure	**presión alta** *(preh-see-'ohn 'ahl-tah)*
physical problems	**problemas físicos** *(proh-'bleh-mahs 'fee-see-kohs)*
respiratory problems	**problemas respiratorios** *(proh-'bleh-mahs reh-spee-rah-'toh-ree-ohs)*
visual problems	**problemas de visión** *(proh-'bleh-mahs deh vee-see-'ohn)*
seizures	**ataques** *(ah-'tah-kehs)*
Do you need...?	¿Necesita usted...? *(neh-seh-'see-tah oo-'stehd)*
special care	**cuidado especial** *(kwee-'dah-doh eh-speh-see-'ahl)*
glasses	**lentes** *('lehn-tehs)*
handicapped parking	**estacionamiento para minusválidos** *(eh-stah-see-oh-nah-mee-'ehn-toh 'pah-rah mee-noos-'vah-lee-dohs)*

a wheelchair	**una silla de ruedas** *('oo-nah 'see-yah deh roo-'eh-dahs)*
hearing aids	**prótesis auditiva** *('pro-teh-sees ow-dee-'tee-vah)*
a cane	**un bastón** *(oon bah-'stohn)*
contact lenses	**lentes de contacto** *('lehn-tehs deh kohn-'tahk-toh)*
crutches	**muletas** *(moo-'leh-tahs)*

• Update the personal information in each file!

What's your...?	**¿Cuál es su...?** *(kwahl ehs soo)*
age	**edad** *(eh-'dahd)*
blood type	**tipo de sangre** *('tee-poh deh 'sahn-greh)*
hair color	**color de pelo** *(koh-'lohr deh 'peh-loh)*
height	**altura** *(ahl-'too-rah)*
weight	**peso** *('peh-soh)*

Family members
Los miembros de la familia
(lohs mee-'ehm-brohs deh lah fah-'mee-lee-ah)

In the Hispanic culture, family life is often the focus of everyday activities. For the Human Resources manager, it is extremely important that employee records include as much family information as possible. Here are some of the well-known members:

aunt	**la tía** *(lah 'tee-ah)*
brother	**el hermano** *(ehl ehr-'mah-noh)*
brother-in-law	**el cuñado** *(ehl koo-'nyah-doh)*
cousin	**el primo** *(ehl 'pree-moh)*
daughter	**la hija** *(lah 'ee-hah)*
daughter-in-law	**la nuera** *(lah 'nweh-rah)*
father	**el padre** *(ehl 'pah-dreh)*
father-in-law	**el suegro** *(ehl 'sweh-groh)*
granddaughter	**la nieta** *(lah nee-'eh-tah)*
grandfather	**el abuelo** *(ehl ah-'bweh-loh)*
grandmother	**la abuela** *(lah ah-'bweh-lah)*
grandson	**el nieto** *(ehl nee-'eh-toh)*

husband	**el esposo** *(ehl eh-'spoh-soh)*
mother	**la madre** *(lah 'mah-dreh)*
mother-in-law	**la suegra** *(lah 'sweh-grah)*
nephew	**el sobrino** *(ehl soh-'bree-noh)*
niece	**la sobrina** *(lah soh-'bree-nah)*
sister	**la hermana** *(lah ehr-'mah-nah)*
sister-in-law	**la cuñada** *(lah koo-'nyah-dah)*
son	**el hijo** *(ehl 'ee-hoh)*
son-in-law	**el yerno** *(ehl 'yehr-noh)*
uncle	**el tío** *(ehl 'tee-oh)*
wife	**la esposa** *(lah eh-'spoh-sah)*

- And don't get these two confused:

| parents | **los padres** *(lohs 'pah-drehs)* |
| relatives | **los parientes** *(lohs pah-ree-'ehn-tehs)* |

Temas culturales

Because the traditional Hispanic family includes more than just its immediate members, you may want to consider learning the names for "relations" outside the immediate family:

boyfriend	**el novio** *(ehl 'noh-vee·oh)*
close friend	**el compañero** *(ehl kohm-pah-'nyeh-roh)*
girlfriend	**la novia** *(lah 'noh-vee·ah)*
godchild	**el ahijado** *(ehl ah-ee-'hah-doh)*
godfather	**el compadre** *(ehl kohm-'pah-dreh)*
godmother	**la comadre** *(lah koh-'mah-dreh)*
godparents	**los padrinos** *(lohs pah-'dree-nohs)*

Childcare
El cuidado de los niños
(ehl kwee-'dah-doh deh lohs 'nee-nyohs)

As a service to their employees, more and more businesses are providing on-site care for younger children while their parents are at work. The childcare option is usually considered part of the benefits package.

In reference to kids, why not play around with these Spanish words that Hispanic children understand:

Where is the...?	¿Dónde está...? ('dohn-deh eh-'stah)
ball	la pelota (lah peh-'loh-tah)
bassinet	el bacinete (ehl bah-see-'neh-teh)
bib	el babero (ehl bah-'beh-roh)
blanket	la cobija (lah koh-'bee-hah)
crib	la cuna (lah 'koo-nah)
diaper	el pañal (ehl pah-'nyahl)
doll	la muñeca (lah moo-'nyeh-kah)
game	el juego (ehl hoo-'eh-goh)
nursing bottle	el biberón (ehl bee-beh-'rohn)
pacifier	el chupete (ehl choo-'peh-teh)
stroller	el cochecillo (ehl koh-cheh-'see-yoh)
toy	el juguete (ehl hoo-'geh-teh)

Children's chatter
La charla de los niños
(lah 'chahr-lah deh lohs 'nee-nyohs)

Word forms and phrases are altered slightly whenever you address younger children in Spanish. Only use these one-liners around the little ones:

How cute!	¡Qué precioso! (keh pre-see-'oh-soh)
How funny!	¡Qué cómico! (keh 'koh-mee-koh)
How pretty!	¡Qué bonito! (keh boh-'nee-toh)
What a beautiful face!	¡Qué linda cara! (keh 'leen-dah 'kah-rah)
What a beautiful outfit!	¡Qué linda la ropa! (keh 'leen-dah lah 'roh-pah)
What a beautiful smile!	¡Qué linda la sonrisa! (keh 'leen-dah lah sohn-'ree-sah)
What a beautiful voice!	¡Qué linda la voz! (keh 'leen-dah lah vohs)

Action words also change when you chat with children. Hispanics use the informal tú form:

Come here, darling.	Ven acá, mi querido. (vehn ah-'kah mee keh-'ree-doh)

Come here, my love.	**Ven acá, mi amor.**
	(vehn ah-'kah, mee ah-'mohr)
Come here, sweetie.	**Ven acá, mi dulce.**
	(vehn ah-'kah mee 'dool-seh)
Don't be afraid.	**No tengas miedo.**
	(noh 'tehn-gahs mee-'eh-doh)
Don't cry.	**No llores.** *(noh 'yoh-rehs)*
Give me a hug.	**Dame un abrazo.**
	('dah-meh oon ah-'brah-soh)
Give me a kiss.	**Dame un beso.** *('dah-meh oon 'beh-soh)*
It's lots of fun.	**Es muy divertido.**
	(ehs 'moo-ee dee-vehr-'tee-doh)
It's for you.	**Es para ti.** *(ehs 'pah-rah tee)*

Listos para practicar

Finish the list by following the simple pattern:

hermano *(ehr-'mah-noh)*	**hermana** *(ehr-'mah-nah)*
yerno *('yehr-noh)*	**nuera** *('nweh-rah)*
nieto *(nee-'eh-toh)*	_____
padre *('pah-dreh)*	_____
abuelo *(ah-'bweh-loh)*	_____
esposo *(eh-'spoh-soh)*	_____

Name three objects that you might find in a baby's crib:

_____

_____

_____

What are three nice things you could say when you greet a young child:

_____

_____

_____

Verbs for benefits
Verbos para beneficios
('vehr-bohs 'pah-rah beh-neh-'fee-see-ohs)

All kinds of new verbs are required when the topic is employee benefits. Many of these you've seen before:

to accrue	**acumular** *(ah-koo-moo-'lahr)*
to add	**añadir** *(ah-nyah-'deer)*
to adjust	**ajustar** *(ah-hoo-'stahr)*
to approve	**aprobar** *(ah-proh-'bahr)*
to authorize	**autorizar** *(ow-toh-ree-'sahr)*
to borrow	**pedir prestado** *(peh-'deer preh-'stah-doh)*
to calculate	**calcular** *(kahl-koo-'lahr)*
to cancel	**cancelar** *(kahn-seh-'lahr)*
to change	**cambiar** *(kahm-bee-'ahr)*
to charge	**cobrar** *(koh-'brahr)*
to check	**averiguar** *(ah-veh-ree-'gwahr)*
to close	**cerrar** *(seh-'rrahr)*
to collect	**recolectar** *(reh-koh-lehk-'tahr)*
to contribute	**contribuir** *(kohn-tree-boo-'eer)*
to count	**contar** *(kohn-'tahr)*
to cover	**cubrir** *(koo-'breer)*
to deliver	**repartir** *(reh-pahr-'teer)*
to deposit	**depositar** *(deh-poh-see-'tahr)*
to distribute	**distribuir** *(dee-stree-boo-'eer)*
to do	**hacer** *(ah-'sehr)*
to earn	**ganar** *(gah-'nahr)*
to enroll	**matricularse** *(mah-tree-koo-'lahr-seh)*
to exchange	**cambiar** *(kahm-bee-'ahr)*
to expire	**vencer** *(vehn-'sehr)*
to file	**reportar** *(reh-pohr-'tahr)*
to get	**conseguir** *(kohn-seh-'geer)*
to grow	**crecer** *(kreh-'sehr)*
to invest	**invertir** *(een-vehr-'teer)*
to leave	**salir** *(sah-'leer)*
to lose	**perder** *(pehr-'dehr)*

to notify	**notificar** *(noh-tee-fee-'kahr)*
to open	**abrir** *(ah-'breer)*
to pay	**pagar** *(pah-'gahr)*
to put in	**meter** *(meh-'tehr)*
to receive	**recibir** *(reh-see-'beer)*
to remove	**sacar** *(sah-'kahr)*
to rent	**alquilar** *(ahl-kee-'lahr)*
to save	**ahorrar** *(ah-oh-'rrahr)*
to share	**compartir** *(kohm-pahr-'teer)*
to spend	**gastar** *(gah-'stahr)*
to take away	**quitar** *(kee-'tahr)*
to think	**pensar** *(pehn-'sahr)*
to transfer	**transferir** *(trahns-feh-'reer)*
to use	**usar** *(oo-'sahr)*
to verify	**verificar** *(veh-ree-fee-'kahr)*
to withdraw	**sacar** *(sah-'kahr)*

Ready for another tip on how to use Spanish action words? Try out this new pattern with the verbs **querer** *(keh-'rehr)* (to want) and **preferir** *(preh-feh-'reer)* (to prefer). Can you translate each sample sentence all by yourself?

To want	**Querer** *(keh-'rehr)*
I want	**Quiero** *(kee-'eh-roh)*
	Quiero abrir una cuenta.
	(kee-'eh-roh ah-'breer 'oo-nah 'kwehn-tah)
You want; He/She wants	**Quiere** *(kee-'eh-reh)*
	Quiere recibir su dinero.
	(kee-'eh-reh reh-see-'beer soo dee-'neh-roh)
You (pl.) want; They want	**Quieren** *(kee-'eh-rehn)*
	Quieren usar el seguro.
	(kee-'eh-rehn oo-'sahr ehl seh-'goo-roh)
We want	**Queremos** *(keh-'reh-mohs)*
	Queremos conseguir los beneficios.
	(keh-'reh-mohs kohn-seh-'geer lohs beh-neh-'fee-see-ohs)

To prefer	**Preferir** *(preh-feh-'reer)*
I prefer	**Prefiero** *(preh-fee-'eh-roh)*
	Prefiero cambiar todo.
	(preh-fee-'eh-roh kahm-bee-'ahr 'toh-doh)
You prefer; He/She prefers	**Prefiere** *(preh-fee-'eh-reh)*
	Prefiere depositar la paga. *(preh-fee-'eh-reh deh-poh-see-'tahr lah 'pah-gah)*
You (pl.) prefer; They prefer	**Prefieren** *(preh-fee-'eh-rehn)*
	Prefieren invertir en la compañía.
	(preh-fee-'eh-rehn een-vehr-'teer ehn lah kohm-pah-'nyee-ah)
We prefer	**Preferimos** *(preh-feh-'ree-mohs)*
	Preferimos pagar con la tarjeta.
	(preh-feh-'ree-mohs pah-'gahr kohn lah tahr-'heh-tah)

¡Información!

Here are three other ways to discuss one's likes and dislikes. Again, learn these shortcuts as soon as you can:

Do you like ..?	**¿Le gusta...?** *(leh 'goo-stah)*
Yes, I like ...	**Sí, me gusta...** *(see, meh 'goo-stah)*
Would you like ...?	**¿Quisiera...?** *(kee-see-'eh-rah)*
Yes, I'd like ...	**Sí, quisiera...** *(see, kee-see-'eh-rah)*
Do you wish ...?	**¿Desea...?** *(deh-'seh-ah)*
Yes, I wish ...	**Sí, deseo...** *(see, deh-'seh-oh)*

Palabras activas

The last time we looked at Spanish infinitive verb forms, we learned how to talk about "everyday" activities. We discovered that the endings of action words must change according to the TENSE and the PERSON, and that most forms follow a familiar pattern:

AR verbs: *to work*	**Trabajar**
I work	**Trabajo** *(trah-'bah-hoh)*
You work, he, she works	**Trabaja** *(trah-'bah-hah)*
You (pl.), They work	**Trabajan** *(trah-'bah-hahn)*
we work	**Trabajamos** *(trah-bah-'hah-mohs)*

However, some verbs have irregular changes that you have to study a little more carefully. The following examples will help you talk about more "everyday" actions around the office.

Notice that the four forms below each infinitive refer to the same persons as the translated forms above. And remember that this is only a brief selection of irregular patterns. To learn more, buy a Spanish grammar textbook.

to count	*to close*
Contar *(kohn-'tahr)*	**Cerrar** *(seh-'rrahr)*
cuento *('kwehn-toh)*	**cierro** *(see-'eh-rroh)*
cuenta *('kwehn-tah)*	**cierra** *(see-'eh-rrah)*
cuentan *('kwehn-tahn)*	**cierran** *(see-'eh-rrahn)*
contamos *(kohn-'tah-mohs)*	**cerramos** *(seh-'rrah-mohs)*
to go	*to laugh*
Ir *(eer)*	**Reír** *(reh-'eer)*
voy *('voh-ee)*	**río** *('ree-oh)*
va *(vah)*	**ríe** *('ree-eh)*
van *(vahn)*	**ríen** *('ree-ehn)*
vamos *('vah-mohs)*	**reímos** *(reh-'ee-mohs)*
to hear	*to do*
Oír *(oh-'eer)*	**Hacer** *(ah-'sehr)*
oigo *('oh-ee-goh)*	**hago** *('ah-goh)*
oye *('oh-yeh)*	**hace** *('ah-seh)*
oyen *('oh-yehn)*	**hacen** *('ah-sehn)*
oímos *(oh-'ee-mohs)*	**hacemos** *(ah-'seh-mohs)*

Watch:
They do taxes.

Hacen los impuestos.
('ah-sehn lohs eem-'pweh-stohs)

I count the deposits.

Cuento los depósitos.
('kwehn-toh lohs deh-'poh-see-tohs)

We go to this bank.

Vamos a este banco.
('vah-mohs ah 'eh-steh 'bahn-'koh)

Listos para practicar

Connect the opposites:

cerrar *(seh-'rrahr)*   **gastar** *(gah-'stahr)*
meter *(meh-'tehr)*   **salir** *(sah-'leer)*
ganar *(gah-'nahr)*   **sacar** *(sah-'kahr)*
entrar *(ehn-'trahr)*   **perder** *(pehr-'dehr)*
ahorrar *(ah-oh-'rrahr)*   **abrir** *(ah-'breer)*

Do you know the meanings of these words below? Finish the phrases using the verbs of your choice:

Quiero *(kee-'eh-roh)* _____
Prefiero *(preh-fee-'eh-roh)* _____
Me gusta *(meh 'goo-stah)* _____
Deseo *(deh-'seh-oh)* _____
Quisiera *(kee-see-'eh-rah)* _____

Translate each sentence, using the irregular verbs you just learned:

She counts the money.   _____
We go to the office.   _____
I hear the manager.   _____
They close at five.   _____
She does the work.   _____

¡Ordenes!

Everything you say should be repeated, and that includes your key command words. This group will be needed as you discuss new employee procedures. Care to fill in your own examples?

add	**añada** (ah-'nyah-dah)	**Añada los beneficios.** (ah-'nyah-dah lohs beh-neh-'fee-see·ohs)
take away	**quite** ('kee-teh)	**Quite los impuestos.** ('kee-teh lohs eem-'pweh-stohs)
use	**use** ('oo-seh)	**Use el banco de crédito.** ('oo-seh ehl 'bahn-koh deh 'kreh-dee-toh)
change	**cambie** ('kahm-bee-eh)	_____
close	**cierre** (see-'eh-reh)	_____
count	**cuente** ('kwehn-teh)	_____
enter	**entre** ('ehn-treh)	_____
get	**consiga** (kohn-'see-gah)	_____
hear	**oiga** ('oh-ee-gah)	_____
open	**abra** ('ah-brah)	_____
pay	**pague** ('pah-geh)	_____
put	**ponga** ('pohn-gah)	_____
put in	**meta** ('meh-tah)	_____
remove	**saque** ('sah-keh)	_____

Chapter Four

Capítulo Cuatro
(kah-'pee-too-loh 'kwah-troh)

The Workplace
El lugar de trabajo
(ehl loo-'gahr deh trah-'bah-hoh)

At work

En el trabajo *(ehn ehl trah-'bah-hoh)*

In many parts of the country, staff members at businesses are required to speak Spanish on a regular basis. As an HR professional, it's always a good idea to learn those words which describe the workplace.

Begin by helping out those clients or customers who are unfamiliar with your location. Can you send them to the right place?

Where's (the)...?	¿Dónde está...? *('dohn-deh eh-'stah)*
agency	**la agencia** *(lah ah-'hehn-see-ah)*
area	**el área** *(ehl 'ah-reh-ah)*
branch	**la sucursal** *(lah soo-koor-'sahl)*
building	**el edificio** *(ehl eh-dee-'fee-see-oh)*
business	**el negocio** *(ehl neh-'goh-see-oh)*
company	**la compañía** *(lah kohm-pah-'nyee-ah)*
department	**el departamento**
	(ehl deh-pahr-tah-'mehn-toh)
division	**la división** *(lah dee-vee-see-'ohn)*
facility	**la instalación** *(lah eens-tah-lah-see-'ohn)*
factory	**la fábrica** *(lah 'fah-bree-kah)*
firm	**la empresa** *(lah ehm-'preh-sah)*
franchise	**la concesión** *(lah kohn-seh-see-'ohn)*
institution	**la institución** *(lah een-stee-too-see-'ohn)*
organization	**la organización**
	(lah ohr-gah-nee-sah-see-'ohn)
plant	**la planta** *(lah 'plahnta)*
property	**la propiedad** *(lah proh-pee-eh-'dahd)*
shop	**el taller** *(ehl tah-'yehr)*
station	**la estación** *(lah eh-stah-see-'ohn)*
store	**la tienda** *(lah tee-'ehn-dah)*
warehouse	**el almacén** *(ehl ahl-mah-'sehn)*
zone	**la zona** *(lah 'soh-nah)*

Now, be a little more specific:

They're in the _____	**Están en el cuarto de _____.**
	(eh-'stahn ehn ehl 'kwahr-toh deh ____)
room conference	**conferencias** *(kohn-feh-'rehn-see-ahs)*
copying	**copias** *('koh-pee-ahs)*
mail	**correo** *(koh-'rreh-oh)*
storage	**depósito** *(deh-'poh-see-toh)*
training	**entrenamiento** *(ehn-treh-nah-mee-'ehn-toh)*
waiting	**espera** *(eh-'speh-rah)*

Go to the ___	**Vaya al departamento de___.**
department.	*('vah-yah ahl deh-pahr-tah-'mehn-toh deh ____)*
administration	**administración** *(ahd-mee-nee-strah-see-'ohn)*
billing	**contabilidad** *(kohn-tah-bee-lee-'dahd)*
customer service	**servicio para clientes**
	(sehr-'vee-see-oh 'pah-rah klee-'ehn-tehs)
finance	**finanzas** *(fee-'nahn-sahs)*
human resources	**recursos humanos**
	(reh-'koor-sohs oo-'mah-nohs)
marketing	**mercadeo** *(mehr-kah-'deh-oh)*
personnel	**personal** *(pehr-soh-'nahl)*
sales	**ventas** *('vehn-tahs)*

Businesses vary, so pull from this group if the words apply:

advertising	**la publicidad** *(lah poo-blee-see-'dahd)*
assembly	**el montaje** *(ehl mohn-'tah-heh)*
communications	**las comunicaciones**
	(lahs koh-moo-nee-kah-see-'oh-nehs)
credit	**el crédito** *(ehl kreh-dee-'toh)*
custodial	**la limpieza** *(lah leem-pee-'eh-sah)*
inspection	**la inspección** *(lah een-spehk-see-'ohn)*
laboratory	**el laboratorio** *(ehl lah-boh-rah-'toh-ree-oh)*
maintenance	**el mantenimiento**
	(ehl mahn-teh-nee-mee-'ehn-toh)
manufacturing	**la fabricación** *(lah fah-bree-kah-see-'ohn)*
operations	**las operaciones**
	(lahs oh-peh-rah-see-'oh-nehs)

packaging	**el embalaje** *(ehl ehm-bah-'lah-heh)*
production	**la producción** *(lah proh-dook-see-'ohn)*
quality control	**el control de calidad**
	(ehl kohn-'trohl deh kah-lee-'dahd)
receiving	**la admisión** *(lah ahd-mee-see-'ohn)*
research	**la investigación**
	(lah een-veh-stee-gah-see-'ohn)
security	**la seguridad** *(lah seh-goo-ree-'dahd)*
shipping	**el transporte** *(ehl trahns-'pohr-teh)*

Listos para practicar

Translate these useful terms:

warehouse _____
factory _____
storage room _____
advertising _____
sales department _____

The building
El edificio *(ehl eh-dee-'fee-see·oh)*

This time, name a few parts of the office building. Follow the pattern as you give directions:

It's next to (the)...	**Está al lado de...** *(eh-'stah ahl 'lah-doh deh)*
aisle	**el pasillo** *(ehl pah-'see-yoh)*
basement	**el sótano** *(ehl 'soh-tah-noh)*
cafeteria	**la cafetería** *(lah kah-feh-teh-'ree-ah)*
elevator	**el ascensor** *(ehl ah-sehn-'sohr)*
entrance	**la entrada** *(lah ehn-'trah-dah)*
escalator	**la escalera mecánica**
	(lah eh-skah-'leh-rah meh-'kah-nee-kah)
exit	**la salida** *(lah sah-'lee-dah)*
garage	**el garaje** *(ehl gah-'rah-heh)*
hallway	**el corredor** *(ehl koh-rreh-'dohr)*

lobby	**el vestíbulo** *(ehl veh-'stee-boo-loh)*
office	**la oficina** *(lah oh-fee-'see-nah)*
reception desk	**la recepción** *(lah reh-sehp-see-'ohn)*
restroom	**el baño** *(ehl 'bah-nyoh)*
room	**el cuarto** *(ehl 'kwahr-toh)*
stairs	**las escaleras** *(lahs eh-'skah-'leh-rahs)*
steps	**los escalones** *(lohs eh-skah-'loh-nehs)*

In order to describe the workplace in detail, you'll need to identify the structures on the property:

It has the big ____.	**Tiene ____ grande.**
	(tee-'eh-neh ____ 'grahn-deh)
ceiling	**el techo** *(ehl teh-'choh)*
door	**la puerta** *(lah 'pwehr-tah)*
floor	**el piso** *(ehl 'pee-soh)*
roof	**el tejado** *(ehl teh-'hah-doh)*
wall	**la pared** *(lah pah-'rehd)*
window	**la ventana** *(lah vehn-'tah-nah)*
It's near the...	**Está cerca de...** *(eh-'stah 'sehr-kah deh)*
cash register	**la registradora** *(lah reh-hee-strah-'doh-rah)*
cigarette machine	**la máquina de cigarrillos**
	(lah 'mah-kee-nah deh see-gah-'ree-yohs)
clerk's window	**la ventanilla** *(lah vehn-tah-'nee-yah)*
double doors	**las puertas dobles**
	(lahs 'pwehr-tahs 'doh-blehs)
front counter	**el mostrador principal**
	(ehl moh-'strah-dohr preen-see-'pahl)
front desk	**la mesa de recepción**
	(lah 'meh-sah deh reh-sehp-see-'ohn)
public telephone	**el teléfono público**
	(ehl teh-'leh-foh-noh 'poo-blee-koh)
vending machine	**la máquina vendedora**
	(lah 'mah-kee-nah vehn-deh-'doh-rah)
water fountain	**la fuente de agua**
	(lah 'fwehn-teh deh 'ah-gwah)

Check all around the grounds. How many of these words can you put into practice?

Walk to (the)...	**Camine a...** *(kah-'mee-neh ah)*
balcony	**el balcón** *(ehl bahl-'kohn)*
bridge	**el puente** *(ehl 'pwehn-teh)*
deck	**la terraza** *(lah teh-'rrah-sah)*
dock	**el muelle** *(ehl 'mweh-yeh)*
driveway	**la entrada para carros**
	(lah ehn-'trah-dah 'pah-rah 'kah-rrohs)
fence	**la cerca** *(lah 'sehr-kah)*
garden	**el jardín** *(ehl hahr-'deen)*
gate	**el portón** *(ehl pohr-'tohn)*
lot	**el lote** *(ehl 'loh-teh)*
parking lot	**el estacionamiento**
	(ehl eh-stah-see-oh-nah-mee-'ehn-toh)
porch	**el portal** *(ehl pohr-'tahl)*
ramp	**la rampa** *(lah 'rahm-pah)*
sidewalk	**la acera** *(lah ah-'seh-rah)*
tower	**la torre** *(lah 'toh-rreh)*

¡Información!

Tell your employees about the restroom!

Please use (the)...	**Favor de usar...** *(fah-'vohr deh oo-'sahr)*
dispenser	**el distribuidor** *(ehl dees-tree-buh-ee-'dohr)*
mirror	**el espejo** *(ehl eh-'speh-hoh)*
paper towel	**la toalla de papel**
	(lah toh-'ah-yah deh pah-'pehl)
sink	**el lavamanos** *(ehl lah-vah-'mah-nohs)*
soap	**el jabón** *(ehl hah-'bohn)*
toilet	**el excusado** *(ehl ehks-'koo-'sah-doh)*
toilet paper	**el papel higiénico**
	(ehl pah-'pehl ee-hee-'eh-nee-koh)
urinal	**el orinal** *(ehl oo-ree-'nahl)*

Temas culturales

In every language, people use slang to talk about routine activities. If you're having trouble understanding certain words or expressions, use the phrase, **¿Qué significa eso?** *(keh seeg-nee-'fee-kah 'eh-soh)*, which translates *What does that mean?* Chances are they'll come up with the Spanish words that are more familiar to you.

Slang might include some not-so-nice words as well. Make it clear that no foul language will be allowed around your workplace. Use this line:

Please don't use foul language.
Por favor, no diga groserías.
 (pohr fah-'vohr, noh 'dee-gah groh-seh-'ree-ahs)

All the previous vocabulary can combine with the following "location" words:

It's...	**Está...** *(eh-'stah)*
in back	**atrás** *(ah-'trahs)*
in front	**al frente** *(ahl 'frehn-teh)*
in the middle	**al medio** *(ahl 'meh-dee-oh)*
underground	**subterráneo** *(soob-teh-'rrah-neh-oh)*

Office furniture
Los muebles de la oficina
(lohs 'mweh-blehs deh lah oh-fee-'see-nah)

Your everyday workplace vocabulary has to include the names for furniture and décor. To keep these words fresh in your mind, apply removable labels so that you can read the Spanish as you walk by.

It's behind (the)...	**Está detrás de...** *(eh-'stah deh-'trahs deh)*
armchair	**el sillón** *(ehl see-'yohn)*
bench	**el banco** *(ehl 'bahn-koh)*
bookshelf	**el librero** *(ehl lee-'breh-roh)*
chair	**la silla** *(lah 'see-yah)*
chest	**el baúl** *(ehl bah-'ool)*

desk	**el escritorio** *(ehl eh-skree-'toh-ree·oh)*
file cabinet	**el archivo** *(ehl ahr-'chee-voh)*
lamp	**la lámpara** *(lah 'lahm-pah-rah)*
sofa	**el sofá** *(ehl soh-'fah)*
stool	**el banquillo** *(ehl bahn-'kee-yoh)*
table	**la mesa** *(lah 'meh-sah)*
trash basket	**el cesto de basura**
	(ehl ceh-'stoh deh bah-'soo-rah)

¡Información!

• Sit down at your desk and start naming the supplies that fill your office. You never know when these items might be required:

Bring (the)...	**Traiga...** *('trah·ee-gah)*
binder	**el encuadernador**
	(ehl ehn-kwah-dehr-nah-'dohr)
calendar	**el calendario** *(ehl kah-lehn-'dah-ree·oh)*
card	**la tarjeta** *(lah tahr-'heh-tah)*
eraser	**el borrador** *(ehl boh-rrah-'dohr)*
folders	**las carpetas** *(lahs kahr-'peh-tahs)*
ink	**la tinta** *(lah 'teen-tah)*
label	**la etiqueta** *(lah eh-tee-'keh-tah)*
laminations	**las hojas laminadas**
	(lahs 'oh-hahs lah-mee-'nah-dahs)
marker	**el marcador** *(ehl mahr-kah-'dohr)*
paper	**el papel** *(ehl pah-'pehl)*
paper clips	**los clips** *(lohs kleeps)*
pen	**el lapicero** *(ehl lah-pee-'seh-roh)*
pencil	**el lápiz** *(ehl 'lah-pees)*
ribbon	**la cinta** *(lah 'seen-tah)*
scissors	**las tijeras** *(lahs tee-'heh-rahs)*
stapler	**la engrapadora**
	(lah ehn-grah-pah-'doh-rah)
stationery	**los objetos de escritorio**
	(lohs ohb-'heh-tohs dehl eh-skree-'toh-ree-oh)

tacks	**las tachuelas** *(lahs tah-choo-'eh-lahs)*
tape	**la cinta engomada**
	(lah 'seen-tah ehn-goh-'mah-dah)
transparencies	**las hojas transparentes**
	(lahs 'oh-hahs trahns-pah-'rehn-tehs)

• And keep speaking Spanglish!

el whiteout
el glue-stick
el post-it

Listos para practicar

Fill in the word that completes each series:

lavabo, mesa, ascensor, florero, lápiz, cerca, techo
(lah-'vah-boh, 'meh-sah, ah-sehn-'sohr, floh-'reh-roh, 'lah-pees, 'sehr-kah, 'teh-choh)

    escalones, escaleras, _____
    (eh-skah-'loh-nehs, eh-skah-'leh-rahs)

    jabón, toalla _____
    (hah-'bohn, toh-'ah-yah)

    pared, tejado _____
    (pah-'rehd, teh-'hah-doh)

    acera, portón _____
    (ah-'seh-rah, pohr-'tohn)

    maceta, estatua _____
    (mah-'seh-tah, eh-'stah-too-ah)

    escritorio, silla _____
    (eh-skree-'toh-ree-oh, 'see-yah)

    borrador, lapicero, *(boh-rrah-'dohr, lah-pee-'seh-roh)* _____

Remember that some things inside your building can be practiced in the plural form. Take what you need from the list below:

Do you like (the)...?	**¿Le gustan...?** *(leh 'goo-stahn)*
blinds	**las persianas** *(lahs pehr-see-'ah-nahs)*
cabinets	**los gabinetes** *(lohs gah-bee-'neh-tehs)*

carpeting	**las alfombras** *(lahs ahl-'fohm-brahs)*
compartments	**los compartimientos**
	(lohs kohm-pahr-tee-mee-'ehn-tohs)
curtains	**las cortinas** *(lahs kohr-'tee-nahs)*
drains	**los desagües** *(lohs deh-'sah-gwehs)*
drawers	**los cajones** *(lohs kah-'hoh-nehs)*
faucets	**los grifos** *(lohs 'gree-fohs)*
shelves	**las repisas** *(lahs reh-'pee-sahs)*
shutters	**los postigos** *(los poh-'stee-gohs)*

Can you put a few words together?

side entrance	**la entrada lateral**
	(lah ehn-'trah-dah lah-teh-'rahl)
glass doors	**las puertas de vidrio**
	(lahs 'pwehr-tahs deh 'vee-dree·oh)
back window	**la ventana trasera**
	(lah vehn-'tah-nah trah-'seh-rah)

Electrical equipment

El equipo eléctrico *(ehl eh-'kee-poh eh-'lehk-tree-koh)*

Training Spanish speakers in the use of electrical equipment can be a challenge, so go ahead and use this page as a reference guide. Read each command phrase aloud:

Plug in (the)...	**Enchufe...** *(ehn-'choo-feh)*
Unplug (the)...	**Desenchufe...** *(dehs-ehn-'choo-feh)*
Turn on (the)...	**Prenda...** *('prehn-dah)*
Turn off (the)...	**Apague...** *(ah-'pah-geh)*
adding machine	**la sumadora** *(lah soo-mah-'doh-rah)*
air conditioner	**el acondicionador de aire**
	(ehl ah-kohn-dee-see-oh-nah-'dohr deh 'ah-ee-reh)
alarm	**la alarma** *(lah ah-'lahr-mah)*
answering machine	**el contestador telefónico**
	(ehl kohn-teh-stah-'dohr teh-leh-'foh-nee-koh)
calculator	**la calculadora** *(lah kahl-koo-lah-'doh-rah)*
camera	**la cámara** *(lah 'kah-mah-rah)*

cash register	la **registradora** *(lah reh-hee-strah-'doh-rah)*
clock	el **reloj** *(ehl reh-'loh)*
computer	la **computadora** *(lah kohm-poo-tah-'doh-rah)*
copier	la **copiadora** *(lah koh-pee·ah-'doh-rah)*
dryer	la **secadora** *(lah seh-kah-'doh-rah)*
fan	el **ventilador** *(ehl vehn-tee-lah-'dohr)*
heater	el **calentador** *(ehl kah-lehn-tah-'dohr)*
hot water heater	el **calentador de agua** *(ehl kah-lehn-tah-'dohr deh 'ah-gwah)*
intercom	el **interfono** *(ehl een-tehr-'foh-noh)*
lamp	la **lámpara** *(lah 'lahm-pah-rah)*
light	la **luz** *(lah loos)*
microphone	el **micrófono** *(ehl mee-'kroh-foh-noh)*
printer	la **impresora** *(lah eem-preh-'soh-rah)*
projector	el **proyector** *(ehl proh-yehk-'tohr)*
radio	la **radio** *(lah 'rah-dee·oh)*
speaker	el **parlante** *(ehl pahr-'lahn-teh)*
stereo	el **estéreo** *(ehl eh-'steh-reh-oh)*
turbine	la **turbina** *(lah toor-'bee-nah)*
TV	el **televisor** *(ehl teh-leh-vee-'sohr)*
typewriter	la **máquina de escribir** *(lah 'mah-kee-nah deh eh-skree-'beer)*
vacuum cleaner	la **aspiradora** *(lah ah-spee-rah-'doh-rah)*
VCR	la **videocasetera** *(lah vee-deh-oh-kah-seh-'teh-rah)*
washer	la **lavadora** *(lah-vah-'doh-rah)*

Find a way to get these systems in operation!

Turn on...	**Prenda...** *('prehn-dah)*
air conditioning	el **aire acondicionado** *(ehl 'ah-ee-reh ah-kohn-dee-see-oh-'nah-doh)*
communications system	el **sistema de comunicación** *(ehl sees-'teh-mah deh koh-moo-nee-kah-see-'ohn)*
heating	la **calefacción** *(lah kah-leh-fahk-see-'ohn)*
security system	el **sistema de seguridad** *(ehl see-'steh-mah deh seh-goo-ree-'dahd)*
sprinkler system	el **sistema para regar** *(ehl see-'steh-mah 'pah-rah reh-'gahr)*

Listos para practicar

Choose the best word to complete these sentences:

la computadora, el refrigerador, el parlante, las cortinas, el dormitorio *(lah kohm-poo-tah-'doh-rah, ehl reh-free-heh-rah-'dohr, ehl pahr-'lahn-teh, lahs kohr-'tee-nahs, ehl dohr-mee-'toh-ree-oh)*

La comida está en _____.
(lah koh-'mee-dah eh-'stah ehn_____)

La secretaria tiene _____.
(lah seh-kreh-'tah-ree-ah tee-'eh-neh_____)

El estéreo necesita _____.
(ehl eh-'steh-reh-oh neh-seh-'see-tah_____)

La cama está en _____.
(lah 'kah-mah eh-stah ehn _____)

La ventana tiene _____.
(lah vehn-'tah-nah tee-'eh-neh _____)

Electricity!

¡La electricidad! *(lah eh-lehk-tree-see-'dahd)*

Care to add words to your list of electrical devices? This time, say *no*, using this helpful pattern:

Don't use (the)...	**No use...** *(noh 'oo-seh)*
battery	**la batería** *(lah bah-teh-'ree-ah)*
charger	**el cargador** *(ehl kahr-gah-'dohr)*
circuit	**el circuito** *(ehl seer-koo-'ee-toh)*
electrical cable	**el cable eléctrico** *(ehl 'kah-bleh eh-'lehk-tree-koh)*
electrical outlet	**el enchufe** *(ehl ehn-'choo-feh)*
extension cord	**el cable de extensión** *(ehl 'kah-bleh deh ehks-tehn-see-'ohn)*
generator	**el generador** *(ehl heh-neh-rah-'dohr)*
master switch	**el conmutador principal** *(ehl kohn-moo-tah-'dohr preen-see-'pahl)*
meter	**el medidor** *(ehl meh-dee-'dohr)*
switch	**el interruptor** *(ehl een-teh-rroop-'tohr)*

transformer	**el transformador** *(ehl trahns-fohr-mah-'dohr)*
wire	**el alambre** *(ehl ah-'lahm-breh)*
Don't press (the)...	**No oprima...** *(noh oh-'pree-mah)*
button	**el botón** *(ehl boh-'tohn)*
dial	**el marcador** *(ehl mahr-kah-'dohr)*
key	**la tecla** *(lah 'teh-klah)*
knob	**el tirador** *(ehl tee-rah-'dohr)*
timer	**el reloj** *(ehl reh-'loh)*
Don't touch (the)...	**No toque...** *(noh 'toh-keh)*
fusebox	**la caja de fusibles** *(lah 'kah-hah deh foo-'see-blehs)*
gas meter	**el medidor de gas** *(ehl meh-dee-'dohr deh gahs)*
smoke alarm	**el detector de humo** *(ehl deh-tehk-'tohr deh 'oo-moh)*
thermometer	**el termómetro** *(ehl tehr-'moh-meh-troh)*
thermostat	**el termostato** *(ehl tehr-moh-'stah-toh)*
water valve	**la válvula de agua** *(lah 'vahl-voo-lah deh 'ah-gwah)*

☞ **¡Información!**

When working around electricity, every word counts, so take this list seriously:

AC	**corriente alterna** *(koh-rree-'ehn-teh ahl-tehr-nah)*
amp	**el amperaje** *(ehl ahm-peh-'rah-heh)*
DC	**corriente continua** *(koh-rree-'ehn-teh kohn-'tee-nwah)*
electric current	**la corriente eléctrica** *(lah koh-rree-'ehn-teh eh-'lehk-tree-kah)*
high voltage	**la alto voltaje** *(lah 'ahl-toh vohl-'tah-heh)*
horsepower	**el caballo de fuerza** *(ehl kah-'bah-yoh deh 'fwehr-sah)*
low voltage	**la bajo voltaje** *(lah 'bah-hoh vohl-'tah-heh)*
watt	**el vatio** *(ehl 'vah-tee-oh)*

The warehouse
El almacén *(ehl ahl-mah-'sehn)*

Walk around any warehouse, factory, or workshop, and you're bound to see most of the items below. Practice with these commands:

Bring (the)...	**Traiga...** *('trah-ee-gah)*
Use (the)...	**Use...** *('oo-seh)*
Move (the)...	**Mueva...** *('mweh-vah)*
blade	**la navaja** *(lah nah-'vah-hah)*
block	**el bloque** *(ehl 'bloh-keh)*
brace	**el grapón** *(ehl grah-'pohn)*
cart	**la carreta** *(lah kah-'rreh-tah)*
cast	**el molde** *(ehl 'mohl-deh)*
dolley	**el travelín** *(ehl trah-veh-'leen)*
filter	**el filtro** *(ehl 'feel-troh)*
hoist	**la grúa** *(lah 'groo-ah)*
hook	**el gancho** *(ehl 'gahn-choh)*
hose	**la manguera** *(lah mahn-'geh-rah)*
ladder	**la escalera** *(lah eh-skah-'leh-rah)*
ladle	**el cucharón** *(ehl koo-chah-'rohn)*
net	**la red** *(lah rehd)*
pallet	**el soporte de madera** *(ehl soh-'pohr-teh deh mah-'deh-rah)*
plate	**la plancha** *(lah 'plahn-chah)*
pulley	**la polea** *(lah poh-'leh-ah)*
scaffold	**el andamio** *(ehl ahn-'dah-mee-oh)*
scale	**la báscula** *(lah 'bah-skoo-lah)*
scrap	**el desecho** *(ehl dehs-'eh-choh)*
seat	**el asiento** *(ehl ah-see-'ehn-toh)*
stake	**la estaca** *(lah eh-'stah-kah)*
stick	**el palo** *(ehl 'pah-loh)*
stool	**el banquillo** *(ehl bahn-'kee-yoh)*
tray	**la bandeja** *(lah bah-'deh-hah)*
tripod	**el trípode** *(ehl 'tree-poh-deh)*
wheel	**la rueda** *(lah roo-'eh-dah)*

Some things can't be moved easily, so utilize these command words instead:

Look at (the)...	**Mire...** *('mee-reh)*
Go to (the)...	**Vaya a...** *('vah-yah ah)*
booth	**el puesto** *(ehl 'pweh-stoh)*
duct	**el conducto** *(ehl kohn-'dook-toh)*
partition	**el divisor** *(ehl dee-vee-'sohr)*
platform	**la plataforma** *(lah plah-tah-'fohr-mah)*
post	**el poste** *(ehl 'poh-steh)*
rafter	**la viga** *(lah 'vee-gah)*
railing	**la baranda** *(lah bah-'rahn-dah)*
ramp	**la rampa** *(lah 'rahm-pah)*
shed	**el cobertizo** *(ehl koh-behr-'tee-soh)*
track	**el carril** *(ehl kah-'rreel)*
workstation	**la estación de trabajo**
	(lah eh-'stah-see-'ohn deh trah-'bah-hoh)
worktable	**la mesa de trabajo**
	(lah 'meh-sah deh trah-'bah-hoh)

Temas culturales

Spanglish is an unavoidable trend to blend Spanish words with English words.

English	*Spanglish*	*Spanish*
carpet	la carpeta	**la alfombra**
	(lah kahr-'peh-tah)	*(lah ahl-'fohm-brah)*
lunch	el lonche	**el almuerzo**
	(ehl 'lohn-cheh)	*(ehl ahl-moo-'ehr-soh)*
muffler	el mofle	**el silenciador**
	(ehl 'moh-fleh)	*(ehl see-lehn-see-ah-'dohr)*
pie	el pay	**el pastel**
	(ehl 'pah-ee)	*(ehl pah-'stehl)*
truck	la troca	**el camión**
	(lah 'troh-kah)	*(ehl kah-mee-'ohn)*
typing	el taipín	**escribir a máquina**
	(ehl tah-ee-'peen)	*(eh-skree-'beer ah 'mah-kee-nah)*

¡Información!

Do you see a pattern here?

It's...	Es... *(ehs)*
atomic	**atómico** *(ah-'toh-mee-koh)*
automatic	**automático** *(ow-toh-'mah-tee-koh)*
electrical	**eléctrico** *(eh-'lehk-tree-koh)*
electronic	**electrónico** *(eh'lehk-'troh-nee-koh)*
mechanical	**mecánico** *(meh-'kah-nee-koh)*
scientific	**científico** *(see-ehn-'tee-fee-koh)*
technical	**técnico** *('tehk-nee-koh)*

Listos para practicar

Circle the word in each group that doesn't belong with the others:

botón, marcador, madera, tecla
(boh-'tohn, mahr-kah-'dohr, mah-'deh-rah, 'tehk-lah)
asiento, silla, banquillo, gancho
(ah-see-'ehn-toh, 'see-yah, bahn-'kee-yoh, 'gahn-choh)
gancho, vatio, voltaje, amperaje
('gahn-choh, 'vah-tee-oh, vohl-'tah-heh, ahm-peh-'rah-heh)

Connect the words that go well together:

grúa *('groo-ah)*	**gas** *(gahs)*
cable *('kah-bleh)*	**alambre** *(ah-'lahm-breh)*
carreta *(kah-'rreh-tah)*	**rueda** *(roo-'eh-dah)*
humo *('oo-moh)*	**polea** *(poh-'leh-ah)*

The machinery
La maquinaria *(lah mah-kee-'nah-ree·ah)*

It isn't likely that you'll find every crucial piece of machinery listed in this guidebook. These are only samples of the mechanical equipment found around the warehouse or factory, but they all can be used to help train Spanish speakers at your place of employment.

You'll be working with (the)...	**Va a trabajar con...** *(vah ah trah-bah-'hahr kohn)*
blast furnace	**el alto horno** *(ehl 'ahl-toh 'ohr-noh)*
blower	**el soplador** *(ehl soh-plah-'dohr)*
compressor	**el compresor** *(ehl kohm-preh-'sohr)*
conveyor belt	**la correa transportadora** *(lah koh-'rreh-ah trahns-pohr-tah-'doh-rah)*
forge	**la fragua** *(lah 'frah-gwah)*
forklift	**la carretilla elevadora** *(lah kah-rreh-'tee-yah eh-leh-vah-'doh-rah)*
mill	**el molino** *(ehl moh-'lee-noh)*
monitor	**el monitor** *(ehl moh-nee-'tohr)*
press	**la prensa** *(lah 'prehn-sah)*
pump	**la bomba** *(lah 'bohm-bah)*
robot	**el robot** *(ehl roh-'boht)*
simulator	**la simuladora** *(lah see-moo-lah-'doh-rah)*
torch	**la antorcha** *(lah ahn-'tohr-chah)*

The pieces

Las piezas *(lahs pee-'eh-sahs)*

In time, you'll pick up all the names for machine and product parts lying around the worksite. Now pronounce these:

Take (the)...	**Tome...** *('toh-meh)*
bar	**la barra** *(lah 'bah-rrah)*
bearing	**el cojinete** *(ehl koh-hee-'neh-teh)*
board	**la tabla** *(lah 'tah-blah)*
cage	**la jaula** *(lah 'hah·oo-lah)*
case	**la caja** *(lah 'kah-hah)*
cartridge	**el cartucho** *(ehl kahr-'too-choh)*
casing	**la cubierta** *(lah koo-bee-'ehr-tah)*
cell	**la célula** *(lah 'seh-loo-lah)*
chassis	**el bastidor** *(ehl bah-stee-'dohr)*
coil	**el rollo** *(ehl 'roh-yoh)*
crank	**la manivela** *(lah mah-nee-'veh-lah)*
handle	**la perilla** *(lah peh-'ree-yah)*

knob	**el botón** *(ehl boh-'tohn)*
lever	**la palanca** *(lah pah-'lahn-kah)*
lightbulb	**el foco** *(ehl 'foh-koh)*
panel	**el panel** *(ehl pah-'nehl)*
peg	**la clavija** *(lah klah-'vee-hah)*
piston	**el émbolo** *(ehl 'ehm-boh-loh)*
propeller	**la hélice** *(lah 'eh-lee-seh)*
ratchet	**el trinquete** *(ehl treen-'keh-teh)*
rivet	**el remache** *(ehl reh-'mah-cheh)*
rod	**la varilla** *(lah vah-'rree-yah)*
roller	**el rodillo** *(ehl roh-'dee-yoh)*
shaft	**el astil** *(ehl ah-'steel)*
sheet	**la hoja** *(lah 'oh-hah)*
spool	**el carrete** *(ehl kah-'rreh-teh)*
spring	**el resorte** *(ehl reh-'sohr-teh)*
valve	**la válvula** *(lah 'vahl-voo-lah)*

¡Información!

• When you can't recall the name for something, use one of these one-liners:

Bring (the)...	**Traiga...** *('trah-ee-gah)*
component	**el componente** *(ehl kohm-poh-'nehn-teh)*
engine	**el motor** *(ehl moh-'tohr)*
machine	**la máquina** *(lah 'mah-kee-nah)*
part	**la parte** *(lah 'pahr-teh)*
piece	**la pieza** *(lah pee-'eh-sah)*
section	**la sección** *(lah sehk-see-'ohn)*
thing	**la cosa** *(lah 'koh-sah)*

• These concepts are tough, but are needed to explain the equipment's purpose or function:

friction	**el roce** *(ehl 'roh-seh)*
function	**la función** *(lah foonk-see-'ohn)*
hydraulics	**la hidráulica** *(lah ee-'drow-lee-kah)*
inertia	**la inercia** *(lah een-'ehr-see-ah)*

load	**la carga** *(lah 'kahr-gah)*
pressure	**la presión** *(lah preh-see-'ohn)*
propulsion	**la propulsión** *(lah proh-pool-see-'ohn)*
scanning	**la exploración** *(lah ehks-ploh-rah-see-'ohn)*
speed	**la velocidad** *(lah veh-loh-see-'dahd)*
static	**la estática** *(lah eh-'stah-tee-kah)*
temperature	**la temperatura** *(lah tehm-peh-rah-'too-rah)*
torque	**el esfuerzo de torsión**
	(ehl ehs-'fwehr-soh deh tohr-see-'ohn)

• When it comes to training, you'll have to mention all the details:

Be careful with the...	**Tenga cuidado con...** *('tehn-gah kwee-'dah-doh kohn)*
bottom	**el fondo** *(ehl 'fohn-doh)*
side	**el lado** *(ehl 'lah-doh)*
top	**el tope** *(ehl 'toh-peh)*

• And these three words all have similar meanings:

hole	**el hoyo** *(ehl 'oh-yoh)*
opening	**la abertura** *(lah ah-'behr-'too-rah)*
socket	**el hueco** *(ehl 'weh-koh)*

Spanish for technicians
Español para técnicos
(eh-spah-'nyohl 'pah-rah 'tehk-nee-kohs)

It's not that difficult talking in Spanish to employees in the hi-tech fields because most scientific terminology looks a lot like English.

Notice the word patterns in these examples:

They are...	**Son...** *(sohn)*
capacitors	**los capacitores** *(lohs kah-pah-see-'toh-rehs)*
condensors	**los condensadores** *(lohs kohn-dehn-sah-'doh-rehs)*
detectors	**los detectores** *(lohs deh-tehk-'toh-rehs)*
insulators	**los aisladores** *(lohs ah·ee-slah-'doh-rehs)*
integrated circuits	**los circuitos integrados** *(lohs seer-'koo·ee-tohs een-teh-'grah-dohs)*

microprocessors	**los microprocesadores**
	(lohs mee-kroh-proh-seh-sah-'doh-rehs)
oscillators	**los osciladores** *(lohs oh-see-lah-'doh-rehs)*
resistors	**los resistores** *(lohs reh-see-'stoh-rehs)*
semi-conductors	**los semiconductores**
	(lohs seh-mee-kohn-dook-'toh-rehs)
sensors	**los sensores** *(lohs sehn-'soh-rehs)*
transformers	**los transformadores**
	(lohs trahns-fohr-mah-'doh-rehs)
transistors	**los transistores** *(lohs trahn-see-'stoh-rehs)*

Listos para practicar

la temperatura, el elemento, la bomba, la perilla, el transistor, la abertura *(lah tehm-peh-rah-'too-rah, ehl eh-leh-'mehn-toh, lah 'bohm-bah, lah peh-'ree-yah, ehl trahn-see-'stohr, lah ah-behr-'too-rah)*

Which word fits *best* into each of these sentences?

_____ **necesita agua.** *(neh-seh-'see-tah 'ah-gwah)*
_____ **es un compuesto.** *(ehs oon kohm-pweh-stoh)*
_____ **es muy alta.** *(ehls 'moo·ee 'ahl-tah)*
_____ **está en la puerta.** *(eh-'stah ehn lah 'pwehr-tah)*
_____ **está en la radio.** *(eh-'stah ehn lah 'rah-dee·oh)*
_____ **es un hueco.** *(ehs oon 'weh-koh)*

Common containers
Los recipientes comunes
(lohs reh-see-pee-'ehn-tehs koh-'moo-nehs)

Containers, too, fill the workshop. Many times, these words are used more than any others. Instruct your employees how to handle or carry the merchandise:

Fill the...	**Llene...** *('yeh-neh)*
Empty the...	**Vacíe...** *(vah-'see-'eh)*
Carry the...	**Lleve...** *('yeh-veh)*
bag	**la bolsa** *(lah 'bohl-sah)*

barrel	**el barril** *(ehl bah-'rreel)*
basket	**la canasta** *(lah kah-'nah-stah)*
bottle	**la botella** *(lah boh-'teh-yah)*
box	**la caja** *(lah 'kah-hah)*
bucket	**el balde** *(ehl 'bahl-deh)*
canister	**el recipiente** *(ehl reh-see-pee-'ehn-teh)*
crate	**la caja para el transporte** *(lah 'kah-hah 'pah-rah ehl trahns-'pohr-teh)*
cup	**la taza** *(lah 'tah-sah)*
glass	**el vaso** *(ehl 'vah-soh)*
jar	**la jarra** *(lah 'hah-rrah)*
package	**el paquete** *(ehl pah-'keh-teh)*
packet	**el bolsillo** *(ehl bohl-'see-yoh)*
tank	**el tanque** *(ehl 'tahn-keh)*
thermos	**el termo** *(ehl 'tehr-moh)*
tub	**la tina** *(lah 'tee-nah)*
tube	**el tubo** *(ehl 'too-boh)*

The toolbox
La caja de herramientas
(lah 'kah-hah deh eh-rrah-mee-'ehn-tahs)

Nobody works without some kind of tool. This selection includes many objects used by workers around the world. Let everyone know what they're supposed to do:

You need (the)...	**Necesita...** *(neh-seh-'see-tah)*
chisel	**el cincel** *(ehl seen-'sehl)*
drill	**el taladro** *(ehl tah-'lah-droh)*
file	**la lima** *(lah 'lee-mah)*
hack saw	**la sierra para cortar metal** *(lah see-'eh-rrah 'pah-rah kohr-'tahr meh-'tahl)*
hammer	**el martillo** *(ehl mahr-'tee-yoh)*
hand saw	**la serrucho** *(lah seh-'rroo-choh)*
level	**el nivel** *(ehl nee-'vehl)*
paintbrush	**la brocha** *(lah 'broh-chah)*
pliers	**el alicate** *(ehl ah-lee-'kah-teh)*

sandpaper	**la lija** *(lah 'lee-hah)*
scraper	**el raspador** *(ehl rah-spah-'dohr)*
screwdriver	**el atornillador** *(ehl ah-tohr-nee-yah-'dohr)*
tape measure	**la cinta para medir**
	(lah 'seen-tah 'pah-rah meh-'deer)
tongs	**las tenazas** *(lahs teh-'nah-sahs)*
trowel	**la paleta** *(lah pah-'leh-tah)*
wrench	**la llave inglesa** *(lah 'yah-veh een-'gleh-sah)*

Notice the little objects, too. Everything needs a name!

Look for (the)...	**Busque...** *('boo-skeh)*
bit	**el taladro** *(ehl tah-'lah-droh)*
bolt	**el perno** *(ehl 'pehr-noh)*
nail	**el clavo** *(ehl 'klah-voh)*
needle	**la aguja** *(lah ah-'goo-hah)*
nut	**la tuerca** *(lah 'twehr-kah)*
pin	**el alfiler** *(ehl ahl-fee-'lehr)*
ring	**el anillo** *(ehl ah-'nee-yoh)*
screw	**el tornillo** *(ehl tohr-'nee-yoh)*
staple	**la grapa** *(lah 'grah-pah)*
washer	**la arandela** *(lah ah-rahn-'deh-lah)*

When it's time for clean-up, call the crew together:

Clean with (the)...	**Limpie con...** *('leem-pee-eh kohn)*
broom	**la escoba** *(lah eh-'skoh-bah)*
brush	**el cepillo** *(ehl seh-'pee-yoh)*
detergent	**el detergente** *(ehl deh-tehr-'hehn-teh)*
dust pan	**la pala de basura** *(lah 'pah-lah deh bah-'soo-rah)*
mop	**el trapeador** *(ehl trah-peh-ah-'dohr)*
rag	**el trapo** *(ehl 'trah-poh)*
soap	**el jabón** *(ehl hah-'bohn)*
sponge	**la esponja** *(lah eh-'spohn-hah)*
towel	**la toalla** *(lah toh-'ah-yah)*

¡Información!

- Label all your tools with removable stickers!
- Over in the lab, the techs need some assistance:

Where's (the)...?	¿Dónde está...? *('dohn-deh eh-'stah)*
lens	el lente *(ehl 'lehn-teh)*
magnet	el imán *(ehl ee-'mahn)*
magnifying glass	la lupa *(lah 'loo-pah)*
microscope	el microscopio *(ehl mee-kroh-'skoh-pee·oh)*
test tube	el tubo de ensayo
	(ehl 'too-boh deh ehn-'say-yoh)

- And in the kitchen, the employees are familiar with a completely different set of objects. Here's a little Spanish for training cooks:

Take out the...	Saque... *('sah-keh)*
Wash the...	Lave... *('lah-veh)*
Dry the...	Seque... *('seh-keh)*
Put away the...	Guarde... *('gwahr-deh)*
bowl	el plato hondo *(ehl 'plah-toh 'ohn-doh)*
coffeepot	la cafetera *(lah kah-feh-'teh-rah)*
cup	la taza *(lah 'tah-sah)*
fork	el tenedor *(ehl teh-neh-'dohr)*
glass	el vaso *(ehl 'vah-soh)*
grill	la parrilla *(lah pah-'rree-yah)*
knife	el cuchillo *(ehl koo-'chee-yoh)*
napkin	la servilleta *(lah sehr-vee-'yeh-tah)*
pan	el sartén *(ehl sahr-'tehn)*
pepper shaker	el pimentero *(ehl pee-mehn-'teh-roh)*
plate	el plato *(ehl 'plah-toh)*
platter	la fuente *(lah 'fwehn-teh)*
pot	la olla *(lah 'oh-yah)*
salt shaker	el salero *(ehl sah-'leh-roh)*
saucer	el platillo *(ehl plah-'tee-yoh)*
spoon	la cuchara *(lah kooh-'chah-rah)*
tablecloth	el mantel *(ehl mahn-'tehl)*

Listos para practicar

List three common containers:

_____ _____ _____

List three tools used in construction:

_____ _____ _____

List three tools used in gardening:

_____ _____ _____

List three kinds of dishes:

_____ _____ _____

List three items needed for cleaning:

_____ _____ _____

The materials

Los materiales *(lohs mah-teh-ree-'ah-lehs)*

Are your materials in order? Tell each trainee what they need to know. Look at the sample sentence next to each item and continue the pattern on your own:

alloy	**la aleación** *(lah ah-leh-ah-see-'ohn)*	_____
aluminum	**el aluminio** *(ehl ah-loo-'mee-nee·oh)*	_____
asbestos	**el asbesto** *(ehl ahs-'beh-stoh)*	_____
asphalt	**el asfalto** *(ehl ahs-'fahl-toh)*	_____
bleach	**el cloro** *(ehl 'kloh-roh)*	_____
brass	**el latón** *(ehl lah-'tohn)*	_____
brick	**el ladrillo** *(ehl lah-'dree-yoh)*	_____
bronze	**el bronce** *(ehl 'brohn-seh)*	_____
canvas	**la lona** *(lah 'loh-nah)*	_____
cardboard	**el cartón** *(ehl kahr-'tohn)*	_____
cement	**el cemento** *(ehl seh-'mehn-toh)*	**No usamos el cemento.** *(noh oo-'sah-mohs ehl seh-'mehn-toh)*
chain	**la cadena** *(lah kah-'deh-nah)*	_____
cloth	**la tela** *(lah 'teh-lah)*	_____

coal	el **carbón** (*ehl kahr-'bohn*)	
copper	el **cobre** (*ehl 'koh-breh*)	
cotton	el **algodón** (*ehl ahl-goh-'dohn*)	
fuel	el **combustible** (*ehl kohm-boo-'stee-bleh*)	
gas	el **gas** (*ehl gahs*)	
glass	el **vidrio** (*ehl 'vee-dree-oh*)	
glue	el **pegamento** (*ehl peh-gah-'mehn-toh*)	**Usamos el pegamento.** (*oo-'sah-mohs ehl peh-gah-'mehn-toh*)
gold	el **oro** (*ehl 'oh-roh*)	
grease	la **grasa** (*lah 'grah-sah*)	
ice	el **hielo** (*ehl 'yeh-loh*)	
iron	el **hierro** (*ehl 'yeh-roh*)	
leather	el **cuero** (*ehl 'kweh-roh*)	
mesh	la **malla** (*lah 'mah-yah*)	
metal	el **metal** (*ehl meh-'tahl*)	
oil	el **aceite** (*ehl ah-'seh-ee-teh*)	
paint	la **pintura** (*lah peen-'too-rah*)	
pipe	la **tubería** (*lah too-beh-'ree-ah*)	
plaster	el **yeso** (*ehl 'yeh-soh*)	
plastic	el **plástico** (*ehl 'plah-stee-koh*)	
plywood	la **madera terciada** (*lah mah-'deh-rah tehr-see-'ah-dah*)	
putty	la **masilla** (*lah mah-'see-yah*)	
rope	la **soga** (*lah 'soh-gah*)	
rubber	la **goma** (*lah 'goh-mah*)	
sand	la **arena** (*lah ah-'reh-nah*)	**Usamos la arena.** (*oo-'sah-mohs lah ah-'reh-nah*)
silver	la **plata** (*lah 'plah-tah*)	
steel	el **acero** (*ehl ah-'seh-roh*)	
stone	la **piedra** (*lah pee-'eh-drah*)	
string	la **cuerda** (*lah 'kwehr-dah*)	
thread	el **hilo** (*ehl 'ee-loh*)	
tile	la **baldosa** (*lah bahl-'doh-sah*)	

| wood | **la madera** *(lah mah-'deh-rah)* | _____ |
| wool | **la lana** *(lah 'lah-nah)* | _____ |

¡Información!

• Not everything has been named yet! Memorize this terminology today:

Look at (the)...	**Mire...** *('mee-reh)*
freight	**el flete** *(ehl 'fleh-teh)*
goods	**los bienes** *(lohs 'bee·eh-nehs)*
materials	**los materiales** *(lohs mah-teh-ree-'ah-lehs)*
merchandise	**las mercancías** *(lahs mehr-kahn-'see-ahs)*
payload	**la carga útil** *(ehl 'kahr-gah 'oo-teel)*
product	**el producto** *(ehl proh-'dook-toh)*
raw material	**la materia prima** *(lah mah-'teh-ree-ah 'pree-mah)*
sales items	**las cosas para vender** *(lahs 'koh-sahs 'pah-rah vehn-'dehr)*
supplies	**las provisiones** *(lahs proh-vee-see-'oh-nehs)*
surplus	**el exceso** *(ehl ehk-'seh-soh)*

• Now say something about the new product:

It's (the)...	**Es...** *(ehs)*
demonstration	**la demostración** *(lah deh-moh-strah-see-'ohn)*
prototype	**el prototipo** *(ehl proh-toh-'tee-poh)*
sample	**la muestra** *(lah 'mweh-strah)*

Measure it!
¡Mídalo! *('mee-dah-loh)*

Discussing measurements is a daily routine in most businesses, so learn these powerful words and phrases in Spanish as soon as you can:

It's a/an...	**Es** *(ehs)*
cylinder	**un cilindro** *(oon see-'leen-droh)*
degree	**un grado** *(oon 'grah-doh)*

double	**el doble** *(ehl 'doh-bleh)*
dozen	**una docena** *('oon-ah doh-'seh-nah)*
drop	**una gota** *('oon-ah 'goh-tah)*
gross	**una gruesa** *('oon-ahgroo-'eh-sah)*
half	**una mitad** *('oon-ah mee-'tahd)*
pair	**un par** *(oon pahr)*
portion	**una porción** *('oon-ah pohr-see-'ohn)*
quarter	**un cuarto** *(oon 'kwahr-toh)*
third	**un tercio** *(oon 'tehr-see-oh)*
ton	**una tonelada** *('oon-ah toh-neh-'lah-dah)*
unit	**una unidad** *('oon-ah 'oo-nee-'dahd)*
Take a/an...	**Tome...** *('toh-meh)*
centimeter	**un centímetro** *(oon sehn-'tee-meh-troh)*
foot	**un pie** *(oon 'pee-eh)*
gallon	**un galón** *(oon gah-'lohn)*
gram	**un gramo** *(oon 'grah-moh)*
gross	**una gruesa** *('oon-ah groo-'eh-sah)*
inch	**una pulgada** *('oon-ah pool-'gah-dah)*
kilogram	**un kilógramo** *(oon kee-loh-'grah-moh)*
meter	**un metro** *(oon 'meh-troh)*
millimeter	**un milímetro** *(oon mee-'lee-meh-troh)*
ounce	**una onza** *('oon-ah 'ohn-sah)*
pound	**una libra** *('oon-ah 'lee-brah)*
quart	**un cuarto** *(oon 'kwahr-toh)*
truckload	**una camionada** *('oon-ah kah-mee-oh-'nah-dah)*
yard	**una yarda** *('oon-ah 'yahr-dah)*

Listos para practicar

Throw in these terms to describe the job in more detail:

diagonal	**diagonal** *(dee-ah-goh-'nahl)*	_____
horizontal	**horizontal** *(oh-ree-sohn-'tahl)*	_____
length	**largo** *('lahr-goh)*	_____
level	**nivel** *(nee-'vehl)*	_____
parallel	**paralelo** *(pah-rah-'leh-loh)*	_____

ratio	**proporción** *(proh-pohr-see-'ohn)*	_____
size	**tamaño** *(tah-'mah-nyoh)*	_____
straight	**recto** *('rehk-toh)*	**La madera es recta.** *(lah mah-'deh-rah ehs 'rehk-tah)*
uneven	**desigual** *(dehs-ee-'gwahl)*	**El piso es desigual.** *(ehl 'pee-soh ehs dehs-ee-'gwahl)*
vertical	**vertical** *(vehr-tee-'kahl)*	_____
width	**anchura** *(ahn-'choo-rah)*	_____

Temas culturales

What do you know about the metric system?

⅝ mi. = **un kilómetro** *(oon kee-'loh-meh-troh)*
2.2 lbs. = **un kilógramo** *(oon kee-'loh-grah-moh)*
32°F   = 0°C

Listos para practicar

Link the words that seem to belong together:

plata *('plah-tah)*	**acero** *(ah-'seh-roh)*
soga *('soh-gah)*	**algodón** *(ahl-goh-'dohn)*
hierro *('yeh-roh)*	**pie** *('pee-eh)*
lana *('lah-nah)*	**anchura** *(ahn-'choo-rah)*
pulgada *(pool-'gah-dah)*	**doble** *('doh-bleh)*
largo *('lahr-goh)*	**hielo** *('yeh-loh)*
mitad *(mee-'tahd)*	**hilo** *('ee-loh)*
agua *('ah-gwah)*	**oro** *('oh-roh)*
libra *('lee-brah)*	**onza** *('ohn-sah)*

Más fácil

In most work settings, much of what you hear relates to job activity. Commands and instructions fill the air, and it's a real benefit to know what everyone's trying to say. Out in the warehouse or factory, these are some of the Spanish verbs or "action words" you'll need to be aware of:

Please...	**Favor de...** *(fah-'vohr deh)*
Don't...	**No...** *('noh)*
You have to...	**Tiene que...** *(tee-'eh-neh keh)*
You should...	**Debe...** *('deh-beh)*
I want to...	**Quiero...** *(kee-'eh-roh)*
He prefers to...	**Prefiere...** *(preh-fee-'eh-reh)*
carry	**llevar** *(yeh-'vahr)*
clean	**limpiar** *(leem-pee-'ahr)*
dry	**secar** *(seh-'kahr)*
empty	**vaciar** *(vah-see-'ahr)*
fill	**llenar** *(yeh-'nahr)*
lower	**bajar** *(bah-'hahr)*
move	**mover** *(moh-'vehr)*
pick up	**recoger** *(reh-koh-'hehr)*
plug in	**enchufar** *(ehn-choo-'fahr)*
press	**presionar** *(pre-see-oh-'nahr)*
pull	**jalar** *(hah-'lahr)*
push	**empujar** *(ehm-poo-'hahr)*
put away	**guardar** *(gwahr-'dahr)*
raise	**subir** *(soo-'beer)*
throw away	**tirar** *(tee-'rahr)*
turn	**voltear** *(vohl-teh-'ahr)*
turn off	**apagar** *(ah-pah-'gahr)*
turn on	**prender** *(prehn-'dehr)*
unplug	**desenchufar** *(dehs-ehn-choo-'fahr)*
use	**usar** *(oo-'sahr)*
wash	**lavar** *(lah-'vahr)*

And, here's another shortcut word. It deals with being able to do:

To be able to	**Poder** *(poh-'dehr)*
I can	**Puedo** *('pweh-doh)*
I can begin.	**Puedo comenzar.** *('pweh-doh koh-mehn-'sahr)*
You, She, He can	**Puede** *('pweh-deh)*
She can clean.	**Puede limpiar.** *('pweh-deh leem-pee-'ahr)*
You (pl.), They can	**Pueden** *('pweh-dehn)*
They can wash.	**Pueden lavar.** *('pweh-dehn lah-'vahr)*
We can	**Podemos** *(poh-'deh-mohs)*
We can pull.	**Podemos jalar.** *(poh-'deh-mohs hah-'lahr)*

Palabras activas

Let's learn a quick way in Spanish to discuss *what's going to happen in the future*. It's the same form used to talk about where you are going. These are the basic forms of the verb *to go* (**ir**):

I'm going to...	**Voy a...** *('voh-ee ah)*
You're, He's, She's going to...	**Va a...** *('vah ah)*
You guys are, They're going to...	**Van a...** *(vahn ah)*
We're going to...	**Vamos a...** *('vah-mohs ah)*

Here's how they work! Notice how these statements refer to *future actions:*

I'm going to the bathroom.	**Voy al baño.** *('voh-ee ahl 'bah-nyoh)*
I'm going to clean.	**Voy a limpiar.** *('voh-ee ah leem-pee-'ahr)*
She's going to the office.	**Va a la oficina.** *(vah ah lah oh-fee-'see-nah)*
She's going to call.	**Va a llamar.** *(vah ah yah-'mahr)*
They're going to the room.	**Van al cuarto.** *(vahn ahl 'kwahr-toh)*
They're going to read.	**Van a leer.** *(vahn ah leh-'ehr)*
We're going there.	**Vamos allí.** *('vah-mohs ah-'yee)*
We're going to eat.	**Vamos a comer.** *('vah-mohs ah koh-'mehr)*

This verb form works well whenever you head out the door:

I'll be at this number.
Voy a estar en este número.
('voh-ee ah eh-'stahr ehn 'eh-steh 'noo-meh-roh)
I'll be back soon.
Voy a regresar pronto.
('voh-ee ah reh-greh-'sahr 'prohn-toh)
I won't be late.
No voy a llegar tarde.
(noh 'voh-ee ah yeh-'gahr 'tahr-deh)

¡Ordenes!

This time, we'll just take the Spanish verbs introduced in this chapter and change them to command forms. See if you can notice any pattern:

Carry	**Lleve** *('yeh-veh)*
Clean	**Limpie** *('leem-pee-eh)*
Dry	**Seque** *('seh-keh)*
Empty	**Vacíe** *(vah-'see-eh)*
Fill	**Llene** *('yeh-neh)*
Lower	**Baje** *('bah-heh)*
Move	**Mueva** *('mweh-vah)*
Pick up	**Recoja** *(reh-'koh-hah)*
Plug in	**Enchufe** *(ehn-'choo-feh)*
Press	**Presione** *(pre-see-'oh-neh)*
Pull	**Jale** *('hah-leh)*
Push	**Empuje** *(ehm-'poo-heh)*
Put away	**Guarde** *('gwahr-deh)*
Raise	**Levante** *(leh-'vahn-teh)*
Throw away	**Tire** *('tee-reh)*
Turn	**Voltee** *(vohl-'teh-eh)*
Turn off	**Apague** *(ah-'pah-geh)*
Turn on	**Prenda** *('prehn-dah)*
Unplug	**Desenchufe** *(dehs-ehn-'choo-feh)*
Wash	**Lave** *('lah-veh)*

Listos para practicar

Answer these questions directed at you:

¿Puede subir las escaleras muy rápido?
('pweh-deh soo-'beer lahs eh-skah-'leh-rahs 'moo-ee 'rah-pee-doh)

¿Va a limpiar su casa mañana?
(vah ah leem-pee-'ahr soo 'kah-sah mah-'nyah-nah)

¿Tiene que enchufar su televisor todos los días?
(tee-'eh-neh keh ehn-choo-'fahr soo teh-leh-vee-'sohr 'toh-dohs lohs 'dee-ahs)

¿Sabe lavar su carro?
('sah-beh lah-'vahr soo 'kah-rroh)

¿Va a prender la lámpara en su oficina hoy?
(vah ah prehn-'dehr lah 'lahm-pah-rah ehn soo oh-fee-'see-nah 'oh-ee)

¿Puede usar el teléfono en su trabajo?
('pweh-deh oo-'sahr ehl teh-'leh-foh-noh ehn soo trah-'bah-hoh)

¿Quiere mover su escritorio?
(kee-'eh-reh moh-'vehr soo eh-skree-'toh-ree-oh)

¿Va a guardar este libro más tarde?
(vah ah gwahr-'dahr 'eh-steh 'lee-broh mahs 'tahr-deh)

Connect these opposite commands:

Baje *('bah-heh)*	**Apague** *(ah-'pah-geh)*
Lave *('lah-veh)*	**Vacíe** *(vah-'see-eh)*
Llene *('yeh-neh)*	**Empuje** *(ehm-'poo-heh)*
Jale *('hah-leh)*	**Levante** *(leh-'vahn-teh)*
Prenda *('prehn-dah)*	**Seque** *('seh-keh)*

Chapter Five

Capítulo Cinco
(kah-'pee-too-loh 'seen-koh)

The Training
El entrenamiento
(ehl ehn-treh-nah-mee-'ehn-toh)

Trainer's talk
El vocabulario del entrenador
(ehl voh-kah-boo-'lah-ree·oh dehl ehn-treh-nah-'dohr)

Guiding Spanish-speaking employees through a maze of training procedures can be awkward, unless you've got the appropriate one-liners to assist you.

Do it by hand.	**Hágalo a mano.** *('ah-gah-loh ah 'mah-noh)*
Remember this.	**Recuerde esto.** *(reh-'kwehr-deh 'eh-stoh)*
This is the procedure.	**Este es el procedimiento.** *('eh-steh ehs ehl proh-seh-dee-mee-'ehn-toh)*
This is what I want.	**Esto es lo que quiero.** *('eh-stoh ehs loh keh kee-'eh-roh)*
This way.	**De esta manera.** *(deh 'eh-stah mah-'neh-rah)*
Just a moment.	**Un momento.** *(oon moh-'mehn-toh)*
It doesn't matter.	**No importa.** *(noh eem-'pohr-tah)*
Like this.	**Así.** *(ah-'see)*
Keep going.	**Siga.** *('see-gah)*
Pay attention.	**Preste atención.** *('preh-steh ah-tehn-see-'ohn)*
Is everything OK?	**¿Está bien todo?** *(eh-'stah 'bee·ehn 'toh-doh)*
Say it in English.	**Dígalo en inglés.** *('dee-gah-'loh ehn een-'glehs)*
Put it here.	**Póngalo aquí.** *('pohn-gah-loh ah-'kee)*
And this, too.	**Y esto también.** *(ee 'eh-stoh tahm-bee-'ehn)*
Like this one.	**Uno como éste.** *('oo-noh koh-moh 'eh-steh)*

Sometimes, opposite commands are easier to remember. Try a few:

That's it.	**Así es.** *(ah-'see ehs)*
That's not it.	**Así no es.** *(ah-'see noh ehs)*
A little more.	**Un poco más.** *(oon 'poh-koh mahs)*
A little less.	**Un poco menos.** *(oon 'poh-koh 'meh-nohs)*
Faster.	**Más rápido.** *(mahs 'rah-pee-doh)*
Slower.	**Más despacio.** *(mahs deh-'spah-see·oh)*

More short answers
Más respuestas cortas
(mahs reh-'spweh-stahs 'kohr-tahs)

You are going to need a variety of practical one-word responses to communicate with people who work for you. Scan this list and choose those that suit you best.

alone	**solo** *('soh-loh)*
also	**también** *(tahm-bee-'ehn)*
anyone	**cualquiera** *(kwahl-kee-'ehr-ah)*
anything	**cualquier cosa** *(kwahl-kee-'ehr 'koh-sah)*
anywhere	**en cualquier sitio**
	(ehn kwahl kee-'ehr 'see-tee-oh)
enough	**bastante** *(bah-'stahn-teh)*
everybody	**todos** *('toh-dohs)*
everything	**todo** *('toh-doh)*
everywhere	**por todas partes** *(pohr 'toh-dahs 'pahr-tehs)*
no one	**nadie** *('nah-dee·eh)*
nowhere	**en ningún sitio** *(ehn neen-'goon 'see-tee·oh)*
none	**ninguno** *(neen-'goo-noh)*
nothing	**nada** *('nah-dah)*
only	**solamente** *(soh-lah-'mehn-teh)*
same	**mismo** *('mees-moh)*
someone	**alguien** *('ahl-gee-ehn)*
something	**algo** *('ahl-goh)*
somewhere	**en algún sitio** *(ehn ahl-'goon 'see-tee·oh)*
too much	**demasiado** *(deh-mah-see-'ah-doh)*
most	**la mayor parte** *(lah mah-'yohr 'pahr-teh)*
the rest	**los demás** *(lohs deh-'mahs)*

Practice:

¿Quién? *(kee-'ehn)*	**Nadie.** *('nah-dee·eh)*
¿Cuántos? *('kwahn-tohs)*	**Ninguno.** *(neen-'goo-noh)*
¿Dónde? *('dohn-deh)*	**Por todas partes.**
	(pohr 'toh-dahs 'pahr-tehs)

¡Información!

- Give a warning if you have to:

Do not touch it.	**No lo toque.** *(noh loh 'toh-keh)*
It doesn't work.	**No funciona.** *(noh foonk-see-'oh-nah)*
It's a mistake.	**Es un error.** *(Es oon ehr-'rohr)*
Be very careful.	**Tenga mucho cuidado.**
	('tehn-gah 'moo-choh kwee-'dah-doh)

- Need some more phrases that refer to "time"?

At the same time.	**A la vez.** *(ah lah vehs)*
Not yet.	**Todavía no.** *(toh-dah-'vee-ah noh)*
Not now.	**Ahora no.** *(ah-'oh-rah noh)*

My schedule
Mi horario *(mee oh-'rah-ree-oh)*

Set up a schedule using the following guide words as examples. They can be useful no matter what the job is:

You start ___	**Empieza** ___ *(ehm-pee-'eh-sah)*
You finish ___	**Termina** ___ *(tehr-'mee-nah)*
Day in ___	**Día de entrada** ___
	('dee-ah deh ehn-'trah-dah)
Day out ___	**Día de salida** ___
	('dee-ah deh sah-'lee-dah)
From ___	**De** ___ *(deh)*
Until ___	**Hasta** ___ *('ah-stah)*
Chores ___	**Las tareas** ___ *(lahs tah-'reh-ahs)*
Go to lunch at _____.	**Vaya a almorzar a** _____.
	('vah-yah ah ahl-mohr-'sahr ah ____)
We are closed on _____.	**Estamos cerrados los** _____.
	(eh-'stah-mohs seh-'rrah-dohs lohs ____)
We'll see you on _____.	**Nos vemos el** _____.
	(nohs 'veh-mohs ehl ____)

And here are other ways to express the same instructions:

Be here at _____.	**Esté aquí a** _____.
	(eh-'steh ah-'kee ah ____)
Quit at _____.	**Pare a** _____. *('pah-reh ah ____)*
You may leave at _____.	**Se puede ir a** _____.
	(seh 'pweh-deh eer ah ____)
Take a break at _____.	**Tome un descanso a** _____.
	('toh-meh oon deh-'skahn-soh ah ____)
Come at _____.	**Venga a** _____. *('vehn-gah ah ____)*
You will work at _____.	**Va a trabajar a** _____.
	(vah ah trah-'bah-'hahr ah ____)
You're off at _____.	**Sale a** _____. *('sah-leh ah ____)*

¡Información!

• Now tell them what they'll need to hear:

Listen for (the) _____.	**Escuche por** _____.
	(eh-'skoo-cheh 'pohr____)
bell	**la campana** *(lah kahm-'pah-nah)*
whistle	**el silbato** *(ehl seel-'bah-toh)*
horn	**la bocina** *(lah boh-'see-nah)*
signal	**la señal** *(lah seh-'nyahl)*
announcement	**el anuncio** *(ehl ah-'noon-see·oh)*
buzzer	**el timbre** *(ehl 'teem-breh)*

• Get firm about tardiness and attendance right from the start!

Be here for sure!	**¡Venga aquí sin falta!**
	('vehn-gah ah-'kee seen 'fahl-tah)
Don't be late!	**¡No llegue tarde!**
	(noh 'yeh-geh 'tahr-deh)
Don't be absent!	**¡No se ausente!**
	(noh seh ow-'sehn-teh)

Important instructions
¡Instrucciones importantes!
(een-strook-see-'oh-nehs eem-pohr-'tahn-tehs)

Continue explaining everyday procedures. Just follow the patterns below:

Use (the)...	**Use...** *('oo-seh)*
authorized area	**la zona autorizada** *(lah 'soh-nah ow-toh-ree-'sah-dah)*
badge number	**el número de la insignia** *(ehl 'noo-meh-roh deh lah een-'seeg-nee-ah)*
personal identification	**la identificación personal** *(lah ee-dehn-tee-fee-kah-see-'ohn pehr-soh-'nahl)*
security code	**el código de seguridad** *(ehl 'koh-dee-goh deh seh-goo-ree-'dahd)*
sign-in sheet	**la lista de registración** *(lah 'lee-stah deh reh-hee-strah-see-'ohn)*
time card	**la tarjeta de trabajo** *(lah tahr-'heh-tah deh trah-'bah-hoh)*
time clock	**el reloj de trabajo** *(ehl reh-'loh deh trah-'bah-hoh)*

Use the employee _____.	**Use _____ para los empleados.** *('oo-seh ____ pah-rah lohs ehm-pleh-'ah-dohs)*
cafeteria	**la cafetería** *(lah kah-feh-teh-'ree-ah)*
entrance	**la entrada** *(lah ehn-'trah-dah)*
parking area	**la zona de estacionamiento** *(lah 'soh-nah deh eh-stah-see·oh-'nah-mee-'ehn-toh)*
restroom	**el baño** *(ehl 'bah-nyoh)*
telephone	**el teléfono** *(ehl teh-'leh-foh-noh)*

All staff members should be informed about current activities, policy changes, and upcoming events. Tell the Spanish speakers where they can find the information they need:

Look at (the)...	Mire... *('mee-reh)*
announcement	**el anuncio** *(ehl ah-'noon-see·oh)*
bulletin	**el boletín** *(ehl boh-leh-'teen)*
bulletin board	**el tablón de anuncios** *(ehl tah-'blohn deh ah-'noon-see-ohs)*
calendar	**el calendario** *(ehl kah-lehn-'dah-ree·oh)*
cassette	**el casete** *(ehl kah-'seh-teh)*
chalkboard	**la pizarra** *(lah pee-'sah-rrah)*
chapter	**el capítulo** *(ehl kah-'pee-too-loh)*
chart	**el diagrama** *(ehl dee-ah-'grah-mah)*
disk	**el disco** *(ehl 'dee-skoh)*
film	**la película** *(lah peh-'lee-koo-lah)*
flyer	**el papel** *(ehl pah-'pehl)*
graph	**el gráfico** *(ehl 'grah-fee-koh)*
letter	**la carta** *(lah 'kahr-tah)*
memo	**el memorándum** *(ehl meh-moh-'rahn-doom)*
note	**la nota** *(lah 'noh-tah)*
notice	**la noticia** *(lah noh-'tee-see-ah)*
page	**la página** *(lah 'pah-hee-nah)*
poster	**el cartel** *(ehl kahr-'tehl)*
report	**el reporte** *(ehl reh-'pohr-teh)*
schedule	**el horario** *(ehl oh-'rah-ree·oh)*
sheet	**la hoja** *(lah 'oh-hah)*
sign	**el letrero** *(ehl leh-'treh-roh)*
tape	**la cinta** *(lah 'seen-tah)*
training manual	**el manual de instrucciones** *(ehl mah-noo-'ahl deh een-strook-see-'oh-nehs)*
video	**el vídeo** *(ehl 'vee-deh-oh)*

¡Información!

If things are filed away, make sure your employees can find them:

Look in (the)...	**Busque en...** *('boo-skeh ehn)*
drawer	**el cajón** *(ehl kah-'hohn)*
file	**el archivo** *(ehl ahr-'chee-voh)*
It's in (the)...	**Está en...** *(eh-'stah ehn)*
aisle	**el pasillo** *(ehl pah-'see-yoh)*
group	**el grupo** *(ehl 'groo-poh)*
line	**la línea** *(lah 'lee-neh-ah)*
pack	**el paquete** *(ehl pah-'keh-teh)*
row	**la fila** *(lah 'fee-lah)*
set	**el juego** *(ehl 'hweh-goh)*

Temas culturales

Trust is very important in the Hispanic culture, especially in business relations. Throughout the training process, feel free to open up about yourself, your family, your work, and your home. Since language is a barrier, begin letting your hair down by showing your employees where everything is located. Don't be shy, always be honest, and make them feel at home.

Listos para practicar

Translate:

Pay attention!	_____
This is what I want.	_____
That's it!	_____

Join these opposites:

algo *('ahl-goh)*	**nadie** *('nah-dee-eh)*
alguien *('ahl-gee-ehn)*	**diferente** *(dee-feh-'rehn-teh)*
mismo *('mees-moh)*	**nada** *('nah-dah)*

Refer to a clock as you complete your work schedule for today:

Empiezo a las _____. *(ehm-pee-'eh-soh ah lahs ____)*
Termino a las _____. *(tehr-'mee-noh ah lahs ____)*
Como mi almuerzo a las _____.
('koh-moh mee ahl-moo-'ehr-soh ah lahs _____)

Fill in each blank with the appropriate missing word:

tarjeta, letreros, empleados, hoja, carro
(tahr-'heh-tah, leh-'treh-rohs, ehm-pleh-'ah-dohs, 'oh-hah, 'kah-rroh)
fila de _____ *('fee-lah deh)____)*
bocina de _____ *(boh-'see-nah deh ____)*
_____ **de trabajo** *(____ deh trah-'bah-hoh)*
_____ **de papel** *(____ deh pah-'pehl)*
baño de _____ *('bah-nyoh deh ____)*

The training course
El curso de entrenamiento
(ehl 'koor-soh deh ehn-treh-nah-mee-'ehn-toh)

Before you pass out assignments, hold a meeting to make sure everyone understands the company's goals:

We try to... | **Tratamos de...** *('trah-tah-mohs deh)*
reward our employees | **recompensar a nuestros empleados**
(reh-kohm-pehn-'sahr ah 'nweh-strohs ehm-pleh-'ah-dohs)
satisfy our customers | **dar satisfacción a los clientes**
(dahr sah-tees-fahk-see-'ohn ah lohs klee-'ehn-tehs)
provide excellent service | **proveer servicio excelente**
(proh-veh-'ehr sehr-'vee-see-oh ehk-seh-'lehn-teh)
check our inventory | **inspeccionar nuestro inventario**
(een-spehk-see-oh-nahr 'nweh-stroh een-vehn-'tah-ree-oh)
use new technology | **usar tecnología nueva**
(oo-'sahr tehk-noh-loh-'hee-ah 'nweh-vah)

follow the policies	**seguir los reglamentos** *(seh-'geer lohs reh-glah-'mehn-tohs)*
make a team effort	**hacer un esfuerzo unido** *(ah-'sehr oon ehs-'fwehr-soh oo-'nee-doh)*
improve our skills	**mejorar nuestras habilidades** *(meh-hoh-'rahr 'nweh-strahs ah-bee-lee-'dah-dehs)*

Read (the)...	**Lea...** *('leh-ah)*
concept	**el concepto** *(ehl kohn-'sehp-toh)*
goal	**la meta** *(lah 'meh-tah)*
idea	**la idea** *(lah ee-'deh-ah)*
mission	**la misión** *(lah mee-see-'ohn)*
motto	**el lema** *(ehl 'leh-mah)*
objective	**el objetivo** *(ehl ohb-heh-'tee-voh)*
plan	**el plan** *(ehl plahn)*
purpose	**el propósito** *(ehl proh-'poh-see-toh)*
system	**el sistema** *(ehl see-'steh-mah)*
theme	**el tema** *(ehl 'teh-mah)*

Now pass out the training materials and quickly review what each employee is supposed to do:

Follow (the)...	**Siga...** *('see-gah)*
directions	**las instrucciones** *(lahs een-strook-see-'oh-nehs)*
guidelines	**las guías** *(las 'gee-ahs)*
laws	**las leyes** *(lahs 'leh-yehs)*
procedures	**los procedimientos** *(lohs proh-seh-dee-mee-'ehn-tohs)*
regulations	**los reglamentos** *(lohs reh-glah-'mehn-tohs)*
rules	**las reglas** *(lahs 'reh-glahs)*
steps	**los pasos** *(lohs 'pah-sohs)*

Study (the)...	**Estudie...** *(eh-'stoo-dee-eh)*
drawing	**el dibujo** *(ehl dee-'boo-hoh)*
illustration	**la ilustración** *(lah ee-loos-trah-see-'ohn)*
map	**el mapa** *(ehl 'mah-pah)*
photo	**la foto** *(lah 'foh-toh)*
picture	**el cuadro** *(ehl 'kwah-droh)*

This next series allows you to explain specific information, so focus carefully on each word as you practice. Try out these sample phrases.

Look for (the)...	**Busque...** *('boo-skeh)*
Remember (the)...	**Recuerde...** *(reh-'kwehr-deh)*
See (the)...	**Vea...** *('veh-ah)*
angle	**el ángulo** *(ehl 'ahn-goo-loh)*
circle	**el círculo** *(ehl 'seer-koo-loh)*
cone	**el cono** *(ehl 'koh-noh)*
corner	**la esquina** *(lah eh-'skee-nah)*
cube	**el cubo** *(ehl 'koo-boh)*
curve	**la curva** *(lah 'koor-vah)*
cylinder	**el cilindro** *(ehl see-'leen-droh)*
design	**el diseño** *(ehl dee-'seh-nyoh)*
edge	**el borde** *(ehl 'bohr-deh)*
groove	**la muesca** *(lah 'mweh-skah)*
letter	**la letra** *(lah 'leh-trah)*
line	**la línea** *(lah 'lee-neh-ah)*
mark	**la marca** *(lah 'mahr-kah)*
number	**el número** *(ehl 'noo-meh-roh)*
pattern	**el modelo** *(ehl moh-'deh-loh)*
point	**la punta** *(lah 'poon-tah)*
rectangle	**el rectángulo** *(ehl rehk-'tahn-goo-loh)*
shape	**la forma** *(lah 'fohr-mah)*
space	**el espacio** *(ehl eh-'spah-see·oh)*
square	**el cuadrado** *(ehl kwah-'drah-doh)*
stripe	**la raya** *(lah 'rah-yah)*
symbol	**el símbolo** *(ehl 'seem-boh-loh)*
triangle	**el triángulo** *(ehl tree-'ahn-goo-loh)*

Tell them!
¡Dígales! *('dee-gah-lehs)*

In some cases, HR managers have to tell Spanish-speaking supervisors, chiefs, or lead personnel what needs to be communicated to the rest of the staff. Read over the following sentence patterns and figure out ways to substitute phrases with other key vocabulary:

Tell them that...	**Dígales que...** *('dee-gah-lehs keh)*
they need to begin	**necesitan empezar**
	(neh-seh-'see-tahn ehm-peh-'sahr)
there is a problem	**hay un problema**
	('ah-ee oon proh-'bleh-mah)
they should hurry	**deben apurarse**
	('deh-behn ah-poo-'rahr-seh)
it is very important	**es muy importante**
	(ehs 'moo-ee eem-pohr-'tahn-teh)
we can't wait	**no podemos esperar**
	(noh poh-'deh-mohs eh-speh-'rahr)
everything looks good	**todo se ve bien** *('toh-doh seh veh 'bee-ehn)*
the meeting is	**la reunión está cancelada**
canceled	*(lah reh-oon-ee-'ohn eh-'stah kahn-seh-'lah-dah)*
the schedule is ready	**el horario está listo**
	(ehl oh-'rah-ree-oh eh-'stah 'lee-stoh)
we have more work	**tenemos más trabajo**
	(teh-'neh-mohs mahs trah-'bah-hoh)
they have to finish	**tienen que terminar**
	(tee-'eh-nehn keh tehr-mee-'nahr)

Check out all these other phrases you can use! Read aloud each example and substitute words for practice:

Make sure that (you)...	**Asegúrese de...** *(ah-seh-'goo-reh-seh deh)*
ask me if you	**preguntarme si no entiende**
don't understand	*(preh-goon-'tahr-meh see noh ehn-tee-'ehn-deh)*
call me at this number	**llamarme a este número**
	(yah-'mahr-meh ah 'eh-steh 'noo-meh-roh)
check on the materials	**verificar los materiales**
	(veh-ree-fee-'kahr lohs mah-teh-ree-'ah-lehs)
arrive early	**llegar temprano**
	(yeh-'gahr tehm-'prah-noh)
lock the doors	**cerrar las puertas con llave**
	(seh-'rrahr lahs 'pwehr-tahs kohn 'yah-veh)

read the information	**leer la información**
	(leh-'ehr lah een-fohr-mah-see-'ohn)
turn off the machine	**apagar la máquina**
	(ah-pah-'gahr lah 'mah-kee-nah)
clean up the mess	**limpiar la basura**
	(leem-pee-'ahr lah bah-'soo-rah)
put everything away	**guardar todo** *(gwahr-'dahr 'toh-doh)*

Do me a favor!
Hágame un favor
('ah-gah-meh oon fah-'vohr)

Are you able to formulate your own requests in Spanish? When you need things done, keep your explanations brief:

Please remind me of (the)...	**Por favor, recuérdeme de...**
	(pohr fah-'vohr, reh-'kwehr-deh-meh deh)
date	**la fecha** *(lah 'feh-chah)*
meeting	**la reunión** *(lah reh-oon-ee-'ohn)*
phone call	**la llamada** *(lah yah-'mah-dah)*
problem	**el problema** *(ehl proh-'bleh-mah)*
time	**la hora** *(lah 'oh-rah)*

Specify your needs politely by adding words to the phrases below. These also work well as parts of written notes or messages:

When you finish...
Cuando termine... *('kwahn-doh tehr-'mee-neh)*

If it's possible...
Si es posible... *(see ehs poh-'see-bleh)*

Before you go...
Antes de irse... *('ahn-tehs deh 'eer-seh)*

Translate:

Cuando termine, apague la máquina.
('kwahn-doh tehr-'mee-neh, ah-'pah-geh lah 'mah-kee-nah)

Si es posible, venga temprano.
(see ehs poh-'see-bleh,'vehn-gah tehm-'prah-noh)

Antes de irse, cierre la puerta.
('ahn-tehs deh 'eer-seh, see-'eh-reh lah 'pwehr-tah)

¡Información!

- Copy these down somewhere and add them to the list above:

  I told you that...
  Le dije que... *(leh 'dee-heh keh)*
  Remember that...
  Recuerde que... *(reh-'kwehr-deh)*
  It's important that...
  Es importante que... *(ehs eem-pohr-'tahn-teh keh)*

- And are you telling them what *not* to do?

Please, don't ...	**Favor de no...** *(fah-'vohr deh noh)*
leave them here	**dejarlos aquí** *(deh-'hahr-lohs ah-'kee)*
use this machine	**usar esta máquino**
	(oo-'sahr 'eh-stah 'mah-kee-noh)
park there	**estacionar allí**
	(eh-stah-see·oh-'nahr ah-'yee)
bring that	**traer eso** *(trah-'ehr 'eh-soh)*
move the	**mover el equipo**
equipment	*(moh-'vehr ehl eh-'kee-poh)*
touch it	**tocarlo** *(toh-'kahr-loh)*
turn it off	**apagarlo** *(ah-pah-'gahr-loh)*

Listos para practicar

Circle the word that doesn't belong in the same vocabulary group:

dibujo, fecha, cuadro, foto
(dee-'boo-hoh, 'feh-chah, 'kwah-droh, 'foh-toh)

meta, objetivo, propósito, empleado
('meh-tah, ohb-heh-'tee-voh, proh-'poh-see-toh, ehm-pleh-'ah-doh)

cubo, cuadrado, olor, círculo
('koo-boh, kwah-'drah-doh, oh-'lohr, 'seer-koo-loh)

vestidos, leyes, instrucciones, reglas
(veh-'stee-dohs, 'leh-yehs, een-strook-see-'oh-nehs, 'reh-glahs)

línea, número, letra, carta
('lee-neh-ah, 'noo-meh-roh, 'leh-trah, 'kahr-tah)

Translate, and then add words to complete a sentence:

Hágame *('ah-gah-meh)*	Do for me	**Hágame un favor.** *('ah-gah-meh oon fah-'vohr)*
Dígales *('dee-gah-lehs)*	_____	_____
Asegúrese *(ah-seh-'goo-reh-seh)*	_____	_____
Recuerde *(reh-'kwehr-deh)*	_____	_____

What happened here?

¿Qué pasó aquí? *(keh pah-'soh ah-'kee)*

Things don't always go right during training, so learn those descriptive words and phrases that refer to potential problems and concerns. Try this familiar pattern:

It's...	**Está...** *(eh-'stah)*
bent	**doblado** *(doh-'blah-doh)*
broken	**roto** *('roh-toh)*
burned	**quemado** *(keh-'mah-doh)*
chipped	**astillado** *(ah-stee-'yah-doh)*
crushed	**aplastado** *(ah-plah-'stah-doh)*
cut	**cortado** *(kohr-'tah-doh)*

damaged	**dañado** *(dah-'nyah-doh)*
inoperative	**inoperable** *(een-oh-peh-'rah-bleh)*
lost	**perdido** *(pehr-'dee-doh)*
out of service	**fuera de servicio** *('fweh-rah deh sehr-'vee-see·oh)*
rotten	**podrido** *(poh-'dree-doh)*
stained	**manchado** *(mahn-'chah-doh)*
stuck	**pegado** *(peh-'gah-doh)*
torn	**rasgado** *(rahs-'gah-doh)*
uneven	**desigual** *(dehs-ee-'gwahl)*

Try practicing descriptions as opposites:

I think it's...	**Creo que está...** *('kreh-oh keh eh-'stah)*
twisted	**torcido** *(tohr-'see-doh)*
straight	**recto** *('rehk-toh)*
loose	**suelto** *('swehl-toh)*
tight	**apretado** *(ah-preh-'tah-doh)*
heavy	**pesado** *(peh-'sah-doh)*
light	**ligero** *(lee-'heh-roh)*
neat	**limpio** *('leem-pee·oh)*
dirty	**sucio** *('soo-see-oh)*

Some matters are a bit more serious, so make an effort to review these descriptive terms often:

Be careful—it's...	**Tenga cuidado...** *('tehn-gah kwee-'dah-doh)*
dangerous	**es peligroso** *(ehs peh-lee-'groh-soh)*
defective	**es defectuoso** *(ehs deh-fehk-too-'oh-soh)*
illegal	**es ilegal** *(ehs ee-leh-'gahl)*
poisonous	**es venenoso** *(ehs veh-neh-'noh-soh)*
prohibited	**está prohibido** *(eh-'stah proh-ee-'bee-doh)*
restricted	**está restringido** *(eh-'stah reh-streen-'hee-doh)*
risky	**es arriesgado** *(ehs ah-rree-ehs-'gah-doh)*

¡Información!

- Can you define the object you're working with?

It's a...	**Es un...** *(ehs oon)*
gas	**gas** *(gahs)*
grain	**grano** *('grah-noh)*
liquid	**líquido** *('lee-kee-doh)*
powder	**polvo** *('pohl-voh)*
solid	**sólido** *('soh-lee-doh)*

- Next time, ask a native Spanish speaker what everyone is shouting about. Here's what to say when there's a mechanical problem:

Something's wrong!	**¡Algo está mal!** *('ahl-goh eh-'stah mahl)*
It looks strange!	**¡Se ve raro!** *(seh veh 'rah-roh)*
Let's repair it!	**¡Vamos a repararlo!**
	('vah-mohs ah reh-pah-'rahr-loh)

Check the...!	**¡Verifique...!** *(veh-ree-'fee-keh)*
control	**el control** *(ehl kohn-'trohl)*
cycle	**el ciclo** *(ehl 'see-kloh)*
level	**el nivel** *(ehl nee-'vehl)*
light	**la luz** *(lah loos)*
power	**la potencia** *(lah poh-'tehn-see-ah)*
speed	**la velocidad** *(lah veh-loh-see-'dahd)*
temperature	**la temperatura** *(lah tehm-peh-rah-'too-rah)*
time	**la hora** *(lah 'oh-rah)*
tune	**el tono** *(ehl 'toh-noh)*

I'm going to...!	**¡Voy a...!** *('voh-ee ah)*
cancel it	**cancelarlo** *(kahn-seh-'lahr-loh)*
deactivate it	**desactivarlo** *(dehs-ahk-tee-'vahr-loh)*
pause it	**pausarlo** *(pow-'sahr-loh)*
turn it off	**apagarlo** *(ah-pah-'gahr-loh)*
stop it	**pararlo** *(pah-'rahr-loh)*

Can you drive it?
¿Puede usted manejarlo?
('pweh-deh oo-'stehd mah-neh-'hahr-loh)

Some orientation and training procedures may involve the use of motorized vehicles and heavy machinery.

Please use (the)...	**Favor de usar...** *(fah-'vohr deh oo-'sahr)*
Let's drive (the)...	**Vamos a manejar...** *('vah-mohs ah mah-neh-'hahr)*
You'll need (the)...	**Necesitará...** *(neh-seh-see-tah-'rah)*
boat	**el bote** *(ehl 'boh-teh)*
boxcar	**el vagón** *(ehl vah-'gohn)*
bulldozer	**la niveladora** *(lah nee-veh-lah-'doh-rah)*
bus	**el autobús** *(ehl ow-toh-'boos)*
car	**el carro** *(ehl 'kah-rroh)*
cement truck	**la mezcladora de cemento** *(lah meh-sklah-'doh-rah deh seh-'mehn-toh)*
commercial vehicle	**el vehículo comercial** *(ehl veh-'ee-koo-loh koh-mehr-see-'ahl)*
delivery truck	**el camión de reparto** *(ehl kah-mee-'ohn deh reh-'pahr-toh)*
dump truck	**el volquete** *(ehl vohl-'keh-teh)*
flatbed truck	**el camión de plataforma** *(ehl kah-mee-'ohn deh plah-tah-'fohr-mah)*
pick up	**la camioneta** *(lah kah-mee·oh-'neh-tah)*
semi-trailer	**el semiremolque** *(ehl seh-mee-reh-'mohl-keh)*
tank truck	**el camión cisterna** *(ehl kah-mee-'ohn see-'stehr-nah)*
tow truck	**la grúa** *(lah 'groo-ah)*
tractor	**el tractor** *(ehl trahk-'tohr)*
tractor trailer	**el camión tractor** *(ehl kah-mee-'ohn trahk-'tohr)*
train	**el tren** *(ehl trehn)*
truck	**el camión** *(ehl kah-mee-'ohn)*
van	**la furgoneta** *(lah foor-goh-'neh-tah)*

Vehicle parts
Las partes del vehículo
(lahs 'pahr-tehs dehl veh-'ee-koo-loh)

Many Spanish speakers are able to translate the basic parts of an automobile from Spanish into English, so you shouldn't have too much trouble in dialogues about vehicle care and repair. In an emergency, however, refer to this bonus list:

Clean (the)...	**Limpie...** *('leem-pee-eh)*
Wash (the)...	**Lave...** *('lah-veh)*
Wax (the)...	**Encere...** *(ehn-'seh-reh)*
Replace (the)...	**Reemplace...** *(eh-ehm-'plah-seh)*
Repair (the)...	**Repare...** *(reh-'pah-reh)*
axle	**el eje** *(ehl 'eh-heh)*
brakes	**los frenos** *(lohs 'freh-nohs)*
bumper	**el parachoques** *(ehl pah-rah-'choh-kehs)*
cab	**la cabina** *(lah kah-'bee-nah)*
dashboard	**el tablero** *(ehl tah-'bleh-roh)*
door	**la puerta** *(lah 'pwehr-tah)*
engine	**el motor** *(ehl moh-'tohr)*
fender	**el guardabarro** *(ehl gwahr-dah-'bah-rroh)*
gauge	**el indicador** *(ehl een-dee-kah-'dohr)*
glove compartment	**la guantera** *(lah gwahn-'teh-rah)*
hood	**la cubierta** *(lah koo-bee-'ehr-tah)*
horn	**la bocina** *(lah boh-'see-nah)*
hubcap	**el tapacubos** *(ehl tah-pah-'koo-bohs)*
lights	**las luces** *(lahs 'loo-sehs)*
mirror	**el espejo** *(ehl eh-'speh-hoh)*
muffler	**el silenciador** *(ehl see-lehn-see-ah-'dohr)*
roof	**el techo** *(ehl 'teh-choh)*
seat	**el asiento** *(ehl ah-see-'ehn-toh)*
shock absorber	**el amortiguador** *(ehl ah-mohr-tee-gwah-'dohr)*
spare tire	**el neumático de repuesto** *(ehl neh-oo-'mah-tee-koh deh reh-'pweh-stoh)*
steering wheel	**el volante** *(ehl voh-'lahn-teh)*
tire	**el neumático** *(ehl neh-oo-'mah-tee-koh)*

| trunk | **la maletera** *(lah mah-leh-'teh-rah)* |
| windshield | **el parabrisas** *(ehl pah-rah-'bree-sahs)* |

¡Información!

- You might as well learn what's going on at the airport.

Some businesses use these words all the time:

airport	**el aeropuerto** *(ehl ah-eh-roh-'pwehr-toh)*
terminal	**el terminal** *(ehl tehr-mee-'nahl)*
airstrip	**la pista de aterrizaje**
	(lah 'pee-stah deh ah-teh-rree-'sah-heh)
flight	**el vuelo** *(ehl 'vweh-loh)*
helicopter	**el helicóptero** *(ehl eh-lee-'kohp-teh-roh)*
customs	**la aduana** *(lah ah-'dwah-nah)*
plane	**el avión** *(ehl ah-vee-'ohn)*

- And, not everyone can afford a larger vehicle:

motorcycle	**la motocicleta** *(lah moh-toh-see-'kleh-tah)*
bicycle	**la bicicleta** *(lah bee-see-'kleh-tah)*
moped	**la bicicleta motorizada**
	(lah bee-see-'kleh-tah moh-toh-ree-'sah-dah)

- Can you guess what these words mean in English?

la transmisión *(lah trahns-mee-see-'ohn)*
el radiador *(ehl rah-dee-ah-'dohr)*
el odómetro *(ehl oh-'doh-meh-troh)*
el tanque *(ehl 'tahn-keh)*
la batería *(lah bah-teh-'ree-ah)*
el pedal *(ehl peh-'dahl)*

Temas culturales

If by chance your Spanish-speaking assistant is unfamiliar with English signs and signals, you may want to review some of the key words that are posted on our roadways. And don't forget, these terms are great to know when traveling in another country!

Curve	**CURVA** *('koor-vah)*
Detour	**DESVIACION** *(dehs-vee-ah-see-'ohn)*
Do Not Cross	**NO CRUZAR** *(noh kroo-'sahr)*
Do Not Litter	**NO TIRE BASURA** *(noh 'tee-reh bah-'soo-rah)*
Emergency	**EMERGENCIA** *(eh-mehr-'hehn-see·ah)*
Entrance	**ENTRADA** *(ehn-'trah-dah)*
Exit	**SALIDA** *(sah-'lee-dah)*
Handicapped	**MINUSVALIDOS** *(mee-noos-'vah-lee-dohs)*
Narrow Road	**CAMINO ESTRECHO** *(kah-'mee-noh eh-'streh-choh)*
No Entrance	**PASO PROHIBIDO** *('pah-soh proh-ee-'bee-doh)*
No Passing	**NO PASAR** *(noh pah-'sahr)*
No U Turn	**PROHIBIDA LA VUELTA EN "U"** *(proh-ee-'bee-dah lah 'vwehl-tah ehn oo)*
One Way	**CIRCULACION** *(seer-koo-lah-see-'ohn)*
Parking	**ESTACIONAMIENTO** *(eh-stah-see·oh-nah-mee-'ehn-toh)*
Pedestrian Crossing	**PASO DE PEATONES** *('pah-soh deh peh-ah-'toh-nehs)*
Railroad Crossing	**CRUCE DE VIAS** *('kroo-seh deh 'vee-ahs)*
Slow	**DESPACIO** *(deh-'spah-see·oh)*
Speed Limit	**LIMITE DE VELOCIDAD** *('lee-mee-teh deh veh-loh-see-'dahd)*
Stop	**ALTO** *('ahl-toh)*
Tow Away Zone	**SE USARA GRUA** *(seh oo-sah-'rah 'groo-ah)*
Traffic Circle	**GLORIETA** *(gloh-ree-'eh-tah)*
Wait	**ESPERE** *(eh-'speh-reh)*
Walk	**CAMINE** *(kah-'mee-neh)*
Wrong Way	**VÍA EQUIVOCADA** *('vee-ah eh-kee-voh-'kah-dah)*
Yield	**CEDA EL PASO** *('seh-dah ehl 'pah-soh)*

¡Información!

• What about the signs around the worksite? Post these in two languages today!

Closed	**CERRADO** *(seh-'rrah-doh)*
Danger	**PELIGRO** *(peh-'lee-groh)*
For Rent	**SE ALQUILA** *(seh ahl-'kee-lah)*
For Sale	**SE VENDE** *(seh 'vehn-deh)*
No Smoking	**NO FUMAR** *(noh foo-'mahr)*
Open	**ABIERTO** *(ah-bee-'ehr-toh)*
Out of Order	**DESCOMPUESTO** *(dehs-kohm-'pweh-stoh)*
Pull	**TIRE** *('tee-reh)*
Push	**EMPUJE** *(ehm-'poo-heh)*
Red Cross	**CRUZ ROJA** *(kroos 'roh-hah)*
Restrooms	**SANITARIOS** *(sah-nee-'tah-ree-ohs)*

• Keep going:

Authorized Personnel Only	**Sólo para personal autorizado** *('soh-loh 'pah-rah pehr-'soh-nahl ow-toh-ree-'sah-doh)*
Change Machine	**Máquina para dar cambio** *('mah-kee-nah 'pah-rah dahr 'kahm-bee-oh)*
Customer Parking	**Estacionamiento para clientes** *(eh-stah-see-oh-nah-mee-'ehn-toh 'pah-rah klee-'ehn-tehs)*
Do Not Block Entrance	**No obstruir la entrada** *(noh ohb-stroo-'eer lah ehn-'trah-dah)*
Emergency Exit	**Salida de emergencia** *(sah-'lee-dah deh eh-mehr-'hehn-see-ah)*
Follow The Arrow	**Siga la flecha** *('see-gah lah 'fleh-chah)*
High Power Cables	**Cables de alto voltaje** *('kah-blehs deh 'ahl-toh vohl-'tah-heh)*
Next Window Please	**Pasar a la siguiente ventanilla** *(pah-'sahr ah lah see-gee-'ehn-teh vehn-tah-'nee-yah)*

Now Hiring	**Estamos contratando personal**
	(eh-'stah-mohs kohn-trah-'tahn-doh pehr-soh-'nahl)
Spanish Is Spoken	**Se habla español**
	(seh 'ah-blah eh-spah-'nyohl)
Use Other Door	**Use la otra puerta**
	('oo-seh lah 'oh-trah 'pwehr-tah)
Wet Floor	**Piso mojado** *('pee-soh moh-'hah-doh)*

• Look up the names for each department and hang a sign:

Customer Service	**Asistencia a la clientela**
	(ah-see-'stehn-see-ah ah lah klee-ehn-'teh-lah)
Deliveries	**Entregas** *(ehn-'treh-gahs)*
Shipping	**Envíos** *(ehn-'vee-ohs)*

Listos para practicar

Choose one of these words to complete each sentence:

peligrosa, roto, luz *(peh-lee-'groh-sah, 'roh-toh, loos)*

El teléfono está _____.
(ehl teh-'leh-foh-noh eh-'stah ____)

La electricidad es _____.
(lah eh-lehk-tree-see-'dahd ehs ___)

Hay problemas con la _____.
('ah-ee proh-'bleh-mahs kohn lah___)

In Spanish,

name three signs you can find along most roadways:

_____   _____   _____

name one sign that is posted on most warehouse doors:

_____

name five major auto parts:

_____   _____   _____   _____   _____

name four vehicles that often carry heavy loads:

_____   _____   _____

Put it on!

¡Póngaselo! *('pohn-gah-seh-loh)*

Be firm about the dress code. Start your presentation by telling trainees about certain safety items. Look at the simple pattern:

You need to use (the)...	**Necesita usar...** *(neh-seh-'see-tah oo-'sahr)*
apron	**el delantal** *(ehl deh-lahn-'tahl)*
belt	**el cinturón de seguridad** *(ehl seen-too-'rohn deh seh-goo-ree-'dahd)*
boots	**las botas** *('lahs 'boh-tahs)*
earplugs	**los tapones para los oídos** *(lohs tah-'poh-nehs 'pah-rah lohs oh-'ee-dohs)*
gloves	**los guantes** *(lohs 'gwahn-tehs)*
hair net	**la redecilla** *(lah reh-deh-'see-yah)*
hat	**el sombrero** *(ehl sohm-'breh-roh)*
helmet	**el casco** *(ehl 'kah-skoh)*
jacket	**la chaqueta** *(lah chah-'keh-tah)*
mask	**la máscara** *(lah 'mah-skah-rah)*
mittens	**los mitones** *(lohs mee-'toh-nehs)*
overcoat	**el abrigo** *(ehl ah-'bree-goh)*
raincoat	**el impermeable** *(ehl eem-pehr-meh-'ah-bleh)*
robe	**la bata** *(lah 'bah-tah)*
safety glasses	**las gafas de seguridad** *(lahs 'gah-fahs deh seh-goo-ree-'dahd)*
scarf	**la bufanda** *(lah boo-'fahn-dah)*
strap	**la correa** *(lah koh-'rreh-ah)*
suit	**el traje** *(ehl 'trah-heh)*
uniform	**el uniforme** *(ehl oo-nee-'fohr-meh)*
vest	**el chaleco** *(ehl chah-'leh-koh)*

¡Información!

Provide these answers to their questions about safety wear:

At all times!	**¡Todo el tiempo!** *('toh-doh ehl tee-'ehm-poh)*
Because it's the law!	**¡Porque es la ley!** *(pohr-keh ehs lah 'leh-ee)*
You can get hurt!	**¡Puede hacerse daño!** *('pweh-deh ah-'sehr-seh 'dah-nyoh)*

Clothing
La ropa *(lah 'roh-pah)*

At some businesses, Human Resources professionals are required to assign "appropriate employee attire" at the work site.

You should wear...	**Debe ponerse...** *('deh-beh poh-'nehr-seh)*
a blouse	**una blusa** *('oo-nah 'bloo-sah)*
a brassiere	**un sostén** *(oon soh-'stehn)*
a cap	**una gorra** *('oo-nah 'goh-rrah)*
a dress	**un vestido** *(oon veh-'stee-doh)*
a girdle	**una faja** *('oo-nah 'fah-hah)*
a shirt	**una camisa** *('oo-nah kah-'mee-sah)*
a skirt	**una falda** *('oo-nah 'fahl-dah)*
a sportcoat	**un saco** *(oon 'sah-koh)*
a sweater	**un suéter** *(oon 'sweh-tehr)*
a sweatsuit	**una sudadera** *('oo-nah soo-dah-'deh-rah)*
a T-shirt	**una camiseta** *('oo-nah kah-mee-'seh-tah)*
underwear	**la ropa interior** *(lah 'roh-pah een-teh-ree-'ohr)*

And these things are in the plural form:

pajamas	**un pijama** *(oon pee-'hah-mah)*
panties	**unas bragas** *('oo-nahs 'brah-gahs)*
pants	**unos pantalones** *('oo-nohs pahn-tah-'loh-nehs)*
shorts	**unos calzoncillos** *('oo-nohs kahl-sohn-'see-yohs)*
slippers	**unas zapatillas** *('oo-nahs sah-pah-'tee-yahs)*
socks	**unos calcetines** *('oo-nohs kahl-seh-'tee-nehs)*
stockings	**unas medias** *('oo-nahs 'meh-dee-ahs)*
underpants	**unos calzoncillos** *('oo-nohs kahl-sohn-'see-yohs)*

Personal items
Cosas personales
('koh-sahs pehr-soh-'nah-lehs)

People bring all sorts of interesting things to work with them. The following items are pretty common, so practice each one in the sentence pattern provided:

He/She has (the)...	**Tiene...** *(tee-'eh-neh)*
Did you lose (the)...?	**¿Perdió...?** *(pehr-dee-'oh)*
Don't bring (the)...	**No traiga...** *(noh 'trah·ee-gah)*
cigarettes	**los cigarrillos** *(lohs see-gah-'ree-yohs)*
comb	**el peine** *(oon 'peh·ee-neh)*
hairbrush	**el cepillo** *(ehl seh-'pee-yoh)*
handkerchief	**el pañuelo** *(ehl pah-nyoo-'eh-loh)*
magazine	**la revista** *(lah reh-'vee-stah)*
make-up	**el maquillaje** *(ehl mah-kee-'yah-heh)*
newspaper	**el periódico** *(ehl peh-ree-'oh-dee-koh)*
sunglasses	**los lentes del sol** *(lohs 'lehn-tehs dehl sohl)*
suntan lotion	**el bronceador** *(ehl brohn-seh-ah-'dohr)*
umbrella	**el paraguas** *(ehl pah-'rah-gwahs)*

• At some businesses, employees are asked to avoid wearing jewelry:

Don't wear (the)...	**No use...** *(noh 'oo-seh)*
I like (the)...	**Me gusta...** *('meh 'goo-stah)*
Be careful with (the)...	**Tenga cuidado con...** *('tehn-gah kwee-'dah-doh kohn)*
bracelet	**el brazalete** *(ehl brah-sah-'leh-teh)*
chain	**la cadena** *(lah kah-'deh-nah)*
earring	**el arete** *(ehl ah-'reh-teh)*
jewel	**la joya** *(lah 'hoh-yah)*
necklace	**el collar** *(ehl koh-'yahr)*
ring	**el anillo** *(ehl ah-'nee-yoh)*
watch	**el reloj de pulsera** *(ehl reh-'loh deh pool-'seh-rah)*

Listos para practicar

Name three articles of clothing needed for work in cold weather:

_____   _____   _____

Name three clothing items that are commonly worn by women:

_____   _____   _____

Name three well-known personal or toiletry articles:

_____   _____   _____

The cafeteria

La cafetería *(lah kah-feh-teh-'ree-ah)*

One of the favorite sites on the orientation tour is the local cafeteria, vending machine, lunch truck, or dining area where employees gather throughout the day for coffee or a bite to eat. No matter how big your business is, Human Resource Managers need to explain what kind of food is offered.

You may sit where you want.
Puede sentarse dónde quiera.
('pweh-deh sehn-'tahr-seh 'dohn-deh kee-'eh-rah)

These are the hours of service.
Estas son las horas de servicio.
('eh-stahs sohn lahs 'oh-rahs deh sehr-'vee-see·oh)

You don't have much time to eat.
No tiene mucho tiempo para comer.
(noh tee-'eh-neh 'moo-choh tee-'ehm-poh 'pah-rah koh-'mehr)

The food is very good.
La comida es muy buena.
(lah koh-'mee-dah ehs 'moo·ee 'bweh-nah)

You have to pay over there.
Tiene que pagar ahí.
(tee-'eh-neh keh pah-'gahr ah-'ee)

This time, tell the trainees about the menu:

They sell...	**Venden...** *('vehn-dehn)*
breakfast	**el desayuno** *(ehl deh-sah-'yoo-noh)*
lunch	**el almuerzo** *(ehl ahl-moo-'ehr-soh)*
dinner	**la cena** *(lah 'seh-nah)*
They serve...	**Sirven...** *('seer-vehn)*
bacon	**el tocino** *(ehl toh-'see-noh)*
beef	**la carne** *(lah 'kahr-neh)*
cereal	**el cereal** *(ehl seh-reh-'ahl)*
chicken	**el pollo** *(ehl 'poh-yoh)*
eggs	**los huevos** *(lohs 'weh-vohs)*
fish	**el pescado** *(ehl peh-'skah-doh)*
ham	**el jamón** *(ehl hah-'mohn)*

hamburgers	**las hamburguesas** *(lahs ahm-boor-'geh-sahs)*
hot dogs	**los perros calientes** *(lohs 'peh-rrohs kah-lee-'ehn-tehs)*
noodles	**los fideos** *(lohs fee-'deh-ohs)*
pork	**el cerdo** *(ehl 'sehr-doh)*
rice	**el arroz** *(ehl ah-'rrohs)*
roast beef	**el rósbif** *(ehl rohs-'beef)*
rolls	**los panecillos** *(lohs pah-neh-'see-yohs)*
salad	**la ensalada** *(lah ehn-sah-'lah-dah)*
sandwiches	**los sandwiches** *(lohs 'sahnd-wee-chehs)*
sausage	**la salchicha** *(lah sahl-'chee-chah)*
seafood	**el marisco** *(ehl mah-'ree-skoh)*
soup	**la sopa** *(lah 'soh-pah)*
steak	**el bistec** *(ehl bee-'stehk)*
toast	**el pan tostado** *(ehl pahn toh-'stah-doh)*
tuna	**el atún** *(ehl ah-'toon)*
turkey	**el pavo** *(ehl 'pah-voh)*

Vegetables
Los vegetales *(lohs veh-heh-'tah-lehs)*

They have...	**Tienen...** *(tee-'eh-nehn)*
beans	**los frijoles** *(lohs free-'hoh-lehs)*
beet	**el betabel** *(ehl beh-tah-'behl)*
cabbage	**el repollo** *(ehl reh-'poh-yoh)*
carrot	**la zanahoria** *(lah sah-nah-'oh-ree·ah)*
celery	**el apio** *(ehl 'ah-pee·oh)*
corn	**el maíz** *(ehl mah-'ees)*
cucumber	**el pepino** *(ehl peh-'pee-noh)*
lettuce	**la lechuga** *(lah leh-'choo-gah)*
mushrooms	**los champiñones** *(lohs chahm-pee-'nyoh-nehs)*
onion	**la cebolla** *(lah seh-'boh-yah)*
peas	**las arvejitas** *(lahs ahr-veh-'hee-tahs)*
potato	**la papa** *(lah 'pah-pah)*
radish	**el rábano** *(ehl 'rah-bah-noh)*
spinach	**la espinaca** *(lah eh-spee-'nah-kah)*
tomato	**el tomate** *(ehl toh-'mah-teh)*

Fruit
La fruta
(lah 'froo-tah)

Do you like...?	**¿Le gusta...?** *(leh 'goo-stah)*
apple	**la manzana** *(lah mahn-'sah-nah)*
apricot	**el albaricoque** *(ehl ahl-bah-ree-'koh-keh)*
banana	**el plátano** *(ehl 'plah-tah-noh)*
cantaloupe	**el melón** *(ehl meh-'lohn)*
cherry	**la cereza** *(lah seh-'reh-sah)*
coconut	**el coco** *(ehl 'koh-koh)*
grape	**la uva** *(lah 'oo-vah)*
grapefruit	**la toronja** *(lah toh-'rohn-hah)*
lemon	**el limón** *(ehl lee-'mohn)*
orange	**la naranja** *(lah nah-'rahn-hah)*
peach	**el melocotón** *(ehl meh-loh-koh-'tohn)*
pear	**la pera** *(lah 'peh-rah)*
strawberry	**la fresa** *(lah 'freh-sah)*

Dessert and snacks
El postre y las meriendas
(ehl 'poh-streh ee lahs meh-ree-'ehn-dahs)

You can buy...	**Puede comprar...** *('pweh-deh kohm-'prahr)*
candy	**los dulces** *(lohs 'dool-sehs)*
gum	**el chicle** *(ehl 'chee-kleh)*
cake	**la torta** *(lah 'tohr-tah)*
pie	**el pastel** *(ehl pah-'stehl)*
jello	**la gelatina** *(lah heh-lah-'tee-nah)*
cookie	**la galleta** *(lah gah-'yeh-tah)*
ice cream	**el helado** *(ehl eh-'lah-doh)*
yogurt	**el yogur** *(ehl yoh-'goor)*

Temas culturales

Traditional American foods don't always appeal to a multi-ethnic work-force. Many Hispanics, for example, simply prefer to bring their home-made foods to work with them for lunch. To raise morale, consider asking employees about the foods they enjoy most, and then add those items to the current cafeteria menu.

Listos para practicar

Use the Spanish you just learned to complete this exercise:

List three popular meat products:

_____   _____   _____

List three fruits and three vegetables:

_____   _____   _____

_____   _____   _____

List three dessert items:

_____   _____   _____

Más fácil

Since this chapter targets the needs of managers involved in orientation and training, the list of Spanish verb infinitives is quite extensive. We've already learned that the best method for practicing verbs is by inserting them into short, practical phrases. Here are some that were presented earlier:

Don't...	**No...** *(noh)*
I can...	**Puedo...** *('pweh-doh)*
I like to...	**Me gusta...** *(meh 'goo-stah)*
I'm going to...	**Voy a...** *('voh·ee ah)*
I want to...	**Quiero...** *(kee-'eh-roh)*
I would like to...	**Quisiera...** *(kee-see-'eh-rah)*
One must...	**Hay que...** *('ah·ee keh)*
Please...	**Favor de...** *(fah-'vohr deh)*

You have to...	**Tiene que...** *(tee-'eh-neh keh)*
You need to...	**Necesita...** *(neh-seh-'see-tah)*
You should...	**Debe...** *('deh-beh)*

Check out this next shortcut, along with a full set of verbs for everyday use. As always, start with only the ones you need!

I, You, She, He could...	**Podría...** *(poh-'dree-ah)*
They could...	**Podrían...** *(poh-'dree-ahn)*
We could...	**Podríamos...** *(poh-'dree-ah-mohs)*
to arrive	**llegar** *(yeh-'gahr)*
to ask for	**pedir** *(peh-'deer)*
to bend	**doblar** *(doh-'blahr)*
to check	**verificar** *(veh-ree-fee-'kahr)*
to climb	**subir** *(soo-'beer)*
to cut	**cortar** *(kohr-'tahr)*
to explain	**explicar** *(ehks-plee-'kahr)*
to learn	**aprender** *(ah-prehn-'dehr)*
to let	**dejar** *(deh-'hahr)*
to load	**cargar** *(kahr-'gahr)*
to lose	**perder** *(pehr-'dehr)*
to measure	**medir** *(meh-'deer)*
to pass	**pasar** *(pah-'sahr)*
to pile	**amontonar** *(ah-mohn-'toh-nahr)*
to repair	**reparar** *(reh-pah-'rahr)*
to spray	**rociar** *(roh-see-'ahr)*
to study	**estudiar** *(eh-stoo-dee-'ahr)*
to touch	**tocar** *(toh-'kahr)*
to try	**tratar** *(trah-'tahr)*
to unload	**descargar** *(dehs-kahr-'gahr)*

Jobs require all kinds of actions, so add these verbs to your warehouse one-liners:

to assemble	**armar** *(ahr-'mahr)*
to attach	**unir** *(oo-'neer)*
to connect	**conectar** *(koh-nehk-'tahr)*
to dig	**excavar** *(exhs-kah-'vahr)*

to drill	**taladrar** *(tah-lah-'drahr)*
to glue	**pegar** *(peh-'gahr)*
to grind	**moler** *(moh-'lehr)*
to hang	**colgar** *(kohl-'gahr)*
to heat	**calentar** *(kah-lehn-'tahr)*
to lock	**cerrar con llave** *(seh-'rrahr kohn 'yah-veh)*
to mark	**marcar** *(mahr-'kahr)*
to mix	**mezclar** *(mehs-'klahr)*
to paint	**pintar** *(peen-'tahr)*
to replace	**reemplazar** *(reh-ehm-plah-'sahr)*
to rest	**descansar** *(deh-skahn-'sahr)*
to sand	**limar** *(lee-'mahr)*
to scrub	**fregar** *(freh-'gahr)*
to stamp	**estampar** *(eh-stahm-'pahr)*
to sweep	**barrer** *(bah-'rrehr)*
to weld	**soldar** *(sohl-'dahr)*

Listos para practicar

Here's a little translation practice:

¿Podría usted limar la madera?
(poh-'dree-ah oo-'stehd lee-'mahr lah mah-'deh-rah)

No podríamos calentar el metal.
(noh poh-'dree-ah-mohs kah-lehn-'tahr ehl meh-'tahl)

Ellos podrían sujetar los cables.
('eh-yohs poh-'dree-ahn soo-heh-'tahr lohs 'kah-blehs)

¡Información!

Here are a few more Spanish verbs with **se** *(seh)*:

to fall	**caerse** *(kah-'ehr-seh)*
to forget	**olvidarse** *(ohl-vee-'dahr-seh)*
to wear	**ponerse** *(poh-'nehr-seh)*
to break	**quebrarse** *(keh-'brahr-seh)*
to be sure	**asegurarse** *(ah-seh-goo-'rahr-seh)*
to get dressed	**vestirse** *(veh-'steer-seh)*
to leave	**irse** *('eer-seh)*

Look at how they appear in sentences:

Daniel se pone el uniforme.
(dah-nee-'ehl seh 'poh-neh ehl oo-nee-'fohr-meh)
Se va a las seis.
(seh vah ah lahs 'seh·ees)
Y se olvida su almuerzo.
(ee seh ohl-'vee-dah soo ahl-moo-'ehr-soh)

Palabras activas

So far we have discovered that in order to converse about activities around work, it was necessary to make changes to the basic action verb. Notice the difference in meanings here:

To work	**Trabajar** *(trah-bah-'hahr)*
I'm working.	**Estoy trabajando.**
	(eh-'stoh-ee trah-bah-'hahn-doh)
I work.	**Trabajo.** *(trah-'bah-hoh)*
I'm going to work.	**Voy a trabajar.** *('voh-ee ah trah-bah-'hahr)*

Now, check out this new way to refer to future actions. Just add new endings to the infinitive, as shown. Look at this regular **ar** verb:

I will work	**Trabajaré** *(trah-bah-hah-'reh)*
You, He, She will work	**Trabajará** *(trah-bah-hah-'rah)*

You (pl.), They will work **Trabajarán** *(trah-bah-hah-'rahn)*
We will work **Trabajaremos** *(trah-bah-hah-'reh-mohs)*

The same patterns hold true for the **er** and **ir** verbs:

to eat **(comer)**	I'll eat.	**Comeré** *(koh-meh-'reh)*
to live **(vivir)**	He'll live.	**Vivirá** *(vee-vee-'rah)*
to run **(correr)**	We'll run.	**Correremos** *(koh-rreh-'reh-mohs)*
to receive **(recibir)**	They'll receive.	**Recibirán** *(reh-see-bee-'rahn)*

¡Información!

Beware of those irregular verbs in the future tense! Here are a few examples:

I'll have a job. **Tendré un trabajo.**
(tehn-'dreh oon trah-'bah-hoh)

They'll come soon. **Vendrán luego.** *(vehn-'drahn 'lweh-goh)*
She'll leave. **Saldrá.** *(sahl-'drah)*

Listos para practicar

Show the two ways to talk about the future.

COMER *(ko-'mehr)*   **Voy a comer.   Comeré.** _____
('voh-ee ah koh-'mehr, koh-meh-'reh)

ESPERAR *(eh-speh-'rahr)*   **Voy a esperar.   Esperaré.** _____
('voh-ee ah eh-speh-'rahr, eh-speh-rah-'reh)

LLAMAR *(yah-'mahr)* _____
MEDIR *(meh-'deer)* _____
APRENDER *(ah-prehn-'dehr)* _____
SUBIR *(soo-'beer)* _____
TRATAR *(trah-'tahr)* _____

Now, follow this sample set, change the other verbs in the same manner, and add some vocabulary:

LLEGAR *(yeh-'gahr)*
(to arrive)

Está llegando ahora.
(eh-'stah yeh-'gahn-doh ah-'oh-rah)
Llega todos los días.
('yeh-gah 'toh-dohs lohs 'dee-ahs)
Llegará mañana.
(yeh-gah-'rah mah-'nyah-nah)

ESTUDIAR *(eh-stoo-dee-'ahr)*
(to study)

_____

_____

_____

PINTAR *(peen-'tahr)*
(to paint)

_____

_____

DESCANSAR *(deh-skahn-'sahr)*
(to rest)

_____

_____

¡Ordenes!

Take some of the verbs we just learned and work on their command forms:

Try	**Trate** *('trah-teh)*	**Trate de aprender.** *('trah-teh deh ah-prehn-'dehr)*
Study	**Estudie** *(eh-'stoo-dee-eh)*	**Estudie el español.** *(eh-'stoo-dee-eh ehl eh-spah-'nyohl)*
Ask for	**Pida** *('pee-dah)*	**Pida la información.** *('pee-dah lah een-fohr-mah-see-'ohn)*
Explain	**Explique** *(ehks-'plee-keh)*	_____
Measure	**Mida** *('mee-dah)*	_____
Check	**Verifique** *(veh-ree-'fee-keh)*	_____

Let	**Deje** *('deh-heh)*	_____
Touch	**Toque** *('toh-keh)*	_____
Bend	**Doble** *('doh-bleh)*	_____
Cut	**Corte** *('kohr-teh)*	_____
Pass	**Pase** *('pah-seh)*	_____
Learn	**Aprenda** *(ah-'prehn-dah)*	_____
Repair	**Repare** *(reh-'pah-reh)*	_____
Arrive	**Llegue** *('yeh-geh)*	_____
Load	**Cargue** *('kahr-geh)*	_____
Unload	**Descargue** *(dehs-'kahr-geh)*	_____
Pile	**Amontone** *(ah-mohn-'toh-neh)*	_____
Spray	**Rocíe** *('roh-'see-eh)*	_____
Climb	**Suba** *('soo-bah)*	_____

¡Información!

• Most beginners in Spanish use the command words all the time. Try to keep things simple by using the words *this* **(esto)** *('eh-stoh)* and *that* **(eso)** *('eh-soh):*

Measure this.	**Mida esto.** *('mee-dah 'eh-stoh)*
Cut that.	**Corte eso.** *('kohr-teh 'eh-soh)*

• Generally speaking, the words **lo** *(loh)* or **la** *(lah)* refer to "it" in Spanish (**lo** for masculine, **la** for feminine). They can be very useful when they are added to your commands:

Bring **(Traiga)** *('trah·ee-gah)*
Bring it. **(Tráigala)** *('trah·ee-gah-lah)*
Do **(Haga)** *('ah-gah)*
Do it. **(Hágalo)** *('ah-gah-loh)*

Pick it up and put it in the trash!
¡Recójalo y métalo en la basura!
(reh-'koh-hah-loh ee 'meh-tah-loh ehn lah bah-'soo-rah)

• The word **le** *(leh)* refers to *him, her,* and *you.* Use it when you're working with an interpreter or when you're instructing your staff:

Tell him/her.   **Dígale** *('dee-gah-leh)*

Ask him/her.   **Pregúntele** *(preh-'goon-teh-leh)*

Explain to him/her.   **Explíquele** *(ehks-'plee-keh-leh)*

Create your own commands!
¡Cree sus propias órdenes!

Are you ready to create your own command words? A simple approach to forming a command in Spanish requires knowledge of the three different action word (verb) endings:

ar as in **hablar** *(ah-'blahr)*   (to speak)
er as in **comer** *(koh-'mehr)*   (to eat)
ir as in **escribir** *(eh-skree-'beer)*   (to write)

To make a command, drop the last two letters of the infinitive form, and replace them as follows:

AR   **E**
To speak **hablar** *(ah-'blahr)*   *Speak* **Hable** *('ah-bleh)*
ER   **A**
To eat **comer** *(koh-'mehr)*   *Eat* **Coma** *('koh-mah)*
IR   **A**
To write **escribir** *(eh-skree-'beer)*   *Write* **Escriba** *(eh-'skree-bah)*

Bear in mind that some forms are strange and have to be memorized:

To go **Ir** *(eer)*   *Go* **Vaya** *('vah-yah)*
To come **venir** *(veh-'neer)*   *Come* **Venga** *('vehn-gah)*
To tell **decir** *(deh-'seer)*   *Tell* **Diga** *('dee-gah)*

Your turn:

PASAR *(pah-'sahr)*   _____
APRENDER *(ah-prehn-'dehr)*   _____
CORTAR *(kohr-'tahr)*   _____

Chapter Six

The Problems
and the Solutions

Los problemas
y las soluciones

(lohs proh-'bleh-mahs ee lahs soh-loo-see-'oh-nehs)

What's your problem?
¿Cuál es su problema?
(kwahl ehs soo proh-'bleh-mah)

Maybe the toughest part of working in Human Resources is the unpleasant task of trouble-shooting. It's time to discuss issues such as resolving conflicts, counseling staff members, preventing crime, and treating medical emergencies. Let's open with a list of common concerns. Notice the helpful pattern:

Let's talk about (the)...	**Vamos a hablar de...**
	('vah-mohs ah ah-'blahr deh)
absences	**las ausencias** *(lahs ow-'sehn-see·ahs)*
alcohol	**el alcohol** *(ehl ahl-koh-'ohl)*
attitude	**la actitud** *(lah ahk-tee-'tood)*
conflict	**el conflicto** *(ehl kohn-'fleek-toh)*
crime	**el crimen** *(ehl 'kree-mehn)*
drugs	**las drogas** *(lahs 'droh-gahs)*
harassment	**el acosamiento**
	(ehl ah-koh-sah-mee-'ehn-toh)
illness	**la enfermedad** *(lah ehn-fehr-meh-'dahd)*
injury	**el trauma** *(ehl 'trah-oo-mah)*
tardiness	**las tardanzas** *(lahs tahr-'dahn-sahs)*

Create clusters of word groups for each concern:

There's a problem with (the)...	**Hay un problema con...**
	('ah-ee oon proh-'bleh-mah kohn)
lack of transportation	**la falta de transporte**
	(lah 'fahl-tah deh trahns-'pohr-teh)
language proficiency	**la competencia en el lenguaje**
	(lah kohm-peh-'tehn-see·ah ehn ehl lehn-'gwah-heh)
personality differences	**las diferencias de personalidad**
	(lahs dee-feh-'rehn-see·ahs deh pehr-soh-nah-lee-'dahd)
personal hygiene	**la higiene personal**
	(lah ee-hee-'eh-neh pehr-soh-'nahl)
style of clothing	**el estilo de ropa** *(ehl eh-'stee-loh deh 'roh-pah)*

What do you know about (the)...?	**¿Qué sabe usted de...?** *(keh 'sah-beh oo-'stehd deh)*
discrimination	**la discriminación** *(lah dee-skree-mee-nah-see-'ohn)*
insubordination	**la insubordinación** *(lah een-soob-ohr-dee-nah-see-'ohn)*
lack of cooperation	**la falta de cooperación** *(lah 'fahl-tah deh koo-oh-peh-rah-see-'ohn)*
misconduct	**la mala conducta** *(lah 'mah-lah kohn-'dook-tah)*
procrastination	**las dilaciones** *(lahs dee-lah-see-'oh-nehs)*
I have a question about (the)...	**Tengo una pregunta acerca de...** *('tehn-goh 'oo-nah preh-'goon-tah ah-'sehr-kah deh)*
assignment	**la tarea** *(lah tah-'reh-ah)*
paperwork	**el papeleo** *(ehl pah-peh-'leh-oh)*
skill	**la habilidad** *(lah ah-bee-lee-'dahd)*
It has to do with (the)...	**Tiene que ver con...** *(tee-'eh-neh keh vehr kohn)*
honesty	**la honradez** *(lah ohn-rah-'dehs)*
loyalty	**la lealtad** *(lah leh-ahl-'tahd)*
responsibility	**la responsabilidad** *(lah reh-spohn-sah-bee-lee-'dahd)*
trust	**la confianza** *(lah kohn-fee-'ahn-sah)*
I heard about (the)...	**Escuché de...** *(eh-skoo-'cheh deh)*
accident	**el accidente** *(ehl ahk-see-'dehn-teh)*
argument	**la discusión** *(lah dees-koo-see-'ohn)*
breakdown	**la falla** *(lah 'fah-yah)*
complaint	**la queja** *(lah 'keh-hah)*
confrontation	**la confrontación** *(lah kohn-frohn-tah-see-'ohn)*
disturbance	**el tumulto** *(ehl too-'mool-toh)*
fight	**la pelea** *(lah peh-'leh-ah)*
interruption	**la interrupción** *(lah een-teh-roop-see-'ohn)*
threat	**la amenaza** *(lah ah-meh-'nah-sah)*
violation	**la infracción** *(lah een-frahk-see-'ohn)*

You were...	**Usted fue...** *(oo-'stehd fweh)*
careless	**descuidado** *(dehs-kwee-'dah-doh)*
critical	**crítico** *('kree-tee-koh)*
cruel	**cruel** *(kroo-'ehl)*
dishonest	**deshonesto** *(dehs-oh-'neh-stoh)*
disrespectful	**irrespetuoso** *(ee-reh-speh-too-'oh-soh)*
incompetent	**incompetente** *(een-kohm-peh-'tehn-teh)*
negligent	**negligente** *(nehg-lee-'hehn-teh)*
rude	**grosero** *(groh-'seh-roh)*
sarcastic	**sarcástico** *(sahr-'kah-stee-koh)*

¡Información!

You'll hear these words all the time:

fault	**la culpa** *(lah 'kool-pah)*
guilt	**la culpabilidad** *(lah kool-pah-bee-lee-'dahd)*
shame	**la vergüenza** *(lah vehr-'gwehn-sah)*

Tell me everything!
¡Dígame todo! *('dee-gah-meh 'toh-doh)*

When there's trouble, make sure the employee speaks to the proper authorities. A number of people often should be informed. Do any of these words look familiar?

Tell (the)...	**Dígale a...** *('dee-gah-leh ah)*
administrator	**el administrador** *(ehl ahd-mee-nee-strah-'dohr)*
boss	**el jefe** *(ehl 'heh-feh)*
employer	**el empresario** *(ehl ehm-preh-'sah-ree·oh)*
executive	**el ejecutivo** *(ehl eh-heh-koo-'tee-voh)*
foreman	**el capataz** *(ehl kah-pah-'tahs)*
lead person	**el líder** *(ehl 'lee-dehr)*
manager	**el gerente** *(ehl heh-'rehn-teh)*
officer	**el oficial** *(ehl oh-'fee-see-'ahl)*
owner	**el dueño** *(ehl 'dweh-nyoh)*
secretary	**el secretario** *(ehl seh-kreh-'tah-ree·oh)*
supervisor	**el supervisor** *(ehl soo-pehr-vee-'sohr)*

Now, ask the right questions. Keep things simple, and use those structures that you feel comfortable with:

Are you OK?	¿Está bien?
	(eh-'stah 'bee-ehn)
Are you sick?	¿Está enfermo/a?
	(eh-'stah ehn-'fehr-moh/ah)
Are you injured?	¿Está lastimado/a?
	(eh-'stah lah-stee-'mah-doh/ah)
What's the trouble?	¿Cuál es el problema?
	(kwahl ehs ehl proh-'bleh-mah)
Do you need help?	¿Necesita ayuda?
	(neh-seh-'see-tah ah-'yoo-dah)
Do you wish to talk to me?	¿Desea hablarme?
	(deh-'seh-ah ah-'blahr-meh)
Can you tell me?	¿Puede decirme?
	('pweh-deh deh-'seer-meh)
Do you have information?	¿Tiene información?
	(tee-'eh-neh een-fohr-mah-see-'ohn)
Who is the person?	¿Quién es la persona?
	(kee-'ehn ehs lah pehr-'soh-nah)
How can I help you?	¿Cómo puedo ayudarle?
	('koh-moh 'pweh-doh ah-yoo-'dahr-leh)
What do you want to do?	¿Qué quiere hacer?
	(keh kee-'eh-reh ah-'sehr)
Do you know the procedure?	¿Sabe el procedimiento?
	('sah-beh ehl proh-seh-dee-mee-'ehn-toh)

Notice how these new verb forms below refer to *past actions*. We'll talk more about this verb tense later on in this chapter:

What happened?	¿Qué pasó? *(keh pah-'soh)*
Where did it happen?	¿Dónde pasó eso?
	('dohn-deh pah-'soh 'eh-soh)
Who saw what happened?	¿Quién vio lo que pasó?
	(kee-'ehn vee-'oh loh keh pah-'soh)
When did it happen?	¿Cuándo pasó eso?
	('kwahn-doh pah-'soh 'eh-soh)

How did it happen?	¿Cómo pasó eso?
	('koh-moh pah-'soh 'eh-soh)
Did you argue?	¿Discutió? *(dees-koo-tee-'oh)*
Did you refuse?	¿Se negó? *(seh neh-'goh)*
Did you disobey?	¿Desobedeció?
	(dehs-oh-beh-deh-see-'oh)
Did you steal?	¿Robó? *(roh-'boh)*
Did you break it?	¿Lo quebró usted?
	(loh keh-'broh oos-'tehd)
Did you lie?	¿Mintió? *(meen-tee-'oh)*
Did you lose it?	¿Lo perdió usted?
	(loh pehr-dee-'oh oos-'tehd)
Did you forget it?	¿Lo olvidó usted?
	(loh ohl-vee-'doh oos-tehd)

¡Información!

• Just in case, check over this set of questions related to attendance:

Are you going to miss work?	¿Va a faltar al trabajo?
	(vah ah fahl-'tahr ahl trah-'bah-hoh)
Are you going to be late?	¿Va a llegar tarde?
	(vah ah yeh-'gahr 'tahr-deh)
Did you call the office?	¿Llamó a la oficina?
	(yah-'moh ah lah oh-fee-'see-nah)
Do you have an excuse?	¿Tiene una excusa?
	(tee-'eh-neh 'oo-nah ehk-'skoo-sah)
What's the reason?	¿Cuál es la razón?
	(kwahl ehs lah rah-'sohn)

• And here's what you can say about their performance problems:

The work is...	El trabajo está...
	(ehl trah-bah-hoh eh-'stah)
missing	perdido *(pehr-'dee-doh)*
incomplete	incompleto *(een-kohm-'pleh-toh)*
late	con retraso *(kohn reh-'trah-soh)*

Listos para practicar

Name three Spanish words that refer to a boss:

_____   _____   _____

Connect the words that relate together:

ausencia *(ow-'sehn-see-ah)*	**pelea** *(peh-'leh-ah)*
enfermedad *(ehn-fehr-meh-'dahd)*	**honradez** *(ohn-rah-'dehs)*
conflicto *(kohn-'fleek-toh)*	**cruel** *(kroo-'ehl)*
confianza *(kohn-fee-'ahn-sah)*	**herido** *(eh-'ree-doh)*
grosero *(groh-'seh-roh)*	**tardanza** *(tahr-'dahn-sah)*

Translate into Spanish:

Did you lose it?   _____

Do you need help?   _____

What's the reason?   _____

How did it happen?   _____

Are you injured?   _____

Crime scene
La escena del crimen
(lah eh-'seh-nah dehl 'kree-mehn)

If a crime is committed, all sorts of terminology will be required. Here's a quick overview of some typical crime-related words and one-liners for the workplace:

You have been accused.	**Ha sido acusado.** *(ah 'see-doh ah-koo-'sah-doh)*
You are under arrest.	**Está arrestado.** *(eh-'stah ah-'rreh-stah-doh)*
We are going to search you.	**Le vamos a registrar.** *(leh 'vah-mohs ah reh-hee-'strahr)*
We have the proof.	**Tenemos la evidencia.** *(teh-'neh-mohs lah eh-vee-'dehn-see-ah)*
There will be an investigation.	**Habrá una investigación.** *(ah-'brah 'oo-nah een-veh-stee-gah-see-'ohn)*
I called the police.	**Llamé a la policía.** *(yah-'meh ah lah poh-lee-'see-ah)*

It's (the)...	**Es...** *(ehs)*
abuse	**el abuso** *(ehl ah-'boo-soh)*
assault	**el asalto** *(ehl ah-'sahl-toh)*
battery	**la agresión** *(lah ah-greh-see-'ohn)*
drug	**la droga** *(lah 'droh-gah)*
embezzling	**el desfalco** *(ehl dehs-'fahl-koh)*
fraud	**el fraude** *(ehl 'frow-deh)*
gambling	**el juego de apuestas** *(ehl hoo-'eh-goh deh ah-'pweh-stahs)*
graffiti	**el grafiti** *(ehl grah-'fee-tee)*
hijacking	**el robo en tránsito** *(ehl 'roh-boh ehn 'trahn-see-toh)*
libel	**la difamación** *(lah dee-fah-mah-see-'ohn)*
murder	**el asesinato** *(ehl ah-seh-see-'nah-toh)*
smuggling	**el contrabando** *(ehl kohn-trah-'bahn-doh)*
stabbing	**la puñalada** *(lah poo-nyah-'lah-dah)*
stealing	**el robo** *(ehl 'roh-boh)*
trespassing	**la intrusión** *(lah een-troo-see-'ohn)*
vandalism	**el vandalismo** *(ehl vahn-dah-'lees-moh)*
Who's the...?	**¿Quién es...?** *(kee-'ehn ehs)*
drug dealer	**el vendedor de drogas** *(ehl vehn-deh-'dohr deh 'droh-gahs)*
gang member	**el pandillero** *(ehyl pahn-dee-'yeh-roh)*
loiterer	**el holgazán** *(ehl ohl-gah-'sahn)*
pickpocket	**el carterista** *(ehl kahr-teh-'ree-stah)*
suspect	**el sospechoso** *(ehl soh-speh-'choh-soh)*
thief	**el ladrón** *(ehl lah-'drohn)*
troublemaker	**el perturbador** *(ehl pehr-toor-bah-'dohr)*
victim	**el víctima** *(ehl 'veek-tee-mah)*
witness	**el testigo** *(ehl teh-'stee-goh)*
He has (the)...	**Tiene...** *(tee-'eh-neh)*
bail	**la fianza** *(lah fee-'ahn-sah)*
felony	**el delito mayor** *(ehl deh-'lee-toh mah-'yohr)*
firearm	**el arma de fuego** *(ehl 'ahr-mah deh 'fweh-goh)*
lawsuit	**el pleito** *(ehl 'pleh-ee-toh)*

probation	la libertad provisional
	(lah lee-behr-'tahd proh-vee-see·oh-'nahl)
subpoena	la citación *(lah see-tah-see-'ohn)*
warrant	la orden de la corte
	(lah 'ohr-dehn deh lah 'kohr-teh)
Where's (the)...?	¿Dónde está...? *('dohn-deh eh-'stah)*
jail	la cárcel *(lah 'kahr-sehl)*
law	la ley *(lah 'leh·ee)*
raid	la redada *(lah reh-'dah-dah)*
riot	el tumulto *(ehl too-'mool-toh)*
surveillance	la vigilancia *(lah vee-hee-'lahn-see·ah)*

¡Información!

Ask around for the names of common drugs or alcoholic beverages. You may need to confront someone soon!

There is/are...	Hay... *('ah·ee...)*
alcohol	alcohol *(ahl-koh-'ohl)*
beer	cerveza *(sehr-'veh-sah)*
crack	crac *(crack)*
heroin	heroína *(eh-roh-'ee-nah)*
liquor	licor *(lee-'kohr)*
marijuana	marijuana *(mah-ree-'wah-nah)*
morphine	morfina *(mohr-'fee-nah)*
narcotics	narcóticos *(nahr-'koh-tee-kohs)*
pills	píldoras *('peel-doh-rahs)*
speed	metanfetamina *(meh-tahn-feh-tah-'mee-nah)*
wine	vino *('vee-noh)*

It's very serious!
¡Es muy serio! *(ehs 'moo·ee 'seh-ree·oh)*

Sometimes common concerns become major problems, which often result in serious consequences. In those special cases, get ready for the following statements:

You are fired.	**Está despedido.** *(eh-'stah deh-speh-'dee-doh)*
This is a warning.	**Esta es una advertencia.**
	('eh-stah ehs 'oo-nah ahd-vehr-'tehn-see·ah)
This is going in your file.	**Esto va en su archivo personal.**
	('eh-stoh vah ehn soo ahr-'chee-voh pehr-soh-'nahl)
We are going to make some changes.	**Vamos a hacer algunos cambios.**
	('vah-mohs ah ah-'sehr 'oo-nohs 'kahm-bee·ohs)
Let's talk in my office.	**Vamos a hablar en mi oficina.**
	('vah-mohs ah ah-'blahr ehn mee oh-fee-'see-nah)
This is the last time.	**Esta es la última vez.**
	('eh-stah ehs lah 'ool-tee-mah vehs)
I'm calling security.	**Estoy llamando a los guardias.**
	(eh-'stoh-ee yah-'mahn-doh ah lohs 'gwahr-dee-ahs)

Continue to discuss the situation in detail:

If it happens again,	**Si pasa de nuevo,**
	(see 'pah-sah deh noo-'eh-voh)
you will get a reprimand	**recibirá una represión**
	(reh-see-bee-'rah 'oo-nah reh-prehn-see-'ohn)
you will be dismissed	**será despedido**
	(seh-'rah deh-speh-'dee-doh)
you will be transferred	**será transferido**
	(seh-'rah trahns-feh-'ree-doh)
you will be suspended	**será suspendido**
	(seh-'rah soo-spehn-'dee-doh)
you will be demoted	**será rebajado de rango**
	(seh-'rah reh-bah-'hah-doh deh 'rahn-goh)
you will have to resign	**tendrá que renunciar**
	(tehn-drah keh reh-noon-see-'ahr)

I think you should...	**Creo que debe...**
	('kreh-oh keh 'deh-beh)
get professional help	**buscar ayuda profesional**
	(boo-'skahr ah-'yoo-dah proh-fee-see·oh-'nahl)
call your lawyer	**llamar a su abogado**
	(yah-'mahr ah soo ah-boh-'gah-doh)
stay home until I call you	**quedarse en casa hasta que le llame**
	(keh-'dahr-seh ehn 'kah-sah 'ah-stah keh leh 'yah-meh)

¡Información!

• Maybe there's a problem at your office that hasn't been mentioned yet:

I'm hearing complaints about (the)...
Estoy escuchando quejas acerca de...
(eh-'stoh-ee eh-skoo-'chan-doh 'keh-hahs ah-'sehr-kah deh)

sexual harassment	**el acosamiento sexual**
	(ehl ah-koh-sah-mee-'ehn-toh sehk-soo-'ahl)
physical abuse	**el abuso físico** *(ehl ah-'boo-soh 'fee-see-koh)*
racial conflict	**el conflicto racial**
	(ehl kohn-'fleek-toh rah-see-'ahl)
violent behavior	**el comportamiento violento**
	(ehl kohm-pohr-tah-mee-'ehn-toh vee-oh-'lehn-toh)
poor attitude	**la actitud negativa**
	(lah ahk-tee-'tood neh-gah-'tee-vah)
foul language	**el lenguaje sucio**
	(ehl lehn-'gwah-heh 'soo-see·oh)

• Here are a few things every manager needs to say:

Every person answers to only one supervisor.
Cada persona responde a sólo un supervisor.
('kah-dah pehr-'soh-nah reh-'spohn-deh ah oon soo-pehr-vee-'sohr)

Talk to me if you have a problem.

Hable conmigo si tiene un problema.

('ah-blah kohn-'mee-goh see tee-'eh-neh oon proh-'bleh-mah)

Everything is confidential.

Todo es confidencial. *('toh-doh ehs kohn-fee-dehn-see-'ahl)*

Listos para practicar

Finish these sentences using the words provided:

las píldoras, despedido, el sospechoso, debe, la cárcel, el robo

(lahs 'peel-doh-rahs, deh-speh-'dee-doh, ehl soh-speh-'choh-soh, 'deh-beh, lah 'kahr-sehl, ehl 'roh-boh)

_____ **es un crimen.** *(___ ehs oon 'kree-mehn)*

_____ **está arrestado.** *(___eh-'stah ah-rreh-'stah-doh)*

_____ **llamar a su abogado.** *(___ yah-'mahr ah soo ah-boh-'gah-doh)*

Está tomando _____. *(eh-'stah toh-'mahn-doh ____)*

El criminal está en _____.

(ehl kree-mee-'nahl eh-'stah ehn ____)

Usted está _____. *(oo-'stehd eh-'stah ____)*

Translate these very serious concerns:

sexual harassment _____

physical abuse _____

racial conflict _____

Temas culturales

Most of Latin America is Roman Catholic, so you may notice the religious influence during your association with some Hispanics during a crisis. Using the word *God*, **Dios** *('dee-ohs)* in conversation, attending daily mass, **la misa** *(lah 'mee-sah),* or observing Catholic traditions are simple signs of their faith. Remember that respect and sensitivity are always in demand when topics center around cultural and religious beliefs.

The consultation

La consulta *(lah kohn-'sool-tah)*

When things get out of hand, it's best to meet in private. Once you get the employee alone, try to find out what the real problem is. You'll probably end up asking for an interpreter, but there's still a lot you can say without any help. These next words delve into the heart of the matter.

How do you feel?	**¿Cómo se siente?** *('koh-moh seh see-'ehn-teh)*
It seems you are...	**Parece que está...** *(pah-'reh-seh keh eh-'stah)*
afraid	**asustado** *(ah-soo-'stah-doh)*
angry	**enojado** *(eh-noh-'hah-doh)*
apathetic	**apático** *(ah-'pah-'tee-koh)*
bitter	**amargo** *(ah-'mahr-goh)*
distracted	**distraído** *(dee-strah-'ee-doh)*
frustrated	**frustrado** *(froo-'strah-doh)*
hostile	**hostil** *(oh-'steel)*
in mourning	**de luto** *(deh 'loo-toh)*
nervous	**nervioso** *(nehr-vee-'oh-soh)*
sad	**triste** *('tree-steh)*
tense	**tenso** *('tehn-soh)*

Don't stop talking about how the person feels. One method is to hold up a list of "feelings" in Spanish, and then ask the employee to point to the word that best describes his or her emotions:

Do you feel...?	**¿Se siente...?** *(seh see-'ehn-teh)*
I feel...	**Me siento...** *(meh see-'ehn-toh)*
abused	**abusado** *(ah-boo-'sah-doh)*
bored	**aburrido** *(ah-boo-'rree-doh)*
bothered	**molesto** *(moh-'leh-stoh)*
burned out	**agotado** *(ah-goh-'tah-doh)*
confused	**confundido** *(kohn-foon-'dee-doh)*
desperate	**desesperado** *(dehs-eh-speh-'rah-doh)*
embarrassed	**turbado** *(toor-'bah-doh)*
fed up	**harto** *('ahr-toh)*
furious	**furioso** *(foo-ree-'oh-soh)*
guilty	**culpable** *(kool-'pah-bleh)*

hated	**odiado** *(oh-dee-'ah-doh)*
impatient	**impaciente** *(eem-pah-see-'ehn-teh)*
inferior	**inferior** *(een-feh-ree-'ohr)*
jealous	**celoso** *(seh-'loh-soh)*
overloaded	**sobrecargado** *(soh-breh-kahr-'gah-doh)*
resentful	**resentido** *(reh-sehn-'tee-doh)*
restless	**inquieto** *(een-kee-'eh-toh)*
trapped	**atrapado** *(ah-trah-'pah-doh)*
uncomfortable	**incómodo** *(een-'koh-moh-doh)*
unhappy	**descontento** *(dehs-kohn-'tehn-toh)*
worried	**preocupado** *(preh-oh-koo-'pah-doh)*

A little advice

Un pequeño consejo *(oon peh-'keh-nyoh koh-'seh-hoh)*

If there is need for further counsel or guidance, offer whatever advice you can, and tell them that they may have to get help elsewhere:

You should...	**Debe...** *('deh-beh)*
call your doctor	**llamar a su doctor**
	(yah-'mahr ah soo dohk-'tohr)
calm down	**calmarse** *(kahl-'mahr-seh)*
exercise	**hacer ejercicio** *(ah-'sehr eh-hehr-'see-see·oh)*
get more sleep	**dormir más** *(dohr-'meer mahs)*
manage your stress	**controlar su estrés**
	(kohn-troh-'lahr soo eh-'strehs)
relax	**relajarse** *(reh-lah-'hahr-seh)*
rest	**descansar** *(deh-skahn-'sahr)*
see a psychiatrist	**ver a un psiquiatra**
	(vehr ah oon see-kee-'ah-trah)
take medication	**tomar medicamentos**
	(toh-'mahr meh-dee-kah-'mehn-tohs)
You shouldn't...	**No debe...** *(noh 'deh-beh)*
Please do not...	**Favor de no...** *(fah-'vohr deh noh)*
Do you like to...?	**¿Le gusta...?** *(leh 'goo-stah)*
antagonize	**antagonizar** *(ahn-tah-goh-nee-'sahr)*
argue	**discutir** *(dees-koo-'teer)*

bother	**molestar** *(moh-leh-'stahr)*
curse	**maldecir** *(mahl-deh-'seer)*
gossip	**chismear** *(chees-meh-'ahr)*
humiliate	**humillar** *(oo-mee-'yahr)*
joke	**bromear** *(broh-meh-'ahr)*
tease	**burlarse** *(boor-'lahr-seh)*
yell	**gritar** *(gree-'tahr)*

¡Información!

• Learn to share about more sensitive issues:

Would you like to talk about (the)...?

¿Quisiera hablar sobre...?

(kee-see-'eh-rah ah-'blahr 'soh-breh)

death	**la muerte** *(lah 'mwehr-teh)*
depression	**la depresión** *(lah deh-preh-see-'ohn)*
divorce	**el divorcio** *(ehl dee-'vohr-see-oh)*
incest	**el incesto** *(ehl een-'seh-stoh)*
rape	**la violación** *(lah vee-oh-lah-see-'ohn)*
trauma	**el trauma** *(ehl 'trah-oo-mah)*
You can take (the)...	**Puede tomar...** *('pweh-deh toh-'mahr)*
breath test	**la prueba de aliento** *(lah proo-'eh-bah deh ah-lee-'ehn-toh)*
personality test	**la prueba de personalidad** *(lah proo-'eh-bah deh pehr-soh-nah-lee-'dahd)*
polygraph	**el detector de mentiras** *(ehl deh-tehk-'tohr deh mehn-'tee-rahs)*

• Add these key words to your counseling comments:

There's no...	**No hay...** *(noh 'ah-ee)*
danger	**peligro** *(peh-'lee-groh)*
harm	**daño** *('dah-nyoh)*
obstacle	**obstáculo** *(ohb-'stah-koo-loh)*
pain	**dolor** *(doh-'lohr)*
risk	**riesgo** *(ree-'ehs-goh)*

It's (the)...	**Es...** *(ehs)*
belief	**la creencia** *(lah kreh-'ehn-see-ah)*
dream	**el sueño** *(ehl 'sweh-nyoh)*
feeling	**el sentimiento** *(ehl sehn-tee-mee-'ehn-toh)*
personality	**la personalidad** *(lah pehr-soh-nah-lee-'dahd)*
thought	**el pensamiento** *(ehl pehn-sah-mee-'ehn-toh)*

• Some work-related conditions affect everyone:

downsize	**la reducción de empleados**
	(lah reh-dook-see-'ohn deh ehm-pleh-'ah-dohs)
turnover	**la rotación de personal**
	(lah roh-tah-see-'ohn deh pehr-soh-'nahl)
shortage	**la escasez de personal**
	(lah eh-skah-'sehs deh pehr-soh-'nahl)

Listos para practicar

Join the words that have similar meanings:

aviso *(ah-'vee-soh)*	**relajarse** *(reh-lah-'hahr-seh)*
obstáculo *(ohb-'stah-koo-loh)*	**hostil** *(oh-'steel)*
furioso *(foo-ree-'oh-soh)*	**inquieto** *(een-kee-'eh-toh)*
burlarse *(boor-'lahr-seh)*	**psiquiatra** *(see-kee-'ah-trah)*
nervioso *(nehr-vee-'oh-soh)*	**molestar** *(moh-leh-'stahr)*
doctor *(dohk-'tohr)*	**riesgo** *(ree-'ehs-goh)*
calmarse *(kahl-'mahr-seh)*	**consulta** *(kohn-'sool-tah)*

Medical problems
Los problemas médicos
(lohs proh-'bleh-mahs 'meh-dee-kohs)

Physical pain may also surface as a topic of concern. Whether work-related or otherwise, injuries and illnesses must be addressed. Study these terms that relate to typical medical problems and try them out with a Spanish speaker:

He/She has (the)...	Tiene... *(tee-'eh-neh)*
allergy	**la alergia** *(lah ah-'lehr-hee-ah)*
blister	**la ampolla** *(lah ahm-'poh-yah)*
bruise	**la contusión** *(lah kohn-too-see-'ohn)*
chicken pox	**la varicela** *(lah vah-ree-'seh-lah)*
chill	**el escalofrío** *(ehl eh-skah-loh-'free-oh)*
cold	**el resfriado** *(ehl rehs-free-'ah-doh)*
constipation	**el estreñimiento** *(ehl eh-streh-nyee-mee-'ehn-toh)*
cough	**la tos** *(lah tohs)*
cut	**la cortadura** *(lah kohr-tah-'doo-rah)*
diarrhea	**la diarrea** *(lah dee-ah-'rreh-ah)*
fever	**la fiebre** *(lah fee-'eh-breh)*
flatulence	**la flatulencia** *(lah 'flah-too-'lehn-see-ah)*
flu	**el resfriado** *(ehl rehs-free-'ah-doh)*
gas	**el gas** *(ehl gahs)*
measles	**el sarampión** *(ehl sah-rahm-pee-'ohn)*
mumps	**las paperas** *(lahs pah-'peh-rahs)*
nausea	**la náusea** *(lah 'now-seh-ah)*
pain	**el dolor** *(ehl doh-'lohr)*
phlegm	**la flema** *(lah 'fleh-mah)*
rash	**la erupción** *(lah eh-roop-see-'ohn)*
scratch	**el rasguño** *(ehl rahs-'goo-nyoh)*
sneeze	**el estornudo** *(ehl eh-stohr-'noo-doh)*
sprain	**la torcedura** *(lah tohr-seh-'doo-rah)*
temperature	**la temperatura** *(lah tehm-peh-rah-'too-rah)*
toothache	**el dolor de muelas** *(ehl doh-'lohr deh 'mweh-lahs)*

Body parts
Las partes del cuerpo
(lahs 'pahr-tehs dehl 'kwehr-poh)

You can't talk about health care concerns until you learn the body parts in Spanish. Get everyone in the HR department to help you practice these:

What happened to his/her _____?	¿Qué pasó con _____? *(keh pah-'soh kohn ___)*
My _____ hurts.	**Me duele** _____. *(meh 'dweh-leh ___)*
ankle	**el tobillo** *(ehl toh-'bee-yoh)*
arm	**el brazo** *(ehl 'brah-soh)*
back	**la espalda** *(lah eh-'spahl-dah)*
chest	**el pecho** *(ehl 'peh-choh)*
elbow	**el codo** *(ehl 'koh-doh)*
finger	**el dedo** *(ehl 'deh-doh)*
foot	**el pie** *(ehl 'pee-eh)*
hand	**la mano** *(lah 'mah-noh)*
head	**la cabeza** *(lah kah-'beh-sah)*
hip	**la cadera** *(lah kah-'deh-rah)*
knee	**la rodilla** *(lah roh-'dee-yah)*
neck	**el cuello** *(ehl 'kweh-yoh)*
shoulder	**el hombro** *(ehl 'ohm-broh)*
stomach	**el estómago** *(ehl eh-'stoh-mah-goh)*
thigh	**el muslo** *(ehl 'moos-loh)*
throat	**la garganta** *(lah gahr-'gahn-tah)*
wrist	**la muñeca** *(lah moo-'nyeh-kah)*

Now review these phrases that refer to more physical ailments:

headache	**el dolor de cabeza** *(ehl doh-'lohr deh kah-'beh-sah)*
stomachache	**el dolor de estómago** *(ehl doh-'lohr deh eh-'stoh-mah-goh)*
sore throat	**el dolor de garganta** *(ehl doh-'lohr deh gahr-'gahn-tah)*

And what about this group of important features:

I hurt my _____.	**Me hice daño en** _____. *(meh 'ee-seh 'dah-nyoh ehn ___)*
cheek	**la mejilla** *(lah meh-'hee-yah)*
chin	**la barbilla** *(lah bahr-'bee-yah)*
ear	**el oído** *(ehl oh-'ee-doh)*
eye	**el ojo** *(ehl 'oh-hoh)*
face	**la cara** *(lah 'kah-rah)*

jaw	**la mandíbula** *(lah mahn-'dee-boo-lah)*
mouth	**la boca** *(lah 'boh-kah)*
nose	**la nariz** *(lah nah-'rees)*
tongue	**la lengua** *(lah 'lehn-gwah)*

Add these phrases to some of the words above:

It's...	**Está...** *(eh-'stah)*
broken	**roto** *('roh-toh)*
burned	**quemado** *(keh-'mah-doh)*
infected	**infectado** *(een-fehk-'tah-doh)*
swollen	**hinchado** *(een-'chah-doh)*
twisted	**torcido** *(tohr-'see-doh)*

I feel _____ .	**Me siento _____ .** *(meh see-'ehn-toh ___)*
dizzy	**mareado** *(mah-reh-'ah-doh)*
exhausted	**agotado** *(ah-goh-tah-doh)*
faint	**debilitado** *(deh-bee-lee-'tah-doh)*
poorly	**mal** *(mahl)*
sick	**enfermo** *(ehn-'fehr-moh)*
sleepy	**soñoliento** *(soh-nyoh-lee-'ehn-toh)*
sore	**dolorido** *(doh-loh-'ree-doh)*
tired	**cansado** *(kahn-'sah-doh)*

Listos para practicar

Name three facial features in Spanish:

_____ _____ _____

Name three major parts of the body:

_____ _____ _____

Name three common ailments or illnesses:

_____ _____ _____

Circle the word that doesn't belong:
torcido, hinchado, helado *(tohr-'see-doh, een-'chah-doh, eh-'lah-doh)*
enfermo, camión, mal, *(ehn-'fehr-moh, kah-mee-'ohn, mahl)*
erupción, cortina, rasguño
(eh-rroop-see-'ohn, kohr-'tee-nah, rahs-'goo-nyoh)

In case of emergency!
¡En caso de emergencia!
(ehn 'kah-soh deh eh-mehr-'hehn-see·ah)

In those rare cases when a worker needs professional medical attention, it will become necessary to discuss more serious maladies. To be on the safe side, get acquainted with these expressions:

He/She is bleeding.	**Está sangrando.** *(eh-'stah sahn-'grahn-doh)*
He/She is vomiting.	**Está vomitando.** *(eh-'stah voh-mee-'tahn-doh)*
He/She is unconscious.	**Está inconsciente.**
	(eh-'stah een-kohn-see-'ehn-teh)

I heard about (the)...	**Escuché de...** *(eh-skoo-'cheh deh)*
accident	**el accidente** *(ehl ahk-see-'dehn-teh)*
bad fall	**la mala caída** *(lah 'mah-lah kah-'ee-dah)*
burn	**la quemadura** *(lah keh-mah-'doo-rah)*
choking	**la asfixia** *(lah ahs-'feek-see·ah)*
convulsion	**la convulsión** *(lah kohn-vool-see-'ohn)*
drowning	**el ahogamiento**
	(ehl ah-oh-gah-mee-'ehn-toh)
fatigue	**la fatiga** *(lah fah-'tee-gah)*
overdose	**la sobredosis** *(lah soh-breh-'doh-sees)*
seizure	**el ataque** *(ehl ah-'tah-keh)*
sunstroke	**la insolación** *(lah een-soh-lah-see-'ohn)*
electrocution	**la electrocución**
	(lah eh-lehk-troh-koo-see-'ohn)

You never know what can happen, so keep on pronouncing everything you read!

She's suffering from...	**Sufre de...** *('soo-freh deh)*
dehydration	**la deshidratación**
	(lah dehs-hee-drah-tah-see-'ohn)
shock	**la postración nerviosa**
	(lah poh-strah-see-'ohn nehr-vee-'oh-sah)
frostbite	**el congelamiento**
	(ehl kohn-heh-lah-mee-'ehn-toh)
poisoning	**el envenenamiento**
	(ehl ehn-veh-neh-nah-mee-'ehn-toh)

dog bite	**la mordedura de perro** *(lah mohr-deh-'doo-rah deh 'peh-rroh)*
contagious disease	**la enfermedad contagiosa** *(lah ehn-fehr-meh-'dahd kohn-tah-hee-'oh-sah)*
snake bite	**la mordedura de culebra** *(lah mohr-deh-'doo-rah deh koo-'leh-brah)*
insect bite	**la mordedura de insecto** *(lah mohr-deh-'doo-rah deh een-'sehk-toh)*

☞ ¡Información!

• And all major illnesses should be reviewed often:

AIDS	**SIDA** *('see-dah)*
cancer	**cáncer** *('kahn-sehr)*
heart disease	**enfermedad del corazón** *(ehn-fehr-meh-'dahd dehl koh-rah-'sohn)*

• Why not memorize this key expression? Don't be fooled by its appearance:

She's pregnant!	**¡Está embarazada!** *(eh-'stah ehm-bah-rah-'sah-dah)*

Be careful!
¡Tenga cuidado! *('tehn-gah kwee-'dah-doh)*

Have you reviewed these potentially dangerous items with every employee? If not, do so immediately!

Be careful with (the)...!	¡Tenga cuidado con...! *('tehn-gah kwee-'dah-doh kohn)*
bleach	**el cloro** *(ehl 'kloh-roh)*
chemicals	**los productos químicos** *(lohs proh-'dook-tohs 'kee-mee-kohs)*
detergent	**el detergente** *(ehl deh-tehr-'hehn-teh)*
dye	**el tinte** *(ehl 'teen-teh)*
electricity	**la electricidad** *(lah eh-lehk-tree-see-'dahd)*
exhaust	**el escape** *(ehl eh-'skah-peh)*

fire	**el fuego** *(ehl 'fweh-goh)*
flames	**las llamas** *(lahs 'yah-mahs)*
fumes	**el vapor** *(ehl vah-'pohr)*
gas	**el gas** *(ehl gahs)*
grease	**la grasa** *(lah 'grah-sah)*
hot water	**el agua caliente** *(ehl 'ah-gwah kah-lee-'ehn-teh)*
insecticide	**el insecticida** *(ehl een-sehk-tee-'see-dah)*
paint	**la pintura** *(lah peen-'too-rah)*
pesticide	**la pesticida** *(lah peh-stee-'see-dah)*
oil	**el aceite** *(ehl ah-'seh·ee-teh)*
scraps	**las sobras** *(lahs 'soh-brahs)*
sewage	**las aguas cloacales** *(lahs 'ah-gwahs kloh-ah-'kah-lehs)*
smoke	**el humo** *(ehl 'oo-moh)*
toxic materials	**los materiales tóxicos** *(lohs mah-teh-ree-'ah-lehs 'tohk-see-kohs)*
trash	**la basura** *(lah bah-'soo-rah)*
waste	**los desperdicios** *(lohs dehs-pehr-'dee-see·ohs)*
Call (the) ...	**Llame a ...** *('yah-meh ah)*
911	**el nueve-uno-uno** *(ehl noo-'eh-veh 'oo-noh 'oo-noh)*
ambulance	**la ambulancia** *(lah ahm-boo-'lahn-see·ah)*
clinic	**la clínica** *(lah 'klee-nee-kah)*
dentist	**el dentista** *(ehl dehn-'tee-stah)*
doctor	**el doctor** *(ehl dohk-'tohr)*
fire department	**el departamento de bomberos** *(ehl deh-pahr-tah-'mehn-toh deh bohm-'beh-rohs)*
home	**la casa** *(lah 'kah-sah)*
hospital	**el hospital** *(ehl oh-spee-'tahl)*
neighbor	**el vecino** *(ehl veh-'see-noh)*
office	**la oficina** *(lah oh-fee-'see-nah)*
operator	**la operadora** *(lah oh-peh-rah-'doh-rah)*
paramedic	**el paramédico** *(ehl pah-rah-'meh-dee-koh)*

pharmacy	**la farmacia** *(lah fahr-'mah-see·ah)*
police	**la policía** *(lah poh-lee-'see-ah)*
relative	**el pariente** *(ehl pah-ree-'ehn-teh)*
tow truck	**la grúa** *(lah 'groo-ah)*

¡Información!

• The doctor, nurse, or on-site medical expert may advise the following:

He/She needs (the)...	**Necesita...** *(neh-seh-'see-tah)*
aspirin	**la aspirina** *(lah ah-spee-'ree-nah)*
Band-Aid®	**la curita** *(lah koo-'ree-tah)*
bandage	**el vendaje** *(ehl vehn-'dah-heh)*
cane	**el bastón** *(ehl bah-'stohn)*
capsules	**las cápsulas** *(lahs 'kahp-soo-lahs)*
cast	**la armadura de yeso** *(lah ahr-mah-'doo-rah deh-'yeh-soh)*
cough syrup	**el jarabe para la tos** *(ehl hah-'rah-beh 'pah-rah lah tohs)*
CPR	**la respiración artificial** *(lah reh-spee-rah-see-'ohn ahr-tee-fee-see-'ahl)*
cream	**la crema** *(lah 'kreh-mah)*
crutches	**las muletas** *(lahs moo-'leh-tahs)*
disinfectant	**el desinfectante** *(ehl dehs-een fehk-'tahn-teh)*
drops	**las gotas** *(lahs 'goh-tahs)*
iodine	**el yodo** *(ehl 'yoh-doh)*
liniment	**el linimento** *(ehl lee-nee-'mehn-toh)*
lotion	**la loción** *(lah loh-see-'ohn)*
lozenges	**las pastillas** *(lahs pah-'stee-yahs)*
medicine	**la medicina** *(lah meh-deh-'see-nah)*
penicillin	**la penicilina** *(lah peh-nee-see-'lee-nah)*
pills	**las píldoras** *(lahs 'peel-doh-rahs)*
powder	**el talco** *(ehl 'tahl-koh)*
prescription	**la receta** *(lah reh-'seh-tah)*

a shot	**la inyección** *(lah een-yehk-see-'ohn)*
stitches	**las puntadas** *(lahs poon-'tah-dahs)*
tablets	**las tabletas** *(lahs tah-'bleh-tahs)*
thermometer	**el termómetro** *(ehl tehr-'moh-meh-troh)*
vaseline	**la vaselina** *(lah vah-seh-'lee-nah)*
vitamins	**las vitaminas** *(lahs vee-tah-'mee-nahs)*
wheelchair	**la silla de ruedas** *(lah 'see-yah deh roo-'eh-dahs)*
X-rays	**los rayos equis** *(lohs 'rah-yohs 'eh-kees)*

• Some Spanish words are easier to remember than others:

It's...	**Es...** *(ehs)*
combustible	**combustible** *(kohm-boo-'stee-bleh)*
explosive	**explosivo** *(ehks-ploh-'see-voh)*
flammable	**inflamable** *(een-flah-'mah-bleh)*

• And always mention this concern:

We care about the environment!
¡Nos preocupamos del ambiente!
(nohs preh-oh-koo-'pah-mohs dehl ahm-bee-'ehn-teh)

 ## Listos para practicar

Name three places to call when there's an emergency:

_____ _____ _____

Name three warehouse items that are very flammable:

_____ _____ _____

Name three items found in most first aid kits:

_____ _____ _____

Connect the related vocabulary words:

deshidratación	**basura**
(dehs-hee-drah-tah-see-'ohn)	*(bah-'soo-rah)*
asfixia	**pariente**
(ahs-'feek-see·ah)	*(pah-ree-'ehn-teh)*
linimento	**ahogamiento**
(lee-nee-'mehn-toh)	*(ah-oh-gah-mee-'ehn-toh)*
cápsula	**postración**
('kahp-soo-lah)	*(poh-strah-see-'ohn)*
familia	**loción**
(fah-'mee-lee·ah)	*(loh-see-'ohn)*
desperdicios	**ambulancia**
(dehs-pehr-'dee-see·ohs)	*(ahm-boo-'lahn-see·ah)*
diente	**hueso**
(dee-'ehn-teh)	*('weh-soh)*
hospital	**llamas**
(oh-spee-'tahl)	*('yah-mahs)*
fuego	**tableta**
('fweh-goh)	*(tah-'bleh-tah)*

 ## Temas culturales

Throughout history, we have discovered that certain herbs and spices work wonders on common ailments. In Latin America, the practice of home remedies—**los remedios caseros** *(lohs reh-'meh-dee-ohs kah-'seh-rohs)*—is quite popular, so don't be surprised if your Hispanic employee offers to prepare something when a fellow worker gets sick or injured.

Natural disasters
Los desastres naturales
(lohs deh-'sah-strehs nah-too-'rah-lehs)

Not every problem is under your control. Natural disasters occur, and you may need to take precautions. As you train new staff members, clearly outline the steps to be taken if trouble strikes. Are you prepared to handle the following?

The ___ is coming.	___ viene. *(vee-'eh-neh)*
flood	**la inundación** *(lah een-oon-dah-see-'ohn)*
hurricane	**el huracán** *(ehl oo-rah-'kahn)*
ice	**el hielo** *(ehl 'yeh-loh)*
rain	**la lluvia** *(lah 'yoo-vee-ah)*
snow	**la nieve** *(lah nee-'eh-veh)*
storm	**la tormenta** *(lah tohr-'mehn-tah)*
tornado	**el tornado** *(ehl tohr-'nah-doh)*

Now post labels in both languages on each piece of emergency equipment in your building. Check out the examples:

Use (the)...	**Use...** *('oo-seh)*
binoculars	**los binoculares** *(lohs bee-nohk-koo-'lah-rehs)*
candle	**la vela** *(lah 'veh-lah)*
cone	**el cono** *(ehl 'koh-noh)*
fire extinguisher	**el extintor** *(ehl ehks-teen-'tohr)*
first aid kit	**el botiquín de primeros auxilios** *(ehl boh-tee-'keen deh pree-'meh-rohs owk-'see-lee-ohs)*
flare	**la luz de bengala** *(lah loos deh behn-'gah-lah)*
flashlight	**la linterna** *(lah leen-'tehr-nah)*
hydrant	**la llave de agua** *(lah 'yah-veh deh 'ah-gwah)*
matches	**los fósforos** *(lohs 'fohs-foh-rohs)*

Call security!
¡Llame a los guardias!
('yah-meh ah lohs 'gwar-dee-ahs)

Let the security officers discuss these important items with the Spanish speaking employees:

emergency exit	**la salida de emergencia** *(lah sah-'lee-dah deh eh-mehr-'hehn-see-ah)*

evacuation procedure	**el plan de evacuación** *(ehl plahn deh eh-vah-koo-ah-see-'ohn)*
preventive maintenance	**el mantenimiento preventivo** *(ehl mahn-teh-nee-mee-'ehn-toh preh-vehn-'tee-voh)*
rescue team	**el equipo de rescate** *(ehl eh-'kee-poh deh reh-'skah-teh)*
room capacity	**la capacidad del salón** *(lah kah-pah-see-'dahd dehl sah-'lohn)*
safety manual	**el manual de seguridad** *(ehl mah-noo-'ahl deh seh-goo-ree-'dahd)*
security measure	**la medida de seguridad** *(lah meh-'dee-dah deh seh-goo-ree-'dahd)*

In extreme circumstances, use these command phrases:

Cover yourself!	**¡Cúbrase!** *('koo-brah-seh)*
Danger!	**¡Peligro!** *(peh-'lee-groh)*
Fire!	**¡Fuego!** *('fweh-goh)*
Get under the table!	**¡Póngase debajo de la mesa!** *('pohn-gah-seh deh-'bah-hoh deh lah 'meh-sah)*
Help!	**¡Socorro!** *(soh-'koh-rroh)*
Run outside!	**¡Corra hacia afuera!** *('koh-rrah 'ah-see-ah ah-'fweh-rah)*
Stay away from the windows!	**¡Quédese lejos de las ventanas!** *('keh-deh-seh 'leh-hohs deh lahs vehn-'tah-nahs)*
Watch out!	**¡Ojo!** *('oh-hoh)*

Is everything secured? For safety purposes, these things should be memorized also:

Always use (the)...	**Siempre use...** *(see-'ehm-preh 'oo-seh)*
alarm	**la alarma** *(lah ah-'lahr-mah)*
chain	**la cadena** *(lah kah-'deh-nah)*
deadbolt	**el pestillo** *(ehl peh-'stee-yoh)*
key	**la llave** *(lah 'yah-veh)*

latch	el **cerrojo** *(ehl seh-'roh-hoh)*
lock	la **cerradura** *(lah seh-rrah-'doo-rah)*
padlock	el **candado** *(ehl kahn-'dah-doh)*
safe	la **caja fuerte** *(lah 'kah-hah 'fwehr-teh)*
shelter	el **refugio** *(ehl reh-'foo-hee·oh)*

Weather trouble
Los problemas con el tiempo
(lohs proh-'bleh-mahs kohn ehl tee-'ehm-poh)

In many parts of the world, work schedules can be disturbed by changes in the weather. When there's a conversation about the weather, listen for consistent patterns. These words and phrases will help:

What's the weather like?	¿**Cómo está el tiempo?** *('koh-moh eh-'stah ehl tee-'ehm-poh)*
It's...	**Hace...** *('ah-seh)*
cold	**frío** *('free-oh)*
hot	**calor** *(kah-'lohr)*
nice weather	**buen tiempo** *('bwehn tee-'ehm-poh)*
sunny	**sol** *(sohl)*
windy	**viento** *(vee-'ehn-toh)*
It's...	**Está...** *(eh-'stah)*
clear	**despejado** *(dehs-peh-'hah-doh)*
cloudy	**nublado** *(noo-'blah-doh)*
cool	**fresco** *('freh-skoh)*
drizzling	**lloviznando** *(yoh-vees-'nahn-doh)*
freezing	**helando** *(eh-'lahn-doh)*
raining	**lloviendo** *(yoh-vee-'ehn-doh)*
snowing	**nevando** *(neh-'vahn-doh)*
stormy	**tempestuoso** *(tehm-peh-stoo-'oh-soh)*
I don't like (the)...	**No me gusta...** *(noh meh-'goo-stah)*
earthquake	el **terremoto** *(ehl teh-rreh-'moh-toh)*
flood	la **inundación** *(lah een-noon-dah-see-'ohn)*
frost	la **escarcha** *(lah eh-'skahr-chah)*
hail	el **granizo** *(ehl grah-'nee-soh)*

landslide	**el desprendimiento de tierra**
	(ehl dehs-prehn-dee-mee-'ehn-toh deh tee-'eh-rrah)
lightning	**el relámpago** *(ehl reh-'lahm-pah-goh)*
thunder	**el trueno** *(ehl troo-'eh-noh)*
sleet	**el aguanieve** *(ehl ah-gwah-nee-'eh-veh)*

¡Información!

Write these terms on your calendar!

The seasons	***Las estaciones*** *(lahs eh-stah-see-'oh-nehs)*
spring	**la primavera** *(lah pree-mah-'veh-rah)*
summer	**el verano** *(ehl veh-'rah-noh)*
fall	**el otoño** *(ehl oh-'toh-nyoh)*
winter	**el invierno** *(ehl een-vee-'ehr-noh)*

Listos para practicar

Name the four seasons in Spanish:

_____   _____   _____   _____

Select the correct word for each sentence:
la linterna, la tormenta, la llave
(lah leen-'tehr-nah, lah tohr-'mehn-tah, lah 'yah-veh)

Hay mucha lluvia en _____
('ah·ee 'moo-chah 'yoo-vee·ah ehn ___)

En la noche, usamos _____
(ehn lah 'noh-cheh, oo-'sah-mohs ___)

Abra el candado con _____
('ah-brah ehl kahn-'dah-doh kohn ___)

Answer these three questions aloud:

¿Hace sol en el verano? *('ah-seh sohl ehn ehl veh-'rah-noh)*
¿Está nublado hoy? *(eh-'stah noo-'blah-doh 'oh·ee)*
¿Le gusta a usted el trueno?
(leh 'goo-stah ah oo-'stehd ehl troo-'eh-noh)

Translate these key terms:

Emergency! _____

Help! _____

Rescue! _____

Safety! _____

Security! _____

The outdoors
Al aire libre *(ahl 'ah·ee-reh 'lee-breh)*

Speaking of the weather, you may want to consider learning a little outdoor Spanish. Although most folks in the field of Human Resources work in an office, some activity may be going on outside.

We are near (the)...	Estamos cerca de...
	(eh-'stah-mohs 'sehr-kah deh)
beach	**la playa** *(lah 'plah-yah)*
desert	**el desierto** *(ehl deh-see-'ehr-toh)*
field	**el campo** *(ehl 'kahm-poh)*
forest	**el bosque** *(ehl 'boh-skeh)*
gulch	**la barranca** *(lah bah-'rrahn-kah)*
hill	**el cerro** *(ehl 'seh-rroh)*
jungle	**la selva** *(lah 'sehl-vah)*
lake	**el lago** *(ehl 'lah-goh)*
mountain	**la montaña** *(lah mohn-'tah-nyah)*
pond	**la charca** *(lah 'chahr-kah)*
river	**el río** *(ehl 'ree-oh)*
sea	**el mar** *(ehl mahr)*
stream	**el arroyo** *(ehl ah-'rroh-yoh)*
swamp	**el pantano** *(ehl pahn-'tah-noh)*
valley	**el valle** *(ehl 'vah-yeh)*

Más fácil

A fast effective shortcut to tell someone in Spanish that an activity was just completed is to add the verb infinitives to the following phrase forms:

To just finish	***Acabar de*** *(ah-kah-'bahr deh)*
I just finished...	**Acabo de...** *(ah-'kah-boh deh)*
I just finished eating.	**Acabo de comer.**
	(ah-'kah-boh deh koh-'mehr)
You, He, She just finished...	**Acaba de...** *(ah-'kah-bah deh)*
He just finished calling.	**Acaba de llamar.**
	(ah-'kah-bah deh yah- 'mahr)
They, You (pl.) just finished...	**Acaban de...** *(ah-'kah-bahn deh)*
They just finished talking.	**Acaban de hablar.**
	(ah-'kah-bahn deh ah-'blahr)
We just finished...	**Acabamos de...**
	(ah-kah-'bah-mohs deh)
We just finished working.	**Acabamos de trabajar.**
	(ah-kah-'bah-mohs deh trah-bah-'hahr)

By the way, the verb **acabar** means *to finish,* and can be used as a regular action word:

I'm finishing now.	**Estoy acabando ahora.**
	(eh-'stoh-ee ah-kah-'bahn-doh ah-'oh-rah)
I finish at five.	**Acabo a las cinco.**
	(ah-'kah-boh ah lahs'seen-koh)
I'll finish the job.	**Acabaré el trabajo.**
	(ah-kah-bah-'reh ehl trah-'bah-hoh)

Speaking of verb forms, these are the actions you'll need to discuss topics related to employee concerns and problem-solving:

to advise	**avisar** *(ah-vee-'sahr)*
to bother	**molestar** *(moh-leh-'stahr)*
to counsel	**aconsejar** *(ah-kohn-seh-'hahr)*
to discuss	**conversar** *(kohn-vehr-sahr)*
to feel	**sentir** *(sehn-'teer)*
to grab	**agarrar** *(ah-gah-'rrahr)*
to heal	**curar** *(koo-'rahr)*
to hit	**pegar** *(peh-'gahr)*
to hold	**sostener** *(soh-steh-'nehr)*
to injure	**herir** *(eh-'reer)*

to insist	**insistir** *(een-see-'steer)*
to joke	**bromear** *(broh-meh-'ahr)*
to lie	**mentir** *(mehn-'teer)*
to miss	**faltar** *(fahl-'tahr)*
to obey	**obedecer** *(oh-beh-deh-'sehr)*
to sleep	**dormir** *(dohr-'meer)*
to steal	**robar** *(roh-'bahr)*
to take care of	**cuidar** *(kwee-'dahr)*
to tie	**amarrar** *(ah-mah-'rrahr)*
to worsen	**empeorar** *(ehm-peh-oh-'rahr)*
to yell	**gritar** *(gree-'tahr)*

And file these **se** verbs as well:

to deny	**negarse** *(neh-'gahr-seh)*
to calm down	**calmarse** *(kahl-'mahr-seh)*
to relax	**relajarse** *(reh-lah-'hahr-seh)*
to burn oneself	**quemarse** *(keh-'mahr-seh)*
to faint	**desmayarse** *(dehs-mah-'yahr-seh)*

¡Información!

• Are you keeping a list of verbs that look a lot like English?

to accuse	**acusar** *(ah-koo-'sahr)*
to arrest	**arrestar** *(ah-rreh-'stahr)*
to consult	**consultar** *(kohn-sool-'tahr)*
to converse	**conversar** *(kohn-vehr-'sahr)*
to investigate	**investigar** *(een-veh-stee-'gahr)*
to suspend	**suspender** *(soos-'spehn-dehr)*
to transfer	**transferir** *(trahns-feh-'reer)*

• These two verbs will also come in handy:

to rain	**llover** *(yoh-'vehr)*	**Está lloviendo.** *(eh-'stah yoh-vee-'ehn-doh)*
to snow	**nevar** *(neh-'vahr)*	**Está nevando.** *(eh-'stah neh-'vahn-doh)*

Palabras activas

Up to now, we've been given the skills to converse about current, every-day, and future activities around the worksite.

Now let's take a look at the *past tense* in Spanish. We can start by learning the more commonly used form. Read the following examples and, just as you did with present and future actions, make the changes in your verbs. You won't be perfect at first, but Spanish speakers will know what you're trying to say.

AR verbs:

To speak	***Hablar*** *(ah-'blahr)*
I spoke with the boss.	**Hablé con el jefe.**
	(ah-'bleh kohn ehl 'heh-feh)
You, He, She spoke a lot.	**Habló mucho.** *(ah-'bloh 'moo-choh)*
You (pl.), They spoke English.	**Hablaron inglés.**
	(ah-'blah-rohn een-'glehs)
We spoke a little.	**Hablamos un poco.**
	(ah-'blah-mohs oon poh-'koh)

ER/IR verbs:

To leave	***Salir*** *(sah-'leer)*
I left at eight.	**Salí a las ocho.** *(sah-'lee ah lahs 'oh-choh)*
You, He, She left late.	**Salió tarde.** *(sah-lee-'oh 'tahr-deh)*
You (pl.), They left.	**Salieron.** *(sah-lee-'eh-rohn)*
We left in a car.	**Salimos en el carro.**
	(sah-'lee-mohs ehn ehl 'kah-rroh)

Unfortunately, some common verbs have irregular past tenses, so be on the look-out! These three are very common:

To go	***Ir*** *(eer)*	
I went	**Fui** *(fwee)*	**Fui a la casa.**
		(fwee ah lah 'kah-sah)
You, He, She went	**Fue** *(fweh)*	_____
You (pl.), They went	**Fueron** *('fweh-rohn)*	_____
We went	**Fuimos** *('fwee-mohs)*	_____

To have	Tener *(teh-'nehr)*	
I had	Tuve *('too-veh)*	**Tuve la fiesta.**
		('too-veh lah fee-'eh-stah)
You, He, She had	Tuvo *('too-voh)*	_____
You (pl.), They had	Tuvieron *(too-vee-'eh-rohn)*	_____
We had	Tuvimos *(too-'vee-mohs)*	_____
To say	Decir *(deh-'seer)*	
I said	Dije *('dee-heh)*	**Dije la verdad.**
		('dee-heh lah vehr-'dahd)
You, He, She said	Dijo *('dee-hoh)*	_____
You (pl.), They said	Dijeron *(dee-'heh-rohn)*	_____
We said	Dijimos *(dee-'hee-mohs)*	_____

¡Información!

• This verb form is called the preterit, and it isn't the only *past tense* you're going to need. Although these phrases won't be discussed in detail, check out the spellings and meanings of the examples below:

I used to have	tenía *(teh-'nee-ah)*
I would have	tendría *(tehn-'dree-ah)*
I was having	estaba teniendo
	(eh-'stah-bah teh-nee-'ehn-doh)
I have had	he tenido *(eh teh-'nee-doh)*

• The verb **SER** *(sehr)* (to be) has the same "preterit" forms as the verb **IR** *(eer)* (to go). Take note:

I was	Fui *(fwee)*
You, He, She was	Fue *(fweh)*
You (pl.), They were	Fueron *('fweh-rohn)*
We were	Fuimos *('fwee-mohs)*

Listos para practicar

Follow the pattern in the example:

Acabo de hablar   **Hablé** *(ah-'bleh)*
(ah-'kah-boh deh ah-'blahr)

Acabo de avisar   _____
(ah-'kah-boh deh ah-'vee-sahr)

Acabo de acosejar   _____
(ah-'kah-boh deh ah-kohn-seh-'hahr)

Acabo de arrestar   _____
(ah-'kah-boh deh ah-rreh-'stahr)

Acabo de consultar   _____
(ah-'kah-boh deh kohn-sool-'tahr)

Acabo de gritar   _____
(ah-'kah-boh deh gree-'tahr)

Acabo de insistir   **Insistí** *(een-see-'stee)*
(ah-'kah-boh deh een-see-'steer)

Acabo de discutir   _____
(ah-'kah-boh deh dee-skoo-'teer)

Acabo de mentir   _____
(ah-'kah-boh deh mehn-'teer)

Acabo de dormir   _____
(ah-'kah-boh deh dohr-'meer)

Acabo de sentir   _____
(ah-'kah-boh deh sehn-'teer)

Acabo de escribir   _____
(ah-'kah-boh deh eh-skree-'beer)

¡Ordenes!

Now, let's take some of the verb infinitives we just learned and turn them into powerful HR commands. Learn how to separate the regular forms from the irregular ones. Practice:

Advise!	**¡Aconseje!** *(ah-kohn-'seh-heh)*	**¡Aconseje al empleado!** *(ah-kohn-'seh-heh ahl ehm-pleh-'ah-doh)*
Calm down!	**¡Cálmese!** *('kahl-meh-seh)*	
Discuss!	**¡Converse!** *(kohn-'vehr-seh)*	_____
Grab!	**¡Agarre!** *(ah-'gah-rreh)*	**¡Agarre la mano!** *(ah-'gah-rreh lah 'mah-noh)*
Relax!	**¡Relájese!** *(reh-'lah-heh-seh)*	_____
Tie!	**¡Amarre!** *(ah-'mah-rreh)*	**¡Amarre el paquete!** *(ah-'mah-rreh ehl pah-'keh-teh)*
Warn!	**¡Avise!** *(ah-'vee-seh)*	_____

These forms are a little tricky:

Hit!	**¡Pegue!** *('peh-geh)*	_____
Hold!	**¡Sostenga!** *(soh-'stehn-gah)*	_____
Obey!	**¡Obedezca!** *(oh-beh-'deh-skah)*	_____
Sleep!	**¡Duerma!** *('dwehr-mah)*	_____

¡Información!

Although the duties of Human Resources professionals may vary, most of the following commands will meet your specific needs.

Allow him.	**Permítale.** *(pehr-'mee-tah-leh)*
Call him.	**Llámele.** *('yah-meh-leh)*
Give him.	**Déle.** *('deh-leh)*
Help him.	**Ayúdele.** *(ah-'yoo-deh-leh)*
Leave him.	**Déjele.** *('deh-heh-leh)*
Grab him.	**Agárrele.** *(ah-'gah-rreh-leh)*
Advise him.	**Avísele.** *(ah-'vee-seh-leh)*
Take care of him.	**Cúidele.** *('kwee-deh-leh)*

Temas culturales

The more trust that builds between you and your employee, the more comfortable you will feel around each other. Since hugging is a common form of greeting between friends, don't panic if someone leans forward to embrace you! Healthy touch is an active part of many cultures, and in Latin America, **cariño** *(kah-'ree-nyoh)* (affection) is openly displayed between friends and coworkers.

Chapter Seven

Capítulo Siete
(kah-'pee-too-loh see-'eh-teh)

The Evaluation
La evaluación
(lah eh-vah-loo-ah-see-'ohn)

Let's evaluate
Vamos a evaluar *('vah-mohs ah eh-vah-loo-'ahr)*

Successful businesses evaluate their progress on a regular basis, and one of the best tools is the Performance Appraisal. Beyond training and daily problem-solving is the field of employee assessment. The Spanish that follows will allow you to explain the appraisal process in detail, so you may want to take notes or duplicate parts of this chapter for evaluation purposes.

We are working on (the)...	**Estamos trabajando en...** *(eh-'stah-mohs trah-bah-'hahn-doh ehn)*
We are using (the)...	**Estamos usando...** *(eh-'stah-mohs oo-'sahn-doh)*
analysis	**el análisis** *(ehl ah-'nah-lee-sees)*
audit	**la inspección** *(lah een-spehk-see-'ohn)*
check up	**la comprobación** *(lah kohm-proh-bah-see-'ohn)*
comparison	**la comparación** *(lah kohm-pah-rah-see-'ohn)*
diagnosis	**el diagnóstico** *(ehl dee-ahg-'noh-stee-koh)*
evaluation	**la evaluación** *(lah eh-vah-loo-ah-see-'ohn)*
exam	**el examen** *(ehl ehk-'sah-mehn)*
experiment	**el experimento** *(ehl ehk-speh-ree-'mehn-toh)*
follow-up	**la continuación** *(lah kohn-tee-noo-ah-see-'ohn)*
form	**el formulario** *(ehl fohr-moo-'lah-ree·oh)*
instrument	**el instrumento** *(ehl een-stroo-'mehn-toh)*
proposal	**la propuesta** *(lah proh-'pweh-stah)*
test	**la prueba** *(lah proo-'eh-bah)*
valuation	**la tasación** *(lah tah-sah-see-'ohn)*

And these one-liners will help them prepare!

These are the times and dates.
Estas son las horas y fechas.
('eh-stahs sohn lahs 'oh-rahs ee 'feh-chahs)
You have time to prepare.
Tiene tiempo para prepararse.
(tee-'eh-neh tee-'ehm-poh 'pah-rah preh-pah-'rahr-seh)
The evaluation will last...
La evaluación durará...
(lah eh-vah-loo-ah-see-'ohn doo-rah-'rah)

Let me explain the procedure.
Déjeme explicar el procedimiento.
('deh-heh-meh ehks-plee-'kahr ehl proh-seh-dee-mee-'ehn-toh)
It will help the business.
Ayudará al negocio.
(ah-yoo-dah-'rah ahl neh-'goh-see·oh)
The purpose is to evaluate...
El propósito es evaluar...
(ehl proh-'poh-see-toh ehs eh-vah-loo-'ahr)
decision-making
...la capacidad de hacer decisiones
(lah kah-pah-see-'dahd deh ah-'sehr deh-see-see-'oh-nehs)
job performance
...el rendimiento en el trabajo
(ehl rehn-dee-mee-'ehn-toh ehn ehl trah-'bah-hoh)
job skill
...la habilidad en el trabajo
(lah ah-bee-lee-'dahd ehn ehl trah-'bah-hoh)
performance level
...el nivel de la ejecución
(ehl nee-'vehl deh lah eh-heh-koo-see-'ohn)
reaction time
...el tiempo que se requiere para responder
(ehl tee-'ehm-poh keh seh reh-kee-'eh-reh 'pah-rah reh-spohn-'dehr)
time management
...el mantenimiento del horario
(ehl mahn-teh-nee-mee-'ehn-toh dehl oh-'rrah-ree·oh)

Let's evaluate (the)...	**Vamos a evaluar...** *('vah-mohs ah eh-vah-loo-'ahr)*
goals	**las metas** *(lahs 'meh-tahs)*
needs	**las necesidades** *(lahs neh-seh-see-'dah-dehs)*
objectives	**los objetivos** *(lohs ohb-heh-'tee-vohs)*
responsibilities	**las responsabilidades** *(lahs reh-spohn-sah-bee-lee-'dah-dehs)*
strengths	**los puntos fuertes** *(lohs -poon-tohs 'fwehr-tehs)*
weaknesses	**las debilidades** *(lahs deh-bee-lee-'dah-dehs)*

We are evaluating (the)...	**Estamos evaluando...** *(eh-'stah-mohs eh-vah-loo-'ahn-doh)*
ability	**la habilidad** *(lah ah-bee-lee-'dahd)*
communication	**la comunicación** *(lah koh-moo-nee-kah-see-'ohn)*
control	**el control** *(ehl kohn-'trohl)*
expertise	**la pericia** *(lah peh-'ree-see-ah)*
intelligence	**la inteligencia** *(lah een-teh-lee-'hehn-see-ah)*
knowledge	**el conocimiento** *(ehl koh-noh-see-mee-'ehn-toh)*
language	**el lenguaje** *(ehl lehn-'gwah-heh)*
potential	**la potencial** *(lah poh-tehn-see-'ahl)*
talent	**el talento** *(ehl tah-'lehn-toh)*

Remind the employees who will be involved in the evaluation process. Can you change these terms so that they refer to females?

He's (the)...	**Es...** *(ehs)*	
administrator	**el administrador** *(ehl ahd-mee-nee-strah-'dohr)*	_____
coordinator	**el coordinador** *(ehl koh-ohr-dee-nah-'dohr)*	_____
director	**el director** *(ehl dee-rehk-'tohr)*	**la directora** *(lah dee-rehk-'toh-rah)*
evaluator	**el evaluador** *(ehl eh-vah-loo-ah-'dohr)*	_____
examiner	**el examinador** *(ehl ehk-sah-mee-nah-'dohr)*	_____
teacher	**el maestro** *(ehl mah-'eh-stroh)*	_____
trainer	**el entrenador** *(ehl ehn-treh-nah-'dohr)*	_____

She's going to...	**Ella va a...** *('eh-yah vah ah...)*
analyze	**analizar** *(ah-nah-lee-'sahr)*
appraise	**estimar** *(eh-stee-'mahr)*
check	**verificar** *(veh-ree-fee-'kahr)*
establish	**establecer** *(eh-stah-bleh-'sehr)*
evaluate	**evaluar** *(eh-vah-loo-'ahr)*
identify	**identificar** *(ee-dehn-tee-fee-'kahr)*
implement	**realizar** *(reh-ah-lee-'sahr)*

measure	**medir** *(meh-'deer)*
monitor	**controlar** *(kohn-troh-'lahr)*
observe	**observar** *(ohb-sehr-'vahr)*
prepare	**preparar** *(preh-pah-'rahr)*
prescribe	**prescribir** *(preh-skree-'beer)*
process	**procesar** *(proh-seh-'sahr)*
record	**documentar** *(doh-koo-mehn-'tahr)*
test	**examinar** *(ehk-sah-mee-'nahr)*
write	**escribir** *(eh-skree-'beer)*

¡Información!

Describe the appraisal or evaluation. These words will get the message across:

It is very...	**Es muy...** *(ehs 'moo-ee)*
acceptable	**aceptable** *(ah-sehp-'tah-bleh)*
constructive	**constructivo** *(kohn-strook-'tee-voh)*
convenient	**conveniente** *(kohn-veh-nee-'ehn-teh)*
customized	**personalizado** *(pehr-soh-nah-lee-'sah-doh)*
effective	**eficaz** *(eh-fee-'kahs)*
fair	**justo** *('hoo-stoh)*
generalized	**generalizado** *(heh-neh-rah-lee-'sah-doh)*
important	**importante** *(eem-pohr-'tahn-teh)*
objective	**objetivo** *(ohb-heh-'tee-voh)*
positive	**positivo** *(poh-see-'tee-voh)*
significant	**significativo** *(seeg-nee-fee-kah-'tee-voh)*
subjective	**subjetivo** *(soob-heh-'tee-voh)*

Listos para practicar

Fill in the blanks with the appropriate vocabulary:

la administradora, la evaluación, la pericia *(lah ahd-mee-nee-strah-'doh-rah, lah eh-vah-loo-ah-see-'ohn, lah peh-'ree-see-ah)*

Estamos usando _____.
 (eh-'stah-mohs oo-'sahn-doh___)
Estamos evaluando _____.
 (eh-'stah-mohs eh-vah-loo-'ahn-doh___)
Ella es _____. *('eh-yah ehs _____)*

Look at the Spanish and guess what the word might mean in English:

identificar *(ee-dehn-tee-fee-'kahr)* _____
preparar *(preh-pah-'rahr)* _____
observar *(ohb-sehr-'vahr)* _____
conveniente *(kohn-veh-nee-'ehn-teh)* _____
positivo *(poh-see-'tee-voh)* _____
generalizado *(heh-neh-rah-lee-'sah-doh)* _____

The test
El examen *(ehl ehk-'sah-mehn)*

If some form of testing is part of the evaluation, guide the employee carefully through each phase. Try these lines:

Come on this date.	**Venga en esta fecha.**
	('vehn-gah ehn 'eh-stah 'feh-chah)
Don't be nervous.	**No se ponga nervioso.**
	(noh seh 'pohn-gah nehr-vee-'oh-soh)
It won't take long.	**No se demore mucho.**
	(noh seh deh-'moh-reh 'moo-choh)
This is the appraisal.	**Esta es la evaluación.**
	('eh-stah ehs lah eh-vah-loo-ah-see-'ohn)
Just do the best you can.	**Hágalo lo mejor que pueda.**
	('ah-gah-loh loh meh-'hohr keh 'pweh-dah)
You'll receive the results soon.	**Recibirá los resultados pronto.**
	(reh-see-bee-'rah lohs reh-sool-'tah-dohs 'prohn-toh)

We're trying to improve (the)...	**Estamos tratando de mejorar...** *(eh-'stah-mohs trah-'tahn-doh deh meh-hoh-'rahr)*
production	**la producción** *(lah proh-dook-see-'ohn)*
quality	**la calidad** *(lah kah-lee-'dahd)*
service	**el servicio** *(ehl sehr-'vee-see-oh)*
We will use (the)...	**Usaremos...** *(oo-sah-'reh-mohs)*
approach	**el enfoque** *(ehl ehn-'foh-keh)*
method	**el método** *(ehl 'meh-toh-doh)*
model	**el modelo** *(ehl moh-'deh-loh)*
principle	**el principio** *(ehl preen-'see-pee-oh)*
strategy	**la estrategia** *(lah eh-strah-'teh-hee-ah)*
technique	**el técnico** *(ehl 'tehk-nee-koh)*
You need to read (the)...	**Necesita leer...** *(neh-seh-'see-tah leh-'ehr)*
answers	**las respuestas** *(lahs reh-'spweh-stahs)*
data	**los datos** *(lohs 'dah-tohs)*
examples	**los ejemplos** *(lohs eh-'hehm-plohs)*
facts	**los hechos** *(lohs 'eh-chohs)*
instructions	**las instrucciones** *(lahs een-strook-see-'oh-nehs)*
questions	**las preguntas** *(lahs preh-'goon-tahs)*
results	**los resultados** *(lohs reh-sool-'tah-dohs)*
I will give you (the)...	**Le voy a dar...** *(leh 'voh-ee ah dahr)*
agreement	**el acuerdo** *(ehl ah-'kwehr-doh)*
letter	**la carta** *(lah 'kahr-tah)*
memo	**el memorándum** *(ehl meh-moh-'rahn-doom)*
policy	**la póliza** *(lah 'poh-lee-sah)*
report	**el informe** *(ehl een-'fohr-meh)*
resource	**el recurso** *(ehl reh-'koor-soh)*
study	**el estudio** *(ehl eh-'stoo-dee-oh)*
summary	**el resumen** *(ehl reh-'soo-mehn)*

Continue to talk, but this time get some feedback from everyone about the evaluation. Keep it simple with the patterns shown on the next page.

Are you...?	¿Está...? *(eh-'stah)*
capable	**capaz** *(kah-'pahs)*
confident	**seguro** *(seh-'goo-roh)*
interested	**interesado** *(een-teh-reh-'sah-doh)*
motivated	**motivado** *(moh-tee-'vah-doh)*
optimistic	**optimista** *(ohp-tee-'mee-stah)*
prepared	**preparado** *(preh-pah-'rah-doh)*
qualified	**calificado** *(kah-lee-fee-'kah-doh)*
satisfied	**satisfecho** *(sah-tees-'feh-choh)*

¡Información!

- All kinds of technical words will be required, so keep in store a few of them:

data collection	**el banco de datos** *(ehl 'bahn-koh deh 'dah-tohs)*
final decision	**la decición final** *(lah deh-see-see-'ohn fee-'nahl)*
information processing	**el proceso informativo** *(ehl proh-'seh-soh een-fohr-mah-'tee-voh)*
learning curve	**la curva de aprendizaje** *(lah 'koor-vah deh ah-prehn-dee-'sah-heh)*
pre-test	**el pre-examen** *(ehl preh-ehk-'sah-mehn)*
production rate	**el volumen de producción** *(ehl voh-'loo-mehn deh proh-dook-see-'ohn)*
post-test	**el post-examen** *(ehl pohst-ehk-'sah-mehn)*
quality control	**el control de calidad** *(ehl kohn-'trohl deh kah-lee-'dahd)*
safety standards	**las normas de seguridad** *(lahs 'nohr-mahs deh seh-goo-ree-'dahd)*
self-improvement	**la superación personal** *(lah soo-peh-rah-see-'ohn pehr-soh-'nahl)*
time frame	**el lapso de tiempo** *(ehl 'lahp-soh deh tee-'ehm-poh)*
top priority	**la prioridad máxima** *(lah pree-oh-ree-'dahd 'makh-see-mah)*

track record	**el récord de trabajo** *(ehl 'reh-kohrd deh trah-'bah-hoh)*
work planning	**la planificación de trabajo** *(lah plahn-nee-fee-kah-see-'ohn deh trah-'bah-hoh)*
workload	**la cantidad de trabajo** *(lah kahn-tee-'dahd deh trah-'bah-hoh)*

• Watch for word patterns.

collaboration	**la colaboración** *(lah koh-lah-boh-rah-see-'ohn)*
cooperation	**la cooperación** *(lah koh-oh-peh-rah-see-'ohn)*
correction	**la corrección** *(lah koh-rrehk-see-'ohn)*
deviation	**la desviación** *(lah dehs-vee-ah-see-'ohn)*
implementation	**la implementación** *(lah eem-pleh-mehn-tah-see-'ohn)*
initiation	**la iniciación** *(lah ee-nee-see-ah-see-'ohn)*
inspection	**la inspección** *(lah een-spehk-see-'ohn)*
limitation	**la limitación** *(lah lee-mee-tah-see-'ohn)*
observation	**la observación** *(lah ohb-sehr-vah-see-'ohn)*
operation	**la operación** *(lah oh-peh-rah-see-'ohn)*
preparation	**la preparación** *(lah preh-pah-rah-see-'ohn)*
satisfaction	**la satisfacción** *(lah sah-tees-fahk-see-'ohn)*
specification	**la especificación** *(lah eh-speh-see-fee-kah-see-'ohn)*

But stay alert—not every word follows the rules:

expectation	**la esperanza** *(lah eh-speh-'rahn-sah)*
competition	**la competencia** *(lah kohm-peh-'tehn-see-ah)*
examination	**el examen** *(ehl ehk-'sah-mehn)*

Listos para practicar

Translate these catchy phrases:

quality control	_____
final decision	_____
time frame	_____

Underline the misplaced word from each group:

doblado, seguro, preparado, calificado
(doh-'blah-doh, seh-'goo-roh, preh-pah-'rah-doh, kah-lee-fee-'kah-doh)

método, enfoque, enchufe, principio
('meh-toh-doh, ehn-'foh-keh, ehn-'choo-feh, preen-'see-pee-oh)

medida, cantidad, asiento, nivel
(meh-'dee-dah, kahn-tee-'dahd, ah-see-'ehn-toh, nee-'vehl)

Name three kinds of reading material that can be found in the Human Resources Department:

_____

_____

_____

After the evaluation
Después de la evaluación
(deh-'spwehs deh lah eh-vah-loo-ah-see-'ohn)

Bring in each employee and share a few words about the results. Begin with a group of positive action words. Notice how the word **le** *(leh)* refers to *you:*

I would like to _____ you.	**Quisiera** _____. *(kee-see-'eh-rah)*
assure	**asegurarle** *(ah-seh-goo-'rahr-leh)*
commend	**alabarle** *(ah-lah-'bahr-leh)*
compliment	**felicitarle** *(feh-lee-see-'tahr-leh)*
encourage	**animarle** *(ah-nee-'mahr-leh)*
motivate	**motivarle** *(moh-tee-'vahr-leh)*
persuade	**persuadirle** *(pehr-swah-'deer-leh)*
reward	**recompensarle** *(reh-kohm-pehn-'sahr-leh)*
support	**apoyarle** *(ah-poh-'yahr-leh)*
thank	**agradecerle** *(ah-grah-deh-'sehr-leh)*

Your post-appraisal meeting could last a while, so don't run out of things to say:

I'm going to...	**Voy a...** *('voh-ee ah)*
clarify	**clarificar** *(klah-ree-fee-'kahr)*

confirm	**confirmar** *(kohn-feer-'mahr)*
explain	**explicar** *(ehk-splee-'kahr)*
identify	**identificar** *(ee-dehn-tee-fee-'kahr)*
suggest	**sugerir** *(soo-heh-'reer)*

If you need to reveal test results, try out the following key terms:

It's...

acceptable	**Es aceptable** *(ehs ah-sehp-'tah-bleh)*
adequate	**Es adecuado** *(ehs ah-deh-'kwah-doh)*
appropriate	**Es apropiado** *(ehs ah-proh-pee-'ah-doh)*
approved	**Está aprobado** *(eh-'stah ah-proh-'bah-doh)*
better	**Está mejor** *(eh-'stah meh-'hohr)*
correct	**Está correcto** *(eh-'stah koh-'rrehk-toh)*
excellent	**Es excelente** *(ehs ehk-seh-'lehn-teh)*
good	**Es bueno** *(ehs 'bweh-noh)*
high	**Es alto** *(ehs 'ahl-toh)*
more	**Es más** *(ehs mahs)*
outstanding	**Es fantástico** *(ehs fahn-'tah-stee-koh)*
satisfactory	**Está satisfecho** *(eh-'stah sah-tees-'feh-choh)*

It's (the)...	**Es...** *(ehs)*
average	**el promedio** *(ehl proh-'meh-dee-oh)*
maximum	**el máximo** *(ehl 'mahk-see-moh)*
minimum	**el mínimo** *(ehl 'mee-nee-moh)*

Sometimes, the results aren't very positive:

It's...

less than expected	**Es menos de lo esperado** *(ehs 'meh-nohs deh loh ehs-peh-'rah-doh)*
a low result	**Es un resultado bajo** *(ehs oon reh-sool-'tah-doh 'bah-hoh)*
unacceptable	**Es inaceptable** *(ehs een-ah-sehp-'tah-bleh)*
incorrect	**Está incorrecto** *(eh-'stah een-koh-'rrehk-toh)*
improper	**Es impropio** *(ehs eem-'proh-pee-oh)*
poor	**Está mal** *(eh-'stah mahl)*
worse	**Está peor** *(eh-'stah peh-'ohr)*

☞ **¡Información!**

• Here are more words and phrases that deal with assessments:

I agree.	**Estoy de acuerdo.**
	(eh-'stoh-ee deh ah-'kwehr-doh)
I disagree.	**No estoy de acuerdo.**
	(noh eh-'stoh-ee deh ah-'kwehr-doh)
It needs	**Necesita mejorar.**
improvement.	*(neh-seh-'see-tah meh-hoh-'rahr)*
There were a lot of	**Había muchos errores.**
mistakes.	*(ah-'bee-ah 'moo-chohs eh-'rroh-rehs)*
What's (the)...?	**¿Cuál es...?** *(kwahl ehs)*
score	**la calificación** *(lah kah-lee-fee-kah-see-'ohn)*
grade	**la nota** *(lah 'noh-tah)*
count	**el recuento** *(ehl reh-'kwehn-toh)*

• All kinds of things can go wrong during an appraisal, so don't forget to mention these problem areas:

We found...	**Encontramos...** *(ehn-kohn-'trah-mohs)*
coding errors	**errores de código**
	(eh-'rroh-rehs deh 'koh-dee-goh)
breakage	**cosas rotas** *('koh-sahs 'roh-tahs)*
lost time	**tiempo perdido**
	(tee-'ehm-poh pehr-'dee-doh)
interruptions	**interrupciones** *(een-teh-roop-see-'oh-nehs)*
substandard	**condiciones deficientes**
conditions	*(kohn-dee-see-'oh-nehs deh-fee-see-'ehn-tehs)*
bias	**prejuicio** *(preh-'hoo-ee-see-oh)*
poor decisions	**malas decisiones**
	('mah-lahs deh-see-see-'oh-nehs)
malfunction	**funcionamiento defectuoso** *(foonk-see-oh-nah-mee-'ehn-toh deh-fehk-too-'oh-soh)*

• The phrase, *to make a mistake* is **equivocarse** *(eh-kee-voh-'kahr-seh)*. Look:

You make mistakes sometimes.
A veces usted se equivoca.
(ah 'veh-sehs oo-'stehd seh eh-kee-'voh-kah)

Recommendations
Las recomendaciones
(lahs reh-koh-mehn-dah-see-'oh-nehs)

Address the worker privately as you lend advice. Give suggestions or make a command:

You should...	**Debe...** *('deh-beh)*	
check	**revisar** *(reh-vee-'sahr)*	_____
commit	**comprometerse**	_____
	(kohm-proh-'meh-'tehr-seh)	
continue	**continuar**	
	(kohn-tee-noo-'ahr)	_____
cooperate	**cooperar**	
	(koh-oh-peh-'rahr)	_____
coordinate	**coordinar**	
	(koh-ohr-dee-'nahr)	_____
develop	**desarrollar**	
	(dehs-ah-roh-'yahr)	_____
exceed	**sobrepasar**	
	(soh-breh-pah-'sahr)	_____
exhibit	**exhibir** *(ehk-see-'beer)*	_____
follow	**seguir** *(seh-'geer)*	_____
improve	**mejorar**	_____
	(meh-hoh-'rahr)	
lead	**dirigir** *(dee-ree-'heer)*	_____
maintain	**mantener**	**Debe mantener el mismo**
	(mahn-teh-'nehr)	**nivel.** *('deh-beh mahn-teh-'nehr ehl 'mees-moh nee-'vehl)*
prepare	**preparar**	
	(preh-pah-'rahr)	

English	Spanish	Example
promise	**prometer** *(proh-meh-'tehr)*	_____
recognize	**reconocer** *(reh-koh-noh-'sehr)*	_____
reinforce	**reforzar** *(reh-fohr-'sahr)*	_____
repeat	**repetir** *(reh-peh-'teer)*	_____
review	**repasar** *(reh-pah-'sahr)*	_____
share	**compartir** *(kohm-pahr-'teer)*	**Debe compartir la información.** *('deh-beh kohm-pahr-'teer lah een-fohr-mah-see-'ohn)*
study	**estudiar** *(eh-stoo-dee-'ahr)*	_____
try	**tratar** *(trah-'tahr)*	_____

You should attend (the) ... **Debe asistir a ...** *('deh-beh ah-see-'steer ah)*
- conference **la conferencia** *(lah kohn-feh-'rehn-see-ah)*
- committee **el comité** *(ehl koh-mee-'teh)*
- discussion **la conversación** *(lah kohn-vehr-sah-see-'ohn)*
- meeting **la reunión** *(lah reh-oo-nee-'ohn)*
- seminar **el seminario** *(ehl seh-mee-'nah-ree-oh)*

You should read (the)... **Debe leer...** *('deh-beh leh-'ehr)*
- alternatives **las alternativas** *(lahs ahl-tehr-nah-'tee-vahs)*
- instructions **las instrucciones** *(lahs een-strook-see-'oh-nehs)*
- recommendations **las recomendaciones** *(lahs reh-koh-mehn-dah-see-'oh-nehs)*
- solutions **las soluciones** *(lahs soh-loo-see-'oh-nehs)*
- suggestions **las sugerencias** *(lahs soo-heh-'rehn-see-ahs)*

¡Información!

• Feel free to add a few time-referenced expressions:

beforehand	**de antemano**	
	(deh ahn-teh-'mah-noh)	
in advance	**con anticipación**	
	(kohn ahn-tee-see-pah-see-'ohn)	
periodically	**de vez en cuando**	
	(deh vehs ehn 'kwahn-doh)	
regularly	**regularmente**	**¡Debe leer regularmente!**
	(reh-goo-lahr-'mehn-teh)	*('deh-beh leh-'ehr reh-goo-lahr-'mehn-teh)*

• Now pick up on this easy pattern in Spanish:

durabili*ty*	**durabili*dad***
	(doo-rah-bee-lee-'dahd)
flexibili*ty*	**flexibili*dad***
	(flehk-see-bee-lee-'dahd)
priori*ty*	**priori*dad***
	(pree-oh-ree-'dahd)
responsibili*ty*	**responsabili*dad***
	(reh-spohn-sah-bee-lee-'dahd)
stabili*ty*	**estabili*dad***
	(eh-stah-bee-lee-'dahd)

Listos para practicar

Circle the action words that are usually heard at a post-appraisal meeting:

explicar, correr, apoyar, bailar, identificar, desarrollar, dormir, mejorar, revisar, besar

(ehk-splee-'kahr, koh-'rrehr, ah-poh-'yahr, ba-ee-'lahr, ee-den-tee-fee-'kahr, dehs-ah-roh-'yahr, dohr-'meer, meh-hoh-'rahr, reh-vee-'sahr, beh-'sahr)

Connect the opposites:

alto *('ahl-toh)*	**bueno** *('bweh-noh)*
más *(mahs)*	**dirigir** *(dee-ree-'heer)*
malo *('mah-loh)*	**peor** *(peh-'ohr)*
mínimo *('mee-nee-moh)*	**menos** *('meh-nohs)*
seguir *(seh-'geer)*	**bajo** *('bah-hoh)*
mejor *(meh-'hohr)*	**máximo** *('mahk-see-moh)*

Translate:

I would like to thank you. _____

You should attend the meeting. _____

I'm going to read the suggestions. _____

Effective phrases
Las frases eficaces
(lahs 'frah-sehs eh-fee-'kah-sehs)

To truly impact your Spanish-speaking work force, use a variety of effective communication techniques. These one-liners get employees to respond immediately:

Can you explain what caused the trouble?
¿Puede explicar qué causó el problema?
('pweh-deh ehk-splee-'kahr keh kow-'soh ehl proh-'bleh-mah)
Are you aware there is a problem?
¿Está consciente de que hay un problema?
(eh-'stah kohn-see-'ehn-teh deh keh 'ah-ee oon proh-'bleh-mah)
Can you tell me why this occurred?
¿Puede decirme por qué ocurrió esto?
('pweh-deh deh-'seer-meh pohr keh oh-koo-rree-'oh 'eh-stoh)
What can we do to correct the mistake?
¿Qué podemos hacer para corregir el error?
(keh poh-'deh-mohs ah-'sehr 'pah-rah koh-rreh-'heer ehl eh-'rrohr)
What do you suggest we do?
¿Qué recomienda que hagamos?
(keh reh-koh-mee-'ehn-dah keh ah-'gah-mohs)

I'd like to hear your ideas.
Quisiera escuchar sus ideas.
 (kee-see-'eh-rah eh-skoo-'chahr soos ee-'deh-ahs)
What other possibilities do you see?
¿Cuáles son las otras posibilidades que usted ve?
 ('kwah-lehs sohn lahs 'oh-trahs poh-see-bee-lee-'dah-dehs keh oo-'stehd veh)
What steps would you take to correct the problem?
¿Qué medidas tomaría para corregir el problema?
 (keh meh-'dee-dahs toh-mah-'ree-ah 'pah-rah koh-rreh-'heer ehl proh-'bleh-mah)
Are you convinced that this is the best solution?
¿Está seguro que ésta es la mejor solución?
 (eh-'stah seh-'goo-roh keh 'eh-stah ehs lah meh-'hohr soh-loo-see-'ohn)
How do you feel about it?
¿Cómo se siente acerca de eso?
 ('koh-moh seh see-'ehn-teh ah-'sehr-kah deh 'eh-soh)
Let's analyze and resolve the problem.
Vamos a analizar y resolver al problema.
 ('vah-mohs ah ah-nah-lee-'sahr ee reh-sohl-'vehr ehl proh-'bleh-mah)

I'd like to hear your... **Quisiera escuchar su...**
 (kee-see-'eh-rah eh-skoo-'chahr soo)

comment	**comentario** *(koh-mehn-'tah-ree-oh)*
idea	**idea** *(ee-'deh-ah)*
interpretation	**interpretación** *(een-tehr-preh-tah-see-'ohn)*
opinion	**opinión** *(oh-pee-nee-'ohn)*
response	**respuesta** *(reh-'spweh-stah)*

Let's motivate them!
¡Vamos a motivarlos!
('vah-mohs ah moh-tee-'vahr-lohs)

Employees may be doing their jobs well, but are they really motivated? Periodically, HR professionals check up on each worker's desire to improve, participate, and interact with others. This next group of expressions and vocabulary will help:

You're part of the team!
¡Usted es parte de nuestro equipo!
 (oo-'stehd ehs 'pahr-teh deh 'nweh-stroh eh-'kee-poh)

We can't do it without you!
¡No podemos hacerlo sin usted!
(noh poh-'deh-mohs ah-'sehr-loh seen oo-'stehd)
Everyone must work together!
¡Todos tienen que trabajar juntos!
('toh-dohs tee-'eh-nehn keh trah-bah-'hahr 'hoon-tohs)

Here's another set of expressions that should be practiced regularly. Add a smile as you motivate the folks around you:

How...!	**¡Qué...!** *(keh)*
excellent	**excelente** *(ehk-seh-'lehn-teh)*
exceptional	**excepcional** *(ehk-sehp-see-oh-'nahl)*
fabulous	**fabuloso** *(fah-boo-'loh-soh)*
fantastic	**fantástico** *(fahn-'tah-stee-koh)*
great	**bueno** *('bweh-noh)*
incredible	**increíble** *(een-kreh-'ee-bleh)*
marvelous	**maravilloso** *(mah-rah-vee-'yoh-soh)*
outstanding	**sobresaliente** *(soh-breh-sah-lee-'ehn-teh)*
remarkable	**extraordinario**
	(ehks-trah-ohr-dee-'nah-ree-oh)
stupendous	**estupendo** *(eh-stoo-'pehn-doh)*
tremendous	**magnífico** *(mahg-'nee-fee-koh)*

Nothing works better than encouraging remarks!

What a great job!	**¡Qué buen trabajo!** *(keh bwehn trah-'bah-hoh)*
Very good!	**¡Muy bien!** *('moo·ee 'bee·ehn)*
Good work!	**¡Bien hecho!** *('bee·ehn 'eh-choh)*
You could do it!	**¡Pudo hacerlo!** *('pooh-doh ah-'sehr-loh)*
You're important!	**¡Usted es importante!**
	(oo-'stehd ehs eem-pohr-'tahn-teh)
You learn quickly!	**¡Aprende rápido!** *(ah-'prehn-deh 'rah-pee-doh)*
We need you!	**¡Le necesitamos!** *(leh neh-seh-see-'tah-mohs)*
We can't do it without you!	**¡No podemos hacerlo sin usted!**
	(noh poh-'deh-mohs ah-'sehr-loh seen oo-'stehd)
I trust you!	**¡Confío en usted!** *(kohn-'fee-oh ehn oo-'stehd)*
I respect you!	**¡Le respeto!** *(leh reh-'speh-toh)*
You're valuable!	**¡Usted es valioso!** *(oo-'stehd ehs vah-lee-'oh-soh)*

I like what you did!	**¡Me gusta lo que hizo!** *(meh 'goo-stah loh keh 'ee-soh)*
You have...	**Usted tiene...** *(oo-'stehd tee-'eh-neh)*
I see...	**Yo veo...** *(yoh 'veh-oh)*
There is/are...	**Hay...** *('ah·ee)*
advancement	**ascenso** *(ah-'sehn-soh)*
better approach	**mejor enfoque** *(meh-'hohr ehn-'foh-keh)*
effective solutions	**soluciones efectivas** *(soh-loo-see-'oh-nehs eh-fehk-'tee-vahs)*
excellent achievements	**rendimientos excelentes** *(rehn-dee-mee-'ehn-tohs ehk-seh-'lehn-tehs)*
fast development	**desarrollo rápido** *(dehs-ah-'roh-yoh 'rah-pee-doh)*
good effort	**gran esfuerzo** *(grahn ehs-fwehr-soh)*
great potential	**gran potencial** *(grahn poh-tehn-see-'ahl)*
high morale	**alta motivación** *('ahl-tah moh-tee-vah-see-'ohn)*
high standards	**normas altas** *('nohr-mahs 'ahl-tahs)*
lots of desire	**mucho deseo** *('moo-choh deh-'seh-oh)*
more success	**más éxito** *(mahs 'ehk-see-toh)*
mutual understanding	**entendimiento mutuo** *(ehn-tehn-dee-mee-'ehn-toh 'moo-too-oh)*
obvious progress	**progreso obvio** *(proh-'greh-soh 'ohb-vee-oh)*
outstanding conduct	**conducta destacada** *(kohn-'dook-tah deh-stah-'kah-dah)*
positive feedback	**reacción positiva** *(reh-ahk-see-'ohn poh-see-'tee-vah)*
professionalism	**profesionalismo** *(proh-feh-see-oh-nah-'lees-moh)*
professional pride	**orgullo profesional** *(ohr-'goo-yoh proh-feh-see-oh-'nahl)*
realistic goals	**metas posibles** *('meh-tahs poh-'see-blehs)*
self-motivation	**motivación personal** *(moh-tee-vah-see-'ohn pehr-soh-'nahl)*
sense of accomplishment	**sentido de logro** *(sehn-'tee-doh deh 'loh-groh)*
tremendous growth	**crecimiento tremendo** *(kreh-see-mee-'ehn-toh treh-'mehn-doh)*

useful ideas	**ideas útiles** *(ee-'deh-ahs 'oo-tee-lehs)*

Keep passing out the compliments:

I like the...	**Me gusta...** *(meh 'goo-stah)*
attitude	**la actitud** *(lah ahk-tee-'tood)*
climate	**el clima** *(ehl 'klee-mah)*
environment	**el ambiente** *(ehl ahm-bee-'ehn-teh)*
mood	**el humor** *(ehl oo-'mohr)*
spirit	**el espíritu** *(ehl eh-'spee-ree-'too)*
I have seen...	**He visto...** *(eh 'vee-stoh)*
acceptance	**aceptación** *(ah-sehp-tah-see-'ohn)*
appreciation	**aprecio** *(ah-'preh-see·oh)*
commitment	**compromiso** *(kohm-proh-'mee-soh)*
companionship	**compañerismo** *(kohm-pah-nyeh-'rees-moh)*
confidence	**confianza** *(kohn-fee-'ahn-sah)*
creativity	**creatividad** *(kreh-ah-tee-vee-'dahd)*
dialogue	**diálogo** *(dee-'ah-loh-goh)*
enthusiasm	**entusiasmo** *(ehn-too-see-'ahs-moh)*
friendship	**amistad** *(ah-mee-'stahd)*
harmony	**armonía** *(ahr-moh-'nee-ah)*
honesty	**honradez** *(ohn-rah-'dehs)*
initiative	**iniciativa** *(ee-nee-see-ah-'tee-vah)*
patience	**paciencia** *(pah-see-'ehn-see·ah)*
responsibility	**responsabilidad** *(reh-spohn-sah-bee-lee-'dahd)*
security	**seguridad** *(seh-goo-ree-'dahd)*
trust	**confianza** *(kohn-fee-'ahn-sah)*
value	**valor** *(vah-'lohr)*
This shows me that you are...	**Esto me enseña que usted es...** *('eh-stoh meh ehn-'seh-nyah keh oo-'stehd ehs)*
ambitious	**ambicioso** *(ahm-bee-see-'oh-soh)*
competent	**competente** *(kohm-peh-'tehn-teh)*
creative	**creativo** *(kreh-ah-'tee-voh)*
efficient	**eficiente** *(eh-fee-see-'ehn-teh)*
independent	**independiente** *(een-deh-pehn-dee-'ehn-teh)*
organized	**organizado** *(ohr-gah-nee-'sah-doh)*
punctual	**puntual** *(poon-too-'ahl)*

Temas culturales

Spanish verbs also have the **tú** *(too)* form, which is an informal *you* used between family members, small children, and friends. Since your relationship with Hispanics at work will usually be on a professional level, the only form you'll need for now is the **usted** *(oo-'stehd)* or formal form. Notice these examples:

	Formal	*Informal*
Come.	**Venga usted.**	**Ven tú.**
	('vehn-gah oo-'stehd)	*(vehn too)*
Sit.	**Siéntese usted.**	**Siéntate tú.**
	(see-'ehn-teh-seh oo-'stehd)	*(see-'ehn-tah-teh too)*
You're ready.	**Usted está listo.**	**Tú estás listo.**
	(oo-'stehd eh-'stah 'lee-stoh)	*(too eh-'stahs 'lee-stoh)*

Listos para practicar

Write three effective questions that you could ask an employee when working together on problem resolution:

_____

_____

_____

Write five supportive one-liners that could be used as positive reinforcement:

_____

_____

_____

_____

_____

Translate these sentences:
   I see fast development.

_____

You have lots of desire.

There is more success.

I like the environment.

I have seen patience and trust.

Let's participate!
¡Vamos a participar!
('vah-mohs ah pahr-tee-see-'pahr)

Still another excellent way to fire up the troops is to offer programs or events in which everyone can participate. Here are some examples:

You are invited to (the)...	**Le invitamos a...** *(leh een-vee-'tah-mohs ah)*
Can you attend (the)...?	**¿Puede asistir a...?** *('pweh-deh ah-see-'steer ah)*
Please come to (the)...	**Por favor, venga a...** *(pohr fah-'vohr, 'vehn-gah ah)*
banquet	**el banquete** *(ehl bahn-'keh-teh)*
celebration	**la celebración** *(lah seh-leh-brah-see-'ohn)*
ceremony	**la ceremonia** *(lah seh-reh-'moh-nee·ah)*
conference	**la conferencia** *(lah kohn-feh-'rehn-see·ah)*
demonstration	**la demostración** *(lah deh-moh-strah-see-'ohn)*
event	**el evento** *(ehl eh-'vehn-toh)*
meeting	**la reunión** *(lah reh-oo-nee-'ohn)*
parade	**el desfile** *(ehl dehs-'fee-leh)*
party	**la fiesta** *(lah fee-'eh-stah)*
performance	**la función** *(lah foonk-see-'ohn)*
picnic	**la merienda** *(lah meh-ree-'ehn-dah)*
program	**el programa** *(ehl proh-'grah-mah)*
raffle	**el sorteo** *(ehl sohr-'teh-oh)*
show	**el espectáculo** *(ehl eh-spehk-'tah-koo-loh)*
tribute	**el tributo** *(ehl tree-'boo-toh)*
wedding	**la boda** *(lah 'boh-dah)*

¡Información!

- More motivating vocabulary:

We have...	**Tenemos...** *(teh-'neh-mohs)*
awards	**galardones** *(gah-lahr-'doh-nehs)*
certificates	**certificados** *(sehr-tee-fee-'kah-dohs)*
games	**juegos** *(hoo-'eh-gohs)*
gifts	**regalos** *(reh-'gah-lohs)*
medals	**medallas** *(meh-'dah-yahs)*
prizes	**premios** *('preh-mee-ohs)*
rewards	**recompensas** *(reh-kohm-'pehn-sahs)*
ribbons	**cintas meritorias**
	('seen-tahs meh-ree-'toh-ree-ahs)
trophies	**trofeos** *(troh-'feh-ohs)*

- And these words are used for special occasions:

Let's...	**Vamos a...** *('vah-mohs ah)*
contribute	**contribuir** *(kohn-tree-boo-'eer)*
donate	**donar** *(doh-'nahr)*
volunteer	**ser voluntarios** *(sehr voh-loon-'tah-ree-ohs)*

Temas culturales

To truly motivate everyone, learn the following expressions to greet your Spanish-speaking employees on special occasions:

Happy Easter!	**¡Felices Pascuas!** *(feh-lee-sehs 'pah-skwahs)*
Happy New Year!	**¡Feliz Año Nuevo!**
	(feh-'lees 'ah-nyoh noo-'eh-voh)
Merry Christmas!	**¡Feliz Navidad!** *(feh-'lees nah-vee-'dahd)*

Join the team
Unase al equipo *('oo-nah-seh ahl eh-'kee-poh)*
In some cases, it may be appropriate to assemble company sports teams, which can compete regularly in local tournaments or leagues. By repre-

senting the business in uniform at such a function, morale gets a boost and employees learn the value of team effort and support. Consider these words that refer to sports and related activities:

We play...	**Jugamos...** *(hoo-'gah-mohs)*
baseball	**el béisbol** *(ehl 'beh-ees-bohl)*
basketball	**el básquetbol** *(ehl 'bah-skeht-bohl)*
bowling	**el boliche** *(ehl boh-'ee-cheh)*
boxing	**el boxeo** *(ehl bohk-'seh-oh)*
football	**el fútbol americano**
	(ehl 'foot-bohl ah-meh-ree-'kah-noh)
golf	**el golf** *(ehl gohlf)*
lacrosse	**el lacrosse** *(ehl lah-'kroh-seh)*
soccer	**el fútbol** *(ehl 'foot-bohl)*
tennis	**el tenis** *(ehl 'teh-nees)*
volleyball	**el vólibol** *(ehl 'voh-leh-ee-bohl)*
We go to (the)...	**Vamos a...** *('vah-mohs ah)*
court	**la cancha** *(lah 'kahn-chah)*
field	**el campo** *(ehl 'kahm-poh)*
game	**el juego** *(ehl hoo-'eh-goh)*
golf course	**el campo de golf** *(ehl 'kahm-poh deh gohlf)*
gymnasium	**el gimnasio** *(ehl heem-'nah-see-oh)*
match	**el partido** *(ehl pahr-'tee-doh)*
playground	**el campo de recreo**
	(ehl 'kahm-poh deh reh-'kreh-oh)
pool	**la piscina** *(lah pee-'see-nah)*
practice	**la práctica** *(lah 'prahk-tee-kah)*
stadium	**el estadio** *(ehl eh-'stah-dee-oh)*

Additional training
Entrenamiento adicional
(ehn-treh-nah-mee-'ehn-toh ah-dee-see-oh-'nahl)

Once the appraisal is complete, attempt to set up specialized education programs for those who need extra assistance. This brief series of words and phrases should provide enough vocabulary to conduct intelligent conversations.

You should go to (the)...	**Debe ir a...** *('deh-beh eer ah)*
class	**la clase** *(lah 'klah-seh)*
course	**el curso** *(ehl 'koor-soh)*
program	**el programa** *(ehl proh-'grah-mah)*
school	**la escuela** *(lah eh-'skweh-lah)*
session	**la sesión** *(lah seh-see-'ohn)*
workshop	**el seminario** *(ehl seh-mee-'nah-ree-oh)*
You need to study (the)...	**Necesita estudiar...** *(neh-seh-'see-tah eh-stoo-dee-'ahr)*
copies	**las copias** *(lahs 'koh-pee-ahs)*
data	**los datos** *(lohs 'dah-tohs)*
documents	**los documentos** *(lohs doh-koo-'mehn-tohs)*
instructions	**las instrucciones** *(lahs een-strook-see-'oh-nehs)*
notes	**las anotaciones** *(lahs ah-noh-tah-see-'oh-nehs)*
outlines	**los resúmenes** *(lohs reh-'soo-meh-nehs)*
Bring (the)...	**Traiga...** *('trah-ee-gah)*
You will need (the)...	**Necesitará...** *(neh-seh-see-tah-'rah)*
binder	**la carpeta** *(lah kahr-'peh-tah)*
book	**el libro** *(ehl 'lee-broh)*
equipment	**el equipo** *(ehl eh-'kee-poh)*
folder	**el cuaderno** *(ehl kwah-'dehr-noh)*
information	**la información** *(lah een-fohr-mah-see-'ohn)*
material	**el material** *(ehl mah-teh-ree-'ahl)*
paper	**el papel** *(ehl pah-'pehl)*
pen	**el lapicero** *(ehl lah-pee-'seh-roh)*
tool	**la herramienta** *(lah eh-rrah-mee-'ehn-tah)*

¡Información!

These sentences can be used to express the idea of help.

It will help you.	**Le ayudará.** *(leh ah-yoo-dah-'rah)*
You need extra help.	**Necesita ayuda adicional.** *(neh-seh-'see-tah ah-'yoo-dah ah-dee-see-oh-'nahl)*
The information is helpful.	**La información es útil.** *(lah een-fohr-mah-see-'ohn ehs 'oo-teel)*

Listos para practicar

Fill in the blanks with one of the words provided:

los certificados, los deportes, la fiesta
  (lohs sehr-tee-fee-'kah-dohs, lohs deh-'pohr-tehs, lah fee-'eh-stah)

Por favor, venga a _____.
  (pohr fah-'vohr, 'vehn-gah ah ____)

Van a recibir _____.
  (vahn ah reh-see-'beer ____)

Queremos jugar _____.
  (keh-'reh-mohs hoo-'gahr ____)

List three common sports:

_____

_____

_____

List three popular hobbies:

_____

_____

_____

List three common items in a classroom:

_____

_____

_____

The trade union
El sindicato *(ehl seen-dee-'kah-toh)*

In a number of industries, employees are encouraged to join trade unions or similar organizations. As a result, HR personnel must be thoroughly aware of any union activity at the workplace, especially when questions are raised about procedures and practices related to the performance appraisal. Regardless of the issue, the terminology that follows will be helpful when dealing with Spanish speakers. However, if the topic gets serious, be sure to get assistance from a skilled bilingual interpreter.

Do you want to talk about (the)...?	¿Quiere hablar acerca de...? *(kee-'eh-reh ah-'blahr ah-'sehr-kah deh)*
agreement	el **acuerdo** *(ehl ah-'kwehr-doh)*
amendment	la **enmienda** *(lah ehn-mee-'ehn-dah)*
appeal	la **apelación** *(lah ah-peh-lah-see-'ohn)*
arbitration	el **arbitraje** *(ehl ahr-bee-'trah-heh)*
clause	la **cláusula** *(lah 'klow-soo-lah)*
collective bargaining	la **negociación colectiva** *(lah neh-go-see-ah-see-'ohn koh-lehk-'tee-vah)*
compromise	el **compromiso** *(ehl kohm-proh-'mee-soh)*
contract	el **contrato** *(ehl kohn-'trah-toh)*
election	la **elección** *(lah eh-lehk-see-'ohn)*
guild	el **gremio** *(ehl 'greh-mee-oh)*
leadership	el **liderazgo** *(ehl lee-deh-'rahs-goh)*
membership	la **afiliación** *(lah ah-fee-lee-ah-see-'ohn)*
seniority	el **mayorazgo** *(ehl mah-yoh-'rahs-goh)*
settlement	el **arreglo** *(ehl ah-'rreh-gloh)*
shop	el **taller** *(ehl tah-'yehr)*
Let's discuss (the)...	Vamos a conversar sobre... *('vah-mohs ah kohn-vehr-'sahr 'soh-breh)*
cards	las **tarjetas** *(lahs tahr-'heh-tahs)*
conditions	las **condiciones** *(lahs kohn-dee-see-'oh-nehs)*
demands	las **reclamaciones** *(lahs reh-klah-mah-see-'oh-nehs)*
dues	las **cuotas** *(lahs 'kwoh-tahs)*
grievances	las **quejas** *(lahs 'keh-hahs)*
guidelines	las **pautas** *(lahs 'pah-oo-tahs)*
laws	las **leyes** *(lahs 'leh-yehs)*
rights	los **derechos** *(lohs deh-'reh-chohs)*
terms	los **términos** *(lohs 'tehr-mee-nohs)*
Who is (the)...?	¿Quién es...? *(kee-'ehn-ehs)*
arbitrator	el **árbitro** *(ehl 'ahr-bee-troh)*
candidate	el **candidato** *(ehl kahn-dee-'dah-toh)*
chairperson	el **presidente** *(ehl preh-see-'dehn-teh)*
delegate	el **delegado** *(ehl deh-leh-'gah-doh)*
director	el **director** *(ehl dee-rehk-'tohr)*

lawyer	**el abogado** *(ehl ah-boh-'gah-doh)*
leader	**el líder** *(ehl 'lee-dehr)*
mediator	**el mediador** *(ehl meh-dee-ah-'dohr)*
member	**el miembro** *(ehl mee-'ehm-broh)*
representative	**el representante** *(ehl reh-preh-sehn-'tahn-teh)*
witness	**el testigo** *(ehl teh-'stee-goh)*
Is there...?	**¿Hay...?** *('ah-ee)*
confidence	**confianza** *(kohn-fee-'ahn-sah)*
dialogue	**diálogo** *(dee-'ah-loh-goh)*
discipline	**disciplina** *(dee-see-'plee-nah)*
dissent	**disconformidad** *(dees-kohn-fohr-mee-'dahd)*
enforcement	**inposición** *(eem-poh-see-see-'ohn)*
influence	**influencia** *(een-floo-'ehn-see-ah)*
interest	**interés** *(een-teh-'rehs)*
involvement	**participación** *(pahr-tee-see-pah-see-'ohn)*
peace	**paz** *(pahs)*
persuasion	**persuasión** *(pehr-swah-see-'ohn)*
pressure	**presión** *(preh-see-'ohn)*
respect	**respeto** *(reh-'speh-toh)*
unity	**unidad** *(oo-nee-'dahd)*

Continue creating phrases using these key vocabulary words and focus on how they are similar to English:

What do you know about (the)...?	**¿Qué sabe usted de...?** *(keh 'sah-beh oo-'stehd deh.)*
association	**la asociación** *(lah ah-soh-see-ah-see-'ohn)*
constitution	**la constitución** *(lah kohn-stee-too-see-'ohn)*
negotiation	**la negociación** *(lah neh-goh-see-ah-see-'ohn)*
intervention	**la intervención** *(lah een-tehr-vehn-see-'ohn)*
investigation	**la investigación** *(lah een-veh-stee-gah-see-'ohn)*
jurisdiction	**la jurisdicción** *(lah hoo-rees-deek-see-'ohn)*
obligation	**la obligación** *(lah ohb-lee-gah-see-'ohn)*
organization	**la organización** *(lah ohr-gah-nee-sah-see-'ohn)*
protection	**la protección** *(lah proh-tehk-see-'ohn)*
violation	**la violación** *(lah vee-oh-lah-see-'ohn)*

When problems with the union arise, get set to respond:

Did you hear about (the)...?	¿**Escuchó de...?** *(eh-skoo-'choh deh...)*
boycott	**el boicot** *(ehl boh-ee-'koht)*
deadlock	**el estancamiento** *(ehl ehs-tahn-kah-mee-'ehn-toh)*
dispute	**la disputa** *(lah dee-'spoo-tah)*
march	**la manifestación** *(lah mah-nee-feh-stah-see-'ohn)*
picket	**el piquete** *(ehl pee-'keh-teh)*
protest	**la protesta** *(lah proh-'teh-stah)*
strike	**la huelga** *(lah 'wehl-gah)*
survey	**la encuesta** *(lah ehn-'kweh-stah)*
work stoppage	**el paro de trabajo** *(ehl 'pah-roh deh trah-'bah-hoh)*
They are going to...	**Van a...** *(vahn ah...)*
lockout	**hacer cierre forzoso** *(ah-'sehr see-'eh-reh fohr-'soh-soh)*
cross lines	**cruzar las líneas** *(vahn ah kroo-'sahr lahs 'lee-neh-ahs)*
cut back	**recortar el trabajo** *(reh-kohr-'tahr ehl trah-'bah-hoh)*
It's...	**Es...** *(ehs)*
avoidable	**evitable** *(eh-vee-'tah-bleh)*
local	**local** *(loh-'kahl)*
militant	**militante** *(mee-lee-'tahn-teh)*
national	**nacional** *(nah-see-oh-'nal)*
non-union	**sin sindicato** *(seen seen-dee-'kah-toh)*
official	**oficial** *(oh-fee-see-'ahl)*
political	**político** *(poh-'lee-tee-koh)*
preliminary	**preliminar** *(preh-lee-mee-'nahr)*
regional	**regional** *(reh-hee-oh-'nahl)*
retroactive	**retroactivo** *(reh-troh-ahk-'tee-voh)*
tentative	**tentativo** *(tehn-tah-'tee-voh)*
unfair	**injusto** *(een-'hoo-stoh)*

And, don't forget to add these verbs to your current list of action words. These all have to do with union relations.

accept	**aceptar** *(ah-sehp-'tahr)*	_____
admit	**confesar** *(kohn-feh-'sahr)*	_____
adopt	**adoptar** *(ah-dohp-'tahr)*	_____
coerce	**obligar** *(oh-blee-'gahr)*	_____
control	**controlar** *(kohn-troh-'lahr)*	_____
debate	**debatir** *(deh-bah-'teer)*	_____
defend	**defender** *(deh-fehn-'dehr)*	**Nuestro abogado nos defenderá.** *('nweh-stroh ah-boh-'gah-doh nohs deh-fehn-deh-'rah)*
demand	**demandar** *(deh-mahn-'dahr)*	_____
deny	**negar** *(neh-'gahr)*	_____
enforce	**imponer** *(eem-poh-'nehr)*	_____
file	**archivar** *(ahr-chee-'vahr)*	_____
guarantee	**garantizar** *(gah-rahn-tee-'sahr)*	**No pueden garantizar el contrato.** *(noh 'pweh-dehn gah-rahn-tee-'sahr ehl kohn-'trah-toh)*
interfere	**interferir** *(een-tehr-feh-'reer)*	_____
intervene	**intervenir** *(een-tehr-veh-'neer)*	_____
negotiate	**negociar** *(neh-goh-see-'ahr)*	_____
protect	**proteger** *(proh-teh-'hehr)*	_____
reject	**rechazar** *(reh-chah-'sahr)*	_____
represent	**representar** *(reh-preh-sehn-'tahr)*	_____
restrain	**restringir** *(reh-streen-'heer)*	_____
suspend	**suspender** *(soo-spehn-'dehr)*	_____
vote	**votar** *(voh-'tahr)*	**Votamos en dos semanas.** *(voh-'tah-mohs ehn dohs seh-'mah-nahs)*

¡Información!

Here are some more topics that come up at union meetings:

We talk about...	**Hablamos de...** *(ah-'blah-mohs deh)*
age	**la edad** *(lah eh-'dahd)*
holidays	**los días feriados** *(lohs 'dee-ahs feh-ree-'ah-dohs)*
hours	**las horas** *(lahs 'oh-rahs)*
rehabilitation	**la rehabilitación** *(lah reh-ah-bee-lee-tah-see-'ohn)*
security	**la seguridad** *(lah seh-goo-ree-'dahd)*
training	**el entrenamiento** *(ehl ehn-treh-nah-mee-'ehn-toh)*
treatment	**el tratamiento** *(ehl trah-tah-mee-'ehn-toh)*
wages	**el sueldo** *(ehl 'swehl-doh)*
They know about (the)...	**Saben de...** *('sah-behn deh)*
assignments	**las tareas** *(lahs tah-'reh-ahs)*
benefits	**los beneficios** *(lohs beh-neh-'fee-see-ohs)*
diseases	**las enfermedades** *(lahs ehn-fehr-meh-'dah-dehs)*
incentives	**los incentivos** *(lohs een-sehn-'tee-vohs)*
injuries	**las heridas** *(lahs eh-'ree-dahs)*

The law
La ley *(lah 'leh·ee)*

Dealing with union activity can lead to courtroom concerns. For your own protection, copy this vital selection of items, and then put them away for emergency use:

addendum	**el anexo** *(ehl ah-'nehk-soh)*
affidavit	**el afidávit** *(ehl ah-fee-'dah-veet)*
allegation	**la acusación** *(lah ah-koo-sah-see-'ohn)*
anti trust	**el antimonopolio** *(ehl ahn-tee-moh-noh-'poh-lee-oh)*

case	**el caso** *(ehl 'kah-soh)*
court	**el tribunal** *(ehl tree-boo-'nahl)*
defense	**la defensa** *(lah deh-'fehn-sah)*
evidence	**la evidencia** *(lah eh-vee-'dehn-see·ah)*
injunction	**el interdicto** *(ehl een-tehr-'deek-toh)*
litigation	**el pleito** *(ehl 'pleh·ee-toh)*
plaintiff	**el demandante** *(ehl deh-mahn-'dahn-teh)*
prosecution	**el procesamiento** *(ehl proh-seh-sah-mee-'ehn-toh)*
testimony	**el testimonio** *(ehl teh-stee-'moh-nee·oh)*
affirmative action	**la acción afirmativa** *(lah ahk-see-'ohn ah-feer-mah-'tee-vah)*
civil rights	**los derechos civiles** *(lohs deh-'reh-chohs see-'vee-lehs)*

Now take note of these valuable terms. They are all related:

labor dispute	**la discusión laboral** *(lah dee-skoo-see-'ohn lah-boh-'rahl)*
labor freeze	**la paralización laboral** *(lah pah-rah-lee-sah-see-'ohn)*
labor leader	**el líder laboral** *(ehl 'lee-dehr lah-boh-'rahl)*
labor relations	**las relaciones laborales** *(lahs reh-lah-see-'oh-nehs lah-boh-'rah-lehs)*
labor union	**el sindicato laboral** *(ehl seen-dee-'kah-toh lah-boh-'rahl)*

Listos para practicar

Translate this set of statements that refer to activities within a union:

Do you want to talk about dues and membership?

_____

Let's talk about negotiations with the organization.

_____

Is there peace and unity?

_____

The contract is official, but unfair.

_____

We talk about hours, benefits, and incentives.

_____

The plaintiff went to court.

_____

Name three people who are typically involved in union activities:

_____ _____ _____

Name three major industries that attract union participation:

_____ _____ _____

Name three negative results of union activity:

_____ _____ _____

 ## Temas culturales

Many managers work with new immigrants who are unfamiliar with local, state, or federal laws and regulations. If you plan to establish a long-term relationship, you can prevent potential problems by giving them as much legal information as possible. By contacting a variety of service agencies, one can pick up literature in Spanish concerning citizenship, taxes, health care, education, transportation, and residence, as well as personal rights and privileges.

 ## Más fácil

The easiest shortcut in Spanish is to use infinitives as nouns. No special phrases are required. Look over these examples:

Off to work!	**¡A trabajar!** *(ah-trah-bah-'hahr)*
Reading is important.	**Leer es importante.** *(leh-'ehr ehs eem-pohr-'tahn-teh)*
Shut the door when you leave.	**Al salir, cierre la puerta.** *(ahl sah-'leer, see-'eh-rreh lah 'pwehr-tah)*

Even though dozens of new verb infinitives relating to employee evaluations have already been introduced in patterns throughout this chapter, memorize these key words. Be sure to pronounce each syllable correctly:

to allow	**permitir** *(pehr-mee-'teer)*
to analyze	**analizar** *(ah-nah-lee-'sahr)*
to approve	**aprobar** *(ah-proh-'bahr)*
to attend	**asistir** *(ah-see-'steer)*
to demonstrate	**demostrar** *(deh-moh-'strahr)*
to clarify	**aclarar** *(ah-klah-'rahr)*
to collect	**coleccionar** *(koh-lehk-see-oh-'nahr)*
to correct	**corregir** *(koh-rreh-'heer)*
to evaluate	**evaluar** *(eh-vah-loo-'ahr)*
to improve	**mejorar** *(meh-hoh-'rahr)*
to inspect	**inspeccionar** *(een-spehk-see-oh-'nahr)*
to join	**afiliarse** *(ah-fee-lee-'ahr-seh)*
to motivate	**motivar** *(moh-tee-'vahr)*
to notice	**fijarse** *(fee-'hahr-seh)*
to observe	**observar** *(ohb-sehr-'vahr)*
to plan	**planear** *(plah-neh-'ahr)*
to prove	**probar** *(proh-'bahr)*
to recognize	**reconocer** *(reh-koh-noh-'sehr)*
to remember	**recordar** *(reh-kohr-'dahr)*
to suggest	**sugerir** *(soo-heh-'reer)*
to verify	**verificar** *(veh-ree-fee-'kahr)*

Keep this additional list for those cases involving union members. All of these have been mentioned before. Care to add a phrase?

to accept	**aceptar** *(ah-sehp-'tahr)*	**Aceptamos cheques aquí.** *(ah-sehp-'tah-mohs 'cheh-kehs ah-'kee)*
to admit	**admitir** *(ahd-mee-'teer)*	**Van a admitirlo.** *(vahn ah ahd-mee-'teer-loh)*
to adopt	**adoptar** *(ah-dohp-'tahr)*	**Están adoptando el plan.** *(eh-'stahn ah-dohp-'tahn-doh ehl plahn)*
to appraise	**estimar** *(eh-stee-'mahr)*	_____

to assure	**asegurar** *(ah-seh-goo-'rahr)*	_____
to check	**revisar** *(reh-vee-'sahr)*	_____
to commend	**alabar** *(ah-lah-'bahr)*	_____
to compliment	**felicitar** *(feh-lee-see-'tahr)*	_____
to confirm	**confirmar** *(kohn-feer-'mahr)*	_____
to continue	**continuar** *(kohn-tee-noo-'ahr)*	_____
to cooperate	**cooperar** *(koh-oh-peh-'rahr)*	_____
to coordinate	**coordinar** *(koh-ohr-dee-nahr)*	_____
to debate	**debatir** *(deh-bah-'teer)*	_____
to defend	**defender** *(deh-fehn-'dehr)*	_____
to demand	**demandar** *(deh-mahn-'dahr)*	_____
to deny	**negar** *(neh-'gahr)*	_____
to develop	**desarrollar** *(deh-sahr-roh-'yahr)*	_____
to encourage	**animar** *(ah-nee-'mahr)*	_____
to establish	**establecer** *(eh-stah-bleh-'sehr)*	_____
to exceed	**sobrepasar** *(soh-breh-pah-'sahr)*	_____
to exhibit	**exhibir** *(ehk-see-'beer)*	_____
to explain	**explicar** *(ehks-plee-'kahr)*	_____
to file	**archivar** *(ahr-chee-'vahr)*	_____
to guarantee	**garantizar** *(gah-rahn-tee-'sahr)*	_____
to identify	**identificar** *(ee-dehn-tee-fee-'kahr)*	_____
to interfere	**interferir** *(een-tehr-feh-'reer)*	_____
to intervene	**intervenir** *(een-tehr-veh-'neer)*	_____
to lead	**dirigir** *(dee-ree-'heer)*	_____
to maintain	**mantener** *(mahn-teh-'nehr)*	_____
to manage	**manejar** *(mah-neh-'hahr)*	_____
to measure	**medir** *(meh-'deer)*	_____
to monitor	**controlar** *(kohn-troh-'lahr)*	_____
to negotiate	**negociar** *(neh-goh-see-'ahr)*	_____
to observe	**observar** *(ohb-sehr-'vahr)*	_____
to persuade	**persuadir** *(pehr-swah-'deer)*	_____
to prepare	**preparar** *(preh-pah-'rahr)*	_____
to prescribe	**prescribir** *(preh-skree-'beer)*	_____
to process	**procesar** *(proh-seh-'sahr)*	_____
to promise	**prometer** *(proh-meh-'tehr)*	_____
to protect	**proteger** *(proh-teh-'hehr)*	_____

to recognize	**reconocer** *(reh-koh-noh-'sehr)*	_____
to record	**documentar** *(doh-koo-mehn-'tahr)*	_____
to reject	**rechazar** *(reh-chah-'sahr)*	_____
to repeat	**repetir** *(reh-peh-'teer)*	_____
to represent	**representar** *(reh-preh-sehn-'tahr)*	_____
to restrain	**restringir** *(reh-streen-'heer)*	_____
to review	**repasar** *(reh-pah-'sahr)*	_____
to reward	**recompensar** *(reh-kohm-pehn-'sahr)*	_____
to settle	**arreglar** *(ah-rreh-'glahr)*	_____
to share	**compartir** *(kohm-pahr-'teer)*	_____
to study	**estudiar** *(eh-stoo-dee-'ahr)*	_____
to support	**apoyar** *(ah-poh-'yahr)*	_____
to suspend	**suspender** *(soo-spehn-'dehr)*	_____
to test	**examinar** *(ehk-sah-mee-'nahr)*	_____
to thank	**agradecer** *(ah-grah-deh-'sehr)*	_____
to try	**tratar** *(trah-'tahr)*	_____
to vote	**votar** *(voh-'tahr)*	_____

Palabras activas

Let's check out another simple formula for changing basic verb forms to refer to *past action*. At times, this form can be used in place of the preterit that was presented in the previous chapter.

First, change all the verb endings to **-ndo,** just like you did when you talked about *current action:*

tomar *(toh-'mahr)*	**tomando** *(toh-'mahn-doh)*
comer *(koh-'mehr)*	**comiendo** *(koh-mee-'ehn-doh)*
escribir *(eh-skree-'beer)*	**escribiendo** *(eh-skree-bee-'ehn-doh)*

Next, in place of **estoy, está, están,** and **estamos** *(eh-'stoh-ee, eh-'stah, eh-'stahn, eh-'stah-mohs),* which refer to present time, combine the following past action words with the **-ndo** verb forms:

I was   **estaba** *(eh-'stah-bah)*

I was talking on the phone.

Estaba hablando por teléfono.

(eh-'stah-bah ah-'blahn-doh pohr teh-'leh-foh-noh)

You were; He, She was   **estaba** *(eh-'stah-bah)*

He was using the machine.

Estaba usando la máquina.

(eh-'stah-bah oo-'sahn-doh lah 'mah-kee-nah)

You (pl.) were, They were   **estaban** *(eh-'stah-bahn)*

They were opening the windows.

Estaban abriendo las ventanas.

(eh-'stah-bahn ah-bree-'ehn-doh lahs vehn-'tah-nahs)

We were   **estábamos** *(eh-'stah-bah-mohs)*

We were working here.

Estábamos trabajando aquí.

(eh-'stah-bah-mohs trah-bah-'hahn-doh ah-'kee)

¡Información!

• **"Estaba"** is actually an *imperfect* past tense form. Look at how it's formed with these other **ar** actions:

I used to drive.	**Manejaba.** *(mah-neh-'hah-bah)*
I was working.	**Trabajaba.** *(trah-bah-'hah-bah)*
I walked.	**Caminaba.** *(kah-mee-'nah-bah)*

• Verbs with **se** get treated the same:

They were joining the union!

¡Se estaban afiliando al sindicato!

(seh eh-'stah-bahn ah-fee-lee-'ahn-doh ahl seen-dee-'kah-toh)

¡Ordenes!

Let's continue to add pronouns to our command words, but this time let's see what happens when we shift everything to the negative. We'll only work with a few of the verbs from this chapter, so read each word carefully. Again, the **le** refers to people, while the **lo** and **la** refer to things:

Analyze it.	**Analícelo.** *(ah-nah-'lee-seh-loh)*
Don't analyze it.	**No lo analice.** *(noh loh ah-nah-'lee-seh)*
Observe him.	**Obsérvele.** *(ohb-'sehr-veh-leh)*
Don't observe him.	**No le observe.** *(noh leh ohb-'sehr-veh)*
Verify it.	**Verifíquelo.** *(veh-ree-'fee-keh-loh)*
Don't verify it.	**No lo verifique.** *(noh loh veh-ree-'fee-keh)*
Show her.	**Muéstrele.** *('mweh-streh-leh)*
Don't show her.	**No le muestre.** *(noh leh 'mweh-streh)*
Clarify it.	**Aclárelo.** *(ah-'klah-rreh-loh)*
Don't clarify it.	**No lo aclare.** *(noh loh ah-'klah-reh)*

¡Información!

• In some cases, you can put two pronouns together. Notice the changes:

Clarify it for him.	**Acláreselo.** *(ah-'klah-reh-seh-loh)*
Verify it for me.	**Verifíquemelo.** *(veh-ree-'fee-keh-meh-loh)*
Show it to her.	**Muéstreselo.** *('mweh-streh-seh-loh)*

Listos para practicar

Some verb infinitives in Spanish are harder to remember because they don't look anything like their English equivalent. Take a moment to look up these tricky translations:

mejorar *(meh-hoh-'rahr)* _____
recordar *(reh-kohr-'dahr)* _____
asistir *(ah-see-'steer)* _____
mostrar *(moh-'strahr)* _____
fijar *(fee-'hahr)* _____

Here's a good way to review what you've learned about past actions in Spanish. Follow the pattern of these examples:

Observé *(ohb-sehr-veh)*   **Estaba observando.**
                                    (eh-'stah-bah ohb-sehr-'vahn-doh)

Voté *(voh-'teh)*   **Estaba votando.**
                                        (eh-'stah-bah voh-'tahn-doh)

Evalué *(eh-vah-loo-'eh)*   _____.

Inspeccioné   _____.
(een-spehk-see·oh-'neh)

Planeé *(plah-neh-'eh)*   _____.

Now, put these words together to form a complete command:

lo verifique me   **¡Verifíquemelo!**
                                        (veh-ree-'fee-keh-meh-loh)

se muestre lo   ¡ _____!
(seh mweh-streh loh)

aclare lo se
(ah'klah-reh loh seh)   ¡ _____!

Chapter Eight

Capítulo Ocho
(kah-'pee-too-loh 'oh-choh)

The Business
Los negocios
(lohs neh-'goh-see·ohs)

Let's talk about business
Hablemos de los negocios
(ah-'bleh-mohs deh lohs neh-'goh-see·ohs)

The Human Resources Department generally takes on the responsibilities of hiring, informing, training, counseling, and evaluating each employee. In the previous chapters, we learned how to conduct these activities in Spanish. Now, it's time to familiarize ourselves with words and phrases that help define the business itself. As always, begin with the basics:

Where is (the)...?	**¿Dónde está..?** *('dohn-deh eh-'stah)*
claim	**la reclamación** *(lah reh-klah-mah-see-'ohn)*
invoice	**la factura** *(lah fahk-'too-rah)*
order	**el pedido** *(ehl peh-'dee-doh)*
receipt	**el recibo** *(ehl reh-'see-boh)*
ticket	**el boleto** *(ehl boh-'leh-toh)*
Move (the)...	**Mueva...** *('mweh-vah)*
delivery	**el reparto** *(ehl reh-'pahr-toh)*
inventory	**el inventario** *(ehl een-vehn-'tah-ree-oh)*
merchandise	**la mercancía** *(lah mehr-kahn-'see-ah)*
product	**el producto** *(ehl proh-'dook-toh)*
sample	**la muestra** *(lah 'mweh-strah)*
shipment	**el envío** *(ehl ehn-'vee-oh)*
supply	**la existencia** *(lah ehk-sees-'tehn-see·ah)*

Sometimes asking questions is an easier way to practice. Take a few minutes to read through each of the phrases below:

Who is (the)...?	**¿Quién es...?** *(kee-'ehn ehs)*
cashier	**el cajero** *(ehl kah-'heh-roh)*
clerk	**el oficinista** *(ehl oh-fee-see-'nee-stah)*
customer	**el cliente** *(ehl klee-'ehn-teh)*
manager	**el gerente** *(ehl heh-'rehn-teh)*
manufacturer	**el fabricante** *(ehl fah-bree-'kahn-teh)*
salesperson	**el vendedor** *(ehl vehn-deh-'dohr)*

Did you see (the)...?	¿Vio...? *(vee-'oh)*
bargain	la **ganga** *(lah 'gahn-gah)*
charge	el **cargo** *(ehl 'kahr-goh)*
discount	el **descuento** *(ehl deh-'skwehn-toh)*
down payment	el **pago inicial** *(ehl 'pah-goh ee-nee-see-'ahl)*
installment	el **plazo** *(ehl 'plah-soh)*
loss	la **pérdida** *(lah 'pehr-dee-dah)*
offer	la **oferta** *(lah oh-'fehr-tah)*
payment	el **pago** *(ehl 'pah-goh)*
refund	el **reembolso** *(ehl reh-ehm-'bohl-soh)*
return	la **devolución** *(lah deh-voh-loo-see-'ohn)*
sale	la **venta** *(lah 'vehn-tah)*
tax	el **impuesto** *(ehl eem-'pweh-stoh)*

What is (the)...?	¿Cuál es...? *(kwahl ehs)*
amount	la **cantidad** *(lah kahn-tee-'dahd)*
content	el **contenido** *(ehl kohn-teh-'nee-doh)*
percentage	el **porcentaje** *(ehl pohr-sehn-'tah-heh)*
price	el **precio** *(ehl 'preh-see·oh)*
profit	la **ganancia** *(lah gah-'nahn-see·ah)*
quality	la **calidad** *(lah kah-lee-'dahd)*
quantity	la **cantidad** *(lah kahn-tee-'dahd)*
rate	la **tarifa** *(lah tah-'ree-fah)*
reduction	la **reducción** *(lah reh-dook-see-'ohn)*
subtotal	el **subtotal** *(ehl soob-toh-'tahl)*
sum	la **suma** *(lah 'soo-mah)*
total	el **total** *(ehl toh-'tahl)*
weight	el **peso** *(ehl 'peh-soh)*

Does it have (the)...?	¿Tiene...? *(tee-'eh-neh)*
brand	la **marca** *(lah 'mahr-kah)*
label	la **etiqueta** *(lah eh-tee-'keh-tah)*
logo	el **logotipo** *(ehl loh-goh-'tee-poh)*
patent	la **patente** *(lah pah-'tehn-teh)*
stamp	el **sello** *(ehl 'seh-yoh)*
trademark	la **marca registrada** *(lah 'mahr-kah reh-hee-'strah-dah)*

Keep asking about money, using verbs in both the present and the past tenses:

How much...?	¿Cuánto...? *('kwahn-toh)*
does it cost	cuesta *('kweh-stah)*
is it worth	vale *('vah-leh)*
do I owe you	le debo *(leh 'deh-boh)*
did you order	pidió *(pee-dee-'oh)*
did you pay	pagó *(pah-'goh)*
did you buy	compró *(kohm-'proh)*
did you save	ahorró *(ah-oh-'rroh)*
did you spend	gastó *(gah-'stoh)*

¡Información!

Describe the product or price:

It's...	
damaged	Está dañado *(eh-'stah dah-'nyah-doh)*
delayed	Está retrasado *(eh-'stah reh-trah-'sah-doh)*
free	Es gratis *(ehs 'grah-tees)*
imported	Es importado *(ehs eem-pohr-'tah-doh)*
included	Está incluído *(eh-'stah een-kloo-'ee-doh)*
paid	Está pagado *(eh-'stah pah-'gah-doh)*
retail	Es al por menor *(ehs ahl pohr meh-'nohr)*
used	Es usado *(ehs oo-'sah-doh)*
void	Está cancelado *(eh-'stah kahn-seh-'lah-doh)*
wholesale	Es al por mayor *(ehs ahl pohr mah-'yohr)*

Listos para practicar

Circle the words that belong together in each of the following lists of Spanish vocabulary items:

el carro, el recibo, el agua, la factura, el pedido *(ehl 'kah-rroh, ehl reh-'see-boh, ehl 'ah-gwah, lah fahk-'too-rah, ehl peh-'dee-doh)*

el cliente, el bombero, el vendedor, el gato, el gerente *(ehl klee-'ehn-teh, ehl bohm-'beh-roh, ehl vehn-deh-'dohr, ehl 'gah-toh, ehl heh-'rehn-teh)*

la venta, la ganga, la oferta, la puerta, la calle *(lah 'vehn-tah, lah 'gahn-gah, lah oh-'fehr-tah, lah 'pwehr-tah, lah 'kah-yeh)*

Connect these words with their correct translations:

free	**peso** *('peh-soh)*
weight	**marca** *('mahr-kah)*
price	**impuesto** *(eem-'pweh-stoh)*
brand	**gratis** *('grah-tees)*
tax	**precio** *('preh-see-oh)*

Now use the sample sentence to complete the exercise below. Write in the proper past tense form:

usar *(oo-'sahr)*	**(Yo)** *(yoh)*	**Usé el dinero.**
		(oo-'seh ehl dee-'neh-roh)
pagar *(pah-'gahr)*	**(Ella)** *('eh-yah)*	_____
gastar	**(Nosotros)**	
(gah-'stahr)	*(noh-soh-'trohs)*	_____
ahorrar	**(Ellos)** *('eh-yohs)*	_____
(ah-oh-'rrahr)		
encontrar		
(ehn-kohn-'trahr)	**(Usted)** *(oo-'stehd)*	_____

Talk to the customer
Hable con el cliente
('ah-bleh kohn ehl klee-'ehn-teh)

Practice these one-liners with your sales staff:

Which one do you like?	**¿Cuál le gusta?** *(kwahl leh 'goo-stah)*
Which one do you want?	**¿Cuál quiere?** *(kwahl kee-'eh-reh)*
Which one do you prefer?	**¿Cuál prefiere?** *(kwahl preh-fee-'eh-reh)*

Continue to learn sentences in smaller sets:

We are here to serve you. **Estamos aquí para servirle.**
(eh-'stah-mohs ah-'kee 'pah-rah sehr-'veer-leh)

How may I assist you?	**¿Cómo puedo servirle?** *('koh-moh 'pweh-doh sehr-'veer-leh)*
This is the payment plan.	**Este es el plan de pagos.** *('eh-steh ehs ehl plahn deh 'pah-gohs)*
How many would you like?	**¿Cuántos quisiera?** *('kwahn-tohs kee-see-'eh-rah)*
We can order more.	**Podemos pedir más.** *(poh-'deh-mohs peh-'deer mahs)*
Like this one?	**¿Así como éste?** *(ah-'see 'koh-moh 'eh-steh)*
Here's another one.	**Aquí hay otro.** *(ah-'kee 'ah-ee 'oh-troh)*
Do you like it?	**¿Le gusta?** *(leh 'goo-stah)*
Is that all?	**¿Es todo?** *(ehs 'toh-doh)*
Something else?	**¿Algo más?** *('ahl-goh mahs)*
We accept...	**Aceptamos...** *(ah-sehp-'tah-mohs)*
checks	**los cheques** *(lohs 'cheh-kehs)*
credit cards	**las tarjetas de crédito** *(lahs tahr-'heh-tahs deh 'kreh-dee-toh)*
cash	**el efectivo** *(ehl eh-fehk-'tee-voh)*
money orders	**los giros** *(lohs 'hee-rohs)*
cashier's checks	**los cheques bancarios** *(lohs 'cheh-kehs bahn-'kah-ree-ohs)*
I'm sorry.	**Lo siento.** *(loh see-'ehn-toh)*
We don't have anymore.	**No tenemos más.** *(noh teh-'neh-mohs mahs)*
We sold the last one.	**Vendimos el último.** *(vehn-'dee-mohs ehl 'ool-tee-moh)*
We no longer sell them.	**Ya no los vendemos.** *(yah noh lohs vehn-'deh-mohs)*

¡Información!

And how do you advertise? Note these items of interest:

I saw it in (the)...	**Lo vi en...** *(loh vee ehn)*
advertisement	**el anuncio** *(ehl ah-'noon-see-oh)*

article	**el artículo** *(ehl ahr-'tee-koo-loh)*
billboard	**la cartelera** *(lah kahr-teh-'leh-rah)*
brochure	**el folleto** *(ehl foh-'yeh-toh)*
catalogue	**el catálogo** *(ehl kah-'tah-loh-goh)*
Internet	**el internet** *(ehl een-tehr-'neht)*
magazine	**la revista** *(lah reh-'vee-stah)*
news	**las noticias** *(lahs noh-'tee-see·ahs)*
newspaper	**el periódico** *(ehl peh-ree-'oh-dee-koh)*

Temas culturales

Once a customer or employee establishes a friendly relationship, it's not uncommon for native Hispanics to use nicknames when referring to others. It is meant to show intimacy, and not disrespect. Besides, it might be fun to look up the translations for any terms of endearment that you hear.

Big business

El gran comercio *(ehl grahn koh-'mehr-see·oh)*

Sharing business information in Spanish requires specialized vocabulary. Perhaps you'll need some of these words at your next meeting with employees:

It's...	**Es...** *(ehs)*
confidential	**confidencial** *(kohn-fee-dehn-see-'ahl)*
domestic	**nacional** *(nah-see·oh-'nahl)*
foreign	**extranjero** *(ehks-trahn-'heh-roh)*
global	**mundial** *(moon-dee-'ahl)*
interim	**provisional** *(proh-vee-see·oh-'nahl)*
internal	**interno** *(een-'tehr-noh)*
international	**internacional** *(een-tehr-nah-see·oh-'nahl)*
interstate	**interestatal** *(een-tehr-eh-stah-'tahl)*
national	**nacional** *(nah-see·oh-'nahl)*
public	**público** *('poo-blee-koh)*
seasonal	**estacional** *(eh-stah-see·oh-'nahl)*
universal	**universal** *(oo-nee-vehr-'sahl)*

Let's talk about (the)...	**Hablemos de...** *(ah-'bleh-mohs deh)*
acquisition	**la adquisición** *(lah ahd-kee-see-see-'ohn)*
agenda	**la agenda** *(lah ah-'hehn-dah)*
campaign	**la campaña** *(lah kahm-'pah-nyah)*
embargo	**el embargo** *(ehl ehm-'bahr-goh)*
forecast	**el pronóstico** *(ehl proh-'noh-stee-koh)*
merger	**la fusión de empresas**
	(lah foo-see-'ohn deh ehm-'preh-sahs)
project	**el proyecto** *(ehl proh-'yehk-toh)*
I will explain (the)...	**Explicaré...** *(ehks-plee-kah-'reh)*
criterion	**el criterio** *(ehl kree-'teh-ree-oh)*
cycle	**el ciclo** *(ehl 'see-kloh)*
deadline	**el plazo** *(ehl 'plah-soh)*
exchange	**el cambio** *(ehl 'kahm-bee-oh)*
index	**el índice** *(ehl 'een-dee-seh)*
quota	**la cuota** *(lah 'kwoh-tah)*
risk	**el riesgo** *(ehl ree-'ehs-goh)*
strategy	**la estrategia** *(lah eh-strah-'teh-hee-ah)*
trend	**la tendencia** *(lah tehn-'dehn-see-ah)*
Let's see (the)...	**Vamos a ver...** *('vah-mohs ah vehr)*
design	**el diseño** *(ehl dee-'seh-nyoh)*
layout	**la organización** *(lah ohr-gah-nee-sah-see-'ohn)*
title	**el título** *(ehl 'tee-too-loh)*

¡Información!

Managers are always using business expressions, so don't hesitate to inquire about certain translations. Do any of these sound familiar?

cash flow	**el flujo de caja** *(ehl 'floo-hoh deh 'kah-hah)*
downtime	**el tiempo improductivo**
	(ehl tee-'ehm-poh eem-proh-dook-'tee-voh)
face value	**el valor nominal**
	(ehl vah-'lohr noh-mee-'nahl)

grace period	**el período de gracia**
	(ehl peh-'ree-oh-doh deh 'grah-see-ah)
manpower	**la fuerza de trabajo**
	(lah 'fwehr-sah deh trah-'bah-hoh)
mass production	**la fabricación en serie**
	(lah fah-bree-kah-see-'ohn ehn 'seh-ree-eh)
net sales	**las ventas netas** *(lahs 'vehn-tahs 'neh-tahs)*
network	**la red de contactos**
	(lah rehd deh kohn-'tahk-tohs)
overhead costs	**los gastos indirectos**
	(lohs 'gah-stohs een-dee-'rehk-tohs)
piecework	**el trabajo a destajo**
	(ehl trah-'bah-hoh ah deh-'stah-hoh)
potential sales	**las ventas potenciales**
	(lahs 'vehn-tahs poh-tehn-see-'ah-lehs)
rough estimate	**la estimación aproximada**
	(lah eh-stee-mah-see-'ohn ah-prohk-see-'mah-dah)
sales pitch	**la cháchara publicitaria**
	(lah 'chah-chah-rah poo-blee-see-'tah-ree-ah)

Listos para practicar

Match each of these sentences with its appropriate response:

¿Cuántos quiere?   El grande.
('kwahn-tohs kee-'eh-reh)   *(ehl 'grahn-deh)*
¿Cuál le gusta?   No, gracias.
(kwahl leh 'goo-stah)   *(noh 'grah-see-ahs)*
¿Algo más?   Cinco, por favor.
('ahl-goh mahs)   *('seen-koh pohr fah-'vohr)*

Name three places where most businesses advertise their products:

_____   _____   _____

Translate into Spanish:

The project is international. _____
What's the retail price? _____
Is the cycle seasonal? _____
The strategy includes mass production._____
We accept cash and credit cards. _____

There's work to do
Hay trabajo que hacer
('ah·ee trah-'bah-hoh keh ah-'sehr)

These people may also be involved in your line of work, so explain who they are to Spanish speakers:

I know (the)...	**Conozco a...** *(koh-'noh-skoh ah)*
affiliate	**el afiliado** *(ehl ah-fee-lee-'ah-doh)*
analyst	**el analista** *(ehl ah-nah-'lee-stah)*
buyer	**el jefe de compras** *(ehl 'heh-feh deh 'kohm-prahs)*
carrier	**el transportador** *(ehl trahns-pohr-tah-'dohr)*
consultant	**el consultor** *(ehl kohn-sool-'tohr)*
consumer	**el consumidor** *(ehl kohn-soo-mee-'dohr)*
courier	**el mensajero** *(ehl mehn-sah-'heh-roh)*
dealer	**el concesionario** *(ehl kohn-seh-see·oh-'nah-ree·oh)*
recruiter	**el reclutador** *(ehl reh-kloo-tah-'dohr)*
shipper	**el fletador** *(ehl fleh-tah-'dohr)*
supplier	**el abastecedor** *(ehl ah-bah-steh-seh-'dohr)*

Now, tell all those in packaging and shipping that you're aware of each procedure. Here's a series of phrases you'll probably use right away:

air express	**el correo aéreo** *(ehl koh-'rreh-oh ah-'eh-reh-oh)*
air freight	**el flete aéreo** *(ehl 'fleh-teh ah-'eh-reh-oh)*
air shipments	**los embarques aéreos**
	(lohs ehm-'bahr-kehs ah-'eh-reh-ohs)
back order	**el pedido previo pendiente de entrega**
	(ehl peh-'dee-doh 'preh-vee·oh pehn-dee-'ehn-teh deh ehn-'treh-gah)

bale cargo	**la carga de fardos**
	(lah 'kahr-gah deh 'fahr-dohs)
direct mail	**el correo directo**
	(ehl koh-'rreh-oh dee-'rehk-toh)
dock charge	**el cargo de muelle**
	(ehl 'kahr-goh deh 'mweh-yeh)
drop shipment	**el despacho directo**
	(ehl deh-'spah-choh dee-'rehk-toh)
duty free goods	**los bienes libres de impuestos**
	(lohs bee-'eh-nehs 'lee-brehs deh eem-'pweh-stohs)
flat rate	**la tarifa fija** *(lah tah-'ree-fah 'fee-hah)*
free trade	**el librecomercio** *(ehl lee-breh-koh-'mehr-see·oh)*
mailing list	**la planilla de direcciones**
	(lah plah-'nee-yah deh dee-rehk-see-'oh-nehs)
mail order	**el pedido por correo**
	(ehl peh-'dee-doh pohr koh-'rreh-oh)
packaging	**el empaquetado** *(ehl ehm-pah-keh-'tah-doh)*
rail shipment	**el embarque por tren**
	(ehl ehm-'bahr-keh pohr trehn)
rush order	**el pedido urgente**
	(ehl peh-'dee-doh oor-'hehn-teh)

Each of these patterns target a unique collection of specialized vocabulary. As always, start off with the ones you'll need:

Have you seen (the)...?	**¿Ha visto...?** *(ah 'vee-stoh)*
flow chart	**el cuadro sinóptico**
	(ehl 'kwah-droh see-'nohp-tee-koh)
public opinion	**la encuesta de la opinión pública**
poll	*(lah ehn-'kweh-stah deh lah oh-pee-nee-'ohn 'poo-blee-kah)*
sales report	**el informe de las ventas**
	(ehl een-'fohr-meh deh lahs 'vehn-tahs)
It's (the)...	**Es...** *(ehs)*
board meeting	**la reunión de la junta**
	(lah reh-oo-nee-'ohn deh lah 'hoon-tah)
board of directors	**la junta directiva**
	(lah 'hoon-tah dee-rehk-'tee-vah)

board room	**la sala de conferencias** *(lah 'sah-lah deh kohn-feh-'rehn-see·ahs)*
What's (the)...?	**¿Cuál es...?** *(kwahl ehs)*
base price	**el precio base** *(ehl 'preh-see·oh 'bah-seh)*
closing price	**el precio de cierre** *(ehl 'preh-see·oh deh see-'eh-rreh)*
fixed price	**el precio fijo** *(ehl 'preh-see·oh 'fee-hoh)*
list price	**el precio de catálogo** *(ehl 'preh-see·oh deh kah-'tah-loh-goh)*
price range	**la variación de precio** *(lah vah-ree-ah-see-'ohn deh 'preh-see·oh)*
price rebate	**la rebaja de precio** *(lah reh-'bah-hah deh 'preh-see·oh)*
retail price	**el precio al por menor** *(ehl 'preh-see·oh ahl pohr meh-'nohr)*
Let's discuss (the)...	**Vamos a tratar...** *('vah-mohs ah trah-'tahr)*
cost analysis	**el análisis de costos** *(ehl ah-'nah-lee-sees deh 'koh-stohs)*
cost control	**el control de costos** *(ehl kohn-'trohl deh 'koh-stohs)*
cost effect	**el efecto del costo** *(ehl eh-'fehk-toh dehl 'koh-stoh)*

¡Información!

Guess at the meanings of these words:

promotion	**la promoción** *(lah proh-moh-see-'ohn)*
distribution	**la distribución** *(lah dee-stree-boo-see-'ohn)*
consolidation	**la consolidación** *(lah kohn-soh-lee-dah-see-'ohn)*
innovation	**la innovación** *(lah ee-noh-vah-see-'ohn)*

These four aren't so easy:

amalgamation	**la fusión** *(lah foo-see-'ohn)*
allocation	**la asignación** *(lah ah-seeg-nah-see-'ohn)*
depletion	**el agotamiento** *(ehl ah-goh-tah-mee-'ehn-toh)*
competition	**la competencia** *(lah kohm-peh-'tehn-see·ah)*

More specialized Spanish
Más español especializado
(mahs eh-spah-'nyohl eh-speh-see·ah-lee-'sah-doh)

Throughout this guidebook, much of the vocabulary has been organized into brief situation-specific groups or sets. You may want to consider copying each set onto a 3 × 5 card for faster review and reference. Here are some more areas of interest:

Use these terms to explain the nature of your business:

It's a...	**Es una...** *(ehs 'oo-nah)*
corporation	**corporación** *(kohr-poh-rah-see-'ohn)*
franchise	**franquicia** *(frahn-'kee-see·ah)*
joint ownership	**propiedad conjunta** *(proh-pee-eh-'dahd kohn-'hoon-tah)*
partnership	**sociedad** *(soh-see-eh-'dahd)*
sole proprietorship	**propiedad única** *(proh-pee-eh-'dahd 'oo-nee-kah)*

This time, look for similarities in each group of words as you elaborate in full detail:

overdrawn	**sobregirado** *(soh-breh-hee-'rah-doh)*
overdue	**vencido** *(vehn-'see-doh)*
overcharge	**cobro excesivo** *('koh-broh ehk-seh-'see-voh)*
overnight	**de un día para otro** *(deh oon 'dee-ah 'pah-rah 'oh-troh)*
product analysis	**el análisis del producto** *(ehl ah-'nah-lee-sees dehl proh-'dook-toh)*
product design	**el diseño del producto** *(ehl dee-'seh-nyoh dehl proh-'dook-toh)*
product development	**el desarrollo del producto** *(ehl deh-sah-'roh-yoh dehl proh-'dook-toh)*
sales budget	**el presupuesto de ventas** *(ehl preh-soo-'pweh-stoh deh 'vehn-tahs)*
sales estimate	**el estimado de ventas** *(ehl eh-stee-'mah-doh deh 'vehn-tahs)*
sales force	**el personal de ventas** *(ehl pehr-soh-'nahl deh 'vehn-tahs)*

sales tax	**el impuesto de ventas** *(ehl eem-'pweh-stoh deh 'vehn-tahs)*
sales territory	**el territorio de ventas** *(ehl teh-rree-'toh-ree·oh deh 'vehn-tahs)*
telecommunications	**las telecomunicaciones** *(lahs teh-leh-koh-moo-nee-kah-see-'oh-nehs)*
telemarketing	**el telemercadeo** *(ehl teh-leh-mehr-'kah-deh·oh)*
teleprocessing	**el teleprocesamiento** *(ehl teh-leh-proh-seh-sah-mee-'ehn-toh)*

Notice how these hyphenated expressions are translated below:

across-the-board	**lineal** *(lee-neh-'ahl)*
as-is	**como está** *('koh-moh ehs-'tah)*
break-even	**salir sin ganar ni perder** *(sah-'leer seen gah-'nahr nee pehr-'dehr)*
door-to-door	**de puerta en puerta** *(deh 'pwehr-tah ehn 'pwehr-tah)*
in-the-red	**endeudado** *(ehn-deh-oo-'dah-doh)*
large-scale	**en gran escala** *(ehn grahn eh-'skah-lah)*
mark-up	**el aumento de precio** *(ehl ow-'mehn-toh deh 'preh-see·oh)*
mark-down	**la reducción de precio** *(lah reh-dook-see-'ohn deh 'preh-see·oh)*
on-line	**en línea** *(ehn 'lee-neh-ah)*
on-the-job	**por rutina** *(pohr roo-'tee-nah)*
paid-in-full	**pagado en su totalidad** *(pah-'gah-doh ehn soo toh-tah-lee-'dahd)*
red-tape	**los trámites burocráticos** *(lohs 'trah-mee-tehs boo-roh-'krah-tee-kohs)*
self-service	**el auto servicio** *(ehl ow-toh-sehr-'vee-see·oh)*

Listos para practicar

Circle the three words that belong to the same vocabulary group in each of the following word lists:

jefe de compras, jardinero, concesionario, abastecedor, dormitorio *('heh-feh deh 'kohm-prahs, hahr-dee-'neh-roh, kohn-seh-see·oh-'nah-ree·oh, ah-bah-steh-seh-'dohr, dohr-mee-'toh-ree·oh)*

lápiz, embarque, piso, correo, despacho, botella *('lah-pees, ehm-'bahr-keh, 'pee-soh, koh-'rreh-oh, deh-'spah-choh, boh-'teh-yah)*

escritorio, sociedad, franquicia, corporación, falda *(eh-skree-'toh-ree·oh, soh-see-eh-'dah, frahn-'kee-see·ah, kohr-poh-rah-see-'ohn, 'fahl-dah)*

Complete these sentences with the best response:

vencido, rebaja de precio, de puerta en puerta *(vehn-'see-doh, reh-'bah-hah deh 'preh-see·oh, deh 'pwehr-tah ehn 'pwehr-tah)*

    José trabaja _____. *('hoh-'seh trah-'bah-hah _____)*
    El pago está _____. *(ehl 'pah-goh eh-'stah _____)*
    Hay una _____. *('ah·ee 'oo-nah _____)*

The computer
La computadora *(lah kohm-poo-tah-'doh-rah)*

This brief overview of terminology will help you out with Spanish speakers who work with computers. Most of the basics are here:

byte	**el carácter de memoria** *(ehl kah-'rahk-tehr deh meh-'moh-ree·ah)*
cable	**el cable** *(ehl 'kah-bleh)*
data base	**la base de datos** *(lah 'bah-seh deh 'dah-tohs)*
disk	**el disco** *(ehl 'dee-skoh)*
drive	**el impulsor** *(ehl eem-pool-'sohr)*
hardware	**los elementos físicos** *(lohs eh-leh-'mehn-tohs 'fee-see-kohs)*
input	**la entrada de información** *(lah ehn-'trah-dah deh een-fohr-mah-see-'ohn)*

keyboard	**el teclado** *(ehl teh-'klah-doh)*
language	**el lenguaje** *(ehl lehn-'gwah-heh)*
memory	**la memoria** *(lah meh-'moh-ree·ah)*
microchip	**la microficha** *(lah mee-kroh-'fee-chah)*
microprocessor	**el microprocesador**
	(ehl mee-kroh-proh-seh-sah-'dohr)
monitor	**el monitor** *(ehl moh-nee-'tohr)*
mouse	**el ratón** *(ehl rah-'tohn)*
output	**la salida de información**
	(lah sah-'lee-dah deh een-fohr-mah-see-'ohn)
program	**la programación** *(lah proh-grah-mah-see-'ohn)*
scanner	**el escáner** *(ehl eh-'skah-nehr)*
screen	**la pantalla** *(lah pahn-'tah-yah)*
software	**el programa** *(ehl proh-'grah-mah)*
system	**el sistema** *(ehl see-'steh-mah)*
terminal	**el terminal** *(ehl tehr-mee-'nahl)*
tower	**la torre** *(lah 'toh-rreh)*

The telephone
El teléfono *(ehl teh-'leh-foh-noh)*

Companies can't survive without the telephone. Let's look through various groups of words and phrases in Spanish that relate to **el teléfono** *(ehl teh-'leh-foh-noh)*:

I have (the)...	**Tengo...** *('tehn-goh)*
answering machine	**el contestador telefónico**
	(ehl kohn-teh-stah-'dohr teh-leh-'foh-nee-koh)
answering service	**el servicio telefónico**
	(ehl sehr-'vee-see·oh teh-leh-'foh-nee-koh)
area code	**el código de área**
	(ehl 'koh-dee-goh deh 'ah-reh·ah)
beeper	**el bíper** *(ehl 'bee-pehr)*
cellular phone	**el teléfono celular**
	(ehl teh-'leh-foh-noh seh-loo-'lahr)
conference call	**la llamada de conferencia**
	(lah yah-'mah-dah deh kohn-feh-'rehn-see·ah)

800 number	**el número de ochocientos**
	(ehl 'noo-meh-roh deh oh-choh-see-'ehn-tohs)
E-mail	**el correo electrónico**
	(ehl koh-'rreh-oh eh-lehk-'troh-nee-koh)
extension	**la extensión** *(lah ehks-tehn-see-'ohn)*
fax	**el facsímil** *(ehl fahk-'see-meel)*
headset	**los auriculares con micrófono**
	(lohs ow-ree-koo-'lah-rehs kohn mee-'kroh-foh-noh)
number	**el número** *(ehl 'noo-meh-roh)*
switchboard	**el conmutador** *(ehl kohn-moo-tah-'dohr)*
two-way radio	**el radioteléfono portátil**
	(ehl rah-dee·oh-teh-'leh-foh-noh pohr-'tah-teel)

Making phone calls in Spanish is a tough task, but with the proper one-liners in hand, conversations are much more productive. The same goes for calls coming into your office. Place the phrases you need alongside the phone, and then wait for the chance to practice. These will work for the time being:

Hello, is _____ there?	**¿Aló, está _____?** *(ah-'loh, eh-'stah _____)*
May I speak to _____?	**¿Puedo hablar con _____?**
	('pweh-doh ah-'blahr kohn ___)
Phone call for _____.	**Una llamada para _____.**
	('oo-nah yah-'mah-dah 'pah-rah _____)
I'm calling about _____.	**Estoy llamando acerca de _____.**
	(eh-'stoh-ee yah-'mahn-doh ah-'sehr-kah deh ___)
I'll transfer you to _____.	**Le voy a transferir a _____.**
	(leh 'voh-ee ah trahns-feh-'reer ah ___)
Tell him/her that _____.	**Dígale que _____.** *('dee-gah-leh keh ___)*

Don't forget to say, please:

More slowly, please.	**Más despacio, por favor.**
	(mahs deh-'spah-see·oh, pohr fah-'vohr)
Wait a moment, please.	**Espere un momento, por favor.**
	(eh-'speh-reh oon moh-'mehn-toh, pohr fah-'vohr)
Please, it's very urgent.	**Por favor, es muy urgente.**
	(pohr fah-'vohr, ehs 'moo·ee oor-'hehn-teh)
Your number, please.	**Su número, por favor.**
	(soo 'noo-meh-roh, pohr fah-'vohr)
Your name, please.	**Su nombre, por favor.**
	(soo 'nohm-breh, pohr fah-'vohr)
Could you please repeat that?	**¿Puede repetirlo, por favor?**
	('pweh-deh reh-peh-'teer-loh, pohr fah-'vohr)

Break your one-liners into vocabulary-specific sets:

Can you call later?	**¿Puede llamar más tarde?**
	('pweh-deh yah-'mahr mahs 'tahr-deh)
He/She will call you later.	**Llamará mas tarde.**
	(yah-'mah-'rah mahs 'tahr-deh)
I'll call back later.	**Llamaré más tarde.**
	(yah-mah-'reh mahs 'tahr-deh)
Do you want to leave a message?	**¿Quiere dejar un recado?**
	(kee-'eh-reh deh-'hahr oon reh-'kah-doh)
I'd like to leave a message.	**Quisiera dejar un recado.**
	(kee-see-'eh-rah deh-'hahr oon reh-'kah-doh)
I will give him/her your message.	**Le voy a dejar su mensaje.**
	(leh 'voh-ee ah deh-'hahr soo mehn-'sah-heh)
Is it long distance?	**¿Es de larga distancia?**
	(ehs deh 'lahr-gah dee-'stahn-see·ah)
Is it a local call?	**¿Es una llamada local?**
	(ehs 'oo-nah yah-'mah-dah loh-'kahl)
Is it a collect call?	**¿Es una llamada a cobro revertido?**
	(ehs 'oo-nah yah-'mah-dah ah 'koh-broh reh-vehr-'tee-doh)

In any language, using the phone can be frustrating, too. Here are a few examples:

He/She isn't here.	**No está aquí.** *(noh eh-'stah ah-'kee)*
He/She doesn't work here.	**No trabaja aquí.** *(noh trah-'bah-hah ah-'kee)*
He/She can't come to the phone.	**No puede contestar la llamada.** *(noh 'pweh-deh kohn-teh-'stahr lah yah-'mah-dah)*
He/she is busy.	**Está ocupado(a).** *(eh-'stah oh-koo-'pah-doh/ah)*
Is this the correct number?	**¿Es el número correcto?** *(ehs ehl 'noo-meh-roh koh-'rrehk-toh)*
I have the wrong number.	**Tengo el número equivocado.** *('tehn-goh ehl 'noo-meh-roh eh-kee-voh-'kah-doh)*
You have the wrong number.	**Tiene el número equivocado.** *(tee-'eh-neh ehl 'noo-meh-roh eh-kee-voh-'kah-doh)*
The number has been changed.	**Ha cambiado el número.** *(ah kahm-bee-'ah-doh ehl 'noo-meh-roh)*

¡Información!

* Sometimes there are technical difficulties:

The line is bad.	**La línea está mala.** *(lah 'lee-neh-ah eh-'stah 'mah-lah)*
The line is busy.	**La línea está ocupada.** *(lah 'lee-neh-ah eh-'stah oh-koo-'pah-dah)*
The line is disconnected.	**La línea está desconectada.** *(lah 'lee-neh-ah eh-'stah dehs-koh-nehk-'tah-dah)*

* Now direct others how to handle the calls:

Dial this number.	**Marque este número.** *('mahr-keh 'eh-steh 'noo-meh-roh)*
Press this number.	**Oprima este número.** *(oh-'pree-mah 'eh-steh 'noo-meh-roh)*

Ask for this number.	**Pida este número.**
	('pee-dah 'eh-steh 'noo-meh-roh)
Wait for the tone.	**Espere por el tono.**
	(eh-'speh-reh pohr ehl 'toh-noh)
Hang up the phone.	**Cuelgue el teléfono.**
	('kwehl-geh ehl teh-'leh-foh-noh)

Temas culturales

To get a feel for communication in Spanish, find time to observe a group of Hispanics in public or at a social gathering. Facial expressions, touch, changes in tone, and hand signals are a few of the many nonverbal differences between the Latin American and U.S. cultures.

Listos para practicar

List five words that relate to the world of computers:

_____ _____ _____

_____ _____

Translate this phone conversation:
Hello, is María there? It's very urgent.

_____

No, I'm sorry. Do you want to leave a message?

_____

Yes, thank you. My name is Lupe, and I'm calling about the problem at the office.

_____

Business around town
Los negocios por toda la ciudad
(lohs neh-'goh-see·ohs pohr 'toh-dah lah see·oo-'dahd)

Not all business is conducted on site at the workplace. Human Resource staff members are often required to handle affairs at locations throughout the city. Other employees must travel as well, in order to provide services, make deliveries, or assist management with their assignments.

Go to the...	**Vaya a...** *('vah-yah ah)*
alley	**el callejón** *(ehl kah-yeh-'hohn)*
apartment building	**el edificio de departamentos** *(ehl eh-dee-'fee-see·oh deh deh-pahr-tah-'mehn-tohs)*
avenue	**la avenida** *(lah ah-veh-'nee-dah)*
bridge	**el puente** *(ehl 'pwehn-teh)*
building	**el edificio** *(ehl eh-dee-'fee-see·oh)*
bus stop	**la parada de autobús** *(lah pah-'rah-dah deh ow-toh-'boos)*
city block	**la cuadra** *(lah 'kwah-drah)*
community	**la comunidad** *(lah koh-moo-nee-'dahd)*
house	**la casa** *(lah 'kah-sah)*
condominium	**el condominio** *(el kohn-doh-'mee-nee-oh)*
corner	**la esquina** *(lah eh-'skee-nah)*
crosswalk	**el cruce de peatones** *(ehl 'kroo-seh deh peh- ah-'toh-nehs)*
downtown	**el centro** *(ehl 'sehn-troh)*
elevator	**el ascensor** *(ehl ah-sehn-'sohr)*
entrance	**la entrada** *(lah ehn-'trah-dah)*
escalator	**la escalera mecánica** *(lah eh-skah-'leh-rah meh-'kah-nee-kah)*
exit	**la salida** *(lah sah-'lee-dah)*
fence	**la cerca** *(lah 'sehr-kah)*
highway	**la carretera** *(lah kah-rreh-'teh-rah)*
mailbox	**el buzón** *(ehl boo-'sohn)*
neighborhood	**el barrio** *(ehl 'bah-rree·oh)*
outskirts	**las afueras** *(lahs ah-'fweh-rahs)*

parking lot	**el estacionamiento** *(ehl eh-stah-see·oh-nah-mee-'ehn-toh)*
pool	**la piscina** *(lah pee-'see-nah)*
restroom	**el excusado** *(ehl ehks-koo-'sah-doh)*
road	**el camino** *(ehl kah-'mee-noh)*
sidewalk	**la acera** *(lah ah-'seh-rah)*
sign	**el anuncio** *(ehl ah-'noon-see-oh)*
skyscraper	**el rascacielos** *(ehl rah-skah-see-'eh-lohs)*
stairs	**las escaleras** *(lahs eh-skah-'leh-rahs)*
statue	**la estatua** *(lah eh-'stah-too-ah)*
street	**la calle** *(lah 'kah-yeh)*
traffic	**el tráfico** *(ehl 'trah-fee-koh)*
traffic signal	**el semáforo** *(ehl seh-'mah-foh-roh)*
tunnel	**el túnel** *(ehl 'too-nehl)*

Temas culturales

Do not translate names of businesses, brands, streets. Nor do you have to change your name to Spanish in order to communicate. All over the world, most formal titles in English remain the same.

Más fácil

Here's a review of all the shortcuts you've learned. Translate, and then choose one of the new verbs below to complete a phrase:

Tengo que... *('tehn-goh keh)*
Hay que... *('ah·ee keh)*
Debo... *('deh-boh)*
Necesito... *(neh-seh-'see-toh)*
Quiero... *(kee-'eh-roh)*
Quisiera... *(kee-see-'eh-rah)*
Puedo... *('pweh-doh)*
Me gusta... *(meh 'goo-stah)*
Voy a... *('voh·ee ah)*
Acabo de... *(ah-'kah-boh deh)*

Prefiero... *(preh-fee-'eh-roh)*
Deseo... *(deh-'seh-oh)*
Favor de... *(fah-'vohr deh)*
No... *(noh)*

Palabras activas

Check over this review of verb forms we've studied so far in this guidebook. Note the spelling and pronunciation changes that take place when you shift from one time reference to the next:

I'm working *now.*
Estoy trabajando *ahora.* *(eh-'stoh-ee trah-bah-'hahn-doh ah-oh-rah)*

I work *every day.*
Trabajo *todos los días.* *(trah-'bah-hoh 'toh-dohs lohs 'dee-ahs)*

I will work *tomorrow.*
Trabajaré *mañana.* *(trah-bah-hah-'reh mah-'nyah-nah)*

I worked *yesterday.*
Trabajé *ayer.* *(trah-bah-'heh ah-'yehr)*

Now, study this powerful two-part verb pattern. It's extremely important in work-related conversations because it refers to actions that have already taken place. It's a past action pattern that is used frequently in everyday communication, so pay close attention to each example. Here's how the words go together.

The first part consists of forms of the verb **Haber** *(ah-'behr)*.
The second part consists of the past participle of the action word. Both parts must be used together.

I've	**(He)**	left	**salido**
			(sah-'lee-doh)
		eaten	**comido**
			(koh-'mee-doh)
You've, She's, He's	**(Ha)**	closed	**cerrado**
			(seh-'rrah-doh)
		cleaned	**limpiado**
			(leem-pee-'ah-doh)

You've (pl.), They've	**(Han)**	worked	**trabajado**
			(trah-bah-'hah-doh)
		driven	**manejado**
			(mah-neh-'hah-doh)
We've	**(Hemos)**	painted	**pintado**
			(peen-'tah-doh)

To learn more about these past participle verb forms, consider taking a beginning Spanish class. It's worth the effort, because in management this two-part verb tense can be very useful. Watch:

I've parked here many times.

He estacionado aquí muchas veces.

(eh eh-stah-see·oh-'nah-doh ah-'kee 'moo-chahs 'veh-sehs)

She's driven a truck.

Ella ha manejado un camión.

('eh-yah ah mah-neh-'hah-doh oon kah-mee-'ohn)

We've cleaned engines before.

Hemos limpiado máquinas antes.

('eh-mohs leem-pee-'ah-doh 'mah-kee-nahs 'ahn-tehs)

¡Información!

• Some past participles can be used as descriptive words:

They are parked cars.	**Son carros estacionados.**
	(sohn 'kah-rrohs eh-stah-see·oh-'nah-dohs)
They are painted doors.	**Son puertas pintadas.**
	(sohn 'pwehr-tahs peen-'tah-dahs)
They are washed dishes.	**Son platos lavados.**
	(sohn 'plah-tohs lah-'vah-dohs)

• A handful of past participles are considered irregular. Here are some examples:

| I've broken the glass. | **He roto el vidrio.** |
| | *(eh 'roh-toh ehl 'vee-dree-oh)* |

He's put the money here.	**Ha puesto el dinero aquí.**
	(eh 'pweh-stoh ehl dee-'neh-roh ah-'kee)
We've seen the man.	**Hemos visto al hombre.**
	('eh-mohs 'vee-stoh ahl 'ohm-breh)

¡Ordenes!

In this chapter, we've discussed the topic of using Spanish in the business world. If your Spanish-speaking staff is assisting you at locations throughout the community, you'll probably need many of the command words that have already been presented. Can you think of situations where the following can be useful?

Once again, remember that the word **lo** usually means *it* in English:

Bring it	**Tráigalo** *('trah·ee-gah-loh)*
Buy it	**Cómprelo** *('kohm-preh-loh)*
Charge it	**Cárguelo** *('kahr-geh-loh)*
Choose it	**Escójalo** *(eh-'skoh-hah-loh)*
Deliver it	**Entréguelo** *(ehn-'treh-geh-loh)*
Do it	**Hágalo** *('ah-gah-loh)*
Exchange it	**Cámbielo** *('kahm-bee-eh-loh)*
Get it	**Consígalo** *(kohn-'see-gah-loh)*
Look for it	**Búsquelo** *('boo-skeh-loh)*
Park it	**Estaciónelo** *(eh-stah-see-'oh-neh-loh)*
Pay it	**Páguelo** *('pah-geh-loh)*
Pick it up	**Recójalo** *(reh-'koh-hah-loh)*
Put it	**Póngalo** *('pohn-gah-loh)*
Return it	**Devuélvalo** *(deh-voo·'ehl-vah-loh)*
Sell it	**Véndalo** *('vehn-dah-loh)*
Send it	**Mándelo** *('mahn-deh-loh)*
Sign it	**Fírmelo** *('feer-meh-loh)*
Take it	**Llévelo** *('yeh-veh-loh)*

¡Información!

Be sure to combine all base commands with the vocabulary that was just presented, or any of the other Spanish you already know:

Pick up the product.   **Recoja el producto.**
                          (reh-'koh-hah ehl proh-'dook-toh)

Sell the product.   **Venda el producto.**
                          ('vehn-dah ehl proh-'dook-toh)

Send the product.   **Mande el producto.**
                          ('mahn-deh ehl proh-'dook-toh)

Listos para practicar

This could be the toughest review activity of all since it requires the application of grammar material presented earlier at the close of every chapter. Closely study this example and then try to fill in each blank below with the correct verb form:

to buy	***comprar*** *(kohm-'prahr)*
I'm buying	**Estoy comprando** *(eh-'stoh-ee kohm-'prahn-doh)*
I buy	**Compro** *('kohm-proh)*
I will buy	**Compraré** *(kohm-prahr-'eh)*
I bought	**Compré** *(kohm-'preh)*
I have bought	**He comprado** *(eh kohm-'prah-doh)*
to spend	***gastar*** *(gah-'stahr)*
I'm spending	_____
I spend	_____
I will spend	_____
I spent	_____
I have spent	_____
to save	***ahorrar*** *(ah-oh-'rrahr)*
I'm saving	_____
I save	_____
I will save	_____

I saved _____
I have saved _____

Now translate these Spanish sentences. Turn back a few pages if you need some help!

Pick it up and send it! _____
I can import and export. _____
Please package and ship
the product. _____
Get it and sign it! _____
I would like to advertise
and sell. _____

Final notice!

¡El anuncio final! *(ehl ah-'noon-see·oh fee-'nahl)*

Well, we've come to the end of our Spanish training in this guidebook. I hope that much of what you've read has already been put into practice, and you're excited about learning more. The vocabulary and grammar presentations, along with the language and culture tips were specifically designed to get you started. So now, fellow Spanish speaker, the rest is up to you.

Adiós y buena suerte, *(ah-dee-'ohs ee 'bweh-nah 'swehr-teh)*

Bill Harvey

Appendix

Apéndice
(ah-'pehn-dee-seh)

English-Spanish Vocabulary

All nouns and adjectives with an asterisk indicate that they are in the masculine mode (e.g., **el abastecedor, el abogado**). If you want to change them into the feminine mode, *add* an **a** to the last letter of words ending in a consonant **(la abastecedora)** or *change* the vowel to **a** **(la abogada)**. All nouns and adjectives that remain unchanged carry both articles **(el/la aprendiz).**

a few	**pocos***	*('poh-kohs)*
a little	**poco***	*('poh-koh)*
ability	**habilidad, la**	*(lah ah-bee-lee-'dahd)*
above	**encima**	*(ehn-'see-mah)*
absences	**ausencias, las**	*(lahs ow-'sehn-see·ahs)*
abuse	**abuso, el**	*(ehl ah-'boo-soh)*
acceptable	**aceptable**	*(ah-sehp-'tah-bleh)*
acceptance	**aceptación, la**	*(lah ah-sehp-tah-see-'ohn)*
accident	**accidente, le**	*(ehl ahk-see-'dehn-teh)*
accounting	**contabilidad, la**	*(lah kohn-tah-bee-lee-'dahd)*
acid	**ácido, el**	*(ehl 'ah-see-doh)*
active	**activo***	*(ahk-'tee-voh)*
addendum	**anexo, el**	*(ehl ah-'nehk-soh)*
address	**dirección, la**	*(lah dee-rehk-see-'ohn)*
adequate	**adecuado***	*(ah-deh-'kwah-doh)*
adjustment	**ajuste, el**	*(ehl ah-'hoo-steh)*
administrator	**administrador, el***	*(ehl ahd-mee-nee-strah-'dohr)*
advertisement	**anuncio, el**	*(ehl ah-'noon-see-oh)*
advertising	**publicidad, la**	*(lah poo-blee-see-'dahd)*
advice	**consejo, el**	*(ehl kohn-'seh-hoh)*
aerospace	**aeroespacio, el**	*(ehl ah·eh-roh-eh-'spah-see-oh)*
affidavit	**afidávit, el**	*(ehl ah-fee-'dah-veet)*
affiliate	**afiliado, el***	*(ehl ah-fee-lee-'ah-doh)*
afraid	**asustado***	*(ah-soo-'stah-doh)*
afterward	**después**	*(deh-'spwehs)*
age	**edad, la**	*(lah eh-'dahd)*
agency	**agencia, la**	*(lah ah-'hehn-see·ah)*
agreement	**acuerdo, el**	*(ehl ah-'kwehr-doh)*

agriculture	**agricultura, la**	*(lah ah-gree-kool-'too-rah)*
air conditioning	**aire acondicionado, el**	*(ehl 'ah-ee-reh ah-kohn-dee-see-oh-'nah-doh)*
air mail	**correo aéreo, el**	*(ehl koh-'rreh-oh ah-'eh-reh-oh)*
airport	**aeropuerto, el**	*(ehl ah-eh-roh-'pwehr-toh)*
aisle	**pasillo, el**	*(ehl pah-'see-yoh)*
alarm	**alarma, la**	*(lah ah-'lahr-mah)*
alcohol	**alcohol, el**	*(ehl ahl-koh-'ohl)*
all	**todo***	*('toh-doh)*
allegation	**acusación, la**	*(lah ah-koo-sah-see-'ohn)*
allergy	**alergia, la**	*(lah ah-'lehr-hee-ah)*
alley	**callejón, el**	*(ehl kah-yeh-'hohn)*
alloy	**aleación, la**	*(lah ah-leh-ah-see-'ohn)*
alone	**solo***	*('soh-loh)*
already	**ya**	*(yah)*
also	**también**	*(tahm-bee-'ehn)*
alternatives	**alternativos, las**	*(lahs ahl-tehr-nah-'tee-vohs)*
aluminum	**aluminio, el**	*(ehl ah-loo-'mee-nee-oh)*
always	**siempre**	*(see-'ehm-preh)*
ambitious	**ambicioso***	*(ahm-bee-see-'oh-soh)*
ambulance	**ambulancia, la**	*(lah ahm-boo-'lahn-see-ah)*
amendment	**enmienda, la**	*(lah ehn-mee-'ehn-dah)*
American	**americano***	*(ah-meh-ree-'kah-noh)*
amount	**cantidad, la**	*(lah kahn-tee-'dahd)*
amp	**amperaje, el**	*(ehl ahm-peh-'rah-heh)*
analysis	**análisis, el**	*(ehl ah-'nah-lee-sees)*
analyst	**analista, el***	*(ehl ah-nah-'lee-stah)*
and	**y**	*(ee)*
angle	**ángulo, el**	*(ehl 'ahn-goo-loh)*
angry	**enojado***	*(eh-noh-'hah-doh)*
ankle	**tobillo, el**	*(ehl toh-'bee-yoh)*
anniversary	**aniversario, el**	*(ehl ah-nee-vehr-'sah-ree-oh)*
announcement	**anuncio, el**	*(ehl ah-'noon-see-oh)*
answering machine	**contestador telefónico, el**	*(ehl kohn-'teh-stah-'dohr teh-leh-'foh-nee-koh)*
answers	**respuestas, las**	*(lahs reh-'spweh-stahs)*
ant	**hormiga, la**	*(lah ohr-'mee-gah)*
anti trust	**anti-monopolio, el**	*(ehl ahn-tee-moh-noh-'poh-lee-oh)*
anyone	**cualquier persona**	*(kwahl-kee-'ehr pehr-'soh-nah)*
anything	**cualquier cosa**	*(kwahl-kee-'ehr 'koh-sah)*
anywhere	**en cualquier sitio**	*(ehn kwahl-kee-'ehr 'see-tee-oh)*
apathetic	**apático***	*(ah-'pah-tee-koh)*
appeal	**apelación, la**	*(lah ah-peh-lah-see-'ohn)*
apple	**manzana, la**	*(lah mahn-'sah-nah)*

appliance	electrodoméstico, el	(ehl eh-lehk-troh-doh-'meh-stee-koh)
applicant	solicitante, el/la	(ehl/lah soh-lee-see-'tahn-teh)
application	solicitud, la	(lah soh-lee-see-'tood)
appointment	cita, la	(lah 'see-tah)
appreciation	aprecio, el	(ehl ah-'preh-see-oh)
apprentice	aprendiz, el/la	(ehl/lah ah-prehn-'dees)
approach	enfoque, el	(ehl ehn-'foh-keh)
appropriate	apropiado*	(ah-proh-pee-'ah-doh)
approval	aprobación, la	(lah ah-proh-bah-see-'ohn)
approved	aprobado*	(ah-proh-'bah-doh)
apricot	durazno, el	(ehl doo-'rah-snoh)
April	abril	(ah-'breel)
apron	delantal, el	(ehl deh-lahn-'tahl)
arbitration	arbitraje, el	(ehl ahr-bee-'trah-heh)
arbitrator	árbitro, el/la	(ehl/lah 'ahr-bee-troh)
architect	arquitecto, el	(ehl ahr-kee-'tehk-toh)
area	área, el	(ehl 'ah-reh-ah)
argument	argumento, el	(ehl ahr-goo-'mehn-toh)
arm	brazo, el	(ehl 'brah-soh)
armchair	sillón, el	(ehl see-'yohn)
armoire	armario, el	(ehl ahr-'mah-ree-oh)
art	arte, el	(ehl 'ahr-teh)
article	artículo, el	(ehl ahr-'tee-koo-loh)
artist	artista, el/la	(ehl/lah ahr-'tee-stah)
as	tan	(tahn)
asbestos	asbesto, el	(ehl ahs-'beh-stoh)
ashtray	cenicero, el	(ehl seh-nee-'seh-roh)
asphalt	asfalto, el	(ehl ahs-'fahl-toh)
aspirin	aspirina, la	(lah ah-spee-'ree-nah)
assembly	montaje, el	(ehl mohn-'tah-heh)
assessment	tasación, la	(lah tah-sah-see-'ohn)
assets	bienes, los	(lohs bee-'eh-nehs)
assignment	misión, la; tarea, la	(lah mee-see-'ohn), (lah tah-'reh-ah)
at the bottom	en el fondo	(ehl ehl 'fohn-doh)
atmosphere	atmósfera, la	(lah aht-'mohs-feh-rah)
attic	desván, el	(ehl dehs-'vahn)
attitude	actitud, la	(lah ahk-tee-'tood)
attorney	abogado, el*	(ehl ah-boh-'gah-doh)
audit	revisión, la	(lah reh-vee-see-'ohn)
August	agosto	(ah-'goh-stoh)
aunt	tía, la	(lah 'tee-ah)
authority	autoridad, la	(lah ow-toh-ree-'dahd)
available	disponible	(dees-poh-'nee-bleh)

avenue	avenida, la	(lah ah-veh-'nee-dah)
average	promedio, el	(ehl proh-'meh-dee-oh)
awards	galardones, los	(lohs gah-lahr-'doh-nehs)
awhile	rato, el	(ehl 'rah-toh)
ax	hacha, el	(ehl 'ah-chah)
axle	eje, el	(ehl 'eh-heh)
baby	bebé, el/la	(ehl/lah beh-'beh)
back	espalda, la	(lah eh-'spahl-dah)
bacon	tocino, el	(ehl toh-'see-noh)
bad	malo*	('mah-loh)
badge	divisa, la	(lah dee-'vee-sah)
bag	bolsa, la	(lah 'bohl-sah)
bail	fianza, la	(lah fee-'ahn-sah)
balance	saldo, el	(ehl 'sahl-doh)
balcony	balcón, el	(ehl bahl-'kohn)
bald	calvo*	('kahl-voh)
ball	pelota, la	(lah peh-'loh-tah)
ballet	ballet, el	(ehl bah-'yeht)
balloon	globo, el	(ehl 'gloh-boh)
banana	plátano, el	(ehl 'plah-tah-noh)
Band-Aid®	curita, la	(lah koo-'ree-tah)
bandage	vendaje, el	(ehl vehn-'dah-heh)
bank	banco, el	(ehl 'bahn-koh)
bankruptcy	bancarrota, la	(lah bahn-kah-'rroh-tah)
banquet	banquete, el	(ehl bahn-'keh-teh)
bar	bar, el	(ehl bahr)
bargain	ganga, la	(lah 'gahn-gah)
barrel	barril, el	(ehl bah-'rreel)
barricade	barricada, la	(lah bah-rree-'kah-dah)
bartender	cantinero, el*	(ehl kahn-tee-'neh-roh)
basement	sótano, el	(ehl 'soh-tah-noh)
basket	canasta, la	(lah kah-'nah-stah)
bathroom	baño, el	(ehl 'bah-nyoh)
bathtub	tina, la	(lah 'tee-nah)
battery	batería, la	(lah bah-teh-'ree-ah)
beach	playa, la	(lah 'plah-yah)
beans	frijoles, los	(lohs free-'hoh-lehs)
bear	oso, el*	(ehl 'oh-soh)
bearing	cojinete, el	(ehl koh-hee-'neh-teh)
beauty salon	salón de belleza, el	(ehl sah-'lohn deh beh-'yeh-sah)
bed	cama, la	(lah 'kah-mah)
bedroom	dormitorio, el	(ehl dohr-mee-'toh-ree-oh)
beef	carne, la	(lah 'kahr-neh)

beet	betabel, el	*(ehl beh-tah-'behl)*
beetle	escarabajos, el	*(ehl eh-skah-rah-'bah-hohs)*
before	antes	*('ahn-tehs)*
behavior	comportamiento, el	*(ehl kohm-pohr-tah-mee-'ehn-toh)*
behind	detrás	*(deh-'trahs)*
bell	campana, la	*(lah kahm-'pah-nah)*
bellhop	botones, el/la	*(ehl/lah boh-'toh-nehs)*
belt	cinturón, el	*(ehl seen-too-'rohn)*
bench	banco, el	*(ehl 'bahn-koh)*
benefits	beneficios, los	*(lohs beh-neh-'fee-see-ohs)*
bent	doblado*	*(doh-'blah-doh)*
better	mejor	*(meh-'hohr)*
bias	prejuicio, el	*(ehl preh-hoo-'ee-see-oh)*
big	grande	*('grahn-deh)*
bike	bicicleta, la	*(lah bee-see-'kleh-tah)*
bill	cuenta, la	*(lah 'kwehn-tah)*
billboard	cartelera, la	*(lah kahr-teh-'leh-rah)*
billing	cuentas, las	*(lahs 'kwehn-tahs)*
bills	billetes, los	*(lohs bee-'yeh-tehs)*
binder	carpeta, la	*(lah kahr-'peh-tah)*
bird	pájaro, el	*(ehl 'pah-hah-roh)*
birth	nacimiento, el	*(ehl nah-see-mee-'ehn-toh)*
birthday	cumpleaños, el	*(ehl koom-pleh-'ah-nyohs)*
bit	taladro, el	*(ehl tah-'lah-droh)*
bitter	amargo*	*(ah-'mahr-goh)*
black	negro*	*('neh-groh)*
blade	navaja, la	*(lah nah-'vah-hah)*
blanket	cobija, la	*(lah koh-'bee-hah)*
bleach	cloro, el	*(ehl 'kloh-roh)*
blender	licuadora, la	*(lah lee-kwah-'doh-rah)*
blinds	persianas, las	*(lahs pehr-see-'ah-nahs)*
blister	ampolla, la	*(lah ahm-'poh-yah)*
block	bloque, el	*(ehl 'bloh-keh)*
blond	rubio*	*('roo-bee-oh)*
blood	sangre, la	*(lah 'sahn-greh)*
blouse	blusa, la	*(lah 'bloo-sah)*
blower	soplador, el	*(ehl soh-plah-'dohr)*
blue	azul	*(ah-'sool)*
boat	barco, el	*(ehl 'bahr-koh)*
boating	paseo en bote, el	*(ehl pah-'seh-oh ehn 'boh-teh)*
body	cuerpo, el	*(ehl 'kwehr-poh)*
bolt	perno, el	*(ehl 'pehr-noh)*
bonds	bonos, los	*(lohs 'boh-nohs)*

bone	hueso, el	*(ehl 'weh-soh)*
book	libro, el	*(ehl 'lee-broh)*
bookshelf	librero, el	*(ehl lee-'breh-roh)*
booth	puesto, el	*(ehl 'pweh-stoh)*
boots	botas, las	*(lahs 'boh-tahs)*
bored	aburrido*	*(ah-boo-'rree-doh)*
boss	jefe, el*	*(ehl 'heh-feh)*
bottle	botella, la	*(lah boh-'teh-yah)*
bottom	fondo, el	*(ehl 'fohn-doh)*
bowl	plato hondo, el	*(ehl 'plah-toh 'ohn-doh)*
box	caja, la	*(lah 'kah-hah)*
boxcar	vagón, el	*(ehl vah-'gohn)*
boy	niño, el	*(ehl 'nee-nyoh)*
boycott	boicot, el	*(ehl boh-ee-'koht)*
boyfriend	novio, el	*(ehl 'noh-vee-oh)*
brace	grapón, el	*(ehl grah-'pohn)*
bracelet	brazalete, el	*(ehl brah-sah-'leh-teh)*
brain	cerebro, el	*(ehl seh-'reh-broh)*
brakes	frenos, los	*(lohs 'freh-nohs)*
branches	ramas, las	*(lahs 'rah-mahs)*
brand	marca, la	*(lah 'mahr-kah)*
brass	latón, el	*(ehl lah-'tohn)*
brassiere	sostén, el	*(ehl soh-'stehn)*
brave	valiente	*(vah-lee-'ehn-teh)*
breakdown	falla, la	*(lah 'fah-yah)*
breakfast	desayuno, el	*(ehl deh-sah-'yoo-noh)*
breaks	pausas, las	*(lahs 'pow-sahs)*
brick	ladrillo, el	*(ehl lah-'dree-yoh)*
bridge	puente, el	*(ehl 'pwehn-teh)*
bright	brillante	*(bree-'yahn-teh)*
brochure	folleto, el	*(ehl foh-'yeh-toh)*
broken	roto*	*('roh-toh)*
bronze	bronce, el	*(ehl 'brohn-seh)*
broom	escoba, la	*(lah eh-'skoh-bah)*
brother	hermano, el	*(ehl ehr-'mah-noh)*
brother-in-law	cuñado, el	*(ehl koo-'nyah-doh)*
brown	café	*(kah-'feh)*
bruise	contusión, la	*(lah kohn-too-see-'ohn)*
brush	cepillo, el	*(ehl seh-'pee-yoh)*
budget	presupuesto, el	*(ehl preh-soo-'pweh-stoh)*
building	edificio, el	*(ehl eh-dee-'fee-see-oh)*
bulldozer	niveladora, la	*(lah nee-veh-lah-'doh-rah)*
bulletin	boletín, el	*(ehl boh-leh-'teen)*

bulletin board	tablón de anuncios, el	*(ehl tah-'blohn deh ah-'noon-see-ohs)*
bumper	parachoques, el	*(ehl pah-rah-'choh-kehs)*
burned	quemado*	*(keh-'mah-doh)*
bus	autobús, el	*(ehl ow-toh-'boos)*
bus stop	parada de autobús, la	*(lah pah-'rah-dah deh ow-toh-'boos)*
busboy	ayudante, el/la	*(ehl/lah ah-yoo-'dahn-teh)*
bushes	arbustos, los	*(lohs ahr-'boo-stohs)*
business	negocio, el	*(ehl neh-'goh-see-oh)*
busy	ocupado*	*(oh-koo-'pah-doh)*
but	pero	*('peh-roh)*
butter	mantequilla, la	*(lah mahn-teh-'kee-yah)*
button	botón, el	*(ehl boh-'tohn)*
buyer	jefe de compras, el*	*(ehl 'heh-feh deh 'kohm-prahs)*
buzzer	timbre, el	*(ehl 'teem-breh)*
cab	cabina, la	*(lah kah-'bee-nah)*
cabbage	repollo, el	*(ehl reh-'poh-yoh)*
cabinet	gabinete, el	*(ehl gah-bee-'neh-teh)*
cafeteria	cafetería, la	*(lah kah-feh-teh-'ree-ah)*
cage	jaula, la	*(lah 'hah-oo-lah)*
calculator	calculadora, la	*(lah kahl-koo-lah-'doh-rah)*
calendar	calendario, el	*(ehl kah-lehn-'dah-ree-oh)*
camera	cámara, la	*(lah 'kah-mah-rah)*
can opener	abrelatas, el	*(ehl ah-breh-'lah-tahs)*
Canadian	canadiense	*(kah-nah-dee-'ehn-seh)*
cancer	cáncer, el	*(ehl 'kahn-sehr)*
candidate	candidato, el*	*(ehl kahn-dee-'dah-toh)*
candle	vela, la	*(lah 'veh-lah)*
cane	bastón, el	*(ehl bah-'stohn)*
canister	bote, el	*(ehl 'boh-teh)*
cantaloupe	melón, el	*(ehl meh-'lohn)*
canvas	lona, la	*(lah 'loh-nah)*
cap	gorra, la	*(lah 'goh-rrah)*
capable	capaz	*(kah-'pahs)*
capacity	capacidad, la	*(lah kah-pah-see-'dahd)*
capsule	cápsula, la	*(lah 'kahp-soo-lah)*
car	carro, el	*(ehl 'kah-rroh)*
card	tarjeta, la	*(lah tahr-'heh-tah)*
cardboard	cartón, el	*(ehl kahr-'tohn)*
care	cuidado, el	*(ehl kwee-'dah-doh)*
career	carrera, la	*(lah kah-'rreh-rah)*
careless	descuidado*	*(dehs-kwee-'dah-doh)*
carpenter	carpintero, el*	*(ehl kahr-peen-'teh-roh)*
carpeting	alfombras, las	*(lahs ahl-'fohm-brahs)*

carrier	**transportador, el**	*(ehl trahns-pohr-tah-'dohr)*
carrot	**zanahoria, la**	*(lah sah-nah-'oh-ree-ah)*
cart	**carreta, la**	*(lah kah-'rreh-tah)*
cartridge	**cartucho, el**	*(ehl kahr-'too-choh)*
case	**caso, el**	*(ehl 'kah-soh)*
cash	**efectivo, el***	*(ehl eh-fehk-'tee-voh)*
cash register	**registradora, la**	*(lah reh-hee-strah-'doh-rah)*
cashier	**cajero, el***	*(ehl kah-'heh-roh)*
cashier's checks	**cheques de gerencia, los**	*(lohs 'cheh-kehs deh heh-'rehn-see-ah)*
casing	**cubierta, la**	*(lah koo-bee-'ehr-tah)*
cassette	**casete, el**	*(ehl kah-'seh-teh)*
cast	**molde, el**	*(ehl 'mohl-deh)*
cat	**gato, el***	*(ehl 'gah-toh)*
catalogue	**catálogo, el**	*(ehl kah-'tah-loh-goh)*
Catholic	**católico***	*(kah-'toh-lee-koh)*
ceiling	**techo, el**	*(ehl 'teh-choh)*
celebration	**celebración, la**	*(lah seh-leh-brah-see-'ohn)*
celery	**apio, el**	*(ehl 'ah-pee-oh)*
cell	**célula, la**	*(lah 'seh-loo-lah)*
cement	**cemento, el**	*(ehl seh-'mehn-toh)*
cement truck	**mezcladora de cemento, la**	*(lah meh-sklah-'doh-rah deh seh-'mehn-toh)*
cemetery	**cementerio, el**	*(ehl seh-mehn-'teh-ree-oh)*
centimeter	**centímetro, el**	*(ehl sehn-'tee-meh-troh)*
cents	**centavos, los**	*(lohs sehn-'tah-vohs)*
cereal	**cereal, el**	*(ehl seh-reh-'ahl)*
ceremony	**ceremonia, la**	*(lah seh-reh-'moh-nee-ah)*
certificate	**certificado, el**	*(ehl sehr-tee-fee-'kah-doh)*
chain	**cadena, la**	*(lah kah-'deh-nah)*
chain saw	**motosierra, la**	*(lah moh-toh-see-'eh-rrah)*
chair	**silla, la**	*(lah 'see-yah)*
chairperson	**presidente, el***	*(ehl preh-see-'dehn-teh)*
change	**cambio, el**	*(ehl 'kahm-bee-oh)*
channel	**canal, el**	*(ehl kah-'nahl)*
chapter	**capítulo, el**	*(ehl kah-'pee-too-loh)*
charge	**cargo, el**	*(ehl 'kahr-goh)*
charger	**cargador, el**	*(ehl kahr-gah-'dohr)*
charity	**caridad, la**	*(lah kah-ree-'dahd)*
chart	**diagrama, el**	*(ehl dee-ah-'grah-mah)*
chassis	**bastidor, el**	*(ehl bah-stee-'dohr)*
cheap	**barato***	*(bah-'rah-toh)*
check	**cheque, el**	*(ehl 'cheh-keh)*
check up	**comprobación, la**	*(lah kohm-proh-bah-see-'ohn)*

cheek	**mejilla, la**	*(lah meh-'hee-yah)*
cheese	**queso, el**	*(ehl 'keh-soh)*
chemicals	**productos químicos, los**	*(lohs proh-'dook-tohs 'kee-mee-kohs)*
cherry	**cereza, la**	*(lah seh-'reh-sah)*
chest	**pecho, el**	*(ehl 'peh-choh)*
chicken	**pollo, el**	*(ehl 'poh-yoh)*
child care	**cuidado del niño, el**	*(ehl kwee-'dah-doh dehl 'nee-nyoh)*
chill	**escalofrío, el**	*(ehl eh-skah-loh-'free-oh)*
chimney	**chimenea, la**	*(lah chee-meh-'neh-ah)*
chin	**barbilla, la**	*(lah bahr-'bee-yah)*
chisel	**cincel, el**	*(ehl seen-'sehl)*
Christian	**cristiano***	*(kree-stee-'ah-noh)*
church	**iglesia, la**	*(lah ee-'gleh-see-ah)*
cigarette	**cigarillo, el**	*(ehl see-gah-'ree-yoh)*
circle	**círculo, el**	*(ehl 'seer-koo-loh)*
circuit	**circuito, el**	*(ehl seer-koo-'ee-toh)*
citizen	**ciudadano, el***	*(ehl see-oo-dah-'dah-noh)*
city block	**cuadra, la**	*(lah 'kwah-drah)*
city hall	**municipio, el**	*(ehl moo-nee-'see-pee-oh)*
claim	**reclamación, la**	*(lah reh-klah-mah-see-'ohn)*
clamp	**prensa de sujetar, la**	*(lah 'prehn-sah deh soo-heh-'tahr)*
class	**clase, la**	*(lah 'klah-seh)*
clause	**cláusula, la**	*(lah 'klow-soo-lah)*
clay	**barro, el**	*(ehl 'bah-rroh)*
clean	**limpio***	*('leem-pee-oh)*
clear	**despejado***	*(deh-speh-'hah-doh)*
clerk	**dependiente, el***	*(ehl deh-pehn-dee-'ehn-teh)*
client	**cliente, el**	*(ehl klee-'ehn-teh)*
climate	**clima, el**	*(ehl 'klee-mah)*
clinic	**clínica, la**	*(lah 'klee-nee-kah)*
clock	**reloj, el**	*(ehl reh-'loh)*
closet	**ropero, el**	*(ehl roh-'peh-roh)*
cloth	**tela, la**	*(lah 'teh-lah)*
cloudy	**nublado***	*(noo-'blah-doh)*
coal	**carbón, el**	*(ehl kahr-'bohn)*
coconut	**coco, el**	*(ehl 'koh-koh)*
code	**código, el**	*(ehl 'koh-dee-goh)*
coffee	**café, el**	*(ehl kah-'feh)*
coffeepot	**cafetera, la**	*(lah kah-feh-'teh-rah)*
coil	**rollo, el**	*(ehl 'roh-yoh)*
coins	**monedas, las**	*(lahs moh-'neh-dahs)*
cold	**resfriado, el**	*(ehl rehs-free-'ah-doh)*
college	**universidad, la**	*(lah oo-nee-vehr-see-'dahd)*

color	color, el	*(ehl koh-'lohr)*
comb	peine, el	*(ehl 'peh-ee-neh)*
combustible	combustible	*(kohm-boo-'stee-bleh)*
commercial	comercial	*(koh-mehr-see-'ahl)*
commission	comisión, la	*(lah koh-mee-see-'ohn)*
commitment	compromiso, el	*(ehl kohm-proh-'mee-soh)*
committee	comité, el	*(ehl koh-mee-'teh)*
communication	comunicación, la	*(lah koh-moo-nee-kah-see-'ohn)*
community	comunidad, la	*(lah koh-moo-nee-'dahd)*
company	compañía, la	*(lah kohm-pah-'nyee-ah)*
comparison	comparación, la	*(lah kohm-pah-rah-see-'ohn)*
compensation	indemnización, la	*(lah een-dehm-nee-sah-see-'ohn)*
competition	competencia, la	*(lah kohm-peh-'tehn-see-ah)*
complaint	queja, la	*(lah 'keh-hah)*
completely	completamente	*(kohm-pleh-tah-'mehn-teh)*
component	componente, el	*(ehl kohm-poh-'nehn-teh)*
compound	compuesto, el	*(ehl kohm-'pweh-stoh)*
compressor	compresor de aire, el	*(ehl kohm-preh-'sohr deh 'ah-ee-reh)*
compromise	compromiso, el	*(ehl kohm-proh-'mee-soh)*
computer	computadora, la	*(lah kohm-poo-tah-'doh-rah)*
concept	concepto, el	*(ehl kohn-'sehp-toh)*
condition	condición, la	*(lah kohn-dee-see-'ohn)*
conditioner	acondicionador, el	*(ehl ah-kohn-dee-see-oh-nah-'dohr)*
condominium	condominio, el	*(ehl kohn-doh-'mee-nee-oh)*
cone	cono, el	*(ehl 'koh-noh)*
conference	conferencia, la	*(lah kohn-feh-'rehn-see-ah)*
confidence	confidencia, la	*(lah kohn-fee-'dehn-see-ah)*
conflict	conflicto, el	*(ehl kohn-'fleek-toh)*
confrontation	confrontación, la	*(lah kohn-frohn-tah-see-'ohn)*
constructive	constructivo*	*(kohn-strook-'tee-voh)*
consultant	consultor, el*	*(ehl kohn-sool-'tohr)*
consumer	consumidor, el*	*(ehl kohn-soo-mee-'dohr)*
contact	contacto, el	*(ehl kohn-'tahk-toh)*
contagious	contagioso*	*(kohn-tah-hee-'oh-soh)*
container	recipiente, el	*(ehl reh-see-pee-'ehn-teh)*
content	contenido, el	*(ehl kohn-teh-'nee-doh)*
contract	contrato, el	*(ehl kohn-'trah-toh)*
contribution	contribución, la	*(lah kohn-tree-boo-see-'ohn)*
control	control, el	*(ehl kohn-'trohl)*
convenient	conveniente	*(kohn-veh-nee-'ehn-teh)*
conveyor belt	correa transportadora, la	*(lah koh-'rreh-ah trahns-pohr-tah-'doh-rah)*
cook	cocinero, el*	*(ehl koh-see-'neh-roh)*

cool	**fresco***	*('freh-skoh)*
coordinator	**coordinador, el***	*(ehl koh-ohr-dee-nah-'dohr)*
copier	**copiadora, la**	*(lah koh-pee-ah-'doh-rah)*
copper	**cobre, el**	*(ehl 'koh-breh)*
copy	**copia, la**	*(lah 'koh-pee-ah)*
corn	**maíz, el**	*(ehl mah-'ees)*
corner	**esquina, la**	*(lah eh-'skee-nah)*
correct	**correcto***	*(koh-'rrehk-toh)*
cost	**costo, el**	*(ehl 'koh-stoh)*
costume	**disfraz, el**	*(ehl dees-'frahs)*
cotton	**algodón, el**	*(ehl ahl-goh-'dohn)*
cough	**tos, la**	*(lah tohs)*
count	**cuenta, la**	*(lah 'kwehn-tah)*
courier	**mensajero, el***	*(ehl mehn-sah-'heh-roh)*
course	**curso, el**	*(ehl 'koor-soh)*
court	**tribunal, el**	*(ehl tree-boo-'nahl)*
courthouse	**corte, la**	*(lah 'kohr-teh)*
cousin	**primo, el***	*(ehl 'pree-moh)*
coverage	**cobertura, la**	*(lah koh-behr-'too-rah)*
cow	**vaca, la**	*(lah 'vah-kah)*
crank	**manivela, la**	*(lah mah-nee-'veh-lah)*
crate	**caja para transporte, la**	*(lah 'kah-hah 'pah-rah trahns-'pohr-teh)*
cream	**crema, la**	*(lah 'kreh-mah)*
creativity	**creatividad, la**	*(lah kreh-ah-tee-vee-'dahd)*
credit	**crédito, el**	*(ehl 'kreh-dee-toh)*
credit card	**tarjeta de crédito, la**	*(lah tahr-'heh-tah deh 'kreh-dee-toh)*
Credit Union	**banco de crédito, el**	*(ehl 'bahn-koh deh 'kreh-dee-toh)*
crime	**crimen, el**	*(ehl 'kree-mehn)*
criteria	**criterio, el**	*(ehl kree-'teh-ree-oh)*
critical	**crítico***	*('kree-tee-koh)*
crowbar	**palanca de hierro, la**	*(lah pah-'lahn-kah deh 'yeh-roh)*
cruel	**cruel**	*(kroo-'ehl)*
crushed	**aplastado***	*(ah-plah-'stah-doh)*
crutches	**muletas, las**	*(lahs moh-'leh-tahs)*
Cuban	**cubano***	*(koo-'bah-noh)*
cube	**cubo, el**	*(ehl 'koo-boh)*
cucumber	**pepino, el**	*(ehl peh-'pee-noh)*
cup	**taza, la**	*(lah 'tah-sah)*
curriculum	**currículum, el**	*(ehl koo-ree-koo-'lum)*
curtains	**cortinas, las**	*(lahs kohr-'tee-nahs)*
curve	**curva, la**	*(lah 'koor-vah)*
cushion	**petaca, la**	*(lah peh-'tah-kah)*
custom	**costumbre, la**	*(lah koh-'stoom-breh)*

customer	cliente, el*	*(ehl klee-'ehn-teh)*
customer service	servicio para clientes, el	*(ehl sehr-'vee-see-oh 'pah-rah klee-'ehn-tehs)*
cut	cortada, la	*(lah kohr-'tah-dah)*
cycle	ciclo, el	*(ehl 'see-kloh)*
cylinder	cilindro, el	*(ehl see-'leen-droh)*
daily	diario*	*(dee-'ah-ree-oh)*
damaged	dañado*	*(dah-'nyah-doh)*
dance	baile, el	*(ehl 'bah-ee-leh)*
danger	peligro, el	*(ehl peh-'lee-groh)*
dangerous	peligroso*	*(peh-lee-'groh-soh)*
dark-haired	moreno*	*(moh-'reh-noh)*
darling	querido*	*(keh-'ree-doh)*
dashboard	tablero del carro, el	*(ehl tah-'bleh-roh dehl 'kah-rroh)*
data	datos, los	*(lohs 'dah-tohs)*
date	fecha, la	*(lah 'feh-chah)*
daughter	hija, la	*(lah 'ee-hah)*
daughter-in-law	nuera, la	*(lah 'nweh-rah)*
day	día, el	*(ehl 'dee-ah)*
deadbolt	pestillo, el	*(ehl peh-'stee-yoh)*
deadlock	punto muerto, el	*(ehl 'poon-toh 'mwehr-toh)*
dealer	concesionario, el	*(ehl kohn-seh-see-oh-'nah-ree-oh)*
death	muerte, la	*(lah 'mwehr-teh)*
debt	deuda, la	*(lah deh-'oo-dah)*
December	diciembre	*(dee-see-'ehm-breh)*
deck	terraza, la	*(lah teh-'rrah-sah)*
deep	profundo*	*(proh-'foon-doh)*
deer	venado, el	*(ehl veh-'nah-doh)*
defective	defectuoso*	*(deh-fehk-too-'oh-soh)*
defense	defensa, la	*(lah deh-'fehn-sah)*
degree	grado, el	*(ehl 'grah-doh)*
delay	demora, la	*(lah deh-'moh-rah)*
delegate	delegado, el*	*(ehl deh-leh-'gah-doh)*
delivery	entrega, la	*(lah ehn-'treh-gah)*
delivery truck	camión de reparto, el	*(ehl kah-mee-'ohn deh reh-'pahr-toh)*
demand	reclamo, el	*(ehl reh-'klah-moh)*
demonstration	demostración, la	*(lah deh-moh-strah-see-'ohn)*
density	densidad, la	*(lah dehn-see-'dahd)*
dentist	dentista, el/la	*(ehl/lah dehn-'tee-stah)*
deodorant	desodorante, el	*(ehl dehs-oh-doh-'rahn-teh)*
department	departamento, el	*(ehl deh-pahr-tah-'mehn-toh)*
department store	almacén, el	*(ehl ahl-mah-'sehn)*
depression	desánimo, el	*(ehl dehs-'ah-nee-moh)*
description	descripción, la	*(lah deh-skreep-see-'ohn)*

desert	**desierto, el**	*(ehl deh-see-'ehr-toh)*
design	**diseño, el**	*(ehl dee-'seh-nyoh)*
desk	**escritorio, el**	*(ehl eh-skree-'toh-ree-oh)*
detergent	**detergente, el**	*(ehl deh-tehr-'hehn-teh)*
device	**aparato, el**	*(ehl ah-pah-'rah-toh)*
diagonal	**diagonal**	*(dee-ah-goh-'nahl)*
dial	**marcador, el**	*(ehl mahr-kah-'dohr)*
dialogue	**diálogo, el**	*(ehl dee-'ah-loh-goh)*
difficult	**difícil**	*(dee-'fee-seel)*
dining room	**comedor, el**	*(ehl koh-meh-'dohr)*
dinner	**cena, la**	*(lah-'seh-nah)*
diploma	**diploma, el**	*(ehl dee-'ploh-mah)*
director	**director, el***	*(ehl dee-rehk-'tohr)*
dirt	**tierra, la**	*(lah tee-'eh-rrah)*
dirty	**sucio***	*('soo-see-oh)*
disability	**incapacidad, la**	*(lah een-kah-pah-see-'dahd)*
discipline	**disciplina, la**	*(lah dee-see-'plee-nah)*
discount	**descuento, el**	*(ehl deh-'skwehn-toh)*
discussion	**discurso, el**	*(ehl dee-'skoor-soh)*
dishonest	**deshonesto***	*(dehs-oh-'neh-stoh)*
dishwasher	**lavaplatos, el**	*(ehl lah-vah-'plah-tohs)*
disk	**disco, el**	*(ehl 'dee-skoh)*
dispute	**disputa, la**	*(lah dee-'spoo-tah)*
disrespectful	**irrespetuoso***	*(ee-reh-speh-too-'oh-soh)*
dissent	**disconformidad, la**	*(lah dees-kohn-fohr-mee-'dahd)*
distracted	**distraído***	*(dee-strah-'ee-doh)*
disturbance	**perturbación, la**	*(lah pehr-toor-bah-see-'ohn)*
ditch	**zanja, la**	*(lah 'sahn-hah)*
division	**división, la**	*(lah dee-vee-see-'ohn)*
divorce	**divorcio, el**	*(ehl dee-'vohr-see-oh)*
dizzy	**mareado***	*(mah-reh-'ah-doh)*
dock	**muelle, el**	*(ehl 'mweh-yeh)*
doctor	**doctor, el***	*(ehl dohk-'tohr)*
dog	**perro, el***	*(ehl 'peh-rroh)*
dollar	**dólar, el**	*(ehl 'doh-lahr)*
dolley	**travelín, el**	*(ehl trah-veh-'leen)*
donation	**donación, la**	*(lah doh-nah-see-'ohn)*
door	**puerta, la**	*(lah 'pwehr-tah)*
double	**doble**	*('doh-bleh)*
down	**abajo**	*(ah-'bah-hoh)*
down payment	**pago inicial, el**	*(ehl 'pah-goh ee-nee-see-'ahl)*
downtown	**centro, el**	*(ehl 'sehn-troh)*
dozen	**docena, la**	*(lah doh-'seh-nah)*

drainage	**drenaje, el**	*(ehl dreh-'nah-heh)*
drawers	**cajones, los**	*(lohs kah-'hoh-nehs)*
drawing	**dibujo, el**	*(ehl dee-'boo-hoh)*
dress	**vestido, el**	*(ehl veh-'stee-doh)*
dresser	**tocador, el**	*(ehl toh-kah-'dohr)*
drill	**taladro, el**	*(ehl tah-'lah-droh)*
drinks	**bebidas, las**	*(lahs beh-'bee-dahs)*
drive	**impulsor, el**	*(ehl eem-pool-'sohr)*
driver	**chófer, el/la**	*(ehl/lah 'choh-fehr)*
driver's license	**licencia de manejar, la**	*(lah lee-'sehn-see-ah 'pah-rah mah-neh-'hahr)*
driveway	**entrada para carros, la**	*(lah ehn-'trah-dah 'pah-rah 'kah-rrohs)*
drop	**gota, la**	*(lah 'goh-tah)*
drowning	**ahogo, el**	*(ehl ah-'oh-goh)*
drug dealer	**vendedor de drogas, el**	*(ehl vehn-deh-'dohr deh 'droh-gahs)*
drugs	**drogas, las**	*(lahs 'droh-gahs)*
dry	**seco***	*('seh-koh)*
dryer	**secadora, la**	*(lah seh-kah-'doh-rah)*
duck	**pato, el***	*(ehl 'pah-toh)*
duct	**conducto, el**	*(ehl kohn-'dook-toh)*
dues	**cuotas, las**	*(lahs 'kwoh-tahs)*
dump truck	**volquete, el**	*(ehl vohl-'keh-teh)*
dust	**polvo, el**	*(ehl 'pohl-voh)*
dust pan	**pala para recoger basura, la**	*(lah 'pah-lah 'pah-rah reh-koh-'hehr bah-'soo-rah)*
duty	**deber, el**	*(ehl deh-'behr)*
dye	**tintura, la**	*(lah teen-'too-rah)*
ear	**oído, el**	*(ehl oh-'ee-doh)*
early	**temprano***	*(tehm-'prah-noh)*
earnings	**ganancias, las**	*(lahs gah-'nahn-see-ahs)*
earplugs	**tapones para los oídos, los**	*(lohs tah-'poh-nehs 'pah-rah lohs oh-'ee-dohs)*
earring	**arete, el**	*(ehl ah-'reh-teh)*
earthquake	**terremoto, el**	*(ehl teh-rreh-'moh-toh)*
east	**este**	*('eh-steh)*
easy	**fácil**	*('fah-seel)*
edge	**borde, el**	*(ehl 'bohr-deh)*
education	**educación, la**	*(lah eh-doo-kah-see-'ohn)*
effective	**eficaz**	*(eh-fee-'kahs)*
eggs	**huevos, los**	*(lohs 'weh-vohs)*
eight	**ocho**	*('oh-choh)*
eighteen	**dieciocho**	*(dee-ehs-ee-'oh-choh)*
eighth	**octavo***	*(ohk-'tah-voh)*
eighty	**ochenta**	*(oh-'chehn-tah)*

elbow	codo, el	(ehl 'koh-doh)
election	elección, la	(lah eh-lehk-see-'ohn)
electrical outlet	enchufe, el	(ehl ehn-'choo-feh)
electricity	electricidad, la	(lah eh-lehk-tree-see-'dahd)
elevator	ascensor, el	(ehl ah-sehn-'sohr)
eleven	once	('ohn-seh)
eligible	eligible	(eh-lee-'hee-bleh)
employee	empleado, el*	(ehl ehm-pleh-'ah-doh)
employer	empresario, el*	(ehl ehm-preh-'sah-ree·oh)
employment	empleo, el	(ehl ehm-'pleh-oh)
engagement	compromiso, el	(ehl kohm-proh-'mee-soh)
engine	motor, el	(ehl moh-'tohr)
engineer	ingeniero, el*	(ehl een-heh-nee-'eh-roh)
enough	bastante	(bah-'stahn-teh)
enthusiasm	entusiasmo, el	(ehl ehn-too-see-'ahs-moh)
entrance	entrada, la	(lah ehn-'trah-dah)
envelope	sobre, el	(ehl 'soh-breh)
environment	ambiente, el	(ehl ahm-bee-'ehn-teh)
equipment	equipo, el	(ehl eh-'kee-poh)
eraser	borrador, el	(ehl boh-rrah-'dohr)
errand	encargo, el	(ehl ehn-'kahr-goh)
escalator	escalera mecánica, la	(lah eh-skah-'leh-rah meh-'kah-nee-kah)
estimate	estimado, el	(ehl eh-stee-'mah-doh)
evaluation	evaluación, la	(lah eh-vah-loo-ah-see-'ohn)
evaluator	evaluador, el	(ehl eh-vah-loo-ah-'dohr)
event	evento, el	(ehl eh-'vehn-toh)
everybody	todos*	('toh-dohs)
everything	todo*	('toh-doh)
everywhere	por todas partes	(pohr 'toh-dahs 'pahr-tehs)
evidence	evidencia, la	(lah eh-vee-'dehn-see·ah)
examination	exámen, el	(ehl ehk-'sah-mehn)
examiner	examinador, el*	(ehl ehk-sah-mee-nah-'dohr)
example	ejemplo, el	(ehl eh-'hehm-ploh)
excellent	excelente	(ehk-seh-'lehn-teh)
exceptional	excepcional	(ehk-sehp-see·oh-'nahl)
exchange	cambio, el	(ehl 'kahm-bee·oh)
executive	ejecutivo, el*	(ehl eh-heh-koo-'tee-voh)
exhaust	escape, el	(ehl eh-'skah-peh)
exhausted	agotado*	(ah-goh-'tah-doh)
exit	salida, la	(lah sah-'lee-dah)
expectation	esperanza, la	(lah eh-speh-'rahn-sah)
expenditures	gastos, los	(lohs 'gah-stohs)
expense	gasto, el	(ehl 'gah-stoh)

expensive	**caro***	(*'kah-roh*)
experience	**experiencia, la**	(*lah ehk-speh-ree-'ehn-see-ah*)
experiment	**experimento, el**	(*ehl ehk-speh-ree-'mehn-toh*)
expiration	**vencimiento, el**	(*ehl vehn-see-mee-'ehn-toh*)
explosive	**explosivo***	(*ehk-sploh-'see-voh*)
extension cord	**cable de extensión, el**	(*ehl 'kah-bleh deh ehks-tehn-see-'ohn*)
eye	**ojo, el**	(*ehl 'oh-hoh*)
fabulous	**fabuloso***	(*fah-boo-'loh-soh*)
face	**cara, la**	(*lah 'kah-rah*)
facility	**facilidad, la**	(*lah fah-see-lee-'dahd*)
fact	**hecho, el**	(*ehl 'eh-choh*)
factory	**fábrica, la**	(*lah 'fah-bree-kah*)
fair	**justo***	(*'hoo-stoh*)
fall	**otoño, el**	(*ehl oh-'toh-nyoh*)
family	**familia, la**	(*lah fah-'mee-lee-ah*)
famous	**famoso***	(*fah-'moh-soh*)
fan	**ventilador, el**	(*ehl vehn-tee-lah-'dohr*)
fantastic	**fantástico***	(*fahn-'tah-stee-koh*)
far	**lejos**	(*'leh-hohs*)
farmer	**campesino, el***	(*ehl kahm-peh-'see-noh*)
fast	**rápido***	(*'rah-pee-doh*)
fat	**gordo***	(*'gohr-doh*)
father	**padre, el**	(*ehl 'pah-dreh*)
father-in-law	**suegro, el**	(*ehl 'sweh-groh*)
fatigue	**fatiga, la**	(*lah fah-'tee-gah*)
faucet	**grifo, el**	(*ehl 'gree-foh*)
fault	**culpa, la**	(*lah 'kool-pah*)
February	**febrero**	(*feh-'breh-roh*)
fee	**honorario, el**	(*ehl oh-noh-'rah-ree-oh*)
feeling	**sentimiento, el**	(*ehl sehn-tee-mee-'ehn-toh*)
felony	**delito mayor, el**	(*ehl deh-'lee-toh mah-'yohr*)
feminine napkins	**paños femeninos, los**	(*lohs 'pah-nyohs feh-meh-'nee-nohs*)
fence	**cerca, la**	(*lah 'sehr-kah*)
fender	**guardabarro, el**	(*ehl gwahr-dah-'bah-rroh*)
fever	**fiebre, la**	(*lah fee-'eh-breh*)
field	**campo, el**	(*ehl 'kahm-poh*)
fifteen	**quince**	(*'keen-seh*)
fifth	**quinto***	(*'keen-toh*)
fifty	**cincuenta**	(*seen-'kwehn-tah*)
fight	**pelea, la**	(*lah peh-'leh-ah*)
file	**lima, la**	(*lah 'lee-mah*)
file cabinet	**archivo, el**	(*ehl ahr-'chee-voh*)
film	**película, la**	(*lah peh-'lee-koo-lah*)

filter	filtro, el	(ehl 'feel-troh)
finance	finanzas, las	(lahs fee-'nahn-sahs)
finger	dedo, el	(ehl 'deh-doh)
fire	fuego, el	(ehl 'fweh-goh)
fire department	departamento de bomberos, el	(ehl deh-pahr-tah-'mehn-toh deh bohm-'beh-rohs)
fire extinguisher	extintor, el	(ehl ehks-teen-'tohr)
firearm	arma de fuego, el	(ehl 'ahr-mah deh 'fweh-goh)
fired	despedido*	(deh-speh-'dee-doh)
firefighter	bombero, el*	(ehl bohm-'beh-roh)
fireplace	fogón, el	(ehl foh-'gohn)
firm	empresa, la	(lah ehm-'preh-sah)
first	primero*	(pree-'meh-roh)
first aid kit	botiquín de primeros auxilios, el	(ehl boh-tee-'keen deh pree-'meh-rohs owk-'see-lee-ohs)
fish	pescado, el	(ehl peh-'skah-doh)
fishing	pesca, la	(lah 'peh-skah)
five	cinco	('seen-koh)
fixed	fijo*	('fee-hoh)
flame	llama, la	(lah 'yah-mah)
flammable	inflamable	(een-flah-'mah-bleh)
flare	luz de bengala, la	(lah loos deh behn-'gah-lah)
flashlight	linterna, la	(lah leen-'tehr-nah)
flea	pulga, la	(lah 'pool-gah)
flexible	flexible	(flehk-'see-bleh)
flight	vuelo, el	(ehl 'vweh-loh)
flood	inundación, la	(lah een-oon-dah-see-'ohn)
floor	piso, el	(ehl 'pee-soh)
floor tile	baldosa, la	(lah bahl-'doh-sah)
florist	florería, la	(lah floh-reh-'ree-ah)
flower	flor, la	(lah flohr)
flowerpot	maceta, la	(lah mah-'seh-tah)
flu	resfriado, el	(ehl rehs-free-'ah-doh)
fly	mosca, la	(lah 'moh-skah)
flyer	paper, el	(ehl pah-'pehr)
folder	cuaderno, el	(ehl kwah-'dehr-noh)
foliage	follaje, el	(ehl foh-'yah-heh)
food	comida, la	(lah koh-'mee-dah)
foot	pie, el	(ehl 'pee-eh)
for	para or por	('pah-rah or pohr)
foreman	capataz, el/la	(ehl/lah kah-pah-'tahs)
forest	bosque, el	(ehl 'boh-skeh)
forge	fragua, la	(lah 'frah-gwah)

fork	**tenedor, el**	*(ehl teh-neh-'dohr)*
forklift	**carretilla elevadora, la**	*(lah kah-rreh-'tee-yah eh-leh-vah-'doh-rah)*
form	**formulario, el**	*(ehl fohr-moo-'lah-ree-oh)*
forty	**cuarenta**	*(kwah-'rehn-tah)*
fountain	**fuente, la**	*(lah 'fwehn-teh)*
four	**cuatro**	*('kwah-troh)*
fourteen	**catorce**	*(kah-'tohr-seh)*
fourth	**cuarto***	*('kwahr-toh)*
fox	**zorro, el***	*(ehl 'soh-rroh)*
fraction	**fracción, la**	*(lah frahk-see-'ohn)*
free	**gratis**	*('grah-tees)*
freezer	**congelador, el**	*(ehl kohn-heh-lah-'dohr)*
freight	**flete, el**	*(ehl 'fleh-teh)*
friction	**fricción, la**	*(lah freek-see-'ohn)*
Friday	**viernes**	*(vee-'ehr-nehs)*
friend	**amigo, el***	*(ehl ah-'mee-goh)*
friendship	**amistad, la**	*(lah ah-mee-'stahd)*
frog	**sapo, el**	*(ehl 'sah-poh)*
from	**de**	*(deh)*
frost	**escarcha, la**	*(lah eh-'skahr-chah)*
fruit	**fruta, la**	*(lah 'froo-tah)*
frustrated	**frustrado***	*(froo-'strah-doh)*
fuel	**combustible, el**	*(ehl kohm-boo-'stee-bleh)*
full-time	**tiempo completo, el**	*(ehl tee-'ehm-poh kohm-'pleh-toh)*
fume	**vapor, el**	*(ehl vah-'pohr)*
fun	**divertido***	*(dee-vehr-'tee-doh)*
function	**función, la**	*(lah foonk-see-'ohn)*
funds	**fondos, los**	*(lohs 'fohn-dohs)*
funeral	**funeral, el**	*(ehl foo-neh-'rahl)*
funny	**chistoso***	*(chee-'stoh-soh)*
furniture	**muebles, los**	*(lohs 'mweh-blehs)*
fusebox	**caja de fusibles, la**	*(lah 'kah-hah deh foo-'see-blehs)*
gallon	**galón, el**	*(ehl gah-'lohn)*
game	**juego, el**	*(ehl hoo-'eh-goh)*
gang member	**pandillero, el***	*(ehl pahn-dee-'yeh-roh)*
garage	**garaje, el**	*(ehl gah-'rah-heh)*
garbage disposal	**desechador, el**	*(ehl dehs-eh-chah-'dohr)*
garden	**jardín, el**	*(ehl hahr-'deen)*
gardener	**jardinero, el***	*(ehl hahr-dee-'neh-roh)*
gardening	**jardinería, la**	*(lah hahr-dee-neh-'ree-ah)*
garment	**prenda, la**	*(lah 'prehn-dah)*
gas	**gas, el**	*(ehl gahs)*
gas meter	**medidor de gas, el**	*(ehl meh-dee-'dohr deh gahs)*

gas station	gasolinera, la	*(lah gah-soh-lee-'neh-rah)*
gasoline	gasolina, la	*(lah gah-soh-'lee-nah)*
gate	portón, el	*(ehl pohr-'tohn)*
gauge	indicador, el	*(ehl een-dee-kah-'dohr)*
gear	engranaje, el	*(ehn-grah-'nah-heh)*
generator	generador, el	*(ehl he-neh-rah-'dohr)*
gift	regalo, el	*(ehl reh-'gah-loh)*
girl	niña, la	*(lah 'nee-nyah)*
girlfriend	novia, la	*(lah'noh-vee-ah)*
glass (drinking)	vaso, el	*(ehl 'vah-soh)*
glass (material)	vidrio, el	*(ehl 'vee-dree-oh)*
glasses	lentes, los	*(lohs 'lehn-tehs)*
glove compartment	guantera, la	*(lah gwahn-'teh-rah)*
gloves	guantes, los	*(lohs 'gwahn-tehs)*
glue	pegamento, el	*(ehl peh-gah-'mehn-toh)*
goal	meta, la	*(lah 'meh-tah)*
goat	chivo, el	*(ehl 'chee-voh)*
God	Dios	*('dee-ohs)*
gold	oro, el	*(ehl 'oh-roh)*
golf course	campo de golf, el	*(ehl 'kahm-poh deh gohlf)*
good	bueno*	*('bweh-noh)*
goods	bienes, los	*(lohs bee-'eh-nehs)*
grades	notas, las	*(lahs 'noh-tahs)*
graduate	graduado, el*	*(ehl grah-doo-'ah-doh)*
grain	grano, el	*(ehl 'grah-noh)*
gram	gramo, el	*(ehl 'grah-moh)*
granddaughter	nieta, la	*(lah nee-'eh-tah)*
grandfather	abuelo, el	*(ehl ah-'bweh-loh)*
grandmother	abuela, la	*(lah ah-'bweh-lah)*
grandson	nieto, el	*(ehl nee-'eh-toh)*
grape	uva, la	*(lah 'oo-vah)*
grapefruit	toronja, la	*(lah toh-'rohn-hah)*
graph	gráfico, el	*(ehl 'grah-fee-koh)*
grass	pasto, el	*(ehl 'pah-stoh)*
gravel	grava, la	*(lah 'grah-vah)*
grease	grasa, la	*(lah 'grah-sah)*
great	muy bueno*	*(moo-ee 'bweh-noh)*
green	verde	*('vehr-deh)*
grievance	queja, la	*(lah 'keh-hah)*
grill	parrilla, la	*(lah pah-'rree-yah)*
grinder	molinero, el*	*(ehl moh-lee-'neh-roh)*
groove	muesca, la	*(lah 'mweh-skah)*
gross	gruesa, la	*(lah groo-'eh-sah)*

group	**grupo, el**	*(ehl 'groo-poh)*
growth	**crecimiento, el**	*(ehl kreh-see-mee-'ehn-toh)*
guide	**guía, el**	*(ehl 'gee-ah)*
guidelines	**pautas, las**	*(lahs pahu-'tahs)*
guild	**gremio, el**	*(ehl 'greh-mee-oh)*
guilt	**culpabilidad, la**	*(lah kool-pah-bee-lee-'dahd)*
gulch	**barranca, la**	*(lah bah-'rrahn-kah)*
gymnasium	**gimnasio, el**	*(ehl heem-'nah-see-oh)*
hack saw	**sierra para cortar metal, la**	*(lah see-'eh-rrah 'pah-rah kohr-'tahr meh-'tahl)*
hail	**granizo, el**	*(ehl grah-'nee-soh)*
hair	**pelo, el**	*(ehl 'peh-loh)*
hairbrush	**cepillo del pelo, el**	*(ehl seh-'pee-yoh dehl 'peh-loh)*
hairpin	**horquilla, la**	*(lah ohr-'kee-yah)*
hairspray	**laca, la**	*(lah 'lah-kah)*
half	**mitad, la**	*(lah mee-'tahd)*
hallway	**corredor, el**	*(ehl koh-rreh-'dohr)*
ham	**jamón, el**	*(ehl hah-'mohn)*
hamburger	**hamburguesa, la**	*(lah ahm-boor-'geh-sah)*
hammer	**martillo, el**	*(ehl mahr-'tee-yoh)*
hand	**mano, la**	*(lah 'mah-noh)*
hand saw	**serrucha, la**	*(lah seh-'rroo-chah)*
handicapped	**minusválidos, los***	*(lohs mee-noos-'vah-lee-dohs)*
handkerchief	**pañuelo, el**	*(ehl pah-nyoo-'eh-loh)*
handle	**perilla, la**	*(lah peh-'ree-yah)*
happy	**contento***	*(kohn-'tehn-toh)*
harassment	**acosamiento, el**	*(ehl ah-koh-sah-mee-'ehn-toh)*
hard	**duro***	*('doo-roh)*
harm	**daño**	*(ehl 'dah-nyoh)*
harmony	**armonía, la**	*(lah ahr-moh-'nee-ah)*
hat	**sombrero, el**	*(ehl sohm-'breh-roh)*
hatch	**media puerta, la**	*(lah 'pwehr-tah 'meh-dee-ah)*
hazard	**obstáculo, el**	*(ehl ohb-'stah-koo-loh)*
he	**él**	*(ehl)*
head	**cabeza, la**	*(lah kah-'beh-sah)*
headache	**dolor de cabeza, el**	*(ehl doh-'lohr deh kah-'beh-sah)*
healthy	**saludable**	*(sah-loo-'dah-bleh)*
heater	**calentador, el**	*(ehl kah-lehn-tah-'dohr)*
heating	**calefacción, la**	*(lah kah-leh-fahk-see-'ohn)*
heavy	**pesado***	*(peh-'sah-doh)*
height	**altura, la**	*(lah ahl-'too-rah)*
helicopter	**helicóptero, el**	*(ehl eh-lee-'kohp-teh-roh)*
helmet	**casco, el**	*(ehl 'kah-skoh)*

helper	ayudante, el/la	*(ehl/lah ah-yoo-'dahn-teh)*
here	aquí	*(ah-'kee)*
high	alto*	*('ahl-toh)*
high school	escuela secundaria, la	*(lah eh-'skweh-lah seh-koon-'dah-ree-ah)*
highway	carretera, la	*(lah kah-rreh-'teh-rah)*
hiking	caminata, la	*(lah kah-mee-'nah-tah)*
hill	cerro, el	*(ehl 'seh-rroh)*
hinge	gozne, el	*(ehl 'gohs-neh)*
hip	cadera, la	*(lah kah-'deh-rah)*
hired	contratado*	*(kohn-'trah-tah-doh)*
hoist	grúa, la	*(lah 'groo-ah)*
hole	hoyo, el	*(ehl 'oh-yoh)*
home	casa, la	*(lah 'kah-sah)*
honesty	honradez, la	*(lah ohn-rah-'dehs)*
honey	miel, la	*(lah mee-'ehl)*
hood	cubierta, la	*(lah koo-bee-'ehr-tah)*
hook	gancho, el	*(ehl 'gahn-choh)*
horizontal	horizontal	*(oh-ree-sohn-'tahl)*
horn	bocina, la	*(lah boh-'see-nah)*
horse	caballo, el	*(ehl kah-'bah-yoh)*
horsepower	caballo de fuerza, el	*(ehl kah-'bah-yoh deh 'fwehr-sah)*
hose	manguera, la	*(lah mahn-'geh-rah)*
hospital	hospital, el	*(ehl oh-spee-'tahl)*
hostile	hostil	*(oh-'steel)*
hot dog	perro caliente, el	*(ehl 'peh-rroh kah-lee-'ehn-teh)*
hot pepper	chile, el	*(ehl 'chee-leh)*
hot water heater	calentador de agua, el	*(ehl kah-lehn-tah-'dohr deh 'ah-gwah)*
house	casa, la	*(lah 'kah-sah)*
how	cómo	*('koh-moh)*
hubcap	tapacubos, el	*(ehl tah-pah-'koo-bohs)*
hug	abrazo, el	*(ehl ah-'brah-soh)*
Human Resources	Recursos Humanos, Los	*(lohs reh-'koor-sohs oo-'mah-nohs)*
hundred	cien	*('see-ehn)*
hurricane	huracán, el	*(ehl oo-rah-'kahn)*
husband	esposo, el	*(ehl eh-'spoh-soh)*
hydrant	llave de agua, la	*(lah 'yah-veh deh 'ah-gwah)*
hydraulics	hidráulica, la	*(lah ee-'drow-lee-'kah)*
hygiene	higiene, la	*(lah ee-hee-'eh-neh)*
I	yo	*(yoh)*
ice	hielo, el	*(ehl 'yeh-loh)*
idea	idea, la	*(lah ee-'deh-ah)*
identification	identificación, la	*(lah ee-dehn-tee-fee-kah-see-'ohn)*
if	si	*(see)*

illegal	**ilegal**	*(ee-leh-'gahl)*
illness	**enfermedad, la**	*(lah ehn-fehr-meh-'dahd)*
illustration	**cuadro, el**	*(ehl 'kwah-droh)*
important	**importante**	*(ehl eem-pohr-'tahn-teh)*
imported	**importado***	*(eem-pohr-'tah-doh)*
in front of	**en frente**	*(ehn 'frehn-teh)*
in, on, at	**en**	*(ehn)*
incest	**incesto, el**	*(ehl een-'seh-stoh)*
inch	**pulgada, la**	*(lah pool-'gah-dah)*
included	**incluído***	*(een-kloo-'ee-doh)*
incompetent	**incapaz**	*(een-kah-'pahs)*
incredible	**increíble**	*(een-kreh-'ee-bleh)*
index	**índice, el**	*(ehl 'een-dee-seh)*
industrious	**trabajador***	*(trah-bah-hah-'dohr)*
inertia	**inercia, la**	*(lah ee-'nehr-see-ah)*
influence	**influencia, la**	*(lah een-floo-'ehn-see-ah)*
information	**información, la**	*(lah een-fohr-mah-see-'ohn)*
initial	**inicial**	*(ee-nee-see-'ahl)*
initiative	**iniciativa, la**	*(lah ee-nee-see-ah-'tee-vah)*
injury	**herida, la**	*(lah eh-'ree-dah)*
ink	**tinta, la**	*(lah 'teen-tah)*
inoperative	**inoperable**	*(een-oh-peh-'rah-bleh)*
insects	**insectos, los**	*(lohs een-'sehk-tohs)*
insecticide	**insecticida, el**	*(lah een-sehk-tee-'see-dah)*
inside	**adentro**	*(ah-'dehn-troh)*
inspection	**inspección, la**	*(lah een-spehk-see-'ohn)*
installment	**plazo, el**	*(ehl 'plah-soh)*
institution	**institución, la**	*(lah een-stee-too-see-'ohn)*
instructions	**instrucciones, las**	*(lahs een-strook-see-'oh-nehs)*
instrument	**instrumento, el**	*(ehl een-stroo-'mehn-toh)*
insurance	**seguro, el**	*(ehl seh-'goo-roh)*
intelligence	**inteligencia, la**	*(lah een-teh-lee-'hehn-see-ah)*
intelligent	**inteligente**	*(een-teh-lee-'hehn-teh)*
intercom	**citófono, el**	*(ehl see-'toh-foh-noh)*
interest	**interés, el**	*(ehl een-teh-'rehs)*
interested	**interesado***	*(een-teh-reh-'sah-doh)*
interesting	**interesante**	*(een-teh-reh-'sahn-teh)*
Internet	**internet, la**	*(lah een-tehr-'neht)*
interpretation	**intrepetación, la**	*(lah een-tehr-preh-tah-see-'ohn)*
interpreter	**intérprete, el**	*(ehl een-'tehr-preh-teh)*
interruption	**interrupción, la**	*(lah een-teh-rroop-see-'ohn)*
interview	**entrevista, la**	*(lah ehn-treh-'vee-stah)*
inventory	**inventorio, el**	*(ehl een-vehn-'toh-ree-oh)*

invoice	factura, la	*(lah fahk-'too-rah)*
involvement	participación, la	*(lah pahr-tee-see-pah-see-'ohn)*
iodine	yodo, el	*(ehl 'yoh-doh)*
iron	hierro, el	*(ehl 'yeh-rroh)*
jack hammer	martillo neumático, el	*(ehl mahr-'tee-yoh neh-oo-'mah-tee-koh)*
jacket	chaqueta, la	*(lah chah-'keh-tah)*
jail	cárcel, la	*(lah 'kahr-sehl)*
janitor	conserje, el	*(ehl kohn-'sehr-heh)*
January	enero	*(eh-'neh-roh)*
jar	jarra, la	*(lah 'hah-rrah)*
jaw	mandíbula, la	*(lah mahn-'dee-boo-lah)*
jewel	joya, la	*(lah 'hoh-yah)*
Jewish	judío*	*(hoo-'dee-oh)*
jogging	trote, el	*(ehl 'troh-teh)*
journeyman	artesano, el*	*(ehl ahr-teh-'sah-noh)*
juice	jugo, el	*(ehl 'hoo-goh)*
July	julio	*('hoo-lee-oh)*
June	junio	*('hoo-nee-oh)*
jungle	selva, la	*(lah 'sehl-vah)*
just	apenas	*(ah-'peh-nahs)*
key	llave, la	*(lah 'yah-veh)*
keyboard	teclado, el	*(ehl teh-'klah-doh)*
kidney	riñón, el	*(ehl ree-'nyohn)*
kiss	beso, el	*(ehl 'beh-soh)*
kit	estuche, el	*(ehl eh-'stoo-cheh)*
kitchen	cocina, la	*(lah koh-'see-nah)*
knee	rodilla, la	*(lah roh-'dee-yah)*
knife	cuchillo, el	*(ehl koo-'chee-yoh)*
knob	perilla, la	*(lah peh-'ree-yah)*
knob	botón, el	*(ehl boh-'tohn)*
knowledge	conocimiento, el	*(ehl koh-noh-see-mee-'ehn-toh)*
label	etiqueta, la	*(lah eh-tee-'keh-tah)*
laboratory	laboratorio, el	*(ehl lah-boh-rah-'toh-ree-oh)*
laborer	obrero, el*	*(ehl oh-'breh-roh)*
lack	falta, la	*(lah 'fahl-tah)*
ladder	escalera, la	*(lah eh-skah-'leh-rah)*
ladle	cucharón, el	*(ehl koo-chah-'rohn)*
lake	lago, el	*(ehl 'lah-goh)*
lamp	lámpara, la	*(lah 'lahm-pah-rah)*
land	terreno, el	*(ehl teh-'rreh-noh)*
language	lenguaje, el	*(ehl lehn-'gwah-heh)*
last	último*	*('ool-tee-moh)*
last name	apellido, el	*(ehl ah-peh-'yee-doh)*

last night	**anoche**	*(ah-'noh-cheh)*
latch	**cerrojo, el**	*(ehl seh-'rroh-hoh)*
late	**tarde**	*('tahr-deh)*
later	**luego**	*('lweh-goh)*
law	**ley, la**	*(lah 'leh-ee)*
lawsuit	**pleito, el**	*(ehl pleh-'ee-toh)*
lawyer	**abogado, el***	*(ehl ah-boh-'gah-doh)*
layout	**organización, la**	*(lah ohr-gah-nee-sah-see-'ohn)*
lazy	**perezoso***	*(peh-reh-'soh-soh)*
leader	**líder, el**	*(ehl 'lee-dehr)*
leadership	**liderazgo, el**	*(ehl lee-deh-'rahs-goh)*
learning	**aprendizaje, el**	*(ehl ah-prehn-dee-'sah-heh)*
lease	**alquiler, el**	*(ehl ahl-kee-'lehr)*
leather	**cuero, el**	*(ehl 'kweh-roh)*
leaves	**hojas, las**	*(lahs 'oh-hahs)*
lemon	**limón, el**	*(ehl lee-'mohn)*
lemonade	**limonada, la**	*(lah lee-moh-'nah-dah)*
length	**largo, el**	*(ehl 'lahr-goh)*
lens	**lente, el**	*(ehl 'lehn-teh)*
less	**menos**	*('meh-nohs)*
letter (alphabet)	**letra, la**	*(lah 'leh-trah)*
letter (mail)	**carta, la**	*(lah 'kahr-tah)*
lettuce	**lechuga, la**	*(lah leh-'choo-gah)*
level	**nivel, el**	*(ehl nee-'vehl)*
lever	**palanca, la**	*(lah pah-'lahn-kah)*
library	**biblioteca, la**	*(lah bee-blee-oh-'teh-kah)*
license	**licencia, la**	*(lah lee-'sehn-see-ah)*
light	**luz, la**	*(lah loos)*
light (not heavy)	**ligero***	*(lee-'heh-roh)*
lightening	**relámpago, el**	*(ehl reh-'lahm-pah-goh)*
lights	**luces, las**	*(lahs 'loo-sehs)*
limit	**límite, el**	*(ehl 'lee-mee-teh)*
line	**línea, la**	*(lah 'lee-neh-ah)*
liquid	**líquido, el**	*(ehl 'lee-kee-doh)*
list	**lista, la**	*(lah 'lee-stah)*
liver	**hígado, el**	*(ehl 'ee-gah-doh)*
living room	**sala, la**	*(lah 'sah-lah)*
lizard	**lagarto, el**	*(ehl lah-'gahr-toh)*
load	**carga, la**	*(lah 'kahr-gah)*
loan	**préstamo, el**	*(ehl 'preh-stah-moh)*
lobby	**vestíbulo, el**	*(ehl veh-'stee-boo-loh)*
location	**lugar, el**	*(ehl loo-'gahr)*
lock	**cerradura, la**	*(lah seh-rrah-'doo-rah)*

logo	logotipo, el	*(ehl loh-goh-'tee-poh)*
loiterer	holgazán, el	*(ehl ohl-gah-'sahn)*
long	largo*	*('lahr-goh)*
loose	suelto*	*('swehl-toh)*
loss	pérdida, la	*(lah 'pehr-dee-dah)*
lost	perdido*	*(pehr-'dee-doh)*
lot	lote, el	*(ehl 'loh-teh)*
lotion	loción, la	*(lah loh-see-'ohn)*
loyalty	lealtad, la	*(lah leh-ahl-'tahd)*
lozenges	pastillas, las	*(lahs pah-'stee-yahs)*
lunch	almuerzo, el	*(ehl ahl-moo-'ehr-soh)*
lungs	pulmones, los	*(lohs pool-'moh-nehs)*
machine	máquina, la	*(lah 'mah-kee-nah)*
machinery	maquinaria, la	*(lah mah-kee-'nah-ree·ah)*
magazine	revista, la	*(lah reh-'vee-stah)*
magnet	imán, el	*(ehl ee-'mahn)*
mail	correo, el	*(ehl koh-'rreh-oh)*
mail carrier	cartero, el/la	*(ehl/lah kahr-'teh-roh)*
mailbox	buzón, el	*(ehl boo-'sohn)*
maintenenace	mantenimiento, el	*(ehl mahn-teh-nee-mee-'ehn-toh)*
make-up	maquillaje, el	*(ehl kah-kee-'yah-heh)*
malfunction	avería, la	*(lah ah-veh-'ree-ah)*
man	hombre, el	*(ehl 'ohm-breh)*
management	gerencia, la	*(lah heh-'rehn-see·ah)*
manager	gerente, el*	*(ehl heh-'rehn-teh)*
manual	manual, el	*(ehl mah-noo-'ahl)*
manufactuing	fabricación, la	*(lah fah-bree-kah-see-'ohn)*
manufacturer	fabricante, el/la	*(ehl/lah fah-bree-'kahn-teh)*
many	muchos*	*('moo-chohs)*
map	mapa, el	*(ehl 'mah-pah)*
March	marzo	*('mahr-soh)*
margarine	margarina, la	*(lah mahr-gah-'ree-nah)*
marital status	estado civil, el	*(ehl eh-'stah-doh see-'veel)*
mark	marca, la	*(lah 'mahr-kah)*
marker	marcador, el	*(ehl mahr-kah-'dohr)*
marmalade	mermelada, la	*(lah mehr-meh-'lah-dah)*
married	casado*	*(kah-'sah-doh)*
marvelous	maravilloso*	*(mah-rah-vee-'yoh-soh)*
mask	máscara, la	*(lah 'mah-skah-rah)*
master switch	conmutador principal, el	*(ehl kohn-moo-tah-'dohr preen-see-'pahl)*
mat	tapete, el	*(ehl tah-'peh-teh)*
matches	fósforos, los	*(lohs 'fohs-foh-rohs)*
materials	materiales, los	*(lohs mah-teh-ree-'ah-lehs)*

mature	**maduro***	*(mah-'doo-roh)*
maximum	**máximo, el***	*(ehl 'mahk-see-moh)*
May	**mayo**	*('mah-yoh)*
maybe	**quizás**	*(kee-'sahs)*
mayonnaise	**mayonesa, la**	*(lah mah-yoh-'neh-sah)*
measles	**sarampión, el**	*(ehl sah-rahm-pee-'ohn)*
measurement	**medida, la**	*(lah meh-'dee-dah)*
mechanic	**mecánico, el/la**	*(ehl/lah meh-'kah-nee-koh)*
mediator	**mediador, el***	*(ehl meh-dee-ah-'dohr)*
medicine	**medicina, la**	*(lah meh-dee-'see-nah)*
meeting	**reunión, la**	*(lah reh-oo-nee-'ohn)*
member	**miembro, el/la**	*(ehl/lah mee-'ehm-broh)*
memo	**memorándum, el**	*(ehl meh-moh-'rahn-doom)*
memory	**memoria, la**	*(lah meh-'moh-ree-ah)*
merchandise	**mercancías, las**	*(lahs mehr-kahn-'see-ahs)*
metal	**metal, el**	*(ehl meh-'tahl)*
meter	**medidor, el**	*(ehl meh-dee-'dohr)*
meter	**metro, el**	*(ehl 'meh-troh)*
method	**método, el**	*(ehl 'meh-toh-doh)*
Mexican	**mexicano***	*(meh-hee-'kah-noh)*
microscope	**microscopio, el**	*(ehl mee-kroh-'skoh-pee-oh)*
microwave	**micronda, el**	*(lah mee-kroh-'ohn-dah)*
milk	**leche, la**	*(lah 'leh-cheh)*
mill	**molino, el**	*(ehl moh-'lee-noh)*
million	**millón**	*(mee-'yohn)*
mine	**mío***	*('mee-oh)*
minimum	**mínimo, el***	*(ehl 'mee-nee-moh)*
mining	**minas, las**	*(lahs 'mee-nahs)*
mirror	**espejo, el**	*(ehl eh-'speh-hoh)*
Miss	**Srta.**	*(seh-nyoh-'ree-tah)*
mission	**misión, la**	*(lah mee-see-'ohn)*
mittens	**mitones, los**	*(lohs mee-'toh-nehs)*
mixer	**batidora, la**	*(lah bah-tee-'doh-rah)*
model	**modelo, el**	*(ehl moh-'deh-loh)*
molecule	**molécula, la**	*(lah moh-'leh-koo-lah)*
Monday	**lunes**	*('loo-nehs)*
monitor	**monitor, el**	*(ehl moh-nee-'tohr)*
month	**mes, el**	*(ehl mehs)*
mood	**estado de ánimo, el**	*(ehl ehs-'tah-doh deh 'ah-nee-moh)*
mop	**trapeador, el**	*(ehl trah-peh-ah-'dohr)*
more	**más**	*(mahs)*
morning	**mañana, la**	*(lah mah-'nyah-nah)*
mortgage	**hipoteca, la**	*(lah ee-poh-'teh-kah)*

Moslem	musulmán*	(moo-sool-'mahn)
mosquito	zancudo, el	(ehl sahn-'koo-doh)
most	la mayor parte	(lah mah-'yohr 'pahr-teh)
moth	polilla, la	(lah poh-'lee-yah)
mother	madre, la	(lah 'mah-dreh)
mother-in-law	suegra, la	(lah 'sweh-grah)
motto	lema, el	(ehl 'leh-mah)
mountain	montaña, la	(lah mohn-'tah-nyah)
mouse	ratón, el*	(ehl rah-'tohn)
mouth	boca, la	(lah 'boh-kah)
movie theater	cine, el	(ehl 'see-neh)
movies	películas, las	(lahs peh-'lee-koo-lahs)
Mr.	Sr.	(seh-'nyohr)
Mrs.	Sra.	(seh-'nyoh-rah)
much	mucho*	('moo-choh)
mud	lodo, el	(ehl 'loh-doh)
muffler	silenciador, el	(ehl see-lehn-see-ah-'dohr)
mumps	paperas, las	(lahs pah-'peh-rahs)
museum	museo, el	(ehl moo-'seh-oh)
mushrooms	hongos, los	(lohs 'ohn-gohs)
music	música, la	(lah 'moo-see-kah)
musician	músico, el/la	(ehl/lah 'moo-see-koh)
mustard	mostaza, la	(lah moh-'stah-sah)
my	mi	(mee)
nail	clavo, el	(ehl 'klah-voh)
nail file	lima de uñas, la	(lah 'lee-mah deh 'oo-nyahs)
name	nombre, el	(ehl 'nohm-breh)
napkin	servilleta, la	(lah sehr-vee-'yeh-tah)
narrow	estrecho*	(eh-'streh-choh)
nationality	nacionalidad, la	(lah nah-see-oh-nah-lee-'dahd)
naturalized	naturalizado*	(nah-too-rah-lee-'sah-doh)
near	cerca	('sehr-kah)
neat	limpio*	('leem-pee-oh)
necessary	necesario*	(neh-seh-'sah-ree-oh)
neck	cuello, el	(ehl 'kweh-yoh)
necklace	collar, el	(ehl koh-'yahr)
needle	aguja, la	(lah ah-'goo-hah)
needs	necesidades, las	(lahs neh-seh-see-'dah-dehs)
negligent	negligente	(nehg-lee-'hehn-teh)
neighbor	vecino, el*	(ehl veh-'see-noh)
neighborhood	barrio, el	(ehl 'bah-rree-oh)
nephew	sobrino, el	(ehl soh-'bree-noh)
nervous	nervioso*	(nehr-vee-'oh-soh)

net	**red, la**	*(lah rehd)*
never	**nunca**	*('noon-kah)*
new	**nuevo***	*('nweh-voh)*
news	**noticias, las**	*(lahs noh-'tee-see-ahs)*
newspaper	**periódico, el**	*(ehl peh-ree-'oh-dee-koh)*
next	**próximo***	*('prohk-see-moh)*
next to	**al lado**	*(ahl 'lah-doh)*
nice	**simpático***	*(seem-'pah-tee-koh)*
niece	**sobrina, la**	*(lah soh-'bree-nah)*
nightstand	**mesita de noche, la**	*(lah meh-'see-tah deh 'noh-cheh)*
nine	**nueve**	*('nweh-veh)*
nineteen	**diecinueve**	*(dee-ehs-ee-'nweh-veh)*
ninety	**noventa**	*(noh-'vehn-tah)*
ninth	**noveno***	*(noh-'veh-noh)*
no one	**nadie**	*('nah-dee-eh)*
noise	**ruido, el**	*(ehl roo-'ee-doh)*
none	**ninguno***	*(neen-'goo-noh)*
noodles	**fideos, los**	*(lohs fee-'deh-ohs)*
north	**norte**	*('nohr-teh)*
nose	**nariz, la**	*(lah nah-'rees)*
note	**nota, la**	*(lah 'noh-tah)*
nothing	**nada**	*('nah-dah)*
notice	**noticia, la**	*(lah noh-'tee-see-ah)*
November	**noviembre**	*(noh-vee-'ehm-breh)*
now	**ahora**	*(ah-'oh-rah)*
nozzle	**pitón, el**	*(ehl pee-'tohn)*
number	**número, el**	*(ehl 'noo-meh-roh)*
nurse	**enfermero, el***	*(ehl ehn-fehr-'meh-roh)*
nut	**tuerca, la**	*(lah 'twehr-kah)*
objective	**objetivo, el**	*(ehl ohb-heh-'tee-voh)*
occupation	**ocupación, la**	*(lah oh-koo-pah-see-'ohn)*
October	**octubre**	*(ohk-'too-breh)*
of	**de**	*(deh)*
of the, from the	**del**	*(dehl)*
offer	**oferta, la**	*(lah oh-'fehr-tah)*
office	**oficina, la**	*(lah oh-fee-'see-nah)*
official	**oficio, el**	*(ehl oh-'fee-see-oh)*
oil	**aceite, el**	*(ehl ah-'seh-ee-teh)*
old	**viejo***	*(vee-'eh-hoh)*
older	**mayor**	*(mah-'yohr)*
once	**una vez**	*('oo-nah vehs)*
one	**uno***	*('oo-noh)*
onion	**cebolla, la**	*(lah seh-'boh-yah)*

only	solamente	*(soh-lah-'mehn-teh)*
opening	abertura, la	*(lah ah-behr-'too-rah)*
operations	operaciones, las	*(lahs oh-peh-rah-see-'oh-nehs)*
operator	telefonista, el/la	*(ehl/lah teh-leh-foh-'nee-stah)*
operator	operadora, la*	*(lah oh-peh-rah-'doh-rah)*
opinion	opinión, la	*(lah oh-pee-nee-'ohn)*
opportunity	oportunidad, la	*(lah oh-pohr-too-nee-'dahd)*
or	o	*(oh)*
orange (color)	anaranjado*	*(ah-nah-rahn-'hah-doh)*
orange (fruit)	naranja, la	*(lah nah-'rahn-hah)*
order	pedido, el	*(ehl peh-'dee-doh)*
organization	organización, la	*(lah ohr-gah-nee-sah-see-'ohn)*
ounce	onza, la	*(lah 'ohn-sah)*
our	nuestro	*('nweh-stroh)*
outside	afuera	*(ah-'fweh-rah)*
outskirts	afueras, las	*(lahs ah-'fweh-rahs)*
outstanding	fantástico*	*(fahn-'tah-stee-koh)*
oven	horno, el	*(ehl 'ohr-noh)*
over there	allá	*(ah-'yah)*
overcoat	abrigo, el	*(ehl ah-'bree-goh)*
overdose	sobredosis, la	*(lah soh-'breh-'doh-sees)*
owl	buho, el	*(ehl 'boo-oh)*
owner	dueño, el*	*(ehl 'dweh-nyoh)*
package	paquete, el	*(ehl pah-'keh-teh)*
packaging	embalaje, el	*(ehl ehm-bah-'lah-heh)*
packet	bolsillo, el	*(ehl bohl-'see-yoh)*
padlock	candado, el	*(ehl kahn-'dah-doh)*
page	página, la	*(lah 'pah-hee-nah)*
paid	pagado*	*(pah-'gah-doh)*
pain	dolor, el	*(ehl doh-'lohr)*
paint	pintura, la	*(lah peen-'too-rah)*
paintbrush	brocha, la	*(lah 'broh-chah)*
painter	pintor, el*	*(ehl peen-'tohr)*
painting	cuadro, el	*(ehl 'kwah-droh)*
pair	par, el	*(ehl pahr)*
pajamas	pijama, el	*(ehl pee-'hah-mah)*
pallet	soporte de madera, el	*(ehl soh-'pohr-teh deh mah-'deh-rah)*
pan	sartén, el	*(ehl sahr-'tehn)*
panel	panel, el	*(ehl pah-'nehl)*
panties	bragas, las	*(lahs 'brah-gahs)*
pants	pantalones, los	*(lohs pahn-tah-'loh-nehs)*
paper	papel, el	*(ehl pah-'pehl)*
paper clips	clips, los	*(lohs kleeps)*

paperwork	**papeleo, el**	*(ehl pah-peh-'leh-oh)*
parade	**desfile, el**	*(ehl dehs-'fee-leh)*
parallel	**paralelo***	*(pah-rah-'leh-loh)*
paramedic	**paramédico, el/la**	*(ehl/lah pah-rah-'meh-dee-koh)*
parents	**padres, los**	*(lohs 'pah-drehs)*
park	**parque, el**	*(ehl 'pahr-keh)*
parking lot	**estacionamento, el**	*(ehl eh-stah-see-oh-nah-mee-'ehn-toh)*
part	**parte, la**	*(lah 'pahr-teh)*
part-time	**tiempo parcial, el**	*(ehl tee-'ehm-poh pahr-see-'ahl)*
partition	**divisor, el**	*(ehl dee-vee-'sohr)*
partner	**socio, el***	*(ehl 'soh-see-oh)*
parts	**piezas, las**	*(lahs pee-'eh-sahs)*
party	**fiesta, la**	*(lah fee-'eh-stah)*
passport	**pasaporte, el**	*(ehl pah-sah-'pohr-teh)*
patent	**patente, la**	*(lah pah-'tehn-teh)*
path	**camino, el**	*(ehl kah-'mee-noh)*
patience	**paciencia, la**	*(lah pah-see-'ehn-see-ah)*
patient	**paciente, el/la**	*(ehl/lah pah-see-'ehn-teh)*
pay	**pago, el**	*(ehl 'pah-goh)*
paycheck	**paga, la**	*(lah 'pah-gah)*
payload	**carga útil, la**	*(lah 'kahr-gah 'oo-teel)*
payment	**pago, el**	*(ehl 'pah-goh)*
peace	**paz, la**	*(lah pahs)*
peach	**melocotón, el**	*(ehl meh-loh-koh-'tohn)*
pear	**pera, la**	*(lah 'peh-rah)*
peas	**arvejitas, las**	*(lahs ahr-veh-'hee-tahs)*
peg	**clavija, la**	*(lah klah-'vee-hah)*
pen	**lapicero, el**	*(ehl lah-pee-'seh-roh)*
penalty	**multa, la**	*(lah 'mool-tah)*
pencil	**lápiz, el**	*(ehl 'lah-pees)*
penicillin	**penicilina, la**	*(lah peh-nee-see-'lee-nah)*
people	**gente, la**	*(lah 'hehn-teh)*
pepper	**pimienta, la**	*(lah pee-mee-'ehn-tah)*
percentage	**porcentaje, el**	*(ehl pohr-sehn-'tah-heh)*
performance	**rendimiento, el;**	*(ehl rehn-dee-mee-'ehn-toh),*
	función, la	*(lah foon-see-'ohn)*
perfume	**perfume, el**	*(ehl pehr-'foo-meh)*
perks	**beneficios**	*(lohs beh-neh-'fee-see-ohs*
	adicionales, los	*ah-dee-see-oh-'nah-lehs)*
permit	**permiso, el**	*(ehl pehr-'mee-soh)*
person	**persona, la**	*(lah pehr-'soh-nah)*
personality	**personalidad, la**	*(lah pehr-soh-nah-lee-'dahd)*
personnel	**personal, el**	*(ehl pehr-soh-'nahl)*

persuasion	persuasión, la	*(lah pehr-swah-see-'ohn)*
pesticide	pesticida, el	*(ehl peh-stee-'see-dah)*
pharmacy	farmacia, la	*(lah fahr-'mah-see-ah)*
phone call	llamada, la	*(lah yah-'mah-dah)*
photograph	foto, la	*(lah 'foh-toh)*
photography	fotografía, la	*(lah foh-toh-grah-'fee-ah)*
physician	médico, el	*(ehl 'meh-dee-koh)*
pick	pico, el	*(ehl 'pee-koh)*
pickle	encurtido, el	*(ehl ehn-koor-'tee-doh)*
pickup	camioneta, la	*(lah kah-mee-oh-'neh-tah)*
picnic	merienda, la	*(lah meh-ree-'ehn-dah)*
picture	pintura, la	*(lah peen-'too-rah)*
piece	pieza, la	*(lah pee-'eh-sah)*
pig	puerco, el*	*(ehl 'pwehr-koh)*
pills	píldoras, las	*(lahs 'peel-doh-rahs)*
pilot	piloto, el/la	*(ehl/lah pee-'loh-toh)*
pin	alfiler, el	*(ehl ahl-fee-'lehr)*
pipe	tubo, el	*(ehl 'too-boh)*
piping	tubería, la	*(lah too-beh-'ree-ah)*
piston	émbolo, el	*(ehl 'ehm-boh-loh)*
pitcher	cántaro, el	*(ehl 'kahn-tah-roh)*
place	lugar, el	*(ehl loo-'gahr)*
plaintiff	demandante, el/la	*(ehl/lah deh-mahn-'dahn-teh)*
plan	plan, el	*(ehl plahn)*
plane	avión, el	*(ehl ah-vee-'ohn)*
planning	planificación, la	*(lah plah-nee-fee-kah-see-'ohn)*
plant	planta, la	*(lah 'plahn-tah)*
plaster	yeso, el	*(ehl 'yeh-soh)*
plastic	plástico, el	*(ehl 'plah-stee-koh)*
plate	plato, el	*(ehl 'plah-toh)*
platform	plataforma, la	*(lah plah-tah-'fohr-mah)*
platter	fuente, la	*(lah 'fwehn-teh)*
playground	campo de recreo, el	*(ehl 'kahm-poh deh reh-'kreh-oh)*
pliers	pinzas, las	*(lahs 'peen-sahs)*
plumber	plomero, el*	*(ehl ploh-'meh-roh)*
plumbing	plomería, la	*(lah ploh-meh-'ree-ah)*
pneumonia	pulmonía, la	*(lah pool-moh-'nee-ah)*
point	punta, la	*(lah 'poon-tah)*
poisonous	venenoso*	*(veh-neh-'noh-soh)*
police	policía, la	*(lah poh-lee-'see-ah)*
police officer	policía, el/la	*(ehl/lah poh-lee-'see-ah)*
policy	póliza, la	*(lah 'poh-lee-sah)*
polite	cortés	*(kohr-'tehs)*

pond	**charca, la**	*(lah 'chahr-kah)*
pool	**piscina, la**	*(lah pee-'see-nah)*
poor	**pobre**	*('poh-breh)*
poorly	**mal**	*(mahl)*
porch	**portal, el**	*(ehl pohr-'tahl)*
pork	**cerdo, el***	*(ehl 'sehr-doh)*
portion	**porción, la**	*(lah pohr-see-'ohn)*
position	**posición, la**	*(lah poh-see-see-'ohn)*
positive	**positivo***	*(poh-see-'tee-voh)*
post	**poste, el**	*(ehl 'poh-steh)*
post office	**oficina de correos, la**	*(lah oh-fee-'see-nah deh koh-'rreh-ohs)*
poster	**cartel, el**	*(ehl kahr-'tehl)*
pot	**olla, la**	*(lah 'oh-yah)*
potato	**papa, la**	*(lah 'pah-pah)*
pottery	**alfarería, la**	*(lah ahl-fah-reh-'ree-ah)*
pound	**libra, la**	*(lah 'lee-brah)*
powder	**polvo, el**	*(ehl 'pohl-voh)*
power	**poder, el**	*(ehl poh-'dehr)*
practice	**práctica, la**	*(lah 'prahk-tee-kah)*
pregnant	**embarazada**	*(ehm-bah-rah-'sah-dah)*
prescription	**receta, la**	*(lah reh-'seh-tah)*
president	**presidente, el***	*(ehl preh-see-'dehn-teh)*
press	**prensa, la**	*(lah 'prehn-sah)*
pressure	**presión, la**	*(lah preh-see-'ohn)*
pretty	**bonito***	*(boh-'nee-toh)*
price	**precio, el**	*(ehl 'preh-see-oh)*
priest	**sacerdote, el**	*(ehl 'sah-sehr-'doh-teh)*
principle	**principio, el**	*(ehl preen-'see-pee-oh)*
printer	**impresora, la**	*(lah eem-preh-'soh-rah)*
priority	**prioridad, la**	*(lah pree-oh-ree-'dahd)*
problem	**problema, el**	*(ehl proh-'bleh-mah)*
procedure	**procedimiento, el**	*(ehl proh-seh-dee-mee-'ehn-toh)*
product	**producto, el**	*(ehl proh-'dook-toh)*
production	**producción, la**	*(lah proh-dook-see-'ohn)*
proficiency	**competencia, la**	*(lah kohm-peh-'tehn-see-ah)*
profit	**ganancia, la**	*(lah gah-'nahn-see-ah)*
program	**programa, el**	*(ehl proh-'grah-mah)*
prohibited	**prohibido***	*(proh-ee-'bee-doh)*
projector	**proyector, el**	*(ehl proh-yehk-'tohr)*
promotions	**ascensos, los**	*(lohs ah-'sehn-sohs)*
propeller	**hélice, el**	*(ehl 'eh-lee-seh)*
property	**propiedad, la**	*(lah proh-pee-eh-'dahd)*
proposal	**propuesta, la**	*(lah proh-'pweh-stah)*

propulsion	**propulsión, la**	*(lah proh-pool-see-'ohn)*
protest	**protesta, la**	*(lah proh-'teh-stah)*
Puerto Rican	**puertorriqueño***	*(pwehr-toh-rree-'keh-nyoh)*
pulley	**polea, la**	*(lah poh-'leh-ah)*
pump	**bomba, la**	*(lah 'bohm-bah)*
purchase order	**orden de comprar, la**	*(lah 'ohr-dehn deh kohm-'prahr)*
purification	**purificación, la**	*(lah poo-ree-fee-kah-see-'ohn)*
purple	**morado***	*(moh-'rah-doh)*
purpose	**propósito, el**	*(ehl proh-'poh-see-toh)*
putty	**masilla, la**	*(lah mah-'see-yah)*
puzzle	**rompecabezas, el**	*(ehl rohm-peh-kah-'beh-sahs)*
qualified	**calificado***	*(kah-lee-fee-'kah-doh)*
quality	**calidad, la**	*(lah kah-lee-'dahd)*
quality control	**control de calidad, el**	*(ehl kohn-'trohl deh kah-lee-'dahd)*
quantity	**cantidad, la**	*(lah kahn-tee-'dahd)*
quart	**cuarto, el**	*(ehl 'kwahr-toh)*
questions	**preguntas, las**	*(lahs preh-'goon-tahs)*
quickly	**rápidamente**	*(rah-pee-dah-'mehn-teh)*
quiet	**quieto***	*(kee-'eh-toh)*
quota	**cuota, la**	*(lah 'kwoh-tah)*
rabbit	**conejo, el**	*(ehl koh-'neh-hoh)*
race	**raza, la**	*(lah 'rah-sah)*
radio	**radio, el**	*(ehl 'rah-dee-oh)*
radish	**rábano, el**	*(ehl 'rah-bah-noh)*
raffle	**sorteo, el**	*(ehl sohr-'teh-oh)*
rafter	**viga, la**	*(lah 'vee-gah)*
rag	**trapo, el**	*(ehl 'trah-poh)*
raid	**incursión, la**	*(lah een-koor-see-'ohn)*
railing	**baranda, la**	*(lah bah-'rahn-dah)*
rain	**lluvia, la**	*(lah 'yoo-vee-ah)*
raincoat	**impermeable, el**	*(ehl eem-pehr-meh-'ah-bleh)*
raise	**aumento de sueldo, el**	*(ehl ow-'mehn-toh deh 'swehl-doh)*
rake	**rastrillo, el**	*(ehl rah-'stree-yoh)*
ramp	**rampa, la**	*(lah 'rahm-pah)*
rape	**violación, la**	*(lah vee-oh-lah-see-'ohn)*
rash	**erupción, la**	*(lah eh-roop-see-'ohn)*
rat	**rata, la**	*(lah 'rah-tah)*
rate	**tarifa, la**	*(lah tah-'ree-fah)*
rates	**tasas, las**	*(lahs 'tah-sahs)*
ratio	**proporción, la**	*(lah proh-pohr-see-'ohn)*
raw	**crudo***	*('kroo-doh)*
razor blade	**hoja de afeitar, la**	*(lah 'oh-hah deh ah-feh-ee-'tahr)*
reading	**lectura, la**	*(lah lehk-'too-rah)*

ready	listo*	('lee-stoh)
receipt	recibo, el	(ehl reh-'see-boh)
receiving	admisión, la	(lah ahd-mee-see-'ohn)
reception desk	recepción, la	(lah reh-sehp-see-'ohn)
receptionist	recepcionista, el/la	(ehl/lah reh-sehp-see-oh-'nee-stah)
recommendations	recomendaciones, las	(lahs reh-koh-mehn-dah-see-'oh-nehs)
record	antecedente, el	(ehl ahn-teh-seh-'dehn-teh)
recruit	recluta, el/la	(ehl/lah reh-'kloo-tah)
recruiter	reclutador, el*	(ehl reh-kloo-tah-'dohr)
rectangle	rectángulo, el	(ehl rehk-'tahn-goo-loh)
red	rojo*	('roh-hoh)
red-headed	pelirrojo*	(peh-lee-'rroh-hoh)
reduction	reducción, la	(lah reh-dook-see-'ohn)
reference	referencia, la	(lah reh-feh-'rehn-see-ah)
refrigerator	refrigerador, el	(ehl reh-free-heh-rah-'dohr)
refund	reembolso, el	(ehl reh-ehm-'bohl-soh)
regulation	reglamento, el	(ehl reh-glah-'mehn-toh)
rehabilitation	rehabilitación, la	(lah reh-ah-bee-lee-tah-see-'ohn)
relationship	relación, la	(lah reh-lah-see-'ohn)
relatives	parientes, los	(lohs pah-ree-'ehn-tehs)
religion	religión, la	(lah reh-lee-hee-'ohn)
remarkable	extraordinario*	(ehk-strah-ohr-dee-'nah-ree-oh)
remedies	remedios, los	(lohs reh-'meh-dee-ohs)
report	informe, el	(ehl een-'fohr-meh)
representative	representante, el/la	(ehl/lah reh-preh-sehn-'tahn-teh)
reprimand	reprensión, la	(lah reh-prehn-see-'ohn)
request	petición, la	(lah peh-tee-see-'ohn)
requirement	requisito, el	(ehl reh-kee-'see-toh)
rescue	rescate, el	(ehl reh-'skah-teh)
research	investigación, la	(lah een-veh-stee-gah-see-'ohn)
resource	recurso, el	(ehl reh-'koor-soh)
respect	respeto, el	(ehl reh-'speh-toh)
response	respuesta, la	(lah reh-'spweh-stah)
responsibility	responsabilidad, la	(lah reh-spohn-sah-bee-lee-'dahd)
restaurant	restaurante, el	(ehl reh-stah-oo-'rahn-teh)
restroom	baño, el	(ehl 'bah-nyoh)
results	resultados, los	(lohs reh-sool-'tah-dohs)
resume	curriculum, el	(ehl koo-ree-koo-'loom)
retail	al por menor	(ahl pohr meh-'nohr)
retirement	jubilación, la	(lah hoo-bee-lah-see-'ohn)
return	devolución, la	(lah deh-voh-loo-see-'ohn)
revenue	ingresos, los	(lohs een-'greh-sohs)
reward	recompensas, las	(lahs reh-kohm-'pehn-sahs)

ribbon	**cinta, la**	*(lah 'seen-tah)*
rice	**arroz, el**	*(ehl ah-'rrohs)*
rich	**rico***	*('ree-koh)*
right now	**ahorita**	*(ah-oh-'ree-tah)*
rights	**derechos, los**	*(lohs deh-'reh-chohs)*
ring	**anillo, el**	*(ehl ah-'nee-yoh)*
riot	**tumulto, el**	*(ehl too-'mool-toh)*
risk	**riesgo, el**	*(ehl ree-'ehs-goh)*
river	**río, el**	*(ehl 'ree-oh)*
road	**camino, el**	*(ehl kah-'mee-noh)*
roast beef	**rósbif, el**	*(ehl rohs-'beef)*
robbery	**robo, el**	*(ehl 'roh-boh)*
robe	**bata, la**	*(lah 'bah-tah)*
robot	**robot, el**	*(ehl roh-'boht)*
rock	**roca, la**	*(lah 'roh-kah)*
rod	**varilla, la**	*(lah vah-'ree-yah)*
roller	**rodillo, el**	*(ehl roh-'dee-yoh)*
rolls	**rollos, los**	*(lohs 'roh-yohs)*
roof	**tejado, el**	*(ehl teh-'hah-doh)*
room	**cuarto, el**	*(ehl 'kwahr-toh)*
rope	**soga, la**	*(lah 'soh-gah)*
rough	**áspero***	*('ahs-peh-roh)*
row	**fila, la**	*(lah 'fee-lah)*
rubber	**goma, la**	*(lah 'goh-mah)*
rude	**grosero***	*(groh-'seh-roh)*
sad	**triste**	*('tree-steh)*
safety glasses	**gafas de seguridad, las**	*(lahs 'gah-fahs deh seh-goo-ree-'dahd)*
salad	**ensalada, la**	*(lah ehn-sah-'lah-dah)*
sale	**venta, la**	*(lah 'vehn-tah)*
sales	**ventas, las**	*(lahs 'vehn-tahs)*
salesperson	**vendedor, el***	*(ehl vehn-deh-'dohr)*
salt	**sal, la**	*(lah sahl)*
same	**mismo***	*('mees-moh)*
sample	**muestra, la**	*(lah 'mweh-strah)*
sand	**arena, la**	*(lah ah-'reh-nah)*
sandpaper	**papel de lija, el**	*(ehl pah-'pehl deh 'lee-hah)*
satisfactory	**satisfecho***	*(sah-tees-'feh-choh)*
Saturday	**sábado**	*('sah-bah-doh)*
sauce	**salsa, la**	*(lah 'sahl-sah)*
saucer	**platillo, el**	*(ehl plah-'tee-yoh)*
sausage	**salchicha, la**	*(lah sahl-'chee-chah)*
savings	**ahorros, los**	*(lohs ah-'oh-rrohs)*
scaffold	**andamio, el**	*(ehl ahn-'dah-mee-oh)*

scale	**báscula, la**	*(lah 'bah-skoo-lah)*
scarf	**bufanda, la**	*(lah boo-'fahn-dah)*
schedule	**horario, el**	*(ehl oh-'rah-ree-oh)*
school	**escuela, la**	*(lah eh-'skweh-lah)*
scissors	**tijeras, las**	*(lahs tee-'heh-rahs)*
score	**calificación, la**	*(lah kah-lee-fee-kah-see-'ohn)*
scrap	**desecho, el**	*(ehl dehs-'eh-choh)*
scraper	**raspador, el**	*(ehl rah-spah-'dohr)*
scraps	**sobras, las**	*(lahs 'soh-brahs)*
scratch	**rasguño, el**	*(ehl rahs-'goo-nyoh)*
screen	**pantalla, la**	*(lah pahn-'tah-yah)*
screw	**tornillo, el**	*(ehl tohr-'nee-yoh)*
screwdriver	**atornillador, el**	*(ehl ah-tohr-nee-yah-'dohr)*
sea	**mar, el**	*(ehl mahr)*
seafood	**marisco, el**	*(ehl mah-'ree-skoh)*
seat	**asiento, el**	*(ehl ah-see-'ehn-toh)*
second	**segundo***	*(seh-'goon-doh)*
secretary	**secretario, el***	*(ehl seh-kreh-'tah-ree-oh)*
section	**sección, la**	*(lah sehk-see-'ohn)*
security	**seguridad, la**	*(lah seh-goo-ree-'dahd)*
semi-trailer	**semi-remolque, el**	*(ehl seh-mee-reh-'mohl-keh)*
seminar	**seminario, el**	*(ehl seh-mee-'nah-ree-oh)*
seniority	**categoría, la**	*(lah kah-teh-goh-'ree-ah)*
September	**septiembre**	*(sehp-tee-'ehm-breh)*
servant	**criado, el***	*(ehl kree-'ah-doh)*
service	**servicio, el**	*(ehl sehr-'vee-see-oh)*
session	**sesión, la**	*(lah seh-see-'ohn)*
seven	**siete**	*(see-'eh-teh)*
seventeen	**diecisiete**	*(dee-ehs-ee-see-'eh-teh)*
seventh	**séptimo***	*('sehp-tee-moh)*
seventy	**setenta**	*(seh-'tehn-tah)*
sewage	**aguas servidas, las**	*(lahs 'ah-gwahs sehr-'vee-dahs)*
sex	**sexo, el**	*(ehl 'sehk-soh)*
shaft	**astil, el**	*(ehl ah-'steel)*
shallow	**bajo***	*('bah-hoh)*
shame	**vergüenza, la**	*(lah vehr-'gwehn-sah)*
shampoo	**champú, el**	*(ehl chahm-'poo)*
shape	**forma, la**	*(lah 'fohr-mah)*
shaver	**afeitadora, la**	*(lah ah-feh-ee-tah-'doh-rah)*
she	**ella**	*('eh-yah)*
shed	**cobertizo, el**	*(ehl koh-behr-'tee-soh)*
sheep	**oveja, la**	*(lah oh-'veh-hah)*
sheet	**hoja, la**	*(lah 'oh-hah)*

shelter	refugio, el	*(ehl reh-'foo-hee-oh)*
shelves	repisas, las	*(lahs reh-'pee-sahs)*
shift	turno de trabajo, el	*(ehl 'toor-noh deh trah-'bah-hoh)*
shipment	envío, el	*(ehl ehn-'vee-oh)*
shipping	transporte, el	*(ehl trahns-'pohr-teh)*
shirt	camisa, la	*(lah kah-'mee-sah)*
shock absorber	amortiguador, el	*(ehl ah-mohr-tee-gwah-'dohr)*
shop	taller, el	*(ehl tah-'yehr)*
short (in height)	bajo*	*('bah-hoh)*
short (in length)	corto*	*('kohr-toh)*
shorts	calzoncillos, los	*(lohs kahl-sohn-'see-yohs)*
shot	inyección, la	*(lah een-yehk-see-'ohn)*
shoulder	hombro, el	*(ehl 'ohm-broh)*
shovel	pala, la	*(lah 'pah-lah)*
show	espectáculo, el	*(ehl eh-spehk-'tah-koo-loh)*
shower	ducha, la	*(lah 'doo-chah)*
shutters	postigos, los	*(lohs poh-'stee-gohs)*
sick	enfermo*	*(ehn-'fehr-moh)*
side	lado, el	*(ehl 'lah-doh)*
sidewalk	acera, la	*(lah ah-'seh-rah)*
sign	letrero, el	*(ehl leh-'treh-roh)*
signal	señal, la	*(lah seh-'nyahl)*
signature	firma, la	*(lah 'feer-mah)*
significant	significativo*	*(seeg-nee-fee-kah-'tee-voh)*
silver	plata, la	*(lah 'plah-tah)*
simulator	simuladora, la	*(lah see-moo-lah-'doh-rah)*
sink	lavabo, el	*(ehl lah-'vah-boh)*
sister	hermana, la	*(lah ehr-'mah-nah)*
sister-in-law	cuñada, la	*(lah koo-'nyah-dah)*
six	seis	*('seh-ees)*
sixteen	dieciséis	*(dee-ehs-ee-'seh-ees)*
sixth	sexto*	*('sehks-'toh)*
size	tamaño, el	*(ehl tah-'mah-nyoh)*
skiing	esquí, el	*(ehl eh-'skee)*
skill	habilidad, la	*(lah ah-bee-lee-'dahd)*
skirt	falda, la	*(lah 'fahl-dah)*
skunk	zorrino, el*	*(ehl soh-'rree-noh)*
skyscraper	rascacielos, el	*(ehl rah-skah-see-'eh-lohs)*
sled	trineo, el	*(ehl tree-'neh-oh)*
sledgehammer	acotillo, el	*(ehl ah-koh-'tee-yoh)*
slope	declive, el	*(ehl deh-'klee-veh)*
sloppy	desaliñado*	*(dehs-ah-lee-'nyah-doh)*
slow	lento*	*('lehn-toh)*

slowly	**lentamente**	*(lehn-tah-'mehn-teh)*
small	**pequeño***	*(peh-'keh-nyoh)*
smell	**olor, el**	*(ehl oh-'lohr)*
smoke	**humo, el**	*(ehl 'oo-moh)*
smoke alarm	**detector de humo, el**	*(ehl deh-tehk-'tohr deh 'oo-moh)*
smooth	**liso***	*('lee-soh)*
snail	**caracol, el**	*(ehl kah-rah-'kohl)*
snake	**culebra, la**	*(lah koo-'leh-brah)*
sneeze	**estornudo, el**	*(ehl eh-stohr-'noo-doh)*
snow	**nieve, la**	*(lah nee-'eh-veh)*
soap	**jabón, el**	*(ehl hah-'bohn)*
social security number	**número de seguro social, el**	*(ehl 'noo-meh-roh deh seh-'goo-roh soh-see-'ahl)*
socket	**hueco, el**	*(ehl 'weh-koh)*
socks	**calcetines, los**	*(lohs kahl-seh-'tee-nehs)*
sofa	**sofá, el**	*(ehl soh-'fah)*
soft	**blando***	*('blahn-doh)*
soft drink	**refresco, el**	*(ehl reh-'freh-skoh)*
soldier	**soldado, el/la**	*(ehl/lah sohl-'dah-doh)*
solid	**sólido***	*(soh-lee-doh)*
solution	**solución, la**	*(lah soh-loo-see-'ohn)*
some	**unos***	*('oo-nohs)*
someone	**alguien**	*('ahl-gee-ehn)*
something	**algo**	*('ahl-goh)*
sometimes	**a veces**	*(ah-'veh-sehs)*
son	**hijo, el**	*(ehl 'ee-hoh)*
son-in-law	**yerno, el**	*(ehl 'yehr-noh)*
song	**canción, la**	*(lah kahn-see-'ohn)*
soon	**pronto**	*('prohn-toh)*
sore	**dolorido***	*(doh-loh-'ree-doh)*
sound	**sonido, el**	*(ehl soh-'nee-doh)*
soup	**sopa, la**	*(lah 'soh-pah)*
south	**sur**	*(soor)*
space	**espacio, el**	*(ehl eh-'spah-see-oh)*
Spanish	**español***	*(eh-spah-'nyohl)*
spare tire	**neumático de repuesto, el**	*(ehl neh-oo-'mah-tee-koh deh reh-'pweh-stoh)*
sparks	**chispas, las**	*(lahs 'chee-spahs)*
speaker	**parlante, el**	*(ehl pahr-'lahn-teh)*
special	**especial**	*(eh-speh-see-'ahl)*
specialist	**especialista, el/la**	*(ehl/lah eh-speh-see-ah-'lee-stah)*
speed	**velocidad, la**	*(lah veh-loh-see-'dahd)*
spider	**araña, la**	*(lah ah-'rah-nyah)*

spinach	espinaca, la	*(lah eh-spee-'nah-kah)*
spirit	espíritu, el	*(ehl eh-'spee-ree-too)*
sponge	esponja, la	*(lah eh-'spohn-hah)*
spool	carrete, el	*(ehl kah-'rreh-teh)*
spoon	cuchara, la	*(lah koo-'chah-rah)*
sportcoat	saco, el	*(ehl 'sah-koh)*
sports	deportes, los	*(lohs deh-'pohr-tehs)*
sprain	torcedura, la	*(lah tohr-seh-'doo-rah)*
spring (season)	primavera, la	*(lah pree-mah-'veh-rah)*
spring (tool)	resorte, el	*(ehl reh-'sohr-teh)*
sprinklers	rociadoras, las	*(lahs roh-see-ah-'doh-rahs)*
square	cuadrado, el	*(ehl kwah-'drah-doh)*
squirrel	ardilla, la	*(lah ahr-'dee-yah)*
stadium	estadio, el	*(ehl eh-'stah-dee-oh)*
stairs	escaleras, las	*(lahs eh-skah-'leh-rahs)*
stake	estaca, la	*(lah eh-'stah-kah)*
stamps	estampillas las	*(lahs eh-stahm-'pee-yahs)*
standard	norma, la	*(lah 'norh-mah)*
staple	grapa, la	*(lah 'grah-pah)*
stapler	engrapadora, la	*(lah ehn-'grah-pah-'doh-rah)*
state	estado, el	*(ehl eh-'stah-doh)*
static	estático*	*(eh-'stah-tee-koh)*
station	estación, la	*(lah eh-stah-see-'ohn)*
statue	estatua, la	*(lah eh-'stah-too-ah)*
steak	bistec, el	*(ehl bee-'stehk)*
steel	acero, el	*(ehl ah-'seh-roh)*
steering wheel	volante, el	*(ehl voh-'lahn-teh)*
steps	escalones, los	*(lohs eh-skah-'loh-nehs)*
stereo	estéreo, el	*(ehl eh-'steh-reh-oh)*
stick	palo, el	*(ehl 'pah-loh)*
stitches	puntadas, las	*(lahs poon-'tah-dahs)*
stockings	medias, las	*(lahs 'meh-dee-ahs)*
stocks	acciones, las	*(lahs ahk-see-'oh-nehs)*
stomach	estómago, el	*(ehl eh-'stoh-mah-goh)*
stone	piedra, la	*(lah pee-'eh-drah)*
stool	banquillo, el	*(ehl bahn-'kee-yoh)*
storage	depósito, el	*(ehl deh-'poh-see-toh)*
store	tienda, la	*(lah tee-'ehn-dah)*
storm	tormenta, la	*(lah tohr-'mehn-tah)*
stove	estufa, la	*(lah eh-'stoo-fah)*
straight	recto*	*('rehk-toh)*
strange	raro*	*('rah-roh)*
strap	correa, la	*(lah koh-'rreh-ah)*

strategy	**estrategia, la**	*(lah eh-strah-'teh-hee·ah)*
strawberry	**fresa, la**	*(lah 'freh-sah)*
stream	**arroyo, el**	*(ehl ah-'rroh-yoh)*
street	**calle, la**	*(lah 'kah-yeh)*
strength	**esfuerzo, el**	*(ehl ehs-'fwehr-soh)*
string	**cuerda, la**	*(lah 'kwehr-dah)*
strip	**rayo, el**	*(ehl 'rah-yoh)*
strong	**fuerte**	*('fwehr-teh)*
stub	**talón, el**	*(ehl tah-'lohn)*
student	**estudiante, el/la**	*(ehl/lah eh-stoo-dee-'ahn-teh)*
study	**estudio, el**	*(ehl eh-'stoo-dee-oh)*
style	**estilo, el**	*(ehl eh-'stee-loh)*
sugar	**azúcar, el**	*(ehl ah-'soo-kahr)*
suggestion	**sugerencia, la**	*(lah soo-heh-'rehn-see-ah)*
suit	**traje, el**	*(ehl 'trah-heh)*
suitcase	**maleta, la**	*(lah mah-'leh-tah)*
sum	**suma, la**	*(lah 'soo-mah)*
summary	**resumen, el**	*(ehl reh-'soo-mehn)*
summer	**verano, el**	*(ehl veh-'rah-noh)*
sun	**sol, el**	*(ehl sohl)*
Sunday	**domingo**	*(doh-'meen-goh)*
sunglasses	**lentes del sol, los**	*(lohs 'lehn-tehs dehl sohl)*
supermarket	**supermercado, el**	*(ehl soo-pehr-mehr-'kah-doh)*
supervisor	**supervisor, el***	*(ehl soo-pehr-vee-'sohr)*
supplier	**abastecedor, el***	*(ehl ah-bah-steh-seh-'dohr)*
supplies	**provisiones, las**	*(lahs proh-vee-see-'oh-nehs)*
sure	**seguro***	*(seh-'goo-roh)*
surgery	**cirugía, la**	*(lah see-roo-'hee-ah)*
surplus	**excedente, el**	*(ehl ehk-'seh-dehn-teh)*
surveillance	**vigilancia, la**	*(lah vee-hee-'lahn-see-ah)*
survey	**encuesta, la**	*(lah ehn-'kweh-stah)*
suspect	**sospechoso, el***	*(ehl soh-speh-'choh-soh)*
swamp	**pantano, el**	*(ehl pahn-'tah-noh)*
sweater	**suéter, el**	*(ehl 'sweh-tehr)*
sweatsuit	**sudaderas, las**	*(lahs soo-dah-'deh-rahs)*
switch	**interruptor, el**	*(ehl een-teh-rroop-'tohr)*
symbol	**símbolo, el**	*(ehl seem-boh-loh)*
system	**sistema, el**	*(ehl see-'steh-mah)*
T-shirt	**camiseta, la**	*(lah kah-mee-'seh-tah)*
table	**mesa, la**	*(lah 'meh-sah)*
tablecloth	**mantel, el**	*(ehl mahn-'tehl)*
tablets	**tabletas, las**	*(lahs tah-'bleh-tahs)*
tacks	**tachuelas, las**	*(lahs tah-choo-'eh-lahs)*

talent	talento, el	*(ehl tah-'lehn-toh)*
tall	alto*	*('ahl-toh)*
tank	tanque, el	*(ehl 'tahn-keh)*
tansportation	transporte, el	*(ehl trahns-'pohr-teh)*
tape	cinta, la	*(lah 'seen-tah)*
tape measure	cinta para medir, la	*(lah 'seen-tah 'pah-rah meh-'deer)*
tardiness	tardanza, la	*(lah tahr-'dahn-sah)*
task	tarea, la	*(lah tah-'reh-ah)*
tax	impuesto, el	*(ehl eem-'pweh-stoh)*
tea	té, el	*(ehl teh)*
teacher	maestro, el*	*(ehl mah-'eh-stroh)*
technician	técnico, el/la	*(ehl/lah 'tehk-nee-koh)*
teenager	muchacho, el*	*(ehl moo-'chah-choh)*
telephone	teléfono, el	*(ehl teh-'leh-foh-noh)*
telephone number	número de teléfono, el	*(ehl 'noo-meh-roh deh teh-'leh-foh-noh)*
television	televisión, la	*(lah teh-leh-vee-see-'ohn)*
temperature	temperatura, la	*(lah tehm-peh-rah-'too-rah)*
ten	diez	*('dee-ehs)*
tenth	décimo*	*('deh-see-moh)*
term	término, el	*(ehl 'tehr-mee-noh)*
test	prueba, la	*(lah proo-'eh-bah)*
test tube	tubo de ensayo, el	*(ehl 'too-boh deh ehn-'sah-yoh)*
testimony	testimonio, el	*(ehl teh-stee-'moh-nee-oh)*
textiles	textiles, los	*(lohs tehks-'tee-lehs)*
that	ese*	*('eh-seh)*
the rest	los demás	*(lohs deh-'mahs)*
theme	tema, el	*(ehl 'teh-mah)*
then	entonces	*(ehn-'tohn-sehs)*
there	allí*	*(ah-'yee)*
thermometer	termómetro, el	*(ehl tehr-'moh-meh-troh)*
thermos	termo, el	*(ehl 'tehr-moh)*
thermostat	termostato, el	*(ehl tehr-moh-'stah-toh)*
these	estos*	*('eh-stohs)*
they (feminine)	ellas	*('eh-yahs)*
they (masculine)	ellos	*('eh-yohs)*
thick	grueso*	*(groo-'eh-soh)*
thief	ladrón, el*	*(ehl lah-'drohn)*
thin	delgado*	*(dehl-'gah-doh)*
thing	cosa, la	*(lah 'koh-sah)*
third	tercero*	*(tehr-'seh-roh)*
thirteen	trece	*('treh-seh)*
thirty	treinta	*('treh-een-'tah)*
this	este*	*('eh-steh)*

those	**esos***	('eh-sohs)
thought	**pensamiento, el**	(ehl pehn-sah-mee-'ehn-toh)
thousand	**mil**	(meel)
thread	**hilo, el**	(ehl 'ee-loh)
threat	**amenaza, la**	(lah ah-meh-'nah-sah)
three	**tres**	(trehs)
throat	**garganta, la**	(lah gahr-'gahn-tah)
thunder	**trueno, el**	(ehl troo-'eh-noh)
Thursday	**jueves**	(hoo-'eh-vehs)
ticket	**boleto, el**	(ehl boh-'leh-toh)
time (general)	**tiempo, el**	(ehl tee-'ehm-poh)
time (occurrence)	**vez, la**	(lah vehs)
time (specific)	**hora, la**	(lah 'oh-rah)
time card	**tarjeta de trabajo, la**	(lah tahr-'heh-tah deh trah-'bah-hoh)
time clock	**reloj de trabajo, el**	(ehl reh-'loh deh trah-'bah-hoh)
timer	**reloj, el**	(ehl reh-'loh)
tips	**propinas, las**	(lahs proh-'pee-nahs)
tire	**neumático, el**	(ehl neh-oo-'mah-tee-koh)
title	**título, el**	(ehl 'tee-too-loh)
to	**a**	(ah)
to the	**al**	(ahl)
today	**hoy**	('oh-ee)
together	**juntos***	('hoon-tohs)
toilet	**excusado, el**	(ehl ehks-koo-'sah-doh)
tomato	**tomate, el**	(ehl toh-'mah-teh)
tomorrow	**mañana**	(lah mah-nyah-nah)
ton	**tonelada, la**	(lah toh-neh-'lah-dah)
tongs	**tenazas, las**	(lahs teh-'nah-sahs)
tongue	**lengua, la**	(lah 'lehn-gwah)
tonight	**esta noche**	('eh-stah 'noh-cheh)
too much	**demasiado***	(deh-mah-see-'ah-doh)
tool	**herramienta, la**	(lah eh-rrah-mee-'ehn-tah)
toolbox	**caja de herramientas, la**	(lah 'kah-hah deh eh-rrah-mee-'ehn-tahs)
tooth	**diente, el**	(ehl dee-'ehn-teh)
toothbrush	**cepillo de dientes, el**	(ehl seh-'pee-yoh deh dee-'ehn-tehs)
toothpaste	**pasta de dientes, la**	(lah 'pah-stah deh dee-'ehn-tehs)
top	**tapa, la**	(lah 'tah-pah)
torch	**antorcha, la**	(lah ahn-'tohr-chah)
tornado	**tornado, el**	(ehl tohr-'nah-doh)
torque	**esfuerzo de torsión, el**	(ehl ehs-'fwehr-soh deh tohr-see-'ohn)
total	**total, el**	(ehl toh-'tahl)
tow truck	**grúa, la**	(lah 'groo-ah)
towel	**toalla, la**	(lah toh-'ah-yah)

tower	torre, la	*(lah 'toh-rreh)*
toy	juguete, el	*(ehl hoo-'geh-teh)*
track	carril, el	*(ehl kah-'rreel)*
tractor	tractor, el	*(ehl trahk-'tohr)*
tractor trailer	camión tractor, el	*(ehl kah-mee-'ohn trahk-'tohr)*
trade union	sindicato, el	*(ehl seen-dee-'kah-toh)*
trademark	marca registrada, la	*(lah 'mahr-kah reh-hee-'strah-dah)*
traffic	tráfico, el	*(ehl 'trah-fee-koh)*
traffic signal	semáforo, el	*(ehl seh-'mah-foh-roh)*
train	tren, el	*(ehl trehn)*
trainer	entrenador, el*	*(ehl ehn-treh-nah-'dohr)*
training	entrenamiento, el	*(ehl ehn-treh-nah-mee-'ehn-toh)*
transcripts	transcripcion, la	*(lah trahn-skreep-see-'ohn)*
transfer	transferencia, la	*(lah trahs-feh-'rehn-see-ah)*
transformer	transformador, el	*(ehl trahs-fohr-mah-'dohr)*
translator	traductor, el*	*(ehl trah-dook-'tohr)*
trash	basura, la	*(lah bah-'soo-rah)*
trash basket	cesto de basura, el	*(ehl 'seh-stoh deh bah-'soo-rah)*
trauma	trauma, el	*(ehl 'trah-oo-mah)*
tray	bandeja, la	*(lah bahn-'deh-hah)*
treatment	tratamiento, el	*(ehl trah-tah-mee-'ehn-toh)*
tree	árbol, el	*(ehl 'ahr-bohl)*
tremendous	magnífico*	*(mahg-'nee-fee-koh)*
trend	tendencia, la	*(lah tehn-'dehn-see-ah)*
triangle	triángulo, el	*(ehl tree-'ahn-goo-loh)*
tribute	tributo, el	*(ehl tree-'boo-toh)*
trip (travel)	viaje, el	*(ehl vee-'ah-heh)*
trowel	paleta, la	*(lah pah-'leh-tah)*
truck	camión, el	*(ehl kah-mee-'ohn)*
truck driver	camionero, el*	*(ehl kah-mee-oh-'neh-roh)*
truckload	camionada, la	*(lah kah-mee-oh-'nah-dah)*
trunk	maletera, la	*(lah mah-leh-'teh-rah)*
trust	confianza, la	*(lah kohn-fee-'ahn-sah)*
tub	tina, la	*(lah 'tee-nah)*
tube	tubo, el	*(ehl 'too-boh)*
Tuesday	martes	*('mahr-tehs)*
tuna	atún, el	*(ehl ah-'toon)*
tune	tono, el	*(ehl 'toh-noh)*
tunnel	túnel, el	*(ehl 'too-nehl)*
turkey	pavo, el*	*(ehl 'pah-voh)*
turtle	tortuga, la	*(lah tohr-'too-gah)*
TV	televisor, el	*(ehl teh-leh-vee-'sohr)*
twelve	doce	*('doh-seh)*

twenty	veinte	('veh-een-teh)
two	dos	(dohs)
type	tipo, el	(ehl 'tee-poh)
typewriter	máquina de escribir, la	(lah 'mah-kee-nah deh eh-skree-'beer)
typist	mecanógrafo, el*	(ehl meh-kah-'noh-grah-foh)
ugly	feo*	('feh-oh)
umbrella	paraguas, el	(ehl pah-'rah-gwahs)
uncle	tío, el	(ehl 'tee-oh)
underpants	calzoncillos, los	(lohs kahl-sohn-'see-yohs)
underwear	ropa interior, la	(lah 'roh-pah een-teh-ree-'ohr)
unemployment	desempleo, el	(ehl dehs-ehm-'pleh-oh)
uneven	desigual	(dehs-ee-'gwahl)
uniform	uniforme, el	(ehl oo-nee-'fohr-meh)
unit	unidad, la	(lah oo-nee-'dahd)
up	arriba	(ah-'rree-bah)
upset	enojado*	(eh-noh-'hah-doh)
vacuum cleaner	aspiradora, la	(lah ah-spee-rah-'doh-rah)
valley	valle, el	(ehl 'vah-yeh)
valuable	valioso*	(vah-lee-'oh-soh)
value	valor, el	(ehl vah-'lohr)
valve	válvula, la	(lah 'vahl-voo-lah)
van	furgoneta, la	(lah foor-goh-'neh-tah)
variance	variación, la	(lah vah-ree-ah-see-'ohn)
vase	florero, el	(ehl floh-'reh-roh)
VCR	videocasetera, la	(lah vee-deh-oh-kah-seh-'teh-rah)
vegetables	vegetales, los	(lohs veh-heh-'tah-lehs)
vertical	vertical	(vehr-tee-'kahl)
very	muy	('moo-ee)
vest	chaleco, el	(ehl chah-'leh-koh)
vibration	vibración, la	(lah vee-brah-see-'ohn)
victim	víctima, la	(lah 'veek-tee-mah)
video	vídeo, el	(ehl 'vee-deh-oh)
violation	infracción, la	(lah een-frahk-see-'ohn)
vitamins	vitaminas, las	(lahs vee-tah-'mee-nahs)
vocabulary	vocabulario, el	(ehl voh-kah-boo-'lah-ree-oh)
void	cancelado*	(kahn-seh-'lah-doh)
voltage	voltaje, el	(ehl vohl-'tah-heh)
wages	sueldo, el	(ehl 'swehl-doh)
wagon	carretón, el	(ehl kah-rreh-'tohn)
waiter	mesero, el*	(ehl meh-'seh-roh)
waiver	extención, la	(lah ehks-tehn-see-'ohn)
wall	pared, la	(lah pah-'rehd)
warehouse	almacén, el	(ehl ahl-mah-'sehn)

washer	arandela, la	*(lah ah-rahn-'deh-lah)*
washing machine	lavadora, la	*(lah lah-vah-'doh-rah)*
wasp	avispa, la	*(lah ah-'vee-spah)*
waste	desperdicios, los	*(lohs deh-spehr-'dee-see-ohs)*
watch	reloj de pulsera, el	*(ehl reh-'loh deh pool-'seh-rah)*
water	agua, el	*(ehl 'ah-gwah)*
water valve	válvula de agua, la	*(lah 'vahl-voo-lah deh 'ah-gwah)*
watt	vatio, el	*(ehl 'vah-tee-oh)*
we	nosotros*	*(noh-'soh-trohs)*
weakness	debilidad, la	*(lah deh-bee-lee-'dahd)*
weather	clima, el	*(ehl 'klee-mah)*
wedding	boda, la	*(lah 'boh-dah)*
Wednesday	miércoles	*(mee-'ehr-koh-lehs)*
week	semana, la	*(lah seh-'mah-nah)*
weekend	fin de semana, el	*(ehl feen deh seh-'mah-nah)*
weight	peso, el	*(ehl 'peh-soh)*
welfare	bienestar social, el	*(ehl bee·ehn-eh-'stahr soh-see-'ahl)*
well	bien	*('bee-ehn)*
west	oeste	*(oh-'eh-steh)*
wet	mojado*	*(moh-'hah-doh)*
wheel	rueda, la	*(lah roo-'eh-dah)*
wheelbarrow	carretilla, la	*(lah kah-rreh-'tee-yah)*
wheelchair	silla de ruedas, la	*(lah 'see-yah deh roo-'eh-dahs)*
whistle	silbido, el	*(ehl seel-'bee-doh)*
white	blanco*	*('blahn-koh)*
wholesale	al por mayor	*(ahl pohr mah-'yohr)*
wide	ancho*	*('ahn-choh)*
widowed	viudo*	*(vee-'oo-doh)*
width	anchura, la	*(lah ahn-'choo-rah)*
wife	esposa, la	*(lah eh-'spoh-sah)*
wild	salvaje	*(sahl-'vah-heh)*
window	ventana, la	*(lah vehn-'tah-nah)*
windshield	parabrisas, el	*(ehl pah-rah-'bree-sahs)*
wind	viento	*(ehl vee-'ehn-toh)*
winter	invierno, el	*(ehl een-vee-'ehr-noh)*
wire	alambre, el	*(ehl ah-'lahm-breh)*
with	con	*(kohn)*
without	sin	*(seen)*
witness	testigo, el/la	*(ehl/lah teh-'stee-goh)*
wolf	lobo, el*	*(ehl 'loh-boh)*
woman	mujer, la	*(lah moo-'hehr)*
wood	madera, la	*(lah mah-'deh-rah)*
wool	lana, la	*(lah 'lah-nah)*

work	**trabajo, el***	*(ehl trah-'bah-hoh)*
work station	**estación de trabajo, la**	*(lah eh-stah-see-'ohn deh trah-'bah-hoh)*
work table	**mesa de trabajo, la**	*(lah 'meh-sah deh trah-'bah-hoh)*
worker	**trabajador, el**	*(ehl trah-bah-hah-'dohr)*
worm	**gusano, el**	*(ehl goo-'sah-noh)*
worried	**preocupado***	*(preh-oh-koo-'pah-doh)*
worse	**peor**	*(peh-'ohr)*
wrench	**llave inglesa, la**	*(lah 'yah-veh een-'gleh-sah)*
wrist	**muñeca, la**	*(lah moo-'nyeh-kah)*
X-rays	**rayos equis, los**	*(lohs 'rah-yohs 'eh-kees)*
yard	**yarda, la**	*(lah 'yahr-dah)*
year	**año, el**	*(ehl 'ah-nyoh)*
yellow	**amarillo***	*(ah-mah-'ree-yoh)*
yes	**sí**	*(see)*
yesterday	**ayer**	*(ah-'yehr)*
yet	**todavía**	*(toh-dah-'vee-ah)*
you	**usted**	*(oo-'stehd)*
you (plural)	**ustedes**	*(oo-'steh-dehs)*
your, his, her, their	**su**	*(soo)*
yours, theirs	**suyo***	*('soo-yoh)*
zero	**cero**	*('seh-roh)*
zip code	**zona postal, la**	*(lah 'soh-nah poh-'stahl)*
zone	**zona, la**	*(lah 'soh-nah)*

English-Spanish Verbs

accept, to	**aceptar**	*(ah-sehp-'tahr)*
accrue, to	**acumular**	*(ah-koo-moo-'lahr)*
accuse, to	**acusar**	*(ah-koo-'sahr)*
add, to	**añadir**	*(ah-nyah-'deer)*
adjust, to	**ajustar**	*(ah-hoo-'stahr)*
adopt, to	**adoptar**	*(ah-dohp-'tahr)*
advertise, to	**anunciar**	*(ah-noon-see-'ahr)*
advise, to	**avisar**	*(ah-vee-'sahr)*
allow, to	**permitir**	*(pehr-mee-'teer)*
analyze, to	**analizar**	*(ah-nah-lee-'sahr)*
answer, to	**contestar**	*(kohn-teh-'stahr)*
antagonize, to	**antagonizar**	*(ahn-tah-goh-nee-'sahr)*
apply, to	**solicitar**	*(soh-lee-see-'tahr)*
appraise, to	**estimar**	*(eh-stee-'mahr)*
approve, to	**aprobar**	*(ah-proh-'bahr)*
argue, to	**argumentar**	*(ahr-goo-mehn-'tahr)*
arrive, to	**llegar**	*(yeh-'gahr)*
ask for, to	**pedir**	*(peh-'deer)*
ask, to	**preguntar**	*(preh-goon-'tahr)*
assemble, to	**unir**	*(oo-'neer)*
assure, to	**asegurar**	*(ah-seh-goo-'rahr)*
attach, to	**sujetar**	*(soo-heh-'tahr)*
attend, to	**asistir**	*(ah-see-'steer)*
authorize, to	**autorizar**	*(ow-toh-ree-'sahr)*
be able, to	**poder**	*(poh-'dehr)*
be sure, to	**asegurarse**	*(ah-seh-goo-'rahr-seh)*
begin, to	**empezar**	*(ehm-peh-'sahr)*
bend, to	**doblar**	*(doh-'blahr)*
borrow, to	**prestar**	*(preh-'stahr)*
bother, to	**molestar**	*(moh-leh-'stahr)*
break, to	**quebrarse**	*(keh-'brahr-seh)*
bring, to	**traer**	*(trah-'ehr)*
burn oneself, to	**quemarse**	*(keh-'mahr-seh)*
buy, to	**comprar**	*(kohm-'prahr)*
calculate, to	**calcular**	*(kahl-koo-'lahr)*
call, to	**llamar**	*(yah-'mahr)*
calm down, to	**calmarse**	*(kahl-'mahr-seh)*
cancel, to	**cancelar**	*(kahn-seh-'lahr)*
change, to	**cambiar**	*(kahm-bee-'ahr)*
charge, to	**cobrar**	*(koh-'brahr)*

check, to	**averiguar**	*(ah-veh-ree-'gwahr)*
clarify, to	**aclarar**	*(ah-klah-'rahr)*
clean, to	**limpiar**	*(leem-pee-'ahr)*
climb, to	**subir**	*(soo-'beer)*
close, to	**cerrar**	*(seh-'rrahr)*
coerce, to	**coercer**	*(koh-ehr-'sehr)*
collect, to	**coleccionar**	*(koh-lehk-see-oh-'nahr)*
come, to	**venir**	*(veh-'neer)*
commend, to	**alabar**	*(ah-lah-'bahr)*
commit, to	**comprometer**	*(kohm-proh-meh-'tehr)*
compliment, to	**felicitar**	*(feh-lee-see-'tahr)*
confess, to	**confesar**	*(kohn-feh-'sahr)*
confirm, to	**confirmar**	*(kohn-feer-'mahr)*
connect, to	**conectar**	*(koh-nehk-'tahr)*
consult, to	**consultar**	*(kohn-sool-'tahr)*
continue, to	**continuar**	*(kohn-tee-noo-'ahr)*
contribute, to	**contribuir**	*(kohn-tree-boo-'eer)*
converse, to	**conversar**	*(kohn-vehr-'sahr)*
cooperate, to	**cooperar**	*(koh-oh-peh-'rahr)*
coordinate, to	**coordinar**	*(koh-ohr-dee-'nahr)*
correct, to	**corregir**	*(koh-rreh-'heer)*
counsel, to	**aconsejar**	*(ah-kohn-seh-'hahr)*
count, to	**contar**	*(kohn-'tahr)*
cover, to	**cubrir**	*(koo-'breer)*
curse, to	**blasfemar**	*(blahs-feh-'mahr)*
cut, to	**cortar**	*(kohr-'tahr)*
defend, to	**defender**	*(deh-fehn-'dehr)*
deliver, to	**entregar**	*(ehn-treh-'gahr)*
demand, to	**exigir**	*(ehk-see-'heer)*
demonstrate, to	**mostrar**	*(moh-'strahr)*
deny, to	**negarse**	*(neh-'gahr-seh)*
deposit, to	**depositar**	*(deh-poh-see-'tahr)*
describe, to	**describir**	*(deh-skree-'beer)*
develop, to	**desarrollar**	*(dehs-ah-rroh-'yahr)*
dial, to	**marcar**	*(mahr-'kahr)*
dig, to	**excavar**	*(ehks-kah-'vahr)*
discuss, to	**discutir**	*(dee-skoo-'teer)*
distribute, to	**distribuir**	*(dee-stree-boo-'eer)*
diversify, to	**diversificar**	*(dee-vehr-see-fee-'kahr)*
do, to	**hacer**	*(ah-'sehr)*
drill, to	**taladrar**	*(tah-lah-'drahr)*
drink, to	**beber**	*(beh-'behr)*
drive, to	**manejar**	*(mah-neh-'hahr)*

dry, to	**secar**	*(seh-'kahr)*
earn, to	**ganar**	*(gah-'nahr)*
eat, to	**comer**	*(koh-'mehr)*
empty, to	**vaciar**	*(vah-see-'ahr)*
encourage, to	**animar**	*(ah-nee-'mahr)*
end, to	**terminar**	*(tehr-mee-'nahr)*
enforce, to	**hacer cumplir**	*(ah-'sehr koom-'pleer)*
enroll, to	**matricularse**	*(mah-tree-koo-'lahr-seh)*
enter, to	**entrar**	*(ehn-'trahr)*
establish, to	**establecer**	*(eh-stah-bleh-'sehr)*
evaluate, to	**evaluar**	*(eh-vah-loo-'ahr)*
exceed, to	**sobrepasar**	*(soh-breh-pah-'sahr)*
exchange, to	**cambiar**	*(kahm-bee-'ahr)*
exhibit, to	**exhibir**	*(ehk-see-'beer)*
expire, to	**vencer**	*(vehn-'sehr)*
explain, to	**explicar**	*(ehk-splee-'kahr)*
export, to	**exportar**	*(ehks-'pohr-tahr)*
faint, to	**desmayarse**	*(dehs-mah-'yahr-seh)*
fall, to	**caerse**	*(kah-'ehr-seh)*
feel, to	**sentir**	*(sehn-'teer)*
file, to	**archivar**	*(ahr-chee-'vahr)*
fill, to	**llenar**	*(yeh-'nahr)*
find, to	**encontrar**	*(ehn-kohn-'trahr)*
finish, to	**acabar**	*(ah-kah-'bahr)*
fire, to	**despedir**	*(deh-speh-'deer)*
follow, to	**seguir**	*(seh-'geer)*
forget, to	**olvidarse**	*(ohl-vee-'dahr-seh)*
get dressed, to	**vestirse**	*(veh-'steer-seh)*
get, to	**conseguir**	*(kohn-seh-'geer)*
give, to	**dar**	*(dahr)*
glue, to	**pegar**	*(peh-'gahr)*
go, to	**ir**	*(eer)*
gossip, to	**chismear**	*(chees-meh-'ahr)*
grab, to	**agarrar**	*(ah-gah-'rrahr)*
grind, to	**moler**	*(moh-'lehr)*
grow, to	**crecer**	*(kreh-'sehr)*
guarantee, to	**garantizar**	*(gah-rahn-tee-'sahr)*
hang, to	**colgar**	*(kohl-'gahr)*
have to, to	**tener que**	*(teh-'nehr keh)*
have, to	**tener**	*(teh-'nehr)*
heal, to	**curar**	*(koo-'rahr)*
hear, to	**oír**	*(oh-'eer)*
heat, to	**calentar**	*(kah-lehn-'tahr)*

help, to	**ayudar**	*(ah-yoo-'dahr)*
hire, to	**contratar**	*(kohn-trah-'tahr)*
hit, to	**pegar**	*(peh-'gahr)*
hold, to	**sostener**	*(soh-steh-'nehr)*
identify, to	**identificar**	*(ee-dehn-tee-fee-'kahr)*
implement, to	**realizar**	*(reh-ah-lee-'sahr)*
import, to	**importar**	*(eem-pohr-'tahr)*
improve, to	**mejorar**	*(meh-hoh-'rahr)*
include, to	**incluir**	*(een-kloo-'eer)*
injure, to	**herir**	*(eh-'reer)*
insist, to	**insistir**	*(een-see-'steer)*
inspect, to	**inspeccionar**	*(een-spehk-see·oh-'nahr)*
interfere, to	**interferir**	*(een-tehr-feh-'reer)*
intervene, to	**intervenir**	*(een-tehr-veh-'neer)*
invest, to	**invertir**	*(een-vehr-'teer)*
investigate, to	**investigar**	*(een-veh-stee-'gahr)*
join, to	**juntar**	*(hoon-'tahr)*
joke, to	**bromear**	*(broh-meh-'ahr)*
just finish, to	**acabar de**	*(ah-kah-'bahr deh)*
lead, to	**dirigir**	*(dee-ree-'heer)*
learn, to	**aprender**	*(ah-prehn-'dehr)*
leave, to	**salir**	*(sah-'leer)*
let, to	**dejar**	*(deh-'hahr)*
lie, to	**mentir**	*(mehn-'teer)*
listen, to	**escuchar**	*(eh-skoo-'chahr)*
live, to	**vivir**	*(vee-'veer)*
load, to	**cargar**	*(kahr-'gahr)*
lock, to	**cerrar con llave**	*(seh-'rrahr kohn 'yah-veh)*
look for, to	**buscar**	*(boo-'skahr)*
look, to	**mirar**	*(mee-'rahr)*
lose, to	**perder**	*(pehr-'dehr)*
lower, to	**bajar**	*(bah-'hahr)*
maintain, to	**mantener**	*(mahn-teh-'nehr)*
make, to	**hacer**	*(ah-'sehr)*
manage, to	**manejar**	*(mah-neh-'hahr)*
mark, to	**marcar**	*(mahr-'kahr)*
measure, to	**medir**	*(meh-'deer)*
meet, to	**reunirse**	*(reh-oo-'neer-seh)*
miss, to	**faltar**	*(fahl-'tahr)*
mix, to	**mezclar**	*(meh-'sklahr)*
monitor, to	**controlar**	*(kohn-troh-'lahr)*
move, to	**mover**	*(moh-'vehr)*
negotiate, to	**negociar**	*(neh-goh-see-'ahr)*

notice, to	**fijar**	*(fee-'hahr)*
notify, to	**notificar**	*(noh-tee-fee-'kahr)*
obey, to	**obedecer**	*(oh-beh-deh-'sehr)*
observe, to	**observar**	*(ohb-sehr-'vahr)*
offer, to	**ofrecer**	*(oh-freh-'sehr)*
open, to	**abrir**	*(ah-'breer)*
order, to	**pedir**	*(peh-'deer)*
owe, to	**deber**	*(deh-'behr)*
package, to	**empaquetar**	*(ehm-pah-keh-'tahr)*
paint, to	**pintar**	*(peen-'tahr)*
pass, to	**pasar**	*(pah-'sahr)*
pay, to	**pagar**	*(pah-'gahr)*
persuade, to	**persuadir**	*(pehr-swah-'deer)*
pick up, to	**recoger**	*(reh-koh-'hehr)*
pile, to	**amontonar**	*(ah-mohn-toh-'nahr)*
plan, to	**planear**	*(plah-neh-'ahr)*
plug in, to	**enchufar**	*(ehn-choo-'fahr)*
postpone, to	**posponer**	*(pohs-poh-'nehr)*
practice, to	**practicar**	*(prahk-tee-'kahr)*
prefer, to	**preferir**	*(preh-feh-'reer)*
prepare, to	**preparar**	*(preh-pah-'rahr)*
prescribe, to	**prescribir**	*(preh-skree-'beer)*
press, to	**oprimir**	*(oh-pree-'meer)*
process, to	**procesar**	*(proh-seh-'sahr)*
produce, to	**producir**	*(proh-doo-'seer)*
promise, to	**prometer**	*(proh-meh-'tehr)*
protect, to	**proteger**	*(proh-teh-'hehr)*
prove, to	**probar**	*(proh-'bahr)*
provide, to	**proveer**	*(proh-veh-'ehr)*
pull, to	**jalar**	*(hah-'lahr)*
push, to	**empujar**	*(ehm-poo-'hahr)*
put away, to	**guardar**	*(gwahr-'dahr)*
put in, to	**meter**	*(meh-'tehr)*
quit, to	**renunciar**	*(reh-noon-see-'ahr)*
rain, to	**llover**	*(yoh-'vehr)*
raise, to	**subir**	*(soo-'beer)*
read, to	**leer**	*(leh-'ehr)*
receive, to	**recibir**	*(reh-see-'beer)*
recognize, to	**reconocer**	*(reh-koh-noh-'sehr)*
recommend, to	**recomendar**	*(reh-koh-mehn-'dahr)*
record, to	**documentar**	*(doh-koo-mehn-'tahr)*
recruit, to	**reclutar**	*(reh-kloo-'tahr)*
reject, to	**rechazar**	*(reh-chah-'sahr)*

relax, to	relajarse	*(reh-lah-'hahr-seh)*
remember, to	recordar	*(reh-kohr-'dahr)*
remove, to	sacar	*(sah-'kahr)*
rent, to	alquilar	*(ahl-kee-'lahr)*
repair, to	reparar	*(reh-pah-'rahr)*
repeat, to	repetir	*(reh-peh-'teer)*
replace, to	reemplazar	*(reh-ehm-plah-'sahr)*
represent, to	representar	*(reh-preh-sehn-'tahr)*
rest, to	descansar	*(deh-skahn-'sahr)*
restrain, to	restringir	*(reh-streen-'heer)*
retire, to	retirarse	*(reh-tee-'rahr-seh)*
return, to	regresar	*(reh-greh-'sahr)*
review, to	repasar	*(reh-pah-'sahr)*
reward, to	recompensar	*(reh-kohm-pehn-'sahr)*
run, to	correr	*(koh-'rrehr)*
sand, to	limar	*(lee-'mahr)*
save, to	ahorrar	*(ah-oh-'rrahr)*
scrub, to	fregar	*(freh-'gahr)*
see, to	ver	*(vehr)*
select, to	seleccionar	*(seh-lehk-see-oh-'nahr)*
sell, to	vender	*(vehn-'dehr)*
send, to	mandar	*(mahn-'dahr)*
serve, to	servir	*(sehr-'veer)*
settle, to	arreglar	*(ah-rreh-'glahr)*
share, to	compartir	*(kohm-pahr-'teer)*
ship, to	embarcar	*(ehm-bahr-'kahr)*
sign, to	firmar	*(feer-'mahr)*
sleep, to	dormir	*(dohr-'meer)*
smoke, to	fumar	*(foo-'mahr)*
snow, to	nevar	*(neh-'vahr)*
speak, to	hablar	*(ah-'blahr)*
spend, to	gastar	*(gah-'stahr)*
spray, to	rociar	*(roh-see-'ahr)*
stamp, to	estampar	*(eh-stahm-'pahr)*
steal, to	robar	*(roh-'bahr)*
study, to	estudiar	*(eh-stoo-dee-'ahr)*
suggest, to	sugerir	*(soo-heh-'reer)*
support, to	apoyar	*(ah-poh-'yahr)*
suspend, to	suspender	*(soo-spehn-'dehr)*
sweep, to	barrer	*(bah-'rrehr)*
take away, to	quitar	*(kee-'tahr)*
take care of, to	cuidar	*(kwee-'dahr)*
take, to	tomar	*(toh-'mahr)*

tease, to	**burlarse**	*(boor-'lahr-seh)*
tell, to	**decir**	*(deh-'seer)*
test, to	**examinar**	*(ehk-sah-mee-'nahr)*
thank, to	**agradecer**	*(ah-grah-deh-'sehr)*
think, to	**pensar**	*(pehn-'sahr)*
throw away, to	**tirar**	*(tee-'rahr)*
tie, to	**amarrar**	*(ah-mah-'rrahr)*
touch, to	**tocar**	*(toh-'kahr)*
transfer, to	**transferir**	*(trahns-feh-'reer)*
transport, to	**transportar**	*(trahns-pohr-'tahr)*
try, to	**tratar**	*(trah-'tahr)*
turn off, to	**apagar**	*(ah-pah-'gahr)*
turn, to	**voltear**	*(vohl-teh-'ahr)*
understand, to	**entender**	*(ehn-tehn-'dehr)*
unload, to	**descargar**	*(deh-skahr-'gahr)*
unplug, to	**desenchufar**	*(dehs-ehn-choo-'fahr)*
use, to	**usar**	*(oo-'sahr)*
verify, to	**verificar**	*(veh-ree-fee-'kahr)*
vote, to	**votar**	*(voh-'tahr)*
wait, to	**esperar**	*(eh-speh-'rahr)*
walk, to	**caminar**	*(kah-mee-'nahr)*
want, to	**querer**	*(keh-'rehr)*
wash, to	**lavar**	*(lah-'vahr)*
wear, to	**ponerse**	*(poh-'nehr-seh)*
weld, to	**soldar**	*(sohl-'dahr)*
withdraw, to	**sacar**	*(sah-'kahr)*
work, to	**trabajar**	*(trah-bah-'hahr)*
worsen, to	**empeorar**	*(ehm-peh-oh-'rahr)*
write, to	**escribir**	*(eh-skree-'beer)*
yell, to	**gritar**	*(gree-'tahr)*

English-Spanish Expressions

Above all	**Sobre todo**	*('soh-breh 'toh-doh)*
Again	**Otra vez**	*('oh-trah vehs)*
And you?	**¿Y usted?**	*(ee oo-'stehd)*
Are you injured?	**¿Está lastimado?**	*(eh-'stah lah-stee-'mah-doh)*
Are you OK?	**¿Está bien?**	*(eh-'stah 'bee-ehn)*
Are you sick?	**¿Está enfermo?**	*(eh-'stah ehn-'fehr-moh)*
At first	**Al principio**	*(ahl preen-'see-pee-oh)*
At last	**Por fin**	*(pohr feen)*
At least	**Por lo menos**	*(pohr loh 'meh-nohs)*
At the same time	**A la vez**	*(ah lah vehs)*
At what time?	**¿A qué hora?**	*(ah keh 'oh-rah)*
Be here for sure!	**¡Venga aquí sin falta!**	*('vehn-gah ah-'kee seen 'fahl-tah)*
Be very careful!	**¡Tenga mucho cuidado!**	*('tehn-gah 'moo-choh kwee-'dah-doh)*
Bless you!	**¡Salud!**	*(sah-'lood)*
By the way	**A propósito**	*(ah proh-'poh-see-toh)*
Can you tell me?	**¿Puede decirme?**	*('pweh-deh deh-'seer-meh)*
Congratulations!	**¡Felicitaciones!**	*(feh-lee-see-tah-see-'oh-nehs)*
Cover yourself!	**¡Cúbrase!**	*('koo-brah-seh)*
Danger!	**¡Peligro!**	*(peh-'lee-groh)*
Do not touch it!	**¡No lo toque!**	*(noh loh 'toh-keh)*
Do you have information?	**¿Tiene información?**	*(tee-'eh-neh een-fohr-mah-see-'ohn)*
Do you know the procedure?	**¿Sabe el procedimiento?**	*('sah-beh ehl proh-seh-dee-mee-'ehn-toh)*
Do you need help?	**¿Necesita ayuda?**	*(neh-seh-'see-tah ah-'yoo-dah)*
Do you understand?	**¿Entiende?**	*(ehn-tee-'ehn-deh)*
Do you wish to talk?	**¿Desea hablar?**	*(deh-'seh-ah ah-'blahr)*
Don't be late!	**¡No llegue tarde!**	*(noh 'yeh-geh 'tahr-deh)*
Don't worry!	**¡No se preocupe!**	*(noh seh preh-oh-'koo-peh)*
Excuse me!	**¡Con permiso!**	*(kohn pehr-'mee-soh)*
Fine, thanks!	**¡Bien, gracias!**	*('bee-ehn 'grah-see-ahs)*
Fire!	**¡Fuego!**	*('fweh-goh)*
For example	**Por ejemplo**	*(pohr eh-'hehm-ploh)*
Go ahead!	**¡Pase!**	*('pah-seh)*
Go with God!	**¡Vaya con Dios!**	*('vah-yah kohn 'dee-ohs)*
Good afternoon!	**¡Buenas tardes!**	*('bweh-nahs 'tahr-dehs)*
Good evening!	**¡Buenas noches!**	*('bweh-nahs 'noh-chehs)*
Good idea!	**¡Buena idea!**	*('bweh-nah ee-'deh-ah)*
Good luck!	**¡Buena suerte!**	*('bweh-nah 'swehr-teh)*
Good morning!	**¡Buenos días!**	*('bweh-nohs 'dee-ahs)*
Good work!	**¡Bien hecho!**	*('bee-ehn 'eh-choh)*

Goodbye!	¡Adiós!	*(ah-dee-'ohs)*
Happy Birthday!	¡Feliz cumpleaños!	*(feh-'lees koom-pleh-'ah-nyohs)*
Happy Easter!	¡Felices Pascuas!	*(feh-'lee-sehs 'pah-skwahs)*
Happy New Year!	¡Feliz Año Nuevo!	*(feh-'lees 'ah-nyoh 'nweh-voh)*
Have a nice day!	¡Qué le vaya bien!	*(keh leh 'vah-yah 'bee-ehn)*
Help!	¡Socorro!	*(soh-'koh-rroh)*
Hi!	¡Hola!	*('oh-lah)*
How?	¿Cómo?	*('koh-moh)*
How are you?	¿Cómo está?	*('koh-moh eh-'stah)*
How can I help you?	¿Cómo puedo ayudarle?	*('koh-moh 'pweh-doh ah-yoo-'dahr-leh)*
How do you say it?	¿Cómo se dice?	*('koh-moh seh 'dee-seh)*
How do you spell it?	¿Cómo se deletrea?	*('koh-moh seh deh-leh-'treh-ah)*
How long ago?	¿Hace cuánto?	*('ah-seh 'kwahn-toh)*
How many?	¿Cuántos?	*('kwahn-tohs)*
How much?	¿Cuánto?	*('kwahn-toh)*
How's it going?	¿Qué tal?	*(keh tahl)*
I don't understand!	¡No entiendo!	*(noh ehn-tee-'ehn-doh)*
I like what you did!	¡Me gusta lo que hizo!	*(meh 'goo-stah loh keh 'ee-soh)*
I see!	¡Ya veo!	*(yah 'veh-oh)*
I speak little Spanish!	¡Hablo poquito español!	*('ah-bloh poh-'kee-toh eh-spah-'nyohl)*
I think so!	¡Creo que sí!	*('kreh-oh keh see)*
I'm learning Spanish!	¡Estoy aprendiendo el español!	*(eh-'stoh-ee ah-prehn-dee-'ehn-doh ehl eh-spah-nyohl)*
I'm sorry!	¡Lo siento!	*(loh see-'ehn-toh)*
In general	En general	*(ehn heh-neh-'rahl)*
In other words	Es decir	*(ehs deh-'seer)*
Is everything OK?	¿Está bien todo?	*(eh-'stah 'bee-ehn 'toh-doh)*
It doesn't matter!	¡No importa!	*(noh eem-'pohr-tah)*
It doesn't work!	¡No funciona!	*(noh foonk-see-'oh-nah)*
It was a mistake!	¡Fue un error!	*(fweh oon eh-'rrohr)*
It's important!	¡Es importante!	*(ehs eem-pohr-'tahn-teh)*
Just a moment!	¡Un momento!	*(oon moh-'mehn-toh)*
Keep going!	¡Siga!	*('see-gah)*
Like this!	¡Como así!	*('koh-moh ah-'see)*
Maybe!	¡Quizás!	*(kee-'sahs)*
Merry Christmas!	¡Feliz Navidad!	*(feh-'lees nah-vee-'dahd)*
More or less!	¡Más o menos!	*(mahs oh 'meh-nohs)*
More slowly!	¡Más despacio!	*(mahs deh-'spah-see-oh)*
Nice to meet you!	¡Mucho gusto!	*('moo-choh 'goo-stoh)*
Not now!	¡Ahora no!	*(ah-'oh-rah noh)*
Not yet!	¡Todavía no!	*(toh-dah-'vee-ah noh)*
On the other hand	En cambio	*(ehn 'kahm-bee-oh)*

English	Spanish	Pronunciation
Pay attention!	¡Preste atención!	('preh-steh ah-tehn-see-'ohn)
Please!	¡Por favor!	(pohr fah-'vohr)
Put it here!	¡Póngalo aquí!	('pohn-gah-loh ah-'kee)
Ready?	¿Listo?	('lee-stoh)
Right away!	¡En seguida!	(ehn seh-'gee-dah)
Run outside!	¡Corra hacia afuera!	('koh-rrah 'ah-see·ah ah-'fweh-rah)
Say it in English!	¡Dígalo en inglés!	('dee-gah-loh ehn een-'glehs)
See you later!	¡Hasta luego!	('ah-stah 'lweh-goh)
Sure!	¡Claro!	('klah-roh)
Thanks a lot!	¡Muchas gracias!	('moo-chahs 'grah-see-ahs)
Thanks for your patience!	¡Gracias por su paciencia!	('grah-see·ahs pohr soo pah-see-'ehn-see·ah)
That depends!	¡Depende!	(deh-'pehn-deh)
That's great!	¡Qué bueno!	(keh 'bweh-noh)
Very good!	¡Muy bien!	('moo·ee 'bee·ehn)
Watch out!	¡Ojo!	('oh-hoh)
We can't do it without you!	¡No podemos hacerlo sin usted!	(noh poh-'deh-mohs ah-'sehr-loh seen oo-'stehd)
Welcome!	¡Bienvenidos!	(bee-ehn-veh-'nee-dohs)
What?	¿Qué?	(keh)
What a great job!	¡Qué buen trabajo!	(keh bwehn trah-'bah-hoh)
What a shame!	¡Qué lástima!	(keh 'lah-stee-mah)
What do you want to do?	¿Qué quiere hacer?	(keh kee-'eh-reh ah-'sehr)
What does it mean?	¿Qué significa?	(keh seeg-nee-'fee-kah)
What happened?	¿Qué pasó?	(keh pah-'soh)
What time is it?	¿Qué hora es?	(keh 'oh-rah ehs)
What's happening?	¿Qué pasa?	(keh 'pah-sah)
What's the reason?	¿Cuál es la razón?	(kwahl ehs lah rah-'sohn)
What's the trouble?	¿Cuál es el problema?	(kwahl ehs ehl proh-'bleh-mah)
When?	¿Cuándo?	('kwahn-doh)
Where?	¿Dónde?	('dohn-deh)
Which?	¿Cuál?	(kwahl)
Who?	¿Quién?	(kee-'ehn)
Whose?	¿De quién?	(deh kee-'ehn)
Why?	¿Por qué?	(pohr keh)
Word by word!	¡Palabra por palabra!	(pah-'lah-brah pohr pah-'lah-brah)
	¡Caramba!	(kah-'rahm-bah)
	¡Sí!	(see)
	¡Puede hacerlo!	('pweh-deh ah-'sehr-loh)
	¡De nada!	(deh 'nah-dah)

9, 10, 9
19 9
28

9/28